PRINCIPLES OF
ECONOMICS

ABOUT THE AUTHOR

Clifford L. James obtained the doctorate at Harvard University. Since 1926 he has taught at Ohio State University, where he is currently Professor of Economics. He has served as senior economist for the United States Tariff Commission, as economic consultant to numerous government agencies, and as a specialist in management engineering. He has been a director of research in the fields of commercial arbitration, industrial concentration, international trade, and economic theory. In addition to many articles in technical journals and monographs, he has written a widely used introductory textbook, *Economics: Basic Problems and Analysis.*

COLLEGE OUTLINE SERIES

PRINCIPLES OF ECONOMICS

CLIFFORD L. JAMES

Ninth Edition

BARNES & NOBLE, Inc., New York
Publishers · Booksellers · Founded 1874

©

NINTH EDITION, 1956
Reprinted with minor revisions, 1957
COPYRIGHT 1934, 1936, 1938, 1940, 1948, 1952, 1954, 1956

BY BARNES & NOBLE, INC.

SEVENTEENTH PRINTING, 1957

L. C. CATALOGUE CARD NUMBER: 56-7096

PRINTED IN THE UNITED STATES OF AMERICA

Preface

Principles of Economics is designed to furnish students of elementary economics with a brief, systematic account of fundamental principles and problems. Since the student is assumed to have a general background in the social sciences, the detailed descriptions and explanations found in some economics textbooks are omitted. The essentials of economics, however, are briefly treated.

Principles of Economics may be used in several ways: it may supplement a textbook; it may serve as a syllabus in a reading course for college students or for study groups in various organizations; it may serve as a convenient guide in planning and supervising adult study and discussion clubs. College students will find that use of the Outline offers these further advantages—it will greatly reduce laborious note-taking (lecture notes and a few special notes from the textbook can be added to the margins of the book); it will simplify preparations for quizzes and examinations; and it will enable those in a reading course to organize material systematically. General references at the end of each chapter provide the basis for advanced study of many important problems.

In part the treatment is comparative. The definitions and analyses of widely used textbooks are not in complete agreement. Many of these differences are indicated for the student in order to enable him to follow closely a given text or teacher and at the same time to make him aware of other points of view. The quick reference table to standard textbooks enables the student to extend his readings with regard to controversial points of analysis.

Recent economic changes and new economic interpretations are presented. Of especial importance is the emphasis given to the differences between private capitalism and communism, to all aspects of the monopoly problem in the United States, and to the problem of varying levels of employment and income as viewed domestically and internationally.

— C. L. James

The Ohio State University

TABLE OF CONTENTS

TABULATED BIBLIOGRAPHY
OF STANDARD TEXTBOOKS

This *College Outline* is keyed to standard textbooks in two ways.

1. If you are studying one of the following textbooks, consult the cross references here listed to find which pages of the *Outline* summarize the appropriate chapter of your text. (Roman numerals refer to the textbook chapters, Arabic figures to the corresponding *Outline* pages.)

2. If you are using the *Outline* as your basis for study and need a fuller treatment of a topic, consult the pages of any of the standard textbooks as indicated in the Quick Reference Table on pages xii–xv.

Bach. *Economics*. Prentice-Hall, 1954.
I (1–14); III (29–41); V (205–207); VI (146–160); VII (117–145); VIII–IX (146–160); X (211–221); XI (161–173); XII (42–57); XIII–XVII (80–116); XVIII–XX (257–270); XXI–XXII (174–210); XXIII (235–256); XXIV–XXV (174–210); XXVI (257–270); XXVII (222–234); XXVIII (235–256); XXIX–XXX (285–304); XXXI–XXXIII (161–173); XXXIV (251–256); XXXV–XXXVIII (305–347); XXXIX (29–41).

Baumol and Chandler. *Economic Processes and Policies*. Harper, 1954.
I (1–9); II (8–14, 146–160); III (10–11); IV (22–26, 211–221); V (44–57,86); VI (29–37); VII (37–41, 257–284); VIII (161–173, 235–256); IX (12, 205–207); X (183–191); XI (191–192); XII (162–173); XIII (192–200); XIV (117–129); XV (130–145); XVI (125–129); XVII–XIX (285–304); XX (58–66); XXI (42–44); XXII (67–86, 257–270); XXIII (109–113, 257–284); XXIV (37–41); XXV–XXVIII (305–347); XXIX (174–210, 222–234); App. I (90–116); App. II (164–168, 200–205); App. III (174–200).

Bernhard. *Economics*. Heath, 1954.
I (80–89); II (285–290); III (32–35); IV (30–31, 39–40); V (33, 71–75); VI (8–13, 80–89); VII (174–192); VIII (114–115, 232–234); IX (267–268); X (150–151); XI (15–41); XII (90–95); XIII (58–66, 95–97); XIV (99–116, 257–270); XV (29–41, 58–66); XVI (146–150, 161–164); XVII (200–205, 250); XVIII (169–173); XIX (36–41); XX (211–218, 177, 191); XXI–XXII (42–57); XXIII (52–54, 67–79); XXIV (82–87, 106); XXV (117–145, 153–160); XXVI (75–77, 278–283); XXVII (31–32); XXVIII (37–41, 285–304); XXIX (35–39); XXX–XXXI (235–256); XXXII–XXXIII (305–348); XXXIV–XXXV (5–6, 146–150); XXXVI–XXXVIII (1–14, 40).

Burns, Neal, and Watson. *Modern Economics*. 2nd ed. Harcourt, Brace, 1953.
I (1–14); II (15–28); III–IV (42–57); V (205–210); VI (117–129); VII (80–89); VIII (161–173); IX–XIV (90–116, 146–160); XV–XVII (257–270); XVIII (146–160); XIX–XXIV (174–210); XXV–XXVII (42–80); XXVIII (257–270); XXIX–XXX (235–256); XXXI–XXXIII (285–304); XXXIV–XXXV (130–145); XXXVI (146–160); XXXVII–XXXIX (305–347); XL–XLIII (29–41).

Bye. *Principles of Economics*. 5th ed. Appleton-Century-Crofts, 1956.
I–II (1–13); III–IV (29–41); V (58–61, 211–221); VI (42–56); VII (62–66, 257–269); VIII (71–75); IX (117–129); X (130–136); XI (137–145); XII (146–160); XIII (205–207); XIV–XVI (161–172, 191); XVII–XXII (90–116); XXIII–XXIV (174–176, 192–200); XXV (235–256); XXVI (183–192); XXVII (176–182); XXVIII (200–205); XXIX (205–209); XXX–XXXIII (305–347); XXXIV (29–41).

Dodd and Hasek. *Economics*. 2nd ed. South-Western, 1952.
I (1–14); II (15–28); III (80–89); IV (1–14); V (29–41); VI (67–79); VII (42–57); VIII (58–66, 257–270); IX–XI (90–116); XII–XIII (257–270);

XIV–XIX (174–210); XX (117–129); XXI–XXII (130–145); XXIII (145–160); XXIV (117–129, 305–347); XXV–XXVII (285–304); XXVIII–XXX (235–256); XXXI–XXXII (161–173); XXXIII (251–256); XXXIV (222–234); XXXVI (305–347); XXXVII–XXXIX (29–41).

Fairchild, Buck, and Slesinger. *Principles of Economics.* Macmillan, 1954.
I (1–14); II (15–28); III (29–41); IV (42–57); V (222–234); VI (58–66); VII (75–77, 271–284); VIII (80–89); IX–XIV (90–116); XV (117–129); XVI–XVIII (130–145); XIX (146–160); XX–XXV (174–210); XXVI–XXIX (305–347); XXX–XXXII (285–304); XXXIII–XXXVII (235–256); XXXVIII (161–173); XXXIX–XL (257–270); XLI (29–41).

Gemmell and Balsley. *Principles of Economics.* Heath, 1953.
I (1–14); II (15–28); III (29–41); IV (15–28); V (1–14); VI (205–207); VII–VIII (161–173); IX (285–304); X–XI (42–57); XII (67–79); XIII–XIV (257–270); XV (67–79); XVI–XVIII (90–116); XIX (117–129); XX–XXI (130–145); XXII (146–160); XXIII–XXIV (305–347); XXV–XXVII (174–210); XXVIII–XXX (235–256); XXXI–XXXII (222–234); XXXIII (211–221); XXXIV (29–41).

Gemmill. *Current Introductory Economics.* Rev. ed. Harper, 1955.
I–II (1–13); III (11, 58–61); IV (29–41); V (15–28); VI (44–57, 64–66); VII (73–75); VIII (117–129); IX–X (130–145); XI (205–207); XII (166–168, 191–192); XIII (146–160); XIV (161–172); XV–XVI (250–256); XVII (207–209); XVIII–XXIII (90–116); XXIV–XXV (305–347); XXVI–XXVIII (174–182); XXIX (211–221); XXX–XXXI (183–192, 200–205); XXXII (80–88); XXXIII (26–31).

Gordon. *Elementary Economics.* American Book Co., 1950.
I–II (1–13); III (67–69, 35–40); IV–VI (69–78); VII (222–234); VIII (305–347); IX–XV (80–89, 275–283); XVI (90–116); XVII (285–304); XVIII (117–145); XIX (75–77, 271–284); XX (192–200); XXI (183–192); XXII (176–182); XXIII (200–205); XXIV (161–172); XXV (146–160); XXVI (205–209).

Harriss. *The American Economy.* Rev. ed. Irwin, 1956.
I (1–13); II (29–41); III (11, 19–28, 42–44); IV (211–221); V (205–206); VI (146–160); VII–VIII (44–56); IX (64–66, 257–269); X (117–135); XI (135–145); XII (151–160); XIII (87–88, 191–192); XIV (161–173); XV–XX (90–113, 59–64, 82–86); XXI (113–114, 257–267); XXII (271–284); XXIII (205–209); XXIV (174–176); XXV (192–200); XXVI–XXVII (235–256); XXVIII (176–182); XXIX (183–192); XXX (200–205); XXXI (222–234); XXXII (81–86, 251–256); XXXIII–XXXV (305–347); XXXVI–XXXVIII (285–304); XXXIX (157–160, 169–172, 302–304); XL (22–28, 150–153); XLI (27–31).

Ise. *Economics.* Rev. ed. Harper, 1950.
I (1–14); II (42–57); III (211–221); IV–V (235–256); VI (1–14); VII–VIII (42–57); IX (58–66); X–XIV (90–116); XV (257–284); XVI (257–270); XVII–XIX (90–116); XX (90–116, 271–284); XXI (80–89); XXII (117–129); XXIII–XXIV (130–145); XXV (146–160); XXVI (161–173); XXVIII–XXIX (305–347); XXX (192–200); XXXI–XXXII (235–256); XXXIII (183–192); XXXIV (176–182); XXXV (222–234); XXXVI (200–205); XXXVII–XXXVIII (285–304); XXXIX–XL (305–347).

James, Calderwood, and Quantius. *Economics: Basic Problems and Analysis.* Prentice-Hall, 1951.
I (1–14); II (29–41); III (1–14); IV (80–89); V (42–66, 257–270); VI (15–28); VII (67–79, 130–145); VIII–IX (90–116); XI (271–284); XII (222–234); XIII–XVI (174–210); XVII (146–160); XVIII (161–173); XX (130–145); XXI–XXII (285–304); XXIII (235–256); XXIV (305–347).

Kiekhofer. *Economic Principles, Problems, and Policies.* 4th ed. Appleton-Century-Crofts, 1951.
I (1–14); II (29–41); III (15–28, 222–234); IV (15–28); V (42–57); VI–VII (235–256); VIII (174–210); IX (117–129); X (130–145); XI–XII (305–347); XIII–XIV (67–79); XV–XX (90–116); XXI (90–116, 222–234); XXII–XXV (174–210); XXVI (146–160); XXVII (161–173); XXVIII (80–89); XXIX (161–173); XXX (67–69); XXXI (161–173); XXXII (211–221); XXXIII–XXXVI (285–304); XXXVII–XXXVIII (29–41); XXXIX (271–284); XL (257–270); XLI–XLII (29–41).

Meyers. *Elements of Modern Economics.* 4th ed. Prentice-Hall, 1956.
I (1–13); II (29–41); III–IX (58–64, 82–86, 90–104); X–XII (104–114); XIII (192–200, 235–256); XIV (183–192); XV (176–182); XVI (200–205); XVII (102–104, 107–109, 174–176); XVIII (64–66, 257–262); XIX (130–145); XX (117–129, 153–160); XXII–XXIII (305–347); XXIII (205–207); XXIV (87–88, 191); XXV (164–168); XXVI (169–172, 302–304); XXVII (205–209); XXVIII (161–172).

Mitchell, Murad, Berkowitz, and Bagley. *Basic Economics.* Sloane, 1951.
I–III (1–14, 29–41); V (42–57, 257–270); VI (67–79, 90–116); VII (58–66); VIII (130–145); IX (117–129); X (146–160); XI (174–210); XII (67–79, 174–210); XIII (174–210); XIV (174–210, 235–256); XV (80–89); XVI (161–173); XVII–XVIII (285–304); XIX (235–256); XX–XXII (305–347).

Mitchell, Murad, Berkowitz, and Bagley. *Economics: Experience & Analysis.* Sloane, 1950.
I–V (15–28); VI (15–28, 222–234, 271–284); VII (15–28); VIII (29–41); IX (29–41, 257–270); X–XI (1–14); XIV (42–66); XV–XVI (90–116); XVII (67–79, 257–284); XVIII (130–145); XIX (117–129); XX (146–160); XXI–XXIV (174–210); XXV–XXVII (80–89); XXVIII (161–173); XXIX–XXX (285–304); XXXI (235–256); XXXII (211–221); XXXV–XXXVIII (305–347); XXXIX (29–41).

Morgan. *Introduction to Economics.* 2nd ed. Prentice-Hall, 1956.
I (15–28); II (1–14); III (29–41); IV (80–89); V (42–57); VI (37–40); VII (117–129); VIII (90–116); IX (58–79); X (42–44, 211–217, 97–104); XI–XII (109–116); XIII (257–284); XIV–XV (192–210); XVI–XVII (192–200, 235–256); XVIII (222–234); XIX (174–192, 200–205); XX–XXI (146–160, 206–207, 285–304); XXII (222–256); XXIII (146–160); XXIV (235–256); XXV (130–145); XXVI–XXVII (117–129); XXVIII (80–89, 183–192); XXIX–XXX (161–173, 235–256); XXXI (161–173); XXXII (285–304); XXXIII (146–160); XXXIV–XXXV (305–330); XXXVI–XXXVII (212–213, 330–347); XXXVIII (15–41).

Nordin and Salera. *Elementary Economics.* 2nd ed. Prentice-Hall, 1954.
I–II (1–14); III–IV (29–41); V–VI (174–210); VII (42–57); IX–XII (257–270); XIII (271–284); XIV (222–234); XV–XVI (235–256); XVII (192–200); XVIII (176–182, 222–235); XIX (183–192); XX (200–205); XXI (117–129, 146–160); XXII–XXIII (130–146); XXIV (251–256); XXV (285–304); XXVI (167–168); XXVII–XXXII (161–173); XXXIII–XXXV (305–347); XXXVI–XXXVII (29–41).

Peach. *Principles of Economics.* Irwin, 1955
I (1–41); II–III (211–221); V (29–41); VI–VIII (174–210); IX (161–173); X (285–304); XII (117–129); XIII–XIV (130–145); XV (146–160); XVI–XVII (42–57); XVIII (58–66); XIX (257–270); XX (271–284); XXI–XXV (285–304); XXVI–XXIX (90–116); XXX–XXXIII (174–210); XXXIV–XXXV (235–256); XXXVI (192–200); XXXVII–XL (305–347); XLI (251–256); XLIII (222–234); XLIV–XLVI (22–41).

Peterson. *Economics.* Rev. ed. Holt, 1954.
I (1–14); II (15–28); III (1–14); IV (205–207); V (29–41); VI (211–221);
VII (1–14); VIII–IX (42–66); X (117–129); XI (130–145); XII (146–160);
XIII (305–347); XIV–XVI (161–173); XVII–XVIII (90–116); XIX (80–
89); XX–XXI (58–66); XXII (257–270); XXIII (222–234, 257–284);
XXIV–XXVI (174–210); XXVII (235–256); XXVIII–XXX (174–210,
235–256); XXXI (285–304); XXXII (305–347); XXXIII (29–41).

Pond. *Essential Economics: An Introduction.* Rev. ed. Harcourt, Brace,
1956.
I (1–13); II (42–44); III (22–28, 64–66, 211–218); IV (44–56, 67–75); V–VI
(82–86, 90–115, 257–267); VII (174–209); VIII (80–87); IX (251–256); X
(117–145); XI–XII (285–304); XIII (146–160); XIV (161–172); XV (271–
284); XVI (235–256); XVII (222–234); XVIII–XIX (305–347); XX (22–31,
37–41, 87–88).

Robinson, Adams, and Dillin. *Modern Economics.* Dryden, 1952.
I (1–14); II (15–28); III (29–41); IV (42–57); V (211–221, 250–251);
VI (235–256); VII (42–57); VIII (58–66); IX–X (117–145); XI–XII (130–
145); XIII–XIV (146–160); XV–XIX (90–116); XX–XXIII (174–210);
XXIV (205–209); XXV–XXVI (161–173); XXVII (80–89); XXVIII–
XXX (305–347); XXXI (222–234); XXXII (271–284); XXXIII–XXXVI
(73–77); XXXVII (251–256); XXXVIII (257–270, 285–304); XXXIX–
XLI (285–304); XLII–XLIV (29–41).

Samuelson. *Economics: An Introductory Analysis.* 3rd ed. McGraw-Hill,
1955.
I (1–14); II (1–14, 58–66, 211–221); III (29–41); IV (174–210); V (42–57);
VI–VII (285–304); VIII (235–256); IX (251–256); X (174–210); XI (80–89);
XII (174–210); XIII (146–160); XIV (130–145); XV (117–129); XVI (130–
145); XVII–XVIII (161–173); XIX–XX (58–66, 90–116); XXI (222–234);
XXII (67–79); XXIII (80–89); XXIV (90–116); XXV (90–116, 257–270);
XXVI–XXX (174–210); XXXI–XXXIV (305–347); XXXVI (305–347);
XXXVII (29–41).

Umbreit, Hunt, and Kinter. *Fundamentals of Economics.* 2nd ed. McGraw-
Hill, 1952.
I (1–14); II (29–41); III (42–66); IV (80–89); V (117–129); VI (130–145);
VII (146–160); VIII (205–207); IX–X (161–173); XI–XVII (90–116);
XVIII–XIX (257–270); XX–XXI (174–210); XXII (235–256); XXIII–
XXV (174–210); XXVI (285–304); XXVII (305–347).

Van Sickle and Rogge. *Introduction to Economics.* Van Nostrand, 1954.
I–II (1–14); III–IV (29–41); V (42–57); VI (67–79); VII–XI (80–116);
XII–XV (174–210); XVI–XX (90–116, 257–270); XXI (117–129, 146–160);
XXII–XXIV (130–145); XXV–XXVI (305–347); XXVII–XXIX (161–
173); XXX (257–270); XXXI–XXXIII (235–256); XXXIV–XXXV (222–
234); XXXVI–XXXVII (251–256); XXXVIII–XL (305–347); XLI–XLII
(285–304); XLIII–XLV (29–41).

Italic type indicates pages.

CHAP.	TOPIC	BACH	BAUMOL CHANDLER	BERNHARD	BURNS, et al.	BYE
I	Economic Concepts	1, 2	*1–58*	*3–17* *707–758*	1	1, 2
II	Evolution of Economic Activity		*59–76*	*137–144*	2	*290–292*
III	Modern Economic Systems	3, 39	*103–118* *455–488*	*121–137* *214–227*	40–43	*3–4* *34*
IV	Production Organization	12	*77–102*	*361–418*	3–4 25–27	6
V	Size of Business	15	*375–388*	*170–184* *221*	28	*75–80* *90–107*
VI	Marketing, Risk, and Transportation		*419–426*	*85–94* *419–435*	4	8
VII	Consumption	13	*414–429*	*25–39* *445–455*	7, 10	*430–432* *461–470*
VIII	Individual Prices: Demand and Supply	13–17	*436–454* *603–631*	*145–227*	9–14	*17–22*
IX	Money	6, 31	*259–278* *293–309*	*456–497*	6, 36	9
X	Credit and Banking	7	*279–292*	*464–487*	34–36	10–11
XI	Price Levels: Changing Value of Money	6 8–10	*15–30*	*238–257* *660–706*	9, 11–14 18	12
XII	Business Cycle	11 32–33	*137–162*	*255–257* *285–317*	8	15, 16
XIII	Distribution of Income	21–25	*577–602* *654–674*	*78–84* *258–282*	19–24	4, 13–14 23–29
XIV	Population Problems	10	*42–57*	*337–350*	*52–53*	5
XV	Agricultural Problems	27	*577–602*	*422–435*	*299–301*	*409–411*
XVI	Labor Problems	23, 28 34	*137–162*	*561–604*	29–30	25
XVII	Industrial Concentration, Government Control	18–20	*414–454*	*165–167* *200–205*	15–16 28	*107–113*
XVIII	Public Utilities	26	*436–454*	*498–506*	*437–438*	*112*
XIX	Public Finance	29–30	*310–374*	*527–545*	31–33	*570–574*
XX	International Economic Relations	35–38	*489–576*	*392–444*	37–39	30–33

See pages viii to xi for complete titles.

TO STANDARD TEXTBOOKS

Roman type indicates chapters.

DODD & HASEK	FAIR-CHILD	GEM-MELL BALSLEY	GEMMILL	GORDON	HARRISS	ISE	JAMES
1, 4	1	1, 5	1, 2	1, 16	1	1, 6	1, 3
2	2	2, 4	5				6
5 37–39	3, 41	3, 34	4, 33	3, 17	2, 41	39–49	2
7	4	10–11	3	63–70 358–369	3, 7–8	2, 7–8	101–109
8	6	19–20	6	143–144	134–140	9	120–131
6	7, 9	12, 15	7	4–6, 19	46–47 346–349		161–168
3	8		32	2, 9–15	549–557	21 269–275	4
9–11	9–14	16–18	18–23	16	15–20	10–14 17–20	176–180 8–10
20, 24	15	19	8	18	10	22	168–176
21–22	16–18	20–21	9–10	18	11	23–24	20
23	19	22	13	25	6, 12 40	25	17
31–32	38	7–8	14	24	13–14 39	26	18
14–19	20–25	25–27	11–12, 17 30–31	16 20–23	5, 23–25 28–29	30, 33 34, 36	13–16
703–707		33	29		4	3	
34	5	31–32	102, 287	7	31	35	12
28–30 33	33–37	28–30	585–603 15–16	445–453	26–27 32	4–5 31–32	23
12–13	39–40	13–14	130–134 465–468	209–210	9, 21	15–16	110–120
242–244	7		119–120	205–218 412–428	22	229, 234 288–299	11
25–27	30–32	9		17	36–38	37–38	21–22
36	26–29	23–24	24–25	8	32–35	28–29	24

This table is continued on next page.

QUICK REFERENCE TABLE

Italic type indicates pages.

CHAP.	TOPIC	KIEK-HOFER	MEYERS	MITCH-ELL Basic	MITCH-ELL Econ.	MOR-GAN
I	Economic Concepts	1	1	1–3	10–11	2
II	Evolution of Economic Activity	*40–46*, 4			1–7	1
III	Modern Economic Systems	2, 37–38 41–42	2, 20	2	8–9, 39	6, 38
IV	Production Organization	5	16–21	5	14	5, 10
V	Size of Business		*113–115*	7	14	9–10
VI	Marketing, Risk, and Transportation	13–14, 30	18	*120–122 233–235*	17	9
VII	Consumption	28	*12–15*	15	25–27	4, 28
VIII	Individual Prices: Demand and Supply	15–21	3–12	6	15–16	8, 11–12
IX	Money	9	20	9	19	26–27
X	Credit and Banking	10	19	8	18	25
XI	Price Levels: Changing Value of Money	26	*340–344*	10	20	21, 23 33
XII	Business Cycle	27, 29, 31	24–26 28	16	28	29, 31
XIII	Distribution of Income	8, 22–25	13–17 23, 27	11–14	21–24	4, 14–17 19–20
XIV	Population Problems	32			32	*165–169 732–733*
XV	Agricultural Problems	*46–52 478–483*			*123–129*	18 *420–422*
XVI	Labor Problems	6–7	*219–226*	14, 19	31	16–17 29–30
XVII	Industrial Concentration, Government Control	40	*429–430*	*96–109*	*180–186 350–361*	13
XVIII	Public Utilities	39			*114–116 354–355*	*235–237*
XIX	Public Finance	33–36	*402–403*	17–18	29–30	20–21 32
XX	International Economic Relations	11–12	21–22	20–22	35–38	34–37

Roman type indicates chapters.

NORDIN & SALERA	PEACH	PETER-SON	POND	ROBIN-SON	SAMUEL-SON	UMBREIT et al.	VAN SICKLE
1–2	1	1, 3, 5	1	1	1–2	1	1–2
	1	2	*2, 382*	2			
3 36–37	1, 5 44–46	5, 33	20	3 42–44	3, 37	2	3–4 43–45
7	16–17	8–9	2, 4	4, 7	5	3	5
	18	*153–177* 21	3	8	*20–23*	3	
			91–96	33 35–36	22		6
17	31–32	19	8	27	11, 23	4	7
6, 21	26–29	17–18	5–6	15–19	19–21 24–25	11–17	7–11 16–18
21 *668–672*	12	10, 12	10	9–10	*46–51* 15	5	21 25–26
22–23	13–14	10–11	10	9, 11–12	14, 16	6	22–24
6 20–21	15	12	13	13–14	13	7	21
27–32	9	14–16	14	25–26	17–18	8–10	27–29
5, 18–20 26	6–8 30–33	24–30	7	20–24	4, 10, 12 26–30	20–21 23–25	12–15
696–701	2–3	6	*56–59*	5	*23–31*		*229–236*
8, 14, 18	43	*560–572*	17	31	21		*34–35*
15–17 24	34–36 41	27 *709–718*	9, 16	5, 6 37	8 *179–183*	22	31–33 36–37
9–12	19	22–23	*146–163*	38	*92–94* *467–471*	18–19	20, 30
13	20	*547–559*	15	32			*428–429*
25	10 21–25	31	11–12	38–41	6–7	26	40–41
33–35	37–40	13, 32	18–19	28–30	31–34 36	27	19, 38–40

See pages viii to xi for complete titles.

CHAPTER ONE

ELEMENTARY ECONOMIC CONCEPTS

NATURE OF ECONOMICS

Conditions of Scarcity. Economics is a social science, a classified body of knowledge concerning human relationships clustered about man's effort to earn a living. Nearly all of the goods and services which man desires for mere existence, or a more comfortable existence, are not freely provided by nature. In order to satisfy his elemental needs for food, clothing, and shelter, as well as his ever-expanding desires for comfort and luxuries, man organizes and toils to increase the production of scarce goods and services. In an age of atomic power, output per man-hour of work may be increased tremendously, and the level of consumption for all may be vastly improved. In such an "economy of abundance," however, goods and services which satisfy human wants will remain scarce relative to total demand because people want more and better things including leisure time in which to enjoy them.

Aims and Major Problems of Economic Analysis. Not all wants can be satisfied, and some wants are rated by individuals as more important than others. Human resources and natural resources can be and are used for producing many different things. Few individuals produce directly the things which they use and want. Consequently, in an organized social group, such as a nation, some system exists for adjusting production and consumption priorities.

The primary aim, then, of economics is an explanation of *how* an economic system operates—that is, how are scarce means of production allocated to satisfy human wants of varying importance? Some of the problems are as follows: How are choices made with regard to the kinds and quantities of goods produced? How are decisions reached with regard to the placement of individuals in different production positions and to their remuneration? Are goods and services made available to individuals on the basis of their needs, or on the basis of their contribution and remuneration as producers? Are jobs always available for willing workers? What is the role of government in the process of allocation?

In a system of communism such as prevails in the U.S.S.R., allocation of the means of production and consumers' items is accomplished mainly by choices of party members in formulating plans for governmental production, wages and salaries, and prices. The process is supplemented by consumers' choices in markets—that is, the kinds and quantities of consumers' items produced may be partly adjusted to consumers' purchases. In a system of private capitalism such as prevails in the United States, allocation, except in a war period, is accomplished mainly by choices in markets—that is, by private production and by private buying and selling of all kinds of producers' and consumers' goods. The process is supplemented by governmental regulations and by some governmental allocations, such as educational facilities, based on democratic voting procedures. The latter type of economic system, which depends predominately on markets as an allocating mechanism, is the one usually referred to in subsequent analysis.

The secondary aim of economics is an evaluation of *how well* an allocating system operates with reference to some standard and includes suggestions of policy for improving the system. The standard or ideal type of allocation which is usually employed is that of competitive markets. Such markets theoretically assure that each line of production is expanded until the price consumers are willing to pay for a given output is equal to its minimum cost of production. The competition of many buyers and sellers of a given commodity is assumed to protect each from exploitation and to require governmental intervention largely for the prevention of theft and fraud. Because of this emphasis on individual freedom of action, the competitive standard of allocation-efficiency is frequently preferred to an ideal type of centralized planning of allocation by government.

Some of the problems are as follows: What are the effects of monopolistic markets as compared with competitive ones and how prevalent are the former? What policies are most effective in dealing with monopolistic situations—enforced competition, regulated prices and services, or government ownership and operation? If for social and humanitarian reasons low-income groups are to receive aid, what programs interfere least with the competitive market process of allocation? As programs of social control expand in curbing monopolies; in aiding low-income groups; in providing industrial accident compensation, unemployment insurance, and sickness and old age benefits; what policies are to be adopted with regard to the financing of governmental services?

Evaluations are made in economics and policies suggested because of the belief that individuals in a free society can alter their evolutionary course, when made aware of alternatives. The analysis, however, points the way only to maximum efficiency in the allocation of resources. It is not a technical critique of consumers' wants, of social incentives, of household management, of business strategy, or of engineering efficiency. It does not provide a complete answer to any social problem because public policy usually includes objectives other than economic efficiency, objectives such as political freedom, economic security, and social justice. These objectives are frequently conflicting, and so free citizens must choose the one or ones to be wholly or partially achieved. In this formulation of public policy, other social sciences, philosophy, and biological sciences contribute information and standards for evaluation. Analysis and policies for improving *economic welfare* constitute only one part of the total *social welfare* of a group.

Methods in Economics. The science of economics attempts to use all the available tools of scientific research. It is compelled, however, because of the nature of its problems and data, to rely more heavily upon qualitative, deductive methods than upon quantitative, inductive methods. In the natural sciences, the phenomena to be studied can frequently be isolated within a laboratory and subjected to a controlled experiment. All factors in the experiment, except one, can be held unchanged while the action of the changing factor can be observed and measured. Hypotheses can be tested and rejected, or if quantitative measurements reveal highly uniformed actions and reactions, the sequence can be stated as a law or principle.

In economics, a division of the social sciences, the problem of verification is very difficult and frequently impossible. The phenomena to be studied *cannot be isolated in a laboratory.* Cost-price relations in markets, variations in income and employment, and other changes in a community, a nation, or the family of nations are the objects of investigation. No controlled experiment is possible. If a tariff act is passed, its effects cannot be accurately determined, for too many other changes occur during the same period. Economics, however, achieves some exactness because of the diversity of its methods.

HISTORICAL METHOD. One method is to analyze and compare the historical development of economic activity and institutions. Since conditions change, and history never repeats, the results might seem insignificant. But historical investigation reveals trends and problems which may reappear in different forms with a few essentials repeated. With a historical perspective, economics can make some allowance for altered conditions and can analyze contemporary economic problems on the basis of past experience. The method is not conclusive because the allowance for new conditions and knowledge may be inaccurately estimated with the result that old obstacles are overstated or understated, but at least it affords a point of departure—a means of presenting more clearly issues and probabilities.

DEDUCTIVE METHOD. A second method is an extension of the historical method—namely, the formulation of generalizations based on past and present experience which are then used as principles or tools to analyze contemporary economic problems. For example, from a historical study of economic activity, from personal observation of present economic activity, and from introspection and a variety of opinions, there may be derived (induction) the principle that most people weigh carefully their acts in order to obtain the greatest satisfaction of their desires for goods and services ("economic man" or "hedonistic calculus" concept). In other words, man's self-interest is assumed to make human conduct rational rather than capricious, to make individuals in the aggregate and on the average (some individual exceptions allowed) act to obtain the pleasure of having more goods and services and to avoid the pain of having less goods and services (the "more or less" or marginal concept).

On the basis of the above generalization economics can formulate hypotheses (deduction) or explanations for given conditions. It can assume laboratory conditions under which individuals move freely about (free competition) to satisfy their self-interest for a maximum amount of goods and services, and under which all factors remain constant except the one to be studied (the "one thing at a time" or "all things being equal" method). The action and consequences of the changing factor can then be stated. For example, if all conditions in a given country remain unchanged except that of an increase in the number of laborers, wages are likely to fall. Several changing factors may sometimes be presented under the above assumptions and their mathematical relations calculated. Sometimes the laboratory conditions are presented in the form of a very primitive economic society where fewer and less complex factors are involved (a microcosm, or Robinson Crusoe assumption), and the analysis which is found suitable there is then applied with some modifications to a complex economic system.

These and other variants of the deductive method are based upon assumed static economic conditions. But everyday economic conditions are constantly changing; they are highly dynamic. An attempt, however, is made to fill the gap by reliance upon the generalizations of free competition and self-interest, operating over a long rather than a short period of time—that is, under dynamic economic conditions approximately the same action and reaction are assumed to occur as under static conditions if longer time is allowed to intervene (the short-run and long-run method of analysis). Economic principles, then, are usually stated as long-run tendencies with many individual exceptions and qualifications.

STATISTICAL METHOD. The chief limitation of this method, as stated previously, is the difficulty of testing one economic change when several changes occur at the same time. If disturbing factors could be eliminated, the effects of economic legislation, such as tax measures, could be conclusively verified. Of course, allowances for disturbing factors in the form of averages, correlation charts, and probability curves can be made ; but the results are not conclusive. The use of allowances for other factors approaches the assumption of static conditions. Moreover, the collection of data may be faulty and subtle mathematics cannot correct it. And finally, there is the problem of interpretation. Statistical investigations do not produce explanations or theories ; they merely fit or do not fit certain explanations which the investigator is testing. Unless repeated tests are possible, the results illustrate rather than prove the explanation of the investigator. Nevertheless, the statistical method, properly qualified, is useful to check minor points and may become more effective as raw data improve in quality and quantity.

The critical student of economics will examine carefully all assumptions made in economics or any other social science ; the reasoning based upon given assumptions is usually sound. If the main assumptions seem plausible, he will weigh carefully the qualifications involved in order to determine the probabilities of application to actual problems.

TYPES OF ECONOMICS

General books and texts on economics may be roughly classified into three groups according to the methods of investigation used and the emphasis given to the problems of market allocation of scarce resources versus government allocation.

Price and Private Enterprise Economics. This type of economic analysis is usually mainly deductive and explores on the basis of assumed conditions all kinds of possible market relations. If very little attention is given to probable market relations, it is referred to as *pure theory* and is often expressed in mathematical terms. In this approach existing human wants, present distribution of wealth, and current techniques of production are commonly treated as given conditions or constant factors. Most of the analysis is static and is devoted to a logical demonstration of equilibrium adjustments of maximum production and satisfaction of wants at minimum costs in a sys-

tem of competitive markets and private business en
The analysis includes the uneconomic effects of monopo
the policies of governmental intervention for offsetting
effects. It ignores, however, many of the exceptional a   -a-
tion problems, such as the provision of educational facilities,
the conservation of natural resources, and the assistance to low-
income groups which require governmental rather than competitive market allocation.

Institutional and Welfare Economics. The method used
is largely inductive. It includes historical descriptions of the
development of institutions, such as private property, markets,
and private business enterprise and capitalism. In part the
historical analysis may be in statistical terms showing economic
trends and probable relationships of changing factors. Descriptions, qualitative and statistical, in the form of case studies of
business firms' decisions and policies, business relations within
an industry, and practices in markets are additional characteristics of this type of economics. Because of the unique features
of some markets; the lag of changing institutions behind changing economic conditions; the unavoidable mixture of market
allocations, competitive and monopolistic, and government allocations; and the stream of technological inventions and innovations, the general explanation is in dynamic terms of economic development or evolution and not economic equilibrium.
This approach emphasizes the exceptional cases in which competitive market allocations of private business are usually replaced by government allocations and the probable trends in
the development of additional exceptions. Since these exceptions are based largely on the social needs of the group and not
on what some individuals may want and may be able to buy,
the analysis is sometimes extended to include noneconomic,
especially ethical, considerations. Broad *social welfare* rather
than *economic welfare* is then the goal of suggested policies of
governmental regulation and social control.

Planning and Socialistic Economics. This type of economics may be either deductive or inductive, theoretical or
historical and statistical. It is not characterized so much by
the methods used as by the emphasis on government allocation.
The analysis of the planning approach stresses the wide varia-

tions in total output, income, and employment of a private enterprise system of market allocation. Millions of private firms, according to the analysis, individually plan future output with no quick central clearance or co-ordination of plans other than price changes in markets as the plans unfold. Individual plans for saving and investing may be inconsistent and recurring readjustments entail tremendous business losses and serious unemployment. Proposals for determination by government of production priorities, somewhat as in a war period, and particularly proposals for budgetary and other adjustments by government which would supplement private investment in order to maintain a high level of employment are typical of economic planning. Socialistic analysis stresses variations in employment of a private market-allocation system and the need for centralized planning of production. In addition it contends that such planning can be effective only when the government owns and operates practically all production units.

(The student of economics may be confused by the diversity of method and approach to problems and crave more synthesis and unity. In a science, however, which investigates changing human relationships, several points of view are frequently tenable; proof of any one is not conclusive; and hence, the art of synthesis is partly in the hands of the student. After careful reading of texts on economics, the student can determine their general approach and can supplement them, if necessary, from other special sources.)

TRADITIONAL TERMS IN ECONOMICS

Since methods and emphasis on problems differ in economics, the definitions of terms differ. Most distinctions, moreover, are of degree rather than kind. Although the definitions of any economist are consequently arbitrary, they are necessary to convey his exact meaning. The careful student, then, will master definitions, not as a short cut to truths, but as an aid to a critical evaluation of any economic analysis.

Utility. This is the quality goods and services possess when they satisfy human wants. The wants may be wise or foolish.

Useful Goods and Services. They possess utility and may be divided into the following groups:

FREE GOODS (free services practically nonexistent). Free goods possess utility, but are available in relatively unlimited quantities, such as air, sunlight, rainfall, etc. Individuals obtain them freely with practically no effort or payment; hence they are outside the subject of economics.

ECONOMIC GOODS AND SERVICES. These possess utility but are scarce relative to the demand for them. The scarcity may be the result of natural limitations (e.g., coal or artistic ability), artificial limitations (e.g., monopoly), or social limitations (e.g., conventions). *Private economic goods* or *services* are those which individuals use economically or sparingly because their use is obtained with some individual effort or payment, such as food, clothing, shelter, autos, legal advice, etc. *Public economic goods* and *services* are those which may be partially or entirely free to individual users, but involve effort or payment on the part of the social group, such as parks, museums, roads, public health protection, etc.

Wealth. In a broad sense another name for economic goods and services on hand at a given time is wealth. Individuals or nations are wealthy or poor according to the quantity and quality of the economic goods and services which they possess. Since *property* is merely a legal relationship of persons to goods and services, property claims to goods and services, such as mortgages, bonds, licenses, and contracts, are not included as wealth. *Money* (metallic, paper currency, drafts, etc.) is usually not wealth, but merely a measure of, or claim to, wealth. A gold coin, however, melted into bullion is wealth because there are many uses for gold as a commodity. To a miser a hoard of money is in part wealth (perverted wealth) since it yields him direct satisfaction.

Various Definitions of Wealth. Wealth may be defined in three different ways:

1) Economic goods which are tangible and owned by human beings. (This definition excludes from wealth personal services, except those of slaves; property rights to economic goods; and other intangibles, such as good will, patent rights, etc.)

2) Economic goods and that portion of property rights which may not merely represent or duplicate economic goods,

such as good will, patents, franchises, etc. (This definition excludes from wealth personal services, except those of slaves. It conforms rather closely to the legal and business concept of wealth.)

3) Economic goods and services, as well as free goods, which contribute to human welfare. (This social definition of wealth excludes such items as opium, gambling devices, artificial scarcity created by man, and other goods and services which may be desired by some individuals, but are held to be undesirable by the social group—that is, might have utility, but be socially undesirable.)

Production. *Production* is the *process* of *creating wealth*— that is, making economic goods and services available for the satisfaction of human wants. It involves the creation of form utility (e.g., growing wheat, making flour, baking bread), place utility (e.g., transporting bread to retail stores), time utility (e.g., bread held by grocers and supplied when demanded), ownership utility (e.g., brokers and bankers assist buying and selling in the process of converting wheat into bread), and the utility of personal services (e.g., making medical aid and advice available for workers in the flour industry). In other words production includes such activities as mining, farming, manufacturing, financing, entertaining, advising medically or legally, etc. Production may be either *direct* (e.g., hand production without tools) or *roundabout* (tool, machine, power production), but is now predominately the latter in advanced industrial nations. Since production is roundabout, the goods and services made available by most persons are not for their immediate use, but are *exchanged* for the goods and services which they want.

Factors of Production.

LAND AND NATURAL RESOURCES. These include economic goods (limited in quantity as regards human wants) which exist without the aid of human labor.

LABOR. This includes all human effort (physical or mental, irksome or pleasurable) used in the production of economic goods and services. The *efficiency* of *labor* is largely determined by racial heritage, bodily vigor, training, and social environment. Labor may be of two kinds. *Productive labor* satisfies human wants either by making material goods or by furnishing services. (The earlier English economists considered as productive only the labor given to making material objects.) *Predatory labor* either fails to satisfy human wants (narrow economic interpretation) or satisfies human wants which the social group considers undesirable (broad social or ethical interpretation). The efforts of some advertisers, gamblers, swindlers, patent medicine peddlers, etc., may be viewed as productive according to the narrow economic interpretation if they actually satisfy human wants, but would be viewed as partially or entirely predatory according to the broad social or ethical interpretation.

CAPITAL GOODS OR INTERMEDIATE GOODS (*producers' goods*). These comprise those goods produced by man for use in further production (e.g., tools, machinery, factory buildings, raw materials, etc.). They satisfy human wants indirectly. Capital goods are accumulated by consuming less than is produced or by *saving*. [Sometimes no distinction is made between land and capital goods; both are treated as capital for the reason that investment in either involves similar problems. Capital goods, of course, may be thought of as the money sum which represents or measures it—that is, *capital value*. Both concepts (capital goods, or the monetary expression of capital goods, capital value) are useful, but the exact meaning employed should be carefully distinguished by the student to avoid confusion. Capital value may include intangibles, such as good will and patent rights.] Money capital is savings available for, but not invested in, producers' goods.

THE ENTREPRENEUR (businessman, organizer, enterpriser). He is a special type of laborer. His function or place in production is that of organizing the other three factors into an operating unit, directing its operations, and assuming responsibility for its operations. The entrepreneurial function is basically an initiating and innovating operation rather than a routine managerial one. It may be performed by several persons or groups in a large modern corporation.

Consumption. *Consumption* is the process of using economic goods and services in the direct satisfaction of human wants. It involves the gradual diminution or the destruction of utilities by human beings—diminution if the goods are durable, such as houses, and destruction if the goods are non-durable, such as food. *Consumers' goods* are finished goods capable of satisfying directly the wants of persons who possess them. (Raw materials or machines used up in the process of manufacture are producers' goods. Finished commodities on the shelves of a retailer, such as groceries and cosmetics, are producers' goods, but when sold to customers become consumers' goods.)

Income and Its Distribution. The distribution of money income is the link between production and consumption. Total expenditures in a year for consumers' goods and services, for producers' goods, and for public goods and services represent the value of the *gross national product*. The goods and services are made available and their purchase made possible by the incurring of costs and the collecting of taxes. The bulk of the costs, excluding depreciation and certain business taxes, are income payments or receipts in the form of wages and salaries, rents, interest, and profits. (Costs to one firm because of purchases from another, say raw materials, are gross receipts to the latter and not net income to anyone.) The total amount of these distributive shares of income for the factors of production is *net national income*. A large portion of net national income is spent on consumers' goods and services, a part is saved and invested in the purchase of producers' goods, and a part is paid as personal taxes to provide public goods and services. This disposition of net national income plus provisions for depreciation and certain business taxes are equal to the value of the gross national product.

Distribution of income according to the four general classes of fundamental services needed in production—that is, services of land, labor, capital, and entrepreneurs—is called *factoral or functional distribution of income. Personal distribution of income* refers to the size of incomes received by different individuals and such income for a person may consist of only one factoral type, say wages, or it may be a combination of several. Individual *real income* consists of the goods and services which the money income will buy, and *psychic income,* the satisfaction derived from the real income.

Value. The *value* of a good or service is the quantity of other goods and services which may be obtained in exchange for it. For example, ten bushels of potatoes under a barter or "swapping" system may be exchanged for one pair of shoes. Shoes, then, have a value of ten bushels of potatoes and ten bushels of potatoes the value of one pair of shoes. If ten bushels of potatoes are exchanged for five dollars, then the value of five dollars is ten bushels of potatoes. Since money is a convenient medium of exchange, value is usually expressed in terms of money.

Price. The *price* of a good or service is the amount of money which is obtained in exchange for one unit of it. Price differs from value as follows:

1) Value may be expressed in terms of any good or service—price always in terms of money.

2) Value is used for any quantity of goods and services—price relates only to one unit.

Although economics attempts occasionally to go behind the money measure of goods and services into the realm of real costs, real income, and social welfare, the major analysis is confined to the field of money exchange or price. The reason for this restriction is a practical one—namely, the difficulty, if not impossibility, of finding an objective quantitative measure of ethical values, real welfare, and service. Exchange value or market price is usually the only objective factor on which economics effectively can base its analysis of man's effort to earn a living.

GENERAL REFERENCES

Clark, J. M., *Preface to Social Economics.*

Commons, John R., *Institutional Economics.*

Fraser, L. M., *Economic Thought and Language.*

Galbraith, John K., *Economics and the Art of Controversy.*

Henderson, H. D., *Supply and Demand.*

Hicks, J. R., A. G. Hart, and J. W. Ford, *The Social Framework of the American Economy* (2nd edition).

Higgs, Henry, *Bibliography of Economics.*

Hobson, J. A., *Economics and Ethics.*

Huff, Darrell, and Irving Geis, *How to Lie with Statistics.*

Hutchison, T. W., *The Significance and Basic Postulates of Economic Theory.*

Keynes, John Maynard, *The General Theory of Employment, Interest and Money.*

Knight, F. H., *The Ethics of Competition.*

———, *Freedom and Reform.*

Lerner, A. P., *The Economics of Control.*

Peck, Harvey W., *Economic Thought and Its Institutional Background.*

Pigou, A. C., *Economics of Welfare.*

Robbins, Lionel, *The Economist in the Twentieth Century.*

———, *The Nature and Significance of Economic Science.*

Stonier, A. W., and D. C. Hague, *The Essentials of Economics.*

Wootton, Barbara, *Lament for Economics.*

Wright, David M., *A Key to Modern Economics.*

Chapter Two

EVOLUTION OF ECONOMIC ACTIVITY

EARLY TECHNOLOGICAL CHANGES

The result of man's desire to protect himself and to increase production with the least effort was the invention of tools. Stone tools were used by primitive man as early as 125,000 B.C. At first the majority of tools consisted of weapons—hatchets, flints, and the bow and arrow. As man became less of a nomad he devised agricultural tools—the plow, the hoe, the grindstone, and a wheeled vehicle.

Metal tools marked the transition from barbarism to civilization, the metal age extending from the time of the Pharaohs to the American Revolution (roughly from 3000 B.C. to A.D. 1750.) More elaborate tools could be fashioned from tin, copper, lead, gold, and silver. As life became easier men turned to science where revolutionizing discoveries and inventions took place in mathematics, geography, astronomy, chemistry, and physics. Many civilizations rose and fell; the Dark Ages passed; and with the Renaissance came the Arabic system of notation, the invention of gun powder, printing, and the mariner's compass, which opened the way for the coming commercial revolution.

Machines, as tools, were introduced in the latter half of the 18th century. This significant change in production is referred to as the Industrial Revolution. Since iron and coal were indispensable for machine production, the machine age may well be called the age of iron and coal. Discoveries and inventions, which are still continuing, altered many phases of economic, political, and social life. Hand methods in *agriculture* were in part replaced by the reaper, threshing machine, tractor, and combine. *Communication* was speeded up by the invention of the telephone, wireless, radio, and rotary press. *Transportation,* first by turnpike and canal, was increased in efficiency and swiftness by means of the railroad, automobile, and airplane. Hand machines existing prior to the Industrial Revolution gave way to machines driven by water or steam which produced more goods in less time. *Power* was greatly augmented when steam and water were used to generate electricity, and machines were constructed which not only produced more goods in less time but also produced goods that would have been impossible under any system of hand labor. Jet propulsion, electronic devices, synthetics and plastics, and atomic power characterize recent technological changes and reflect future developments.

DEVELOPMENT OF ECONOMIC ORGANIZATIONS

From early times people organized and co-operated in using tools to produce the goods which they desired or could exchange for other desirable goods. Each organization became less independent economically as tools grew more elaborate and production more roundabout. The following stages in the development of economic organizations merely suggest the changes which occurred in a few countries. Some groups of people never developed all the stages set forth below, developed them in a different order, or at the present time have many of the stages existing side by side.

Prior to the Industrial Revolution.

DIRECT APPROPRIATION TYPE. This economic organization is chiefly concerned with primitive man who satisfied his daily needs directly from nature—hunting, fishing, gathering food, etc.

PASTORAL OR PASTORAL-AGRICULTURE TYPE. This organization occurred when man started to domesticate animals and wild grain for his own use. It may also be called the *household system* when a family, clan, or tribe formed an economic unit. Here was found some division of labor, a little bartering within the group, and complete self-sufficiency. In the order of their complexity we have as examples the nomad tribes, the large estates of the Romans, and the English manor or feudal system.

The English manor with a feudal basis, predominant in the

10th to 14th centuries, was based on land tenure and personal services. The head of the manor was the lord who was subject to the authority of the king, who in turn was subject to the Church. The *Church,* which actively engaged in economic and political matters of the day, became a great unifying force. The lord ruled over a tract of land tenanted by laborers who ranged from serfs, who were bound to the soil, to freemen, who were artisans, blacksmiths, and millers. They were expected to give a certain number of days of agricultural and military work as well as a part of their product to the lord in return for physical protection and courts for settling disputes. Practically everything consumed or used, with the exception of salt, metals, and tar, was produced on the manor. The manor declined as increased trade, a result of the Crusades, and wars broke up its isolation. Money appeared, and serfs bought their freedom or ran away to become free citizens in the towns which were growing up around castles, monasteries, or where trade routes crossed.

THE HANDICRAFT STAGE. In the 14th century when towns began to thrive, the handicraft stage appeared. Here was the beginning of specialization when the cobbler, smith, tailor, weaver, carpenter, etc., began producing quantities of goods not for their own use but for others to consume. Money became increasingly important in the new *commercial revolution.* Towns vied with each other for commercial and political influence. Trade was a privilege of the citizens of the town and outside traders were burdened with restrictions.

Merchant Guilds. Traders within a given town furthered their interests commercially and also politically by uniting in a kind of chamber of commerce called the *merchant guild.* The guilds regulated trade and tried to keep it a monopoly for the town merchants.

Craft Guilds. These united members of special trades— the glass workers' guild, the cobblers' guild, etc.—in the regulation of their trade as well as in religious and social interests. The members of the craft guilds, in order to avoid the severe regulations of the merchants' guilds, began to market their own products and thus gradually brought about the decline of the merchant guilds. Admittance to the craft guilds was difficult; an applicant had to spend several years as apprentice and journeyman before he could become a master. Their aim was to protect members from outside competition and to secure honest workmanship. The guilds were greatly weakened when outsiders began to produce goods and market them surreptitiously and when members, to escape guild regulation, left the towns. In England a further blow came when Henry VIII in the 16th century confiscated all their property which had been used for religious purposes.

The Medieval Fair. The medieval fair, promoted by the guilds, brought traders and buyers together. Commercial disputes were settled according to the *law merchant*—an informal arbitration procedure which avoided antiquated court methods. Later the law merchant became a part of the statutory and common law of various countries.

THE DOMESTIC SYSTEM OR PUTTING-OUT TYPE. This organization (16th to the middle of the 18th century), which followed the guilds, may be called the first step in modern capitalism. It marked the appearance of the middleman who bought raw material, "put it out" to workers, and found a market for the finished product. In some cases he supplied the tools, often simple machines run by hand, and thus began the separation of the craftsman from the ownership of his tools. The middleman had to be a capitalist because he was producing for an unknown market, buying raw materials, and paying wages.

Nationalism. The breakdown of the old economic and political systems caused the rise of nationalism, particularly in England. National states increased their power at the expense of feudal lords, guilds, towns, and the Church.

Mercantilism. The national system of regulation which prevailed in the growing national states of England and Europe was mercantilism. Economic and social activity was regulated with a view to maximizing national wealth. Some of these doctrines were concerned with building up a colonial empire, developing a favorable balance of trade, increasing population, and controlling internal trade.

Laissez Faire. This "let-things-alone" policy was the one which, particularly in England, succeeded mercantilism. The growing commercial class and wealthy traders found that their interests and those of the state were not always in harmony.

They felt that the government should not interfere with individual activity. Adam Smith supported this individualistic policy in his famous "Wealth of Nations" published in 1776. He believed that individual welfare and national prosperity were usually compatible—that is, if everyone were allowed to follow his own self-interest, the greatest national good would result. Gradually many of the old mercantilistic regulations disappeared and men were left with greater freedom to bargain, trade, or enter into contract as they saw fit. Not only domestic trade was to be free from regulation but also foreign trade with other countries was to be freed from tariff restrictions.

Agricultural Changes. There were agricultural changes of great importance occurring during this period. The common fields, which had been disappearing as the need for sheep pasturage increased, continued to be enclosed in order that new methods of agriculture could be tried. Better breeds of cattle, crop rotation, introduction of root crops and hay increased food production with less labor. Wealthy gentlemen, desiring prestige and wishing to build up estates, bought huge tracts of land which pushed out the small farmer and left him free to enter the new factory system appearing on the horizon.

The English Industrial Revolution.

ORIGIN. Great Britain was the scene of the Industrial Revolution (1770–1840) during which the domestic system slowly changed to the *factory system.* The change consisted basically of the introduction of machines and the application of mechanical power. The *geographical isolation* of Great Britain freed her from some of the devastating effects of the continental wars, lessened fear of attack, and enabled her to flourish as a shipping and trading nation. *Accumulated capital,* a necessity in the roundabout process of manufacture, was available in England because of her foreign trade. *Laborers* were available because of their personal freedom—the manors and guilds had been broken down. Skilled laborers also had come from other countries to escape religious persecution. *Coal* and *iron* deposits of good quality were conveniently located. *Inventions* in the textile industries (Kay's shuttle, 1738; Hargreaves' spinning jenny, 1767; Crompton's mule, 1779; and Cartwright's power loom, 1784) and in the iron industry (the steam engine and blast furnace) appeared rapidly because of the mechanical skill developed by British artisans and because the opportunity for supplying larger markets stimulated improvements. Private capitalism had reached the industrial stage in which the emphasis on profit-making shifted from buying and selling hand-produced goods and from leasing property and lending money to pioneering in the development and ownership of machines capable of greatly increasing production.

DESCRIPTION OF THE INDUSTRIAL REVOLUTION.

Factories. These were an outgrowth of the use of power. The earlier hand machines, mostly wooden, could be used in a home or small building, but the new power machines of iron run by water or steam had to be near the source of power supply (waterfalls or coal deposits). The machines were too large and heavy for a small home and too expensive for a laborer to buy. Large industrial towns sprang up where factories were located and where coal and iron were mined.

Laborers. Families, giving up their gardens and live stock, moved to the cities to work for wages. Crowded living conditions, factory discipline, and foul workrooms were distasteful to the laborers, and riots often broke out, resulting in the destruction of machinery. As the demand for goods increased, the new factories became firmly entrenched. Employers vied with each other to turn out the largest quantity of goods. Hours of work were unbearably long; women and children were exploited; living and working conditions were increasingly miserable. But manufacturers who wanted as little interference as possible clung to the laissez-faire doctrine.

Transportation. Increased transportation facilities expanded local markets to national and world markets. Roads in England during the 18th century were very poor and in the winter often impassable. There was great need for transporting coal, iron, and raw materials to the factories as well as for transporting finished goods to the markets. Turnpike trusts were formed to build roads and keep them in repair. Canals provided cheaper transportation for heavy or bulky goods. Railways, in the face of much opposition, increased the speed of transportation and the demand for coal and iron. As foreign demand increased and Great Britain improved her specialization in manufacturing, she became the foremost world trader.

EFFECTS OF THE INDUSTRIAL REVOLUTION.

Production. As new industries sprang up and undeveloped industries became powerful, production increased greatly. Necessities could be had in greater abundance and even a taste of luxury was not impossible for the laboring class. Although population increased very rapidly, the level of consumption rose for society as a whole. Increased consumption and increased leisure followed the introduction of machinery.

Labor and Capital. Labor and capital found that their interests clashed under the new regime. Since tasks were divided into minute operations, the laborer's skill and knowledge were less important in competitive bargaining. Laborers no longer owned their tools nor were they in personal contact with their employer on whom they depended for their entire livelihood. On the other hand, depreciation and interest charges were large on the expensive machinery used, so employers tended to drive sharp bargains with laborers in order to meet the charges and make profits.

Political Control. As the old laissez-faire policy failed to protect the consumer and laborer, political control was found to be necessary. Government inspection of goods to determine quality prevented some adulteration and fraud. A series of laws regulating hours of labor, factory conditions, and types of work for women and children brought about better conditions than existed under the old domestic system. State education, minimum wage laws, workmen's compensation, and social insurance are more recent measures that completely break away from laissez faire. Laws which prevented labor organizations were repealed, and trade-unions rapidly increased in number and bargaining power. Public control has now been extended to the regulation and operation of some industries, such as railroads, public utilities, and parcel post.

Urban Problems. The rapid increase in city population brought about many problems. Workers were crowded together in unsanitary buildings. Filth and disease undermined the health of men, women, and children in slums and tenements. Machines brought noise, smoke, and dirt which cost cities and individuals millions of dollars a year and injured health. Sew age, garbage disposal, water supply, fire and police protection are other common problems to be met by an urban population, an outgrowth of the factory system.

Trade Fluctuations. The national and international markets of an interdependent economic system make it difficult to estimate demand, especially when a rising level of consumption makes demand more fickle. Increasing numbers of producers know little about what others are producing or the total supply of their product. Plans made by some to save, by others to invest, and by still others to produce investment goods are frequently inconsistent. Improvements and innovations are always occurring to upset the stability of some part of the economic system. Thus large-scale production and interdependence have made trade fluctuations increasingly severe for both the wage earner and the businessman.

WORLD-WIDE INDUSTRIALISM

The United States. The Industrial Revolution developed gradually, beginning a half century later in the United States than in England. And in the United States, it was largely an outgrowth of British industrial experience.

PRIOR TO THE CIVIL WAR.

Technological Development. This development was slow in the United States because England, fearing competition, refused to allow machinery or mechanical plans to leave the country; because the United States gained more in producing raw materials to exchange for manufactured goods; and because free land and rich resources absorbed most of the population and left no available labor supply for factories. The United States had a comparative advantage in agriculture and shipping.

The mercantilistic policy of England in regulating colonial trade and commerce and in forcing the colonies to share government expenses was resented by a country where cheap land and pioneering had developed an independent spirit. Certain economic interests in the United States could not be harmonized with British regulatory policy, and the Revolutionary War broke out. Later the economic interests of the growing commercial class were instrumental in forming the Constitution of the United States, because trade had been hampered by state laws and regulations under the Articles of Confederation.

Manufacturing was stimulated when the Revolutionary War and the War of 1812 cut off the supply of foreign goods. In 1789, Slater, a former apprentice to Arkwright, started a cotton mill in Pawtucket; later (1814) Lowell founded a textile factory in Waltham, Massachusetts, and used power looms. New England with meager natural resources, except waterfalls, became the center of manufacturing. Here laborers were more willing to work in factories. Machinery and manufacturing came simultaneously in America and seemed the natural thing. Most of the evils of the English Industrial Revolution were escaped since dissatisfied laborers could pioneer in the West. The new industries received encouragement from tariffs and prizes, but they increased slowly until the time of the Civil War.

Economic Industrial Stages. These were often contemporaneous in the United States. As the frontier was pushed westward, primitive conditions with hunters and trappers existed; near the frontier was the pastoral stage of development; next agriculture; and farther east trade, commerce, and manufacture. Such an economic situation led to sectionalism. The East, the West, the North, and the South had their individual economic interests which clashed in political parties, in the federal government, and finally, in the Civil War. Slavery in the South was dying out until Whitney's invention of the cotton gin in 1793 made slave labor commercially profitable in cotton growing. Merchants and financiers of the more populous East and North dominated the federal government which passed tariff legislation favorable to their industrial interests. To offset the political influence of the northern states, the agricultural South, which desired free trade, attempted to have more slave states admitted to the union. Thus slavery was primarily a political and economic question rather than a moral one.

AFTER THE CIVIL WAR.

The Homestead Act of 1862. This act opened the West to an increased population and gave away thousands of acres of the public domain for little or nothing. Some economists believe that this measure harmed agriculture and delayed urban and industrial development. Better *transportation* was needed to hold together such an extensive country. The United States had passed through the turnpike (1790–1816) and canal (1807–1837) periods. Now the government, by grants of land and other aids, subsidized the building of railroads. Because of the monopolistic tendencies among railroads, which was partly due to overbuilding, government control later became necessary.

Agricultural efficiency was also increasing. Machinery and scientific methods had increased production to such an extent that in 1940 only about 20 per cent of the population needed to work on farms to feed the entire population, whereas in 1860 approximately 60 per cent of the population was required. Declining prices for agricultural products during most of the period, 1865–1897, created discontent among farmers which led to reform movements. After World War I farmers were unable to adjust supplies of basic crops to declining demand. A heavy mortgage burden, taxes, and the tariff aggravated the maladjustment which finally ended in substantial government aids to agriculture.

Manufacturing. After the Civil War there was a rapid increase in manufacturing. The natural increase in population combined with immigration enlarged the market for manufactured articles. Improvements in machinery and power, standardization, and large-scale production lessened unit costs. Since large amounts of capital were needed to finance these huge undertakings, industrial control became concentrated in the corporation. In many industries a few corporations account for most of the output. Since 1880 industrial concentration and monopolistic combinations have been characteristic of American industry. During World War II, however, these industries demonstrated a record capacity for production.

The Labor Movement. In the United States a labor movement, similar to the English one, united trades into unions. The American Federation of Labor later became a confederation of craft unions. The unity and vigor of the English labor movement, however, was lacking, partly because of the better economic opportunities which existed in a new country, and partly because of the difficulty of organizing the flood of immigrants as well as the American Negro. In the great depression of the 30's the Committee for Industrial Organization brought together all types of workers, skilled and unskilled, in mass-production industries and formed industrial unions. These unions were expelled from the AF of L in 1938. The CIO unions have since become active in party politics. No unified labor movement has yet appeared in the United States.

State Regulation. Industry became more widespread as the economy of the country increased in complexity. The free trade policy of the Revolutionary Period gave way to high protective tariffs on manufactures. Governmental commissions were established to regulate prices of monopolistic industries and to place competition on a more equitable basis in other industries. Legislation to protect consumers against impure foods, to safeguard the health of workers in factories, and to promote child welfare increased in importance. Regulation of the banking system, assistance to agriculture, and control of labor unions were other significant activities of the government. After World War II measures to offset economic fluctuations and to preserve a high level of employment without replacing private enterprises with socialistic enterprises became the central objective of public policy.

Trade and Finance Position. The *international trade* and *finance* of the United States developed several significant new features. Manufactured goods gradually supplanted raw materials as the chief exports, whereas imports of manufactured goods gave way to increasing imports of raw materials. As regards international finance (private, long-term investments) citizens of the United States who were net debtors to the extent of three billion dollars in 1913 became net creditors to the extent of about eleven billion dollars in 1930. This new trade and finance position gave the United States a dominant place in world economy, which was demonstrated during World War II by lend-lease shipments valued at about fifty billion dollars. Although the net, private, long-term lending position of the United States declined to a few billion dollars at the end of the war, the government assumed a leading role in providing relief gifts and special reconstruction loans and in promoting international financial and trade organizations for improving the economic relations of nations. The shift in the center of gravity for international trade and finance from London to Washington which began after World War I was completed after World War II.

France. The industrial development of France began after the final defeat of Napoleon in 1815. The country has always been handicapped by the lack of iron and coal resources but in spite of this has developed manufacturing. Handicrafts are also fostered. Agriculture, however, still occupies about one-half of the people. For political and social reasons national policy favors the development of a balanced economy of manufactures and agriculture. France's important position in international finance in the interwar period testified at least in part to the success of the above policy. However, the country's international economic prospects following World War II are for a lower level of exports and imports than formerly because of its inability to regain its former capacity to produce. Devastation of the war in physical plants, in economic organization, and in workers' morale is not likely to be offset quickly by the present program of socialization of a few industries.

Germany. Although Germany lagged a century behind England in industrialization, she rapidly absorbed the factory system. As a result of the War of 1870 with France, the German states achieved political unity. Under a paternalistic government her excellent coal resources and her fair iron resources enabled her, in 1914, to rival the United States in steel production. German industry was encouraged by the government to build up trusts, cartels, and export combinations. International trade was extended by a large merchant marine and an imperialistic foreign policy. Although German industry was weakened by the World War I losses of capital equipment, iron deposits, and colonies, many lines of German industry in the interwar period equalled in efficiency the best plants of other countries. As a result of World War II, Germany will probably never regain her former relative position in international trade and finance.

Japan. The factory system was adopted in Japan as a defense against European industrialism. Although weak in natural resources of coal and iron, the Imperial Government of

Japan systematically fostered industrialization. Aided by semi-automatic machines and new power resources (hydro-electric), Japan became the leading industrial country of the orient during the interwar period. Defeat in World War II is likely to retard Japanese industrial development for many years and to entail a permanent loss of her former relative position in international trade.

Russia. Under the Czars, Russia received little encouragement to industrialize or to take advantage of her huge natural resources. After World War I the Soviet Government launched a series of "Five Year Plans" of industrialization. Practically all means of production were owned by the state, and the Communist party directed production and regulated consumption. Huge factories, power plants, community homes, and transportation facilities were constructed. Industrialization was extremely difficult, however, partly because capital equipment was obtained from abroad by exporting low-priced raw materials, and partly because skilled labor for manufacturing or mechanized agriculture was lacking. Nevertheless, the forced industrialization of the country at the expense of consumers' goods provided the means for stopping the Nazi German war machine and for delivering a powerful contribution to its destruction. Following World War II Soviet Russia emerged as a leading military and industrial power. Because of the diversity and richness of her natural resources and because of her policy of isolation, her position in international trade and finance is likely to be a minor one. Her economic influence in the world, however, as the leading communist state and as a rival of the United States, a country of private capitalism, is the most important development of the postwar period.

England. Today England is confronted with rivals in world trade. As a result of the Industrial Revolution, England had a monopoly of the manufacturing trade of the world for almost a century. She built up a vast colonial empire and the world's largest merchant marine. Her citizens became the world's largest creditors. The spread of the Industrial Revolution to other countries and its development there made necessary a partial reorganization of British industry. This readjustment was underway when World War II placed a crushing burden on the country. Great Britain will probably continue as an important country in international trade and finance, but not in the same relative position as formerly. Since only 10 per cent of her people are engaged in agriculture, Great Britain must continue to manufacture and export in order to feed her large population. In order to meet this grave problem of the postwar period a few industries have been acquired by the government and a semisocialistic direction of production and regulation of consumption has been adopted.

GENERAL REFERENCES

Beard, Charles and Mary, *The Rise of American Civilization.*

Bining, Arthur C., *Rise of American Economic Life.*

Clapham, J. H., *The Economic Development of France and Germany, 1815–1914.*

Faulkner, H. W., *American Economic History.*

Gras, N. S. B., *Introduction to Economic History.*

Heaton, H., *Economic History of Europe.*

Johnson, E. A. J., *Some Origins of the Modern Economic World.*

Kirkland, Edward C., *A History of American Economic Life.*

Lipson, E., *The Economic History of England,* volumes I, II, and III.

Nef, John V., *America and Civilization.*

Shannon, F. A., *Economic History of the People of the United States.*

Usher, A. P., *History of Mechanical Inventions.*

Weber, Max, *General Economic History.*

Wright, Chester W., *Economic History of the United States.*

CHAPTER THREE

CHARACTERISTICS OF MODERN ECONOMIC SYSTEMS

ECONOMIC SYSTEMS

Economic systems may have different forms, but the general aims of each of them must be the same: goods must be produced, efficiency must be encouraged, and individual shares must be distributed in order to provide for consumption. The main difference appears in the mechanism for co-ordinating production and consumption.

Autonomous Economic Order. The autonomous economic order is one in which an individual (Robinson Crusoe) or a family (in pioneer days) is self-sufficing. The individual or unit determines what shall be produced and how it shall be consumed. There is no problem of the interrelation of production and consumption units. This type of economic order, which rarely exists, helps to illustrate the task which every economic order must perform and also demonstrates that in complex economic systems these tasks are divided among millions of production and consumption units and must be co-ordinated.

Free Private Enterprise or Capitalism. The essential element of private enterprise or capitalism, as it exists in the United States, is freedom of individual action in buying and selling goods and services and in owning and organizing the means of production for private gain. Prices which emerge from market transactions provide the main mechanism for co-ordination of production and consumption. Individuals as consumers indicate their preferences for goods and services by using their incomes for purchases; individuals as producers derive their income and engage in production according to the opportunities for gain in the sale of goods and services. Individuals are specialized and not self-sufficing. Largely because of economic interdependence the government protects, assists, and regulates economic activity in order to prevent the free conduct of some from depriving others of their freedom. The direction of economic activity, however, rests primarily with market conditions and the opportunity for profit-making by private enterprise in supplying markets.

Socialism and Communism. The terms socialism and communism are not precise and are often used interchangeably. The Soviet Union, commonly referred to as a communist state, in its constitution calls itself a socialist state. Socialism and communism can best be understood as representing different degrees of state ownership of the means of production and of centralized governmental planning and control of economic activity.

Socialism. Socialism involves the state ownership of natural resources and the means of production in *basic* industries. Production is planned and directed by the government according to the principle of production for use and not for profit. Individuals can own personal property, engage in small private business and agriculture, and work for wages. They are free to choose their own occupations and to make their own choices of goods. By limiting the variety of goods and services planned for production, the government can restrict the freedom of choice of consumers and workers. Markets and prices exist only as a partial co-ordinating mechanism for production and consumption. The United Kingdom is a semisocialistic state.

Communism. In a pure form, communism involves the state ownership of *both producers' and consumers' goods.* Goods and services are distributed not according to ability as a producer but according to *needs.* In Soviet Russia, state ownership and governmental control have been carried further than in any other country. All land and natural resources are owned by the state. Practically all other means of production are owned by the state or by workers' co-operatives. Farms, for example, are either operated by the government in the same manner as state-owned mines, factories, railroads, banks, and stores, or by workers' co-operatives which conform to governmental production plans. Private business is restricted mostly to a few professions and one-man or one-family production units. Private hiring of labor for production of goods for sale is forbidden. Except for professional tools and minor equipment there is practically no private ownership of producers' goods. Consumers' goods, however, may be privately owned. The Soviet Constitution proclaims as its principle of income distribution, "From each according to his ability, to each according to his work." Although the workers are unionized, trade-unions do not bargain with production units as in a free enterprise system. Choices of jobs are partly restricted by plans for expansion of certain industries and for development of particular regions. Choices of consumers in markets are limited by production plans which restrict the kinds and quantities of consumers' goods in favor of more industrial equipment. Special governmental planning agencies co-ordinate production and consumption. Markets and prices largely reflect these decisions; they do not guide the direction of production.

FREE PRIVATE ENTERPRISE

A system of free private enterprise assumes that man's self-interest will induce him to produce at least cost those things for which there is the greatest demand. For the most part, production is determined by prices prevailing in the market place. Competition is the regulator of economic activities. The role of government is primarily to safeguard the operations of markets and to regulate economic activities where competition is imperfect or lacking. The United States is an outstanding example of this system. Certain fundamental institutions and basic features of it are described briefly in the following sections.

Legal Institutions. A system of free enterprise requires certain freedoms and rights in order that the factors of production may be combined to produce goods and services. These rights and privileges are established by law and protected by the courts.

PERSONAL LIBERTY. An individual has the right to choose any occupation in any part of the country (although lack of capital and natural ability may prevent him from doing so). He has the right to produce and consume what he likes (certain exceptions, e.g., drugs). He cannot be made a slave or be imprisoned for debt.

PRIVATE PROPERTY RIGHTS. An individual has the right to acquire property; to consume or to control it; to buy and sell it; to give it away as a gift; and to bequeath it at death. Private property has encouraged the accumulation of capital and has served as a stimulant to individual initiative—both so essential to economic progress. While the government protects private property, it also restricts private property in the interest of common welfare.

CONTRACTS. An individual is allowed to enter into contracts which bind together the economic system and make co-operation among individuals possible. The right to enter contracts is a specific exercise of the rights of private property and personal liberty. Contracts are the legal aspects of the combination of the factors of production. They provide the basis for the exercise of individual initiative in the development of production.

MONEY. Since goods and services are produced to exchange for money, the government has the responsibility of issuing money and supervising monetary and banking activities.

Co-operation. Although there are many areas of economic conflict in a system of private enterprise, a substantial amount of co-operation takes place. Individuals do in part directly and voluntarily work together. Many kinds of religious, charitable, and philanthropic organizations are co-operative production units. Some business firms organized by agricultural producers and consumers are on a co-operative basis. In rural areas farmers frequently engage in simple, direct co-operation in doing some types of work. Most of the co-operation, however, in a private enterprise system is indirect and is the result of specialization, division of labor, and the exchange of goods and services for money in markets.

Division of Labor. Co-operation in the most complex form is called division of labor. While the term is generally coupled with the manufacturing process, division of labor is a characteristic of the entire production system. The larger divisions are the production of raw material, manufacturing, transportation, merchandising and banking, and various professional services. Division of labor makes it possible for a man to find the work for which he is best fitted, an adaptation which was impossible under the manorial system where practically everyone was forced to be an agriculturist. Instead of co-operation in the same kind of work, as in simple co-operation, each laborer is confined to a distinct task. The separation of trades was the earliest form of division of labor. Large-scale production has divided the trades so that each worker performs a minute part. Even the professions are becoming more specialized— e.g., criminal lawyers, corporation lawyers, eye specialists, nerve specialists.

MINUTE SPECIALIZATION. After the wide-spread introduction of machinery, minute specialization developed. An extensive use of machinery is made easier, of course, when division of labor breaks up complex tasks into simple uniform operations. In the performance of a single task the worker acquires great skill and speed. In time, a labor-saving machine may be made to take the place of his few movements, and labor is set free for other tasks or more leisure while the product is being increased. Machinery tends to make industry dynamic, since machine manufacturers constantly improve techniques. The process of production has been lengthened and made roundabout, but total production has been augmented by division of labor and specialization.

Objections to minute division of labor are as follows: it is deadly monotonous; skill is discounted; the specialized worker becomes unfit for other occupations; rare ability commands high returns and thus greater inequality of income results. It is a moot question, however, whether monotony is objectionable to the worker, and occupational change is often made easier because the specialized tasks are easier to learn. While the objections may be true in part, the fact that more goods are produced with less effort and less hours of labor and that the worker's share in the goods has greatly increased offset the objections.

Division of labor into minute operations depends on the possibility of exchanging the goods. If a cobbler could not sell all his surplus shoes, it would be foolish for him to hire a man just to cut out soles. But if his supply were quickly exhausted and more shoes were demanded, it would be economical to hire several men to perform specialized operations. The extensive use of machinery in *transportation* has made vast areas accessible. Thus the larger the extent of the market, the more complex the division of labor may become.

TERRITORIAL OR REGIONAL DIVISION OF LABOR. A more general division depends upon the comparative advantage existing in various sections. The soil, climate, or natural resources of a region make it adaptable for specific industries. Orange growing is more profitable in California; cotton in the southern states; coal mining in Pennsylvania, etc. Effective transportation is essential in such a division and is a further evidence of co-operation. Practically all of the New England region may devote itself to manufacturing and depend for its food supply from the West and South.

The Price System. The function of prices in a private enterprise system is to provide a co-ordinating mechanism for the millions of decentralized production and consumption units. Prices prevailing in markets *in the main* determine what kinds and quantities of goods shall be produced and how they shall be distributed.

PRODUCTION. Profits, the reward received for entrepreneurial ability, guide production. Profits, which depend on the selling price of goods and the cost of making them, indicate to the entrepreneur what people are buying. High prices of a product draw entrepreneurs into that industry; low prices check production by causing entrepreneurs to drop out. In general the conditions of supply and demand determine price and guide production. A small supply raises price, a large supply lowers price. Prices in the form of wages, costs of raw materials, transportation rates, etc., determine where (in the city or country) and how the entrepreneur will produce his goods.

PERSONAL DISTRIBUTION AND CONSUMPTION. The share of each person in the total output is determined by the price of the goods and services he has to sell, or has been able to sell. As goods are produced, costs are incurred. These costs in the form of wages and salaries, rents and royalties, and interest payments are, with the addition of dividends and profits, the sources of incomes for individuals. They spend a large part of these incomes on consumption and save and invest the remainder. Spending and investing provide the markets for consumers' goods and producers' goods. Incomes received as producers enable individuals to share in consumption. These shares are important incentives for maintaining and increasing production. The consumption of various goods is determined by their prices, the income of the individual, and his tastes as a consumer. A millionaire may buy a yacht, the factory worker, a Ford. Goods go to those who are *able and willing* to pay for them.

LIMITATIONS. The price system does not always operate to assure a just distribution of income nor the production of socially desirable goods. Occasionally prices fluctuate substantially, and depressions, business losses, and unemployment ensue. As a result, government regulations have been necessary to define the limits within which the forces of the market place may direct production and consumption.

Significance of Competition.

In an economic system based on private property rights and freedom of business enterprise, *competition* in buying and selling is indispensable for its efficient operation. Competition is the regulator of the economic activities of individuals who are following their self-interests in market transactions. In the United States, markets vary by slight degrees from highly competitive ones to those which are highly monopolistic.

COMPETITIVE MARKETS. Markets which are highly competitive are composed of many buyers and sellers who are trading a homogeneous commodity—that is, a commodity which has one or more uniform grades. No trader is in a position to affect the price appreciably by his individual action, and only one price prevails at a given time for each grade in the market. Under these conditions both buyers and sellers are assured of fair and equal treatment. Individuals in their capacity as workers and consumers are protected from exploitation because of the opportunity to sell their services to numerous buyers and to buy their goods and services from numerous sellers. Costs, including profits, are established at minimum levels, and prices approximately equal costs. Efficient business enterprises receive larger returns than inefficient ones because both sell at the same market price. Some goods may not be produced, or may be produced only in small quantities, because the relation of demand and selling price to costs does not make additional production profitable. Efficiency in the utilization of resources is encouraged, and production is adjusted to consumption.

MONOPOLISTIC MARKETS. Economic self-interest is frequently not closely checked by competition, and private gain fails to correspond with public welfare. Sellers prefer a high price to a low one. Business enterprises form combinations, e.g., pools, trusteeships, holding companies, and mergers, in order to reduce the number of sellers and to control price by limiting supply. Machine production on a large scale which requires vast financial resources and patents account in part for fewness of sellers. Industrial concentration and control by a few producers are characteristic of many markets. Labor organizations attempt to reduce the number of sellers in labor markets by collective bargaining in order to offset the advantage possessed by a few large buyers. Although buyers and sellers may be numerous, markets are often partially monopolistic because the products in a given commodity class are not homogeneous. The constant development of new products makes competition in terms of standardized products impossible in many instances. They are not sold on the basis of grades and uniform units of quantity. Each seller to the extent that his product is, or seems to be, different controls supply and price, the degree of control depending on buyers' estimates of the suitability of similar products as substitutes. Because of the difficulties involved in comparing and testing products, consumers occasionally organize to protect their interests. When monopolistic elements are present in markets, cost and prices are not established at minimum levels, resources are not fully utilized, and consumption is forced to adjust to restricted production. In some instances monopolistic industries may be more efficient than competitive ones, but there is no assurance against arbitrary restriction of buying and selling, the creation of scarcity for private gain, and the exploitation of any group by another.

MARKET MALADJUSTMENTS. In an economic system composed of several million private business enterprises and millions of specialized workers and which operates in a highly interdependent way through markets, the opportunities for maladjustments are numerous. Business enterprises experience great difficulty in anticipating changes in supply, demand, and price. Individuals are free to initiate improvements in the technique of production, to vary products and output, to shift their demand for goods and services, and to alter the proportion of their incomes devoted to consuming, saving, and investing. If these diverse and variable individual plans were quickly and easily adjusted through markets, maladjustments would be temporary and minor. But miscalculations are frequently general in character; commitments cannot be quickly revised, and changes have cumulative repercussions. If several basic industries, for example, expand to a point where some losses are incurred, men and equipment are not smoothly transferred to other work. Instead, unemployment develops, investment is curtailed, incomes decline, and the system as a whole is adversely affected. Waste and insecurity in the form of idle men and machines characterize recurring and prolonged periods of readjustment.

Monopolistic markets and market maladjustments involving unemployment are the two great problems which largely account for the expansion of governmental control in the economy.

GOVERNMENT AND PRIVATE ENTERPRISE

Government in the United States (national, state, and local) protects, assists, and regulates private enterprise; in a few instances, it owns and operates enterprises. Many of the protective services of the government must be present (e.g., enforcement of personal liberty, property rights, and contracts) before private enterprise can operate. The belief, however, that the government should merely act as a policeman and umpire gave way long ago to the insistence by a majority of citizens that it undertake developmental activities in order to promote the general welfare. World War I brought an end to the period of laissez faire.

Reasons for Governmental Control and Public Enterprise.

1) Private enterprise cannot exist without the protection and aid of the government.

2) Private enterprise is unable to perform some essential tasks (e.g., flood control) and fails to perform others because they are not likely to yield immediate private gains (e.g., reforestation).

3) Although private enterprise supplies through markets certain goods and services, the government in order to promote the general welfare supplements the private market allocation of facilities (e.g., education).

4) When competition, the regulator of private enterprise and markets, degenerates, the government intervenes in numerous instances to enforce fair competition by laws preventing adulteration, fraud, unfair methods, and monopolistic combinations; in other cases to regulate private monopolies in order to assure adequate service at reasonable prices; and in a few cases to supply in part goods and services as a basis for comparing the performance of private enterprise.

5) When private enterprise and the market process as a whole become maladjusted, the government attempts to conserve human resources, to provide economic security, and to correct the maladjustments.

Types of Governmental Control and Public Enterprise.

1) The government provides for national defense, police protection, and the administration of justice. It maintains other protective facilities, such as fire departments, forest patrols, coast guards, sanitation codes, construction standards, building and machinery inspection.

2) The government assists private enterprise by providing for bridges, highways, harbors, patents, foreign consular service, the bureau of standards, research, experimentation, and statistics. It also aids certain industries directly, as in protective tariffs for manufacturing and agriculture and subsidies for railroads, shipping, aviation, and agriculture. Special credit facilities are furnished for industry, trade, and agriculture.

3) The government regulates several monopolistic industries, such as transportation, power and light, and communications. It owns and operates a postal system, numerous water utilities, and a few electric utilities. It also regulates many business practices, agricultural production of a few basic products, labor conditions, and financial institutions.

4) The government attempts to promote economic stability and security by controlling money and credit; financing public improvements; providing for dependents, defectives, and unemployed workers; and conserving natural resources.

5) The most important developmental activity of the government is the provision for compulsory education of children. The economic effects of education are important because what is produced and consumed in any nation depends largely on the nature and degree of the culture of its people. Other developmental facilities include libraries, museums, governmental publications, parks, and playgrounds.

Problems of Governmental Control.

PRESSURE GROUPS. Since the government intervenes to protect, assist, and regulate economic activity, the struggle for private gain and economic advantage by individuals and groups depends in part upon public policy. Various groups (e.g., industrialists, farmers, laborers, consumers, etc.) resort to political pressures in order to advance their economic interests. The same group which lobbies for governmental assistance, for example, in the form of tariffs, may oppose similar aid to other groups and may oppose governmental control of its own activities. Under these conditions the formulation of consistent measures of governmental control is extremely difficult.

ECONOMIC PLANNING. As indicated previously, public planning of production in an economic system may vary greatly with regard to the degree of centralized control. In a system consisting predominantly of private enterprise, public planning of production supplements market direction. In the United States, restrictions, prohibitions, regulations, subsidies, and other inducements, and a very small amount of public enterprise provide some general direction for production, especially in agriculture. In addition, the Employment Act of 1946 sets up a program of periodic reports on current economic conditions by the president to Congress which implies governmental recognition of responsibility for the maintenance of a high level of employment and economic stability. On the basis of these reports Congress may enact legislation which would vary tax rates and debt reduction, interest rates and the amount of bank credit, and expenditures on public works in order to offset or to compensate for a decline in private business or for an inflationary expansion of private business. In general the objective is to provide a floor and ceiling for the whole economic system without interfering with private enterprise and market direction of specific production and consumption activities within these limits.

This limited form of economic planning is difficult to administer, especially if co-operation is sometimes weak between government and business, labor, or farm groups. On the other hand a more comprehensive type of planning which effectively prescribed production priorities and rationing of some consumers' items as in a war period would eliminate some of the essential features of private enterprise. Competitive economic efficiency, job security, and economic and political freedom are difficult objectives to achieve in a complex, interdependent system of production.

EVALUATION OF THE PRESENT SYSTEM

Competition today is far from the perfect mechanism often assumed. People are not rational in all of their political and economic actions; the factors of production are not perfectly mobile; price does not always measure quality; serious depressions and vast unemployment are industrial plagues—yet the present system for the most part produces goods which people want, in large quantity, and at prices near the cost of production. Economic freedom has been modified and restricted, but political liberty and democratic processes have been preserved. In view of the complexity of economic society the adjustment is remarkably good. The satisfaction of wants has been accomplished more effectively by private enterprise than by any other system. Many improvements, however, can still be made (as the following chapters indicate), and the private enterprise system may, in time, be superseded by a better one. A fundamental issue for evaluation at all times is freedom versus efficiency and security. State socialism, for example, might improve the efficiency of production and probably would provide greater economic security for many people, but the economic freedom of some individuals (property holders and enterprising innovators) would be lessened under this type of complete government control. On the other hand, economic freedom or opportunity might be enhanced for some classes (nonproperty holders). In the welter of conflicting economic interests, social experimentation offers the only hope for improvement and eternal vigilance the only protection against loss of essential freedoms.

GENERAL REFERENCES

Baykov, Alexander, *The Development of the Soviet Economic System.*
Childs, M. W., *Sweden, the Middle Way.*
Clark, J. M., *Social Control of Business.*
Halm, G. N., *Economic Systems—A Comparative Analysis.*
Hobson, John A., *The Evolution of Modern Capitalism.*
Keezer, Dexter M., *Making Capitalism Work.*
Lerner, A. P., *The Economics of Control.*
Loucks, W. N., and J. W. Hoot, *Comparative Economic Systems.*
Lyon, L. S., and V. Abramson, *Government and Economic Life.*
Marshall, L. C., *Industrial Society.*
Schumpeter, J. A., *Capitalism, Socialism, and Democracy.*
Sweezy, Paul M., *Socialism.*
Tugwell, R. G., and H. C. Hill, *Our Economic Society.*
Veblen, Thorstein, *The Theory of Business Enterprise.*
Ware, C. F., and G. C. Means, *The Modern Economy in Action.*
Webb, Sidney and Beatrice, *Industrial Democracy.*
Wright, David McCord, *Capitalism.*

CHAPTER FOUR

PRODUCTION ORGANIZATION

The organization of production involves two important considerations: (1) the location of the production unit and (2) the form of the particular business unit (individual proprietorship, partnership, corporation, etc.). A third problem, the size of business enterprise, is analyzed in the next chapter.

LOCALIZATION OF INDUSTRY

Localization of industry refers to the tendency for industries to concentrate in particular localities; it is a phase of the territorial division of labor (e.g., silk mills at Paterson, shoe factories at Brockton and Lynn, steel mills at Pittsburgh and Gary, automobile plants at Detroit, etc.). In any particular instance, one or more conditions may account for the localization of an industry; the ideal location is a resultant of competing attractions or a balance of possible economies. A list of important conditions are set forth separately below.

Power Resources. *Availability of cheap and effective power* is an important condition in determining the location of industries.

WATERFALLS. In the early use of machinery, waterfalls which could be harnessed with water wheels especially attracted the textile industries. Today waterfalls are used chiefly to generate electricity, which may be transmitted economically several hundred miles; hence, waterfalls now restrict less than formerly the location of industries.

COAL DEPOSITS. The introduction of steam as a source of power made economical the location of many basic industries, such as iron and steel, near extensive coal deposits. Usually iron ore could be transported more cheaply to coal deposits than coal to iron deposits. Coal deposits, however, now restrict less than formerly the location of industries because steam power developed from coal is converted into electricity and is transmitted long distances.

OIL AND GAS. The development of the internal combustion engine which uses gasoline, gas, or semicrude oil as fuel, makes the location of many industries near energy resources less imperative. These fuels can be cheaply transported, and, consequently, they tend to decentralize industry.

ATOMIC POWER. In the reasonably near future, the availability of atomic power in a package or easily transportable form for industrial use will probably free industry from its need to be near original sources of power.

Raw Materials. *Nearness to raw materials* is sometimes an important influence in the location of an industry. Pulp mills, for example, adjoin spruce and poplar forests. Paper mills, since they are expensive to build and since pulp may be cheaply transported, are likely to be located near power resources and large markets. Other examples are: flour mills near grain-growing regions, meat-packing plants near stock-growing areas, potteries near essential clay, etc.

Markets. *Proximity to large markets* is frequently an important factor in the location of many manufacturing industries which produce finished commodities. Transportation, of course, is fundamental in determining the accessibility to markets. Cheap water transportation, railroads, and highways have always been important factors in the localization of industry. The development of air freight has greatly affected the relation of markets and location, especially with regard to perishable goods or those with great value compared with bulk.

Labor. *Availability of competent labor* is sometimes important in determining the location of industries. Because of sentimental attachments, lack of financial means, etc., labor is not easily attracted from one location to another. In order, then, to be assured of a satisfactory supply of labor, industries are located near large centers of population where a supply of different kinds of labor is usually available. When one or more factors of production are relatively cheaper at another place, an industry may move to the more profitable location. Recently cheaper labor markets have been a prime inducement for such changes.

Industrial Growth. *Industrial growth* or the *momentum* of an early start frequently influences the location of industries. Within a general area which is suitable for several industries one particular location may develop into a shoe-manufacturing center because a skilled shoemaker happened to settle there. If one firm succeeds, others are attracted to the same locality. Sometimes employees of the successful firm establish a business of their own. Financial assistance frequently may be obtained more easily for a given industry in a locality where lenders for a long time have been familiar with that industry. Technical knowledge accumulates as the industry grows. Subsidiary industries spring up to supply the main industry. When an industry has acquired great momentum in one locality, it may persist as the chief center even though other localities offer greater advantages as regards some of the above points.

Planned Location. Considerable attention has been given by industrial planners to the idea of planning the location of an entire industrial community, not merely the industrial plant. Such planning involves not only considerations of increased efficiency, but also the welfare of the workers. Indirectly it may increase efficiency as well.

FORMS OF BUSINESS ORGANIZATION

Individual Proprietorship. The *individual proprietorship* is a one-man type of business enterprise. One individual assumes full responsibility for the conduct of the enterprise (e.g., most farming, many professions, some manufacturing, retailing, etc.). This type of business organization is suitable for production which is better supervised by one individual, which involves a high degree of flexibility, and which requires but a small amount of capital and modest expense of organization. Its chief disadvantage is "unlimited liability" for business debts —that is, if the firm fails, creditors may force the sale of the proprietor's personal property, as well as his business property, to satisfy their claims. Unlimited liability, however, may make some creditors more willing to extend credit.

Partnership. A *partnership* is based upon a written or oral agreement between two or more individuals to assume jointly full responsibility for the conduct of a business enterprise.

Prior to the Civil War it was the prevailing type of business organization in the United States. It superseded the individual proprietorship in many fields of production where additional capital was necessary and where the association of varied abilities in management was desirable. One disadvantage of the partnership is the fact that the bankruptcy, insanity, or death of one partner automatically dissolves the partnership. Another disadvantage is the "unlimited liability" of each partner for all debts contracted by any one of the partners in the conduct of the partnership business.

Sometimes a "limited partnership" is formed in which several of the partners have unlimited personal liability for debts, but one or more partners have their liability limited to the extent of their investment in the business. The "limited partnership" is possible only when provided for by statute law. Moreover, those partners with limited liability lose that protection in the courts if they actively engage in the business. The "limited partnership" offers many advantages, such as obtaining capital without relinquishing control, perpetuating operation by admitting as limited partners the heirs of deceased partners, and avoiding heavier taxes imposed by some states on corporations.

Corporation.

THE CHARTER AND STATE LAWS. The existence of the corporation depends upon a *charter* or certificate of incorporation granted by the state. Charters are granted when individuals meet the requirements of corporation laws. With a few exceptions, such as national banks under federal laws, corporation laws are state laws. These laws are not uniform. Since corporations organized in one state may freely do business in another state under the rule of "interstate comity" (i.e., courtesy among states), they frequently organize in a state with very lax laws and then carry on most of their business activities in other states.

SEPARATE LEGAL ENTITY. Although the corporation is composed of many individuals, they are not the corporation. The corporation is a *separate legal entity* or person, distinct from its owners.

ACTIVITIES. The corporation engages in such activities as its charter specifies. These, however, are sometimes quite general. The charter may be revoked if violated and the corporation dissolved.

CAPITAL. The corporation makes possible large accumulations of capital. The resulting large-scale enterprise may be more efficient, thus lowering the costs of production.

PERMANENCY. Since ownership in the corporation may be transferred by a sale of its stock without the assent of other owners, the corporation is *highly permanent*—in some cases almost perpetual. Since the Dartmouth College case, 1819, in which the United States Supreme Court held that a charter granted by a state to a corporation was a binding contract and could not be altered by the state without the consent of the corporation, state laws limit the life of the corporation, usually to twenty or fifty years. New charters, however, are obtained without much difficulty.

LIMITED LIABILITY. Another distinctive feature of the corporation is the *limited liability* of the owners for corporate debts. If the corporation fails, the owners are liable to lose only what they paid for stock in the corporation; the creditors have no claims on their personal resources.

MANAGEMENT AND DIRECTORS. The management of a corporation is usually delegated by the owners to a *hired manager*. Directors, elected by the owners principally from their own group, usually select the manager. Sometimes there are *dummy directors*—that is, directors with no active participation in the affairs of the corporation and who merely serve to complete the number prescribed in the charter, or directors who represent interests with real power, e.g., banks or competing interests. Directors assist the manager in important decisions, and occasionally they submit matters of unusual importance to the owners for collective action. In large corporations there may be separation of ownership from control because of the use of nonvoting common stock, the use of proxies, and the wide distribution of ownership.

Financial Structure of the Corporation. The *financial structure of corporations* is exceedingly *complex*. The original and permanent investment of the owners, or *shareholders* in the corporation, is ordinarily termed the *capital stock*. A *share of stock* represents one unit of property right in the total investment, and a *certificate of stock* is the document which the owner holds as evidence of his part of the total rights in the corporation. Corporations raise funds by selling stock (i.e., the owners or stockholders furnish funds), by borrowing (i.e., sale of bonds and notes to creditors), and by operating at a profit and retaining part or all of it.

KINDS OF COMMON STOCK. *Common stock* usually carries with it the *exclusive right of voting*. Sometimes, however, a corporation will issue a special class of *nonvoting common stock*. Since each share of stock carries one vote, the owner or owners of slightly more than half of the voting common stock would have absolute control of the corporation. Frequently many small shareholders merely invest in the corporation and have little interest in voting; consequently, a much smaller percentage of common stock will usually suffice to control the corporation. Dividend payments on common stock are controlled by the board of directors.

NATURE OF PREFERRED STOCK. *Preferred stock* under most corporate charters carries with it the right to a prescribed dividend rate but no voice in management. This type of stock has preference over common stock in two ways: first, dividends must be paid on it before any can be declared on common stock; second, many charters provide that, in case of liquidation, the preferred stockholder must be paid in full before the common stockholder receives his share of the assets. Preferred stock may be *cumulative*—that is, if dividends on preferred stock have not been paid one year because funds were not available, these back dividends must be paid up before any dividends can be declared on the common stock (protection for the preferred stockholder against manipulation of accounts to conceal profits). Preferred stock may have other special features as provided for in the charter.

BONDS AND NOTES. *Bonds* and *notes* represent borrowed capital of a corporation; they are certificates of indebtedness. The owners of a corporation (holders of common and preferred stock) borrow funds through the sale of corporation bonds and notes. Holders of bonds and notes are creditors of the corporation. Bonds bear interest at a specified rate. Usually the bonds are secured by a mortgage on the fixed assets of the corporation, and any default in the payment of either interest or principal gives the bondholders the right to foreclose in order to satisfy their claims. Otherwise the bondholders have no control over the corporation.

The bondholder, then, assumes the least risk in the corporation, receives the smallest return, and has no control. He also has the risk of a rising price level which would make his fixed return in dollars buy less goods and services. The preferred stockholder assumes more risk, receives a larger return, and frequently has no control. The common stockholder assumes the greatest risk, may receive the highest return, and usually has control.

THE BALANCE SHEET AND THE INCOME STATEMENT. Two accounting devices, the *balance sheet* and the *income statement* (often called profit and loss statement), are helpful in understanding the setup and operation of a corporation. (These devices may also be used for other types of business units.) A balance sheet lists in one column the money value of a corporation's assets and in another its liabilities (claims against the assets) as of a given date. A balance sheet might show the following items.

BALANCE SHEET

ASSETS		LIABILITIES	
Current assets		CREDITORS' CLAIMS	
Cash	$ 50,000	*Current liabilities*	
Marketable securities	50,000	Accounts payable	$ 50,000
Raw material	100,000	Notes and bills payable	50,000
Finished goods	50,000	*Fixed liabilities*	
Accounts receivable	150,000	Bonds	800,000
Notes receivable	50,000	OWNERS' CLAIMS	
Fixed assets		Capital stock	1,500,000
Real estate and buildings	1,500,000	Surplus	100,000
Machinery and equipment	500,000	Total liabilities	$2,500,000
Patents	50,000		
Total Assets	$2,500,000		

Explanation of the Balance Sheet. In a balance sheet of a solvent corporation, the assets and liabilities are always equal. The successful corporation, of course, owns more than it owes, but any excess of assets over the claims of creditors belongs to the owners of the corporation. The liability side merely shows to whom the assets belong. For example, in the above balance sheet, the total assets minus the claims of the creditors leaves an excess of assets of $1,600,000 (net worth) which belongs to the owners in the form of capital invested in stock and surplus.

In other words, the balance sheet pictures the corporation as a hypothetical person which owns assets of $2,500,000, and owes creditors $900,000 and the owners $1,600,000. If the claims of the creditors exceed the assets, the corporation is insolvent, and the owners' claims, or equity, disappear. With regard to solvency, the distinction between fixed and current assets and liabilities is also important. Although the total assets of a corporation may greatly exceed its total indebtedness, its current assets may be smaller than its current liabilities, and hence, it may soon be insolvent because of inability to realize enough cash from its current assets to meet its current liabilities.

The above balance sheet shows how the corporation accumulates funds of its own in the form of surplus. If a 1 per cent dividend were declared on the capital stock, the cash item in the balance sheet (and the surplus) would be decreased by $15,000. The item of surplus usually indicates a reinvestment of profits in the business. Sometimes, however, the surplus item does not represent the entire amount of reinvested profits, because stock is sometimes issued to represent reinvested earnings—that is, stock dividends are declared. In the above balance sheet a stock dividend would reduce the surplus item and increase correspondingly the capital stock item. Capital stock, then, would represent both original investment and reinvested earnings, whereas the surplus item would represent only that portion of reinvested profits against which no stock had been issued. The transfer from surplus to capital stock does not change the owners' equity. They merely have more certificates of stock as claims against the same assets. Since shares, however, are now worth less, they may be easier to sell, especially to small buyers. A stock dividend is frequently resorted to in order to avoid the appearance of unusually high profits and dividend rates.

Limitations of the Balance Sheet. The balance sheet has certain limitations. It is an interim report and cross section of a business which is changing, and the figures are expressed in monetary units which vary in value. The balance sheet is a set of estimates, and it may conceal as well as reveal the financial condition of a corporation. The stock may be watered. Corporations usually issue stock with a face or par value (e.g., $100) engraved on each certificate. (Its value in the market may be more or less than par.) The law usually provides that the stock must not be issued for less than par, but frequently property and services are paid for with stock instead of cash and the property or services may be overvalued. Since the claims of the owners (or capital stock item) is inflated, the balance sheet is made to balance by simply listing the property acquired with stock on the asset side at its inflated purchase price. Other items, such as patent rights and good will may easily be used to inflate assets. *Watered stock,* then, is *stock issued without full payments* for it and the *discrepancy* is *concealed by overvaluation of assets.*

The balance sheet, on the other hand, may understate the present worth of assets. Usually property items are listed at the price originally paid or present market price—whichever is lower. Consequently, a property now worth $50,000 may be listed in the balance sheet at $10,000 because it was purchased at that price years ago. Furthermore, the value of a corporation to its owners is affected by its present and prospective net income. A corporation, for example, may issue stocks at a par value of $100. After several years each share of stock may have a book value of $110—that is, the assets increased more than the claims of creditors. (The increased value of the owners' equity divided by the number of shares outstanding gives an increased book value, or equity per share, unless capital stock has been correspondingly increased.) The *market value,* however, of each share of stock may be $200 instead of $100 or $110. The high market value is the result of a large present or prospective net income and attractive dividend payments. On the other hand, the market value of each share may be only $80 when the book value is $110 and the par value $100— that is, in the past the corporation made profits which were reinvested in the business, the owners' equity per share (book value) increased, but the corporation ceased to make profits and pay dividends. (Since the value of corporate stocks fluctuates and rarely represents the par value, many states have authorized the issuance of *no-par stock.* Such stocks may aid the investor to understand better the factors which determine stock values. They also make it easier for corporations to sell stock under adverse circumstances which may militate against the interests of the investor.)

The *present* and *prospective net income* of a corporation is *not* the *sole determinate of* the *value* of its stock. For example, one item of asset, such as real estate, may increase so much in value that the value of the stock is high regardless of a low net income. The balance sheet, nevertheless, usually needs to be *supplemented* by the *income statement* in order to determine the financial position of a corporation.

Explanation of the Income Statement. The income, or profit and loss, statement shows the receipts and expenses of a corporation or business unit over a period of usually one year. It varies in form, but the main items given below are commonly included.

INCOME STATEMENT

Net sales	$2,000,000
Operating expenses: cost of goods (labor and material) ; selling expense; general and administrative expense (salaries, office, depreciation, and certain taxes)	1,710,000
Net operating income	$ 290,000
Other income	5,000
	$ 295,000
Other expense (interest on borrowed capital)	10,000
Net income	$ 285,000
Income tax	160,000
Net profit	$ 125,000
Dividends declared	75,000
Added to surplus	$ 50,000

Gross sales and deductions of discounts, allowances, and returns which indicate net sales are usually not shown in the published income statement. The separation of income and expenses into operating and nonoperating is important as a general check on the performance of management. Net income (or loss) for an accounting period such as a year is an estimate. It may be understated or overstated by estimates of depreciation charges and by improper classification of some purchased items as capital investment and others as current expense. The purchase of a machine, for example, which is likely to last for several years is not an operating expense, but an investment. Each year only a portion of the purchase price is included in the expenses in the form of a depreciation charge. Nevertheless, the income statement showing the sources.

amount, and disposition of income is an important supplement to the balance sheet in describing and summing up business operations at stated intervals.

In subsequent chapters costs are frequently referred to as fixed and variable. Although this distinction is not important for the income accounting cited above, some of the expense items, such as administrative salaries, depreciation, certain taxes, and interest on borrowed capital are mostly constant or fixed for a short period of time; whereas cost of goods, including labor and materials and selling expense, varies with the volume of output and sales. Costs are also referred to later as explicit and implicit for economic analysis. Income accounting is usually a record of explicit costs—that is, actual expenses paid during a period plus estimated depreciation. Net income or profit for a business unit in accounting terms may differ with the type of organization and financing. For the sole owner and manager of a business unit, net income or profit is a mixed income of interest on invested capital, salary of management, and profit. The same business unit organized as a corporation would probably pay some interest on borrowed capital and a salary for a hired manager. Net income or profit would then probably consist of interest on the capital invested by stockholders and profit. In economic terms implicit costs are the implied expenses that must be covered by receipts regardless of ownership in order to attract and keep capital and managerial and entrepreneurial ability in a given industry. In economic terms total costs include explicit and implicit costs, and profit under competitive conditions over a long period is an implicit part of total cost.

MARKETING CORPORATE SECURITIES. The security markets are of interest from the point of view of method and the position of the corporation and the purchaser.

Financial Middlemen and Underwriters. Investment bankers are frequently essential in marketing corporate securities. Small corporations, and occasionally even a large one, may be financed by a few individuals who organize the corporation, but most corporations do not build up their own selling agency in order to reach the general investing public. Funds, moreover, are usually needed at once and the investment banker will buy corporate securities in large blocks, will agree to pay a certain sum for them at a given date, and will assume the risk of sell-ing the securities to the public—that is, he *underwrites* the sale. For instance, a corporate bond issue of several million dollars is offered to the investment banker. After investigation he may form a group or syndicate of investment bankers which agrees to pay the corporation 98 per cent per bond of $1000 within a given period. The investment bankers then attempt to sell the bonds to the public at (say) 100 per cent before the end of the period. If successful, they profit from the transac-tion, but any bonds unsold or sold below the purchase price must be paid for by the investment bankers at the agreed time and price.

Stock Exchanges. They assist in the sale of *corporate se-curities already issued.* The New York Stock Exchange, for example, is a voluntary association of more than a thousand members, mostly brokers, which provides a ready sale for stocks and bonds of the better grades. Securities must first be listed on the exchange (approval of the investigation committee needed) before they can be dealt in on the floor, and only members are allowed to buy and sell. Most members, of course, act as brokers and buy and sell at the order of a principal. Cor-porate securities listed on the Exchange are an attractive invest-ment because they may be quickly sold for cash or used as col-lateral for bank loans. The liquidity of investment provided by stock exchanges has some social disadvantages. Loan funds are diverted into short-term rather than long-term investments, which affects adversely the expansion of production. Because of the ease with which securities may be unloaded on the market at the right time, the prices of securities are frequently bid up until they no longer reflect present or prospective earnings. In-stead of security prices serving as a guide to long-term invest-ment, they may thwart and muddle the process.

A substantial volume of bonds and some stocks are bought and sold in the over-the-counter market. Transactions are car-ried out by security houses, and prices are established by in-dividual negotiation.

Investors. The position of the purchaser of corporate stocks has been improved by federal legislation. The Securities Act of 1933 and the Securities Exchange Act of 1934 supplement ineffectual state laws (blue-sky laws) designed to protect investors. The Securities and Exchange Commission created by this legislation attempts to prevent misrepresentation in the sale of securities and to eliminate manipulation of securities on stock exchanges. New issues of all securities (with the exception of securities of domestic steam railroads which are regulated by the Interstate Commerce Commission) along with a statement of fact, which discloses such information as salaries of directors and officers, and detailed balance sheets and income statements must be registered with the Securities and Exchange Commission. If the registration statement is false, any original buyer of such securities may recover any loss sustained by a civil action against the seller. All security exchanges and their listed securities must also be registered with the SEC. Certain types of manipulation (e.g., wash sales and matched orders) are prohibited; other speculative operations (e.g., price pegging) are regulated. The SEC is also empowered to supervise trading in nonlisted securities. The control of credit used in margin accounts is placed with the Board of Governors of the Federal Reserve System.

Modern corporations and stock exchanges offer many opportunities for dishonest practices. Exorbitant salaries in the form of secret additions to the regular salary may be paid to corporate officials. A few large stockholders and directors in control of a corporation may arrange for the purchase of supplies at high prices from another company in which they are interested, or they may buy real estate which the corporation needs and then resell to the corporation at a handsome profit. Sometimes a group of insiders in control of a corporation will form a selling agency which then handles at a substantial profit all the sales of the corporation, or they will manipulate the accounts of the corporation in order to conceal its real position and then buy and sell its stock to their own advantage.

Although the above legislation for the protection of investors is an improvement, effective administration is beset with many difficulties. Fraudulent practices in the sale of securities are not easily separated from the ordinary risks of investment. Elimination of the former is likely to hamper legitimate investment. Vested interests, however, are likely to exaggerate the few adverse effects on legitimate transactions. Other changes are needed. A heavy transfer tax on the sale of securities on stock exchanges would restrict speculation to the wealthy group of professionals. The competition among states to liberalize their incorporation laws could be remedied by federal legislation which required all corporations doing an interstate business to have a federal charter. If all charters required full publicity of accounts, some over-capitalization might be avoided. Corporation control by a few insiders could be lessened by prohibiting the issue of nonvoting common stock and by making voting common stock cumulative—that is, if eight directors were to be chosen, allow each share of stock eight votes which might be cast for one director. Minority interests would then usually have an opportunity to elect at least one director. Another possible remedy would be to change corporation laws so that directors would be responsible as *trustees* for the stockholders.

Co-operatives. A co-operative is a type of business unit through which individuals co-operate in performing certain economic activities. They may be classified as consumers', producers', or credit co-operatives (co-ops). From the beginning of the co-operative movement in Rochdale, England, in 1844, certain basic principles have been followed.

1) Each member has one vote no matter how many shares of stock he may own.

2) Returns on stock are limited to a fixed percentage.

3) The returns over expenses (including interest on stocks) are returned to the members in proportion to their *purchases*.

Co-operatives operate **not only** in retailing but also in wholesaling and manufacturing. Co-operatives enjoy an advantage in their exemption from income taxes. At present, co-operatives are responsible for only a very small part of retailing and wholesaling, but their influence and scope of activities are growing.

Producers' co-operatives, such as marketing associations, have improved the bargaining position of the agricultural producer, enabling him to buy more economically and to eliminate some wastes in distribution.

Credit co-operatives (credit unions and mutual insurance companies) enable their members to pool their funds and invest or lend. Credit unions, which may operate under state or federal charters, are able to provide loans to members at lower rates of interest than would otherwise be possible in commercial lending institutions.

Other types of co-operatives include the New York Stock Exchange and the Associated Press.

Government Corporations. Governments (federal, state, and local) carry on a number of business enterprises (post office, liquor stores, public utilities). Some enterprises of government are organized into government-owned corporations (the Panama Canal Company of the U.S.A., the Tennessee Valley Authority, the Federal Deposit Insurance Corporation, the Export-Import Bank, the credit agencies under the Farm Credit Administration, etc.). These government-owned corporations are organized under special acts of Congress or are incorporated under the laws of the states or the District of Columbia. At one time, federal corporations enjoyed a good deal of independence in obtaining income and in making expenditures, but the Corporation Act of 1945 established complete control over their activities. At present, these corporations, like any other governmental agency, must secure their funds from appropriations made by the Congress, and unexpended balances revert to a general fund at the close of the fiscal year. Statistics concerning the assets and liabilities of federal government corporations and credit agencies may be found in the Federal Reserve Bulletin.

Other special forms and problems of business organizations, such as trusts, holding companies, trade associations, and political units, will be discussed in succeeding chapters.

GENERAL REFERENCES

Berle, A. A., *The Twentieth Century Capitalist Revolution.*

Berle, A. A., and G. C. Means, *The Modern Corporation and Private Property.*

Dean, J., *Managerial Economics.*

Dewing, A. S., *Financial Policy of Corporations.*

Dice, C. A., and W. J. Eiteman, *The Stock Market.*

Digby, Margaret, *The World Cooperative Movement.*

Hoover, Edgar M., *The Location of Economic Activity.*

Hoover Commission (Commission on Reorganization of the Executive Branch of the Government), *Reports*.

Jordan, D. F., *Investments*.

McDiarmid, John, *Government Corporations and Federal Funds*.

Paton, W. A., *Accountants' Handbook*.

Ripley, W. Z., *Main Street and Wall Street*.

Schumacher, Herman, "Location of Industry," *Encyclopedia of the Social Sciences*.

Van Dorn, H. A., *Government Owned Corporations*.

Weber, Alfred, *Theory of Location of Industries*.

CHAPTER FIVE

THE SIZE OF BUSINESS ENTERPRISES

The size of business enterprises may be influenced by a number of conditions, such as the type of business, technical knowledge, the possibility of division of labor, the use of capital equipment, market and financial opportunities, and the desire to maximize profits. The fundamental consideration here is to examine how the most efficient allocation of the factors of production may be achieved. Land, labor, capital, and entrepreneurship are combined to produce output. One factor may be substituted for another. For example, less labor and more capital may be used in a production unit. Under certain conditions a maximum profit is associated with an output produced at a minimum cost.

In the formation of a business, the entrepreneur makes a choice concerning the size of the business unit which reflects costs of the factors used and selling prices of the output prevailing at the time. Subsequent changes in costs or selling prices may induce him to use a different combination of the factors to obtain the most profitable combination. Thus, given a certain scale of enterprise and certain costs and selling prices, the entrepreneur tries to achieve a least-cost or most profitable combination of the factors. If possible, he may also seek to lower unit costs of a given output through the economies made possible by large-scale production—that is, by changing the scale of production. Another possibility of reducing costs, technological improvements, is not discussed in this chapter.

When technological improvements, or qualitative changes, are being made in the factors of production, no precise analysis can be made of quantitative relationships. The relationship discussed here is quantitative.

NONPROPORTIONAL RETURNS AND FACTORAL PROPORTIONS

In a preliminary way, a cost for a given output may be explained in terms of the quantity of input required to produce it and the price paid for the different factors of input. The principle of nonproportional returns (diminishing returns or productivity) refers to the relationship between input and output. When these physical quantities are translated into money costs, the least-cost combination of factors or the most profitable combination may be ascertained.

Nonproportional Returns. If there is no change in production methods and successive units of one or more factors (variable) are added to fixed amounts of other factors, the increase in the total output will not be proportional to the amount of the successive units of the variable factors. At first, there will be an increasing average output per unit of variable factor (stage of increasing returns); later, a decreasing average output per unit of variable factor (stage of diminishing returns). If the stage of diminishing returns is carried far enough, additional units of input will eventually bring about a decrease in the total output. The following example illustrates these points.

Fixed Factor (one acre of land)	Variable Factor (labor and capital)	Total Output (bushels)	Average Output (per unit of variable factor)	Marginal Output (addition to total output by increase in variable)
1	1	2	2	0
1	2	6	3	4
1	3	12	4	6
1	4	20	5	8
1	5	27	5.4	7
1	6	32	5.3	5
1	7	35	5	3
1	8	36	4.5	1
1	9	34	3.8	−2

REASONS FOR NONPROPORTIONAL RETURNS. On the basis of the above assumptions, the reason for nonproportional returns is the difference in factors which makes them imperfect substitutes for each other. In the above table if more than five units of the variable are used to increase output, labor and capital are an imperfect substitute for more land. To produce more than twenty-seven bushels, both more land and labor and capital in the same proportion of one to five should be used. This would simply be more production units of the optimum size.

One man on a one-acre vegetable farm cannot tend effectively the entire patch. Two men can produce more than twice as much as one man because of the division of labor and co-operation in difficult tasks. The addition of several more men might, for the same reasons, increase the average output per laborer, but finally, the average output per laborer decreases although the total product still increases. The decrease in the average output per laborer finally occurs simply because more division of labor and co-operation on one acre is proportionately less advantageous. Laborers may be added until the total product decreases—that is, until laborers get in one another's way.

OPTIMUM RETURNS. It is that combination in which the average yield per variable factor is at a maximum (five-labor combination in the preceding example). The combination yielding optimum returns is the last one in the stage of increasing returns; thereafter average returns diminish.

Sometimes increasing and diminishing returns are defined in terms of marginal output per variable factor instead of average output. In terms of the table, optimum returns would then be the four-labor combination. The two definitions are not identical, as the above example indicates, because numerically the marginal product per variable factor decreases before the average product decreases. *Although marginal output or product is not usually made the basis of a definition of diminishing returns, it influences, as discussed later, the price paid for the use of the variable factor.*

NONPROPORTIONAL RETURNS AND HISTORICAL TRENDS IN PRODUCTION. The reason for using agricultural production as illustration of diminishing returns is largely historical. A century and a half ago many economists believed that since the total supply of land was fixed, diminishing returns in the production of foodstuffs would make it extremely difficult to feed an increasing population. They underestimated, at least to date, the productivity of new agricultural regions, the possibilities of economies of large-scale production, and the possibility of technological improvements in agricultural production. Eventually the exhaustion of natural resources may restrict per capita production and consumption unless population decreases proportionately, or human ingenuity creates synthetic materials. From a broad social point of view, land (natural resources) seems to be more limited than the other factors of production. The important point to note is that the principle of nonproportional returns does not apply to historical production trends in which many offsetting changes may operate. It describes at a given time the relation of fixed and variable factors in the absence of offsetting economies of scale and of technological improvement, or of accentuating tendencies in the form of depleted resources.

If, in a given enterprise, any one factor of production is held constant while others are increased, diminishing returns will result. For instance, if increasing numbers of laborers are employed in a factory with no change of management or machines, increases and decreases in output per variable factor, similar to the land illustration, will occur. In all cases, however, the principle of nonproportional returns does not indicate the best combination in terms of costs. Although the ratio of physical inputs to outputs, or physical efficiency, establishes limits for a least-cost combination, the relative prices of the factors determine that combination. The cost analysis involves what is usually referred to as the principle of factoral proportions.

Factoral Proportions. The principle of factoral proportions refers to the balance of production factors in a business enterprise which will constitute the least-cost combination, or most profitable combination. Since all factors of production usually cost something and since the amounts used can be varied, the lowest total cost per unit of output is achieved in an enterprise by using relatively less of the expensive factors and more of the cheap ones. For example, if the acre of land in the above illustration costs $10 and each unit of variable factor, $1, the lowest total cost per unit of output will be reached with the seven-labor combination. The figures are as follows:

Total Output	Total Fixed Cost	Total Variable Cost	Total Cost	Fixed Cost per Unit of Output	Variable Cost per Unit of Output	Total Cost per Unit of Output
2	$10	$1	$11	$5.00	$.50	$5.50
6	10	2	12	1.66	.34	2.00
12	10	3	13	.83	.25	1.08
20	10	4	14	.50	.20	.70
27	10	5	15	.37	.18	.55
32	10	6	16	.31	.19	.50
35	10	7	17	.28	.20	.48
36	10	8	18	.27	.23	.50
34	10	9	19	.29	.27	.56

The combination yielding optimum returns is not the least-cost combination. This point and other implications of the table are important.

LEAST-COST COMBINATION. For any enterprise under the assumed conditions, the *least-cost combination is always somewhere in the stage of diminishing returns.* Variable factors can always be profitably added until that stage is reached, because the cost per unit of output is decreasing until then for both the fixed and variable factors (note example above). The cost per unit of output of the fixed factor decreases as long as total output increases—that is, the fixed costs are spread over more units of output. The cost per unit of output of the variable factor, however, decreases only up to the point where the average output per variable factor declines—that is, where the stage of diminishing average returns is reached. Of course the variable factor cannot be profitably added to a point where the total output declines because the cost per unit of output for the fixed as well as the variable factor would increase. The *least-cost combination,* therefore, *for any enterprise will be reached at that point in the stage of diminishing average returns when the increasing costs of the variable factor per unit of output is no longer offset by the decreasing cost of the fixed factor per unit of output.* If the fixed factor (e.g., plant and equipment, or farm and implements) is expensive while the variable factor (labor) is cheap, the least-cost combination will occur far in the stage of diminishing returns—that is, the fixed factor will be used intensively in order to spread its costs over more units of output. If the fixed factor is relatively cheap while the variable factor is expensive, the least-cost combination will occur early in the stage of diminishing returns—that is, the fixed factor is used extensively because the high cost of the variable factor per unit of output quickly offsets the slight decrease in the cost of the fixed factor per unit of output.

MOST PROFITABLE COMBINATION. The relationship of cost and profit involves the prices at which different outputs can be sold and is analyzed later in terms of different market situations (Chapter Eight). In a preliminary way the important point is that the *least-cost combination is not always the most profitable combination for an enterprise.* Under competitive conditions, each firm in the long run is compelled to operate at its least-cost combination because that is also its most profitable combination. In this case fixed costs would include a normal profit sufficient to induce firms to remain in the industry, and competition among firms would result in an output for the industry large enough to make the price equal to the lowest total cost per unit of output for each firm. An attempt to sell at any higher price would eliminate a firm from the industry. Under monopolistic conditions, however, output is restricted so that total cost per unit is above the minimum cost of the firm in order to obtain a maximum profit. The smaller output sells for a sufficiently larger sum so that the higher costs per unit are more than offset. Also in the short run under competitive conditions, fluctuations in demand may sometimes make it profitable for an enterprise to extend its production beyond the least-cost combination, because the slightly increased total unit costs will be more than offset by the larger volume of sales (elastic demand). On the other hand, if demand declines sharply, entrepreneurs may make some profit, or lose less money, by producing less goods than is required to attain the least-cost combination—the higher total unit costs of restricted output reduce profits less than would the losses incurred on a declining market with a larger volume of output from the least-cost combination. In the event that either a lessened or increased demand remained permanent over a period of years, entrepreneurs would gradually vary their factors of production until a least-cost combination would be attained under the new demand. Some firms, however, may operate for a long time even though no net profits are made, because as long as returns pay the variable expenses (excluding depreciation) and part of the fixed costs, the owners lose less than they would by scrapping a plant. New firms are frequently unable to operate at the least-cost combination for a long time, because their capacity is designed for a prospective market which may or may not be gradually built up.

MARGINAL COSTS AND MARGINAL RECEIPTS. In any market situation the variation of output by a firm in order to maximize profits or to minimize losses may be summarized in a simple rule. Entrepreneurs find it profitable to increase the variable factors in an enterprise as long as the selling price of the additional output will more than pay the cost of the additional variable factor. When the two amounts (marginal costs and marginal receipts) become equal, further expansion of output is not profitable. Up to that point expansion of output adds more to receipts than to costs. Marginal cost is the amount added to total cost by a one-unit increase in output, or for a range of output, the addition to total cost divided by the additional units of output. Marginal receipts or revenues are the addition to total receipts resulting from a one-unit increase in the output sold. The relationship of marginal cost and total cost per unit of output (average total unit cost) and the relationship of marginal receipts and price are indicated later (Chapter Eight).

ECONOMIES OF SCALE AND LARGE–SCALE ENTERPRISE

As already noted, the entrepreneur not only combines the factors of production in a given scale of enterprise so as to yield the greatest profit, but he also seeks economies in the use of the factors through a larger scale of enterprise. An expansion of the production units in an industry sometimes permits greater specialization in both the use of labor and capital equipment. Such economies of large-scale production result in new, lower, minimum-cost combinations of the factors. The basic change is not a variation in the proportion of factors; more of all factors are used, and the total output increases more than the increase in factors. Specialized labor and capital equipment can be added frequently to a production unit only in large, indivisible amounts. Because of this indivisibility of certain, specialized factors, they cannot be profitably employed in small-scale operations. They cannot be fully utilized, or in some cases cannot be used at all.

Increases, however, in the scale of production with consequent lower costs may result in some form of monopoly (see Chapter Eight). In that event some of the advantages of large-scale business discussed below are monopoly advantages. Lower costs may then contribute more to monopoly profits than to lower prices. Although the drift toward large-scale production and combination during the past sixty years is the dominant trend in industry, many small enterprises still exist to supply local and sometimes national markets.

Advantages of Large-scale Business Enterprises.

SIZE AND UNIT COSTS. Small plants may grow into large ones mainly because of the opportunity to use machinery more effectively and to subdivide labor more minutely. Large plants, moreover, are frequently able to manufacture by-products or reclaim waste material which would be unprofitable for a small plant. Large plants also buy on more favorable terms than small plants and are financially able to hire exceptionally capable managers, technical experts, and research staffs.

ECONOMIES OF HORIZONTAL COMBINATIONS. Large business units may be formed by a combination of *separate plants of the same kind under one management* (*horizontal combination,* e.g., chain stores) and may obtain many of the advantages of a large plant cited above, such as able managers, research work, and quantity discounts on purchases. Horizontal combination may obtain other advantages, such as large-scale operation for one stage of production in which it is suitable while other stages remain small-scale; stimulation of efficient operation of each plant by comparison with the others; full time operation of several plants during slack periods while one or more is completely closed; and large reductions in marketing expenses.

ECONOMIES OF VERTICAL COMBINATIONS. Large business units sometimes develop by *integration of plants performing successive steps in production under* the *same management* (*vertical combination,* e.g., from raw materials to finished product). Special advantages, such as reliable delivery of uniform quality raw materials, elimination of selling expense for raw materials, and more regular production of raw materials are frequently obtained by vertical combination.

ECONOMIES OF COMPLEMENTARY COMBINATIONS. Several *plants which make different products may be combined* into a large business unit under one management (*complementary combination,* e.g., railroads, steamships, resort hotels). Large business units of this kind obtain advantages, such as large quantity buying, efficient management, and economies in marketing (one salesman or agent handles several items instead of one).

Disadvantages of Large Business Enterprises. These arise largely because of the scarcity of managerial ability. As a business expands a capable manager experiences increasing difficulties in making proper decisions and in controlling effectively his force. Delegation of authority to subordinates develops red tape and bureaucratic methods. Personal supervision of performance is impossible, and statistical devices which are not only expensive but also unreliable are set up to measure efficiency.

Chiefly because of these managerial difficulties, small firms still exist in many industries in competition with large firms. There are, in addition, several industries in which the small firm predominates and in which it is likely to retain most of the business, such as professional services, retailing, farming, repairing, and the making of women's clothes. In the latter group of industries the small firm usually has the advantage because the market is local; the product cannot be standardized, and hence cannot be produced by machinery; demand shifts often and the small firm can more easily cater to it; most of the work may be done by the family; and finally, supervision must frequently be personal.

GENERAL REFERENCES

Black, J. D., and A. G. Black, *Production Organization.*
Buchanan, N. S., *The Economics of Corporate Enterprise.*
Clark, J. M., *The Economics of Overhead Costs.*
Devine, Carl T., *Cost Accounting and Analysis.*
Encyclopedia of the Social Sciences, "Diminishing Returns," "Large-Scale Production," "Increasing Returns," "Production."
Stigler, George J., *The Theory of Price.*
U. S. Temporary National Economic Committee, Hearings: *Technology and Concentration of Economic Power;* Monographs: *Measurement of the Social Performances of Business; Relative Efficiency of Large, Medium-Sized and Small Business; The Structure of Industry.*

CHAPTER SIX

MARKETING, RISK, AND TRANSPORTATION

MARKETS AND MARKETING

Important parts of the production process are marketing, risk-bearing, and transporting. In economic analysis the term "production" means that a good is not "produced" until the consumer gets it. Marketing is, therefore, one stage in production. Similarly, the risk and transportation involved in marketing are also parts of production. A market need not be an organized, established meeting place; wherever rights to goods and services are bought and sold, a market exists. The variety of markets and market practices are almost limitless because of the kind, number, and location of competitors (both buyers and sellers); the nature of the commodities or services (seasonal goods or staples, raw materials or finished products, standardized products, perishables, etc.); and the general organizational structure. The structure may be very simple as in the local farmers' markets where home-grown products are brought into town and sold at a stand; or market structures may be elaborate, such as an organized commodity exchange. These exchanges in cotton, wool, wheat, and other basic raw materials are sometimes called the "perfect market." Perishable goods or goods quickly reproduced are unsuitable for elaborate market organization. A group of individuals dealing in large quantities of a commodity that is easily graded, sampled, and stored may form a voluntary market association. Rules are formulated to govern sales, settle trade disputes, set up standards of grading, and give statistical and ticker service. Sales are transacted on the basis of samples. Such markets are exceptional.

Classification of Markets. In economic analysis the primary aim is to examine markets in terms of how prices are established under various conditions of demand and supply. Markets are viewed as mechanisms for allocating the means of production and consumers' goods and services. A general classification of markets from a price-making point of view is based largely on different degrees of competition or monopoly. Such a classification is presented later with an analysis of cost-price relations (Chapter Eight).

In this chapter the classification and analysis of markets are mainly in terms of marketing channels, organization of marketing activities, and the technical functions performed. For example, specialization in marketing in the form of wholesaling and retailing is described without reference to degree of competition. Such functions as assembling, storing, and standardizing commodities are described in order to indicate the complex technical elements of markets. Viewed historically, marketing has become an important part of the production process in recent times and a part which is frequently viewed as unnecessary and unproductive.

Development of Marketing. Modern marketing, which involves the activity of all those engaged in transferring goods from producer to consumer through numerous commercial channels, is the result of a high degree of specialization in modern industry. When man was producing only those things which he himself needed there was little or no trade. Today an individual may spend his entire life producing something which he will never use, depending on others to supply his needs. Ancient cities and nations (Egypt, Phoenicia, etc.), which history lists as great traders, offered only luxuries and foreign products to a few of the wealthiest citizens. During the Middle Ages towns grew up, crafts and trades developed, and townspeople found it convenient to trade their wares for country produce. At first small shops and the *traveling merchant* or peddler facilitated this exchange; later a *town market* was held on a certain day and place, but the variety and quantity of goods were small. Dukes or bishops, seeing a chance to become wealthy, promoted great *fairs* at important places. They often received gratifying profits from the special fees or taxes assessed on all the merchants who traded at the fair. To make the fair popular many customary restrictions to trade were removed and some semblance of freedom of trade existed. They came to be known as "free fairs." In the more backward countries great fairs still exist. In the United States fairs provide entertainment and information rather than trade, but our great department stores and supermarkets represent a kind of continuous fair.

The modern specialization of industry increased the importance of marketing. To a considerable extent the degree of specialization depends upon the size of markets. Thus, large-scale production and large-scale marketing developed simultaneously. Specialists appeared who devoted all their time to transferring goods from the initial producers to consumers. Normally about 20 per cent of the gainfully employed are engaged in marketing, and a little over one-half of the consumer's dollar goes for marketing costs. The volume of wholesale trade in the United States in 1948 was $190,480,000,000; the volume of retail trade was $130,521,000,000.

MARKETING AGENTS

The opportunities for making profit in distributing goods have led to the development of a complex system of middlemen. The typical channel of distribution is from producer to wholesaler to retailer, but no two systems are alike and several other middlemen (sales agents, brokers, etc.) may have a part. About 45 per cent of consumers' goods is channeled through wholesalers; 33 per cent goes direct from factory to retailer; about 15 per cent is handled by the manufacturers' own wholesale branches; and about 7 per cent moves directly from factory to homes. While some economies may occasionally be achieved by eliminating middlemen in the distribution of goods, for the most part these costs must be incurred for certain functions. Reduction of the number of middlemen does not reduce the number of functions. Even if the costs of distribution were less, it would be doubtful whether consumers would benefit in many instances from lower prices. An increase in the profits for owners would be the probable result, at least for a short period of time, because of semimonopoly conditions and the obstacles to new competitors.

Wholesalers.

THE WHOLESALER OR JOBBER. He buys goods in large quantities from one or several manufacturers and sells them to retailers. While the goods are in his hands he undertakes the tasks of sorting, grading, packing, storing, and financing. He may sell small amounts or huge quantities to many different kinds of retailers (e.g., canvassers, local stores, department stores), extend them credit, and transport the goods to them. The wholesaler can usually do these things cheaper than either the manufacturer or retailer because he is a specialist. By handling large quantities he saves on freight charges, clerical service, and time. By handling many commodities graded and ready for sale, such as raw materials, he enables the manufacturer to buy more efficiently. The wholesaler, then, assumes some of the risks and costs of marketing more cheaply than any other agent.

In the early history of American industry the wholesaler was dominant. Manufacturers operated on a small scale, were unorganized, and lacked market information. The wholesaler, aware of their weakness, played one manufacturer off against another. The wholesaler needed transportation facilities and encouraged canal and railroad building. With the improvement in transportation, machinery, and large-scale production, the manufacturer acquired the dominant position.

COMMISSION MERCHANT. The commission merchant or commission house is very important in some trades, especially farm products. The commission merchant handles the entire output for one or more producers, sells it where he can, and receives a commission on his sales. Very often he sells the goods under his own brands.

MANUFACTURER'S AGENT. The manufacturer's agent sells goods under the manufacturer's name, is usually restricted in territory, and receives a commission for his sales.

BROKER. The broker is found in several types of industries—where the volume of sales is extremely large, where sales are seasonal, and where the producers are small and the market scattered. The broker is an intermediary who may represent either buyer or seller and never has actual possession of the goods. He places orders where he will get the best price and receives a commission for his services.

CO-OPERATIVE MARKETING. In agriculture, particularly, producers have joined together to sell their goods co-operatively (e.g., creameries, grain elevator associations, etc.).

Retailers.

SINGLE-STORE INDEPENDENT. The local retail store keeps goods in stock, extends credit, and often delivers goods to customers' homes. Formerly the independents sold virtually all the consumption goods. They had in 1948 about 67 per cent of the total sales; retail chains about 23 per cent; department stores 8 per cent; mail order houses about 1 per cent; and other types about 1 per cent.

DEPARTMENT STORE. The large department store assumes more marketing functions. It may be its own wholesaler, buy directly from manufacturers, assemble, rearrange, have its own brands, train salespeople, and carry on other functions.

CHAIN STORE. The chain stores' major expansion took place following World War I. Since their sales are mostly confined to standardized goods, great economies in purchasing and management can be effected. Capital and ability are united. Skillful purchasing executives know the market and bargain with the manufacturer. Delivery service and credit extension are often dispensed with. This, too, helps make lower priced goods possible.

MAIL ORDER HOUSES. Mail order houses flourished when transportation facilities were meager. Rural customers had more and better choices for less money from a catalogue than from the local general store. With the advent of good roads and the automobile, however, mail order houses lost business. To offset this, some of them (e.g., Sears, Roebuck and Montgomery Ward) have opened retail stores in the larger cities.

CO-OPERATIVES. Consumer co-operatives have played an important role in retail trade in Europe and are expanding in retail marketing in the United States.

OTHER TYPES. Other types of retail markets include such units as factory outlet stores, huckstering, public markets, and roadside stands.

MARKETING FUNCTIONS

Assembling. Assembling or buying a quantity of goods from a variety of sources is a task for a specialist. In order

to make a profit he must estimate demand and foresee events
that may affect supply. Climatic changes, labor troubles, and
other disturbances may change the usual supply of a commodity. The task of assembling is easy when only a few large
firms produce a commodity (e.g., steel), but difficult when
many scattered individuals produce small but necessary amounts
(tea). The advantages derived from specialization in assembling are substantial. Estimates of market conditions are
more accurate. Manufacturers may buy more efficiently from
a collected supply. Large volume handling permits lower freight
costs.

Storage. Storing goods while they are being gradually used
up creates *time utility* and aids in the stabilization of prices.
Production may take place for only a short time during the
year, but the consumption of many products is continuous. Or
demand may be seasonal while production is continuous. To
ship a large quantity of goods and store it may be cheaper
than to ship small lots as they are demanded. In order to have
goods on hand when they are wanted (at fairly stable prices)
someone must undertake the function of storage.

Standardization. Standardization or rearrangement is still
another important division of marketing. Goods must be
cleaned and sorted; rearranged into uniform kinds, qualities,
and sizes; packed and labelled before they are ready for the
market. The Bureau of Standards, the Federal Trade Commission, other governmental agencies, and professional organizations (American Standards Association, etc.) have set up many
standards for various products that are generally accepted.
Such organization enables goods to be sold by description or
sample and eliminates the cost of personal inspection.

Selling. Selling, or the *creation of demand,* has become increasingly difficult, expensive, and important since large-scale
production began. Selling activity takes many forms (e.g.,
personal solicitation, letters and circulars, free samples, ex-
hibitions, and advertising). Customers are told of new products, new styles, and new uses for old products; a desire to own
them is aroused. Advertising is the most important part of
selling. Total expenditures for all types of advertising in 1950

were estimated at $5,700,000,000. The object of advertising is to take an article out of competition by having a customer accept it as unique. A quasi monopoly is formed by the use of brands and trade-marks. Manufacturers advertise not only to push new products but also to prevent consumption changes and to modify the market to fit their production program. The economic effects of advertising are referred to later, especially in Chapter Eight.

Financing. Financing is a marketing function which is necessary because rearrangement, storage, shipping, and transfering of ownership take time. Money is tied up in stocks of goods until they are sold. Credit extension by commercial banks, discount houses, note brokers, or the middleman himself facilitates the flow of goods to the consumer. Throughout the marketing process a system of deferred payments is found.

Assumption of Risk. Assumption of risk in production is the special function of the entrepreneur. Of course, the laborer assumes risks of unemployment, death, or injury; the capitalist and land owner are not absolutely certain of their return; but the entrepreneur contracts to pay for labor, capital, and the use of land in the production of goods which yield an uncertain future return. Because of the uncertainty of future markets, the unpredictability of natural forces and human behavior, risk is universal. The entrepreneur must produce goods in anticipation of future wants. Fire, theft, deterioration, or price changes may decrease or destroy the value of his goods. Profits are in part a return covering these risks but entrepreneurs also endeavor to reduce risk as much as possible and to shift part of the burden to others.

REDUCTION OF RISKS. Reducing risks (1) by preventive measures (e.g., fireproof buildings, dykes, preventive medicine, etc.); (2) by increased knowledge (e.g., weather, statistical, and commercial bureaus); and (3) by consolidation (e.g., selling or insuring over a large area) is one method to prevent loss and injury.

SHIFTING RISKS. Professionals who are specialists in risk-bearing enable the entrepreneur to avoid some of the risks in production.

Hedging. Speculators estimate the movement of prices and on the basis of their estimates buy or sell in the hope of making a profit. In the great commodity exchanges (e.g., wheat, cotton, wool) commodities may be bought outright for cash (cash or spot sales), but the larger portion of sales are based on contracts for future delivery (speculative sales or futures). The speculator who thinks the price is going to rise (bull) "buys long" (i.e., goods are to be delivered to him at a future date) to sell again at a higher price. The speculator who thinks the price is going to fall (bear) "sells short" (goods are to be delivered by him at a future date) to buy later when the price is low. When the time comes to settle these contracts goods may be actually delivered, but usually the money difference between the contracted price and the prevailing price at the time of delivery is the only transaction made.

Such speculative markets enable traders to take a position on both sides of the market as a way of avoiding risk. Two contracts are made which neutralize each other. A miller who wishes to protect his milling profit from price changes may contract to deliver in the future (sell short) the same amount of wheat which he must buy at once to manufacture into flour. If the wheat price rises, he loses on his futures contract but gains on his past one; if the wheat price falls, he gains on his futures contract but loses on his past contract. In both cases he makes no profit on his speculative activity, but his trade profit from milling is protected, which is the function of hedging. A successful hedge depends upon a change in spot prices equal to a change in futures prices. That the futures price may be above or below the spot price on a given day has no effect on hedging, provided the spread between the two prices remains the same over a period of time. The futures price, however, which is usually quoted, is the spot price plus the costs of holding and storage. As a rule the spot price and futures price *do* move up or down together, but any change in the cost of holding and storage would change the spread between the two prices and the miller would profit or lose on the hedge (i.e., a decrease in the spread would give the miller a speculative profit; an increase in the spread would give him a speculative loss).

There is a tendency in such speculative markets to stabilize price. Buying when prices are low decreases available stocks on hand and tends to raise future price; selling when prices are high increases available stocks and tends to lower future price. And there is a tendency to stabilize consumption; goods are taken off the market when they are cheap and put back when they are expensive. These benefits, however, are derived only when speculative activity is based on accurate information. If speculators' estimates are incorrect, price fluctuations are even more severe than would otherwise be the case.

Insurance. A method of pooling risks is found in insurance. Loss for an individual is a possibility; for a group of individuals, it is a certainty. The individual substitutes small, certain losses (premiums) for a probable loss uncertain in time and amount. In the event of a future loss he has a certain indemnification (benefits). An insurance company can calculate from past experiences the probabilities of such losses and can adjust the premiums to cover the total sum of them. Insurance is based on the *law of large numbers.* It is applied to a great variety of risks affecting persons and property. When only a few risks are combined, average losses cannot be calculated, and any insurance for them would be mere gambling.

Insurance probably originated in the 13th century and has existed in America since pre-Revolutionary days. A *mutual* type of insurance is provided when a group of people in a town, county, state, or country incorporate for the purpose of pooling individual risks. If the premiums each year exceed the amount of loss, they are lowered or a dividend is declared. When insurance is organized as a stock company, it is run as any private business—to make profits for its stockholders. The various states have many laws regulating insurance companies; they may stipulate the minimum amount of capital stock, the kinds of investments, risks, and other conditions.

Transportation. In the United States transportation has developed into the largest and most important function of marketing. Transportation, or the physical movement of goods from those who initially produce or manufacture them to those who use them, creates *place utility.* Specialization, division of labor, large-scale production, and the extent of the market depend on transportation. Before trade became extensive, middlemen undertook their own transportation. But the movement of goods became so important that they turned over this function of marketing to specialized agents more capable of handling the problem.

BEFORE 1850. Transportation in the United States before 1850 was difficult and costly. The Appalachian Mountains cut off the eastern seaboard from the fertile Middle West. Navigable rivers were few, and roads were local luxuries. After the Revolutionary War the new government realized the need for a means of communication and transport to unite the country. *Road building* (the Cumberland Road was most important) by private companies and by state governments flourished, and a network of highways developed. Transportation, however, remained costly, and the roads were often impassable. Following Fulton's practical demonstration of the steamboat in 1807, trade immediately increased. The steamboat was first used on the Ohio River in 1811.

Although transportation costs decreased on the important navigable rivers, rates for transportation between waterways were still extremely high. To solve the problem, private individuals and local and state governments plunged into an *era of canal building* (about 1812–1850). The Erie Canal (1825) was a great success and paid for itself in ten years. Freight rates from New York to Buffalo fell from $100 per ton to $15; shipping time fell from twenty days to eight.

Transportation was still far from perfect since most of the rivers ran north and south, the canals froze in winter, and transportation by road was costly. The need for east and west transportation was solved by the railroads. Between 1830 and 1850 steam railroads passed through a period of experimentation in construction and operation. There was no common width of track, roads were local, rails wooden, and freight traffic small. An adequate means of transportation, however, was inevitable. The South was raising cotton; the Middle West, grain; Kentucky and Tennessee, tobacco; and the East was manufacturing. Such geographical specialization brought about by the development of the waterways was recognized to be mutually advantageous and was a constant pressure for improvements.

AFTER 1850. *Transportation* improved greatly because of the rapid development of the railroads (increased mileage, iron rails, and heavy cars and engines). The eastern and mid-western cities were linked by the New York Central, Erie, and Pennsylvania railroads. Railroad building was interrupted by the Civil War. During the years 1870–1880 the mileage increased two and a half times as fast as the population. Both private and public capital were used freely. By means of land grants, subsidies, and direct aid, the local, state, and federal governments expanded the railroads. It is estimated that government investment in stocks and bonds of railroad companies amounted to about $700,000,000.

Progress in construction and operation continued in the seventies—consolidation and through trunk lines to the Pacific, steel rails, and uniform gauge brought about long distance hauling and many economies. The railroads definitely became the carriers for the grain trade. The canals were doomed. This period is also noted for its flagrant manipulation of railroad securities; favoritism; scorn of public interests; and destructive competition which later led to government regulation.

From 1880 to 1930 railroads developed in the West and Southwest, and transcontinental lines were built. By 1910 expansion was dwindling and by World War I had almost ceased. With more than 250,000 miles of track in 1920 rail connections were adequate.

Other means of transportation are found on *rivers, lakes, highways,* and *ocean* and in the *air.* Because of extensive government improvements (dredging, flood control, locks, etc.), traffic on rivers and lakes has been revived during the last ten years.

The development of the automobile industry has brought with it a tremendous expansion in road building. Commercial trucking has given the railroads significant competition, especially in short hauls. Coastwise shipping which is satisfactory for bulky goods and slow shipments is less important. Pipe lines have become important transportation agencies for petroleum and gas. Air transportation, a late-comer, promises to be a major type of transportation for perishables and other goods on which a premium for fast transportation can be paid. Finally, the United States Merchant Marine, stimulated by World War II, has made the United States at least temporarily a leader in world shipping.

MARKETING TRENDS

The pressure to sell goods has been intensified by large-scale methods of production, by technological changes, by changes in the habits of consumers, and by keen competition of rival firms. The *area of* the *market* for goods has been increased by modern transportation and by world-wide advertising. *Installment selling* has appeared because of the necessity for marketing huge supplies of goods, especially durable consumption goods. It enables consumers to pay for goods as they are being used. Installment selling, however, may artificially stimulate demand. The future income of consumers is overestimated and more of certain commodities is produced than can be sold. Co-operation in marketing is now found among farmers, among single-store independents, and between manufacturers and middlemen. Consumer co-operatives are continuing to grow. Because of the effective retail selling of chain stores, super markets, and other independent stores, consumer co-operatives probably will not obtain a large share of the market. The uncertainty of their future tax status is also important.

Large manufacturers who have built up a quasi-monopoly product and good will tend to *dominate* many markets. Wholesalers, retailers, and consumers have less independence in buying when goods are standardized in appearance, quality, and price by the manufacturer. *Large department* and *chain stores,* however, with sufficient capital to hire a purchasing agent and buy in huge quantities can deal more effectively with the manufacturer. Wholesalers' activities are changing in order to offset the manufacturers' dominance. Some have started to manufacture and handle their own products. Some confine themselves to small trading areas around their headquarters. Others are co-operating with the independent retailer (especially in the grocery line), and still others are becoming specialists in a small line of goods.

And finally, the role of government in marketing has greatly increased during the last half century and is likely to become even greater. Its responsibilities extend from antitrust legislation, regulation of trade practices, and the establishment of standards to the support of certain prices, the control of exports and imports and domestic and foreign credit.

GENERAL REFERENCES

Beckman, T. N., and N. H. Engle, *Wholesaling Principles and Practice*.

Clark, F. E., and C. P. Clark, *Principles of Marketing*.

Converse, P. D., and H. W. Huegy, *The Elements of Marketing*.

Dearing, C. L., and W. Owen, *National Transportation Policy*.

Fair, M. L., and E. W. Williams, *Economics of Transportation*.

Hardy, C. O., *Risk and Risk-Bearing*.

Marshall, L. C., *Industrial Society*.

Maynard, H. H., and T. N. Beckman, *Principles of Marketing*.

Stewart, P. W., J. F. Dewhurst, and Louise Field, *Does Distribution Cost Too Much?*

Warbasse, J. P., *Co-operative Democracy*.

CHAPTER SEVEN

CONSUMPTION

NATURE OF CONSUMPTION

Consumption is the process of using up and enjoying economic goods and services in the *direct satisfaction* of human wants. The process of using up goods and services *indirectly* —that is, in production—is sometimes referred to as *productive consumption*. *Final consumption,* or the direct satisfaction of human wants, is the problem to be analyzed here.

The measure of consumption is exceedingly difficult and only partially obtainable. For example, a measure of the satisfaction derived by individuals from the consumption of goods and services would greatly help in the promotion of general welfare, but such a measure is impossible to obtain. Consumption is determined by the tastes of the consumers and their incomes. A study of consumption involves the analysis of real wages, the personal distribution of income, consumer spending patterns and savings, the marketing and financial agencies which serve the consumer, and consumer education and protection.

Real Wages. Real incomes or real wages are the terms used to indicate the purchasing power of money income or money wages. They roughly measure consumption. For instance, money wages might double over a period of ten years, but the prices of goods and services consumed might also double which would leave real wages and consumption unchanged. Real wages are calculated by dividing the index number of money wages by the index numbers of the consumers' price index (see Chapter Eleven for a discussion of index numbers). Index numbers, however, must be used with caution since they usually do not cover family incomes, do not measure the effect of unemployment, and may not reflect changes in consumption, quality of goods, nor the size of the community in which the income receiver spends his money.

The term, standard of living, should likewise be used with caution. Frequently the term is used to designate a tolerable scale of consumption for a given group (minimum standard for health and decency). Sometimes it is used to designate an actual scale of consumption for a given group (plane of living). Many economists use the term to denote an ideal or desired scale of living which is above the actual scale of consumption in a given group.

Income and Expenditures. The personal distribution of income (Chapter Thirteen) affects the spending patterns. Certain items of consumption vary with the size of income as is indicated by studies of household budgets. At higher incomes a much smaller proportion is spent for food and a larger proportion on clothing, automobiles, and education. About the same proportion is spent on housing, household equipment, personal and medical care, reading, and other items, regardless of the size of the income. It is also very significant that the rate of savings increases the higher the income.

The relation of income to expenditures may also be studied in the aggregate by comparing the size of the gross national product (the dollar value of all goods and services produced in a given year) with the total consumers' purchases. Before the war consumers purchased well over two-thirds of the gross national product. During the war the government's share rose enormously and will likely remain much higher than its prewar proportion. It must not be forgotten that government expenditures, for the most part, represent collective consumer expenditures (education, protection, etc.).

Trends in Consumption. Over a period of time, there are certain trends in consumption. From 1909–1941, nearly a third of a century, total consumption expenditures increased by more than 75 per cent (measured in dollars of constant purchasing power). Food, liquor, and tobacco expenditures represented about one-third; expenditures for clothing and personal care remained stable at about 15 per cent; the proportion for housing declined from about one-fourth to one-sixth; outlays for consumer transportation, recreation, medical care, insurance, etc., showed marked gains; a smaller proportion was expended for religious and welfare purposes.

Trend changes are also apparent in the American diet. Increases have occurred in the consumption of fruits, vegetables, sugar, and dairy products and decreases in foods furnishing heat and energy for active work (cereals, meats, potatoes). There has been a decrease in the use of coarser and lower priced clothing materials (cottons and woolens) and an increase in the finer, light, and more expensive materials (rayons, silks, etc.). A remarkable increase has taken place in the use of automobiles, radios, and electrical appliances.

RELATION OF CONSUMPTION TO PRODUCTION

Consumption in a competitive system based upon free private enterprise is a guide to production and a reward for efficient production. Through the medium of money, consumers make their wants known to producers in the form of prices which they are willing to pay for goods and services. Consumers cast dollar votes which determine what firms shall produce and how the factors of production shall be allocated. Those producers which effectively satisfy the wants of consumers are encouraged by large monetary returns which enable them in turn to buy the goods and services which they require. Several important qualifications, however, need to be attached to the above statements with regard to the position of the consumer in our present economic system.

Producers' Influence on Consumption. *Producers influence the choice of consumers* in several ways. First, producers take the initiative in changing the technique of production which increases the variety and volume of consumption goods, changes the quality of consumption goods (less artistic, more standardized, perhaps more serviceable), and provides additional leisure and recreation. Second, producers use skillful marketing methods which influence the consumers' choice of brands (one make of cigarette rather than another) and sometimes even products (cigarettes rather than candies), which accelerate changes in consumption and sometimes even initiate them. The net effect of producers' influence upon the choice of consumers cannot be accurately determined, but a review of the possible gains and losses indicates that producers' influence is not entirely beneficial.

SALES PROMOTION AND MASS PRODUCTION. High pressure selling and elaborate advertising are frequently defended as beneficial because they promote mass production in a few large efficient plants. In part the defense is sound, but many inefficient plants have skillful sales methods. Modern selling technique, moreover, may be more a result of mass production than a cause of it. Some selling devices actually discourage mass production because they encourage style changes, permit a small sales volume at high prices rather than a large sales volume at low prices, and create the impression that many brands of a given product are unique. Furthermore, if selling methods do encourage mass production, prices are not necessarily lower because selling costs may offset production economies.

SALES PROMOTION AND EDUCATION. Persuasive sales methods are of some educational value. New products are introduced. The multitude of competing opportunities to spend which are offered consumers tend to make some buyers more careful in their purchases—a few perhaps become totally indifferent to the pleas of sellers. Advertising wars between industries competing for the consumers' dollar may produce a few facts about each. On the other hand, the so-called educational work may be designed merely to stimulate conspicuous consumption, such as a correct hat for every occasion, or a style change for each hour of the day. Consumers are goaded to maintain superficial appearances at the expense of more fundamental needs. Success, or one's position in society, tends to be measured in terms of wasteful expenditures.

SALES PROMOTION AND QUALITY OF PRODUCT. Lavish sales promotion on a national scale may force improvement in the quality of a product. If repeat sales are needed and the consumer has some check on the quality of the article, the expense of a national appeal and the difficulty of pleasing a national market will compel many producers to offer high quality products. Sometimes, however, newness rather than durability in quality is the main plea. Although consumers are willing to pay the price for advertised newness or uniqueness, they are not necessarily satisfied with the purchase after serious reflection. For this reason many commodities are returned to sellers.

Ignorance of Consumers. *Consumers are frequently very ignorant buyers.* They are uninformed about countless items which they buy; they are unable to hire specialized purchasing agents; hence, they usually buy on the basis of guess and emotion. Some consumers, of course, may prefer to spend money carelessly rather than undergo the inconvenience of studying their purchases. Two important consequences result from the ignorance of consumers.

WASTE OF BUYING POWER. Consumers frequently purchase inferior or harmful goods at high prices. Differences in the qualities of goods are a deep mystery for most consumers. Retailers buy from wholesalers according to grades, but consumers buy with little knowledge of grade distinctions. If consumers do recognize differences in the quality of certain products, they face the almost impossible task of determining whether or not a given item is sufficiently superior to another article to justify a higher price. The relation of price to quality is further complicated since the same article is sometimes sold at different prices by different retailers, or merchants offer at so-called bargain sales articles at the regular price or even at a higher price. Many harmful or ineffective health restorers are foisted upon a gullible public. Price, then, is not always a reliable index of quality, and hence, consumers waste part of their income in the purchase of harmful or inferior goods and services.

INEFFICIENT PRODUCTION SUBSIDIZED. Since the consumer often fails to distinguish between superior and inferior purchases, many inefficient plants are virtually subsidized by ignorant buyers. If consumers were more discriminating buyers, competition would eliminate inefficient, shoddy production; less capital and labor would be required to carry on production in the more efficient plants; total production would increase.

Protection for the Consumer. Some forms of *protection for* the *consumer* which will reduce the wastes of haphazard consumption do exist and may be further improved.

GOVERNMENT AGENCIES. The consumers' interests are a natural responsibility for government. Weights and measures used in many business transactions are regulated and supervised. Federal, state, and local laws seek to protect the consumer against unhealthy conditions in bakeries and dairies and in vegetable-handling and against harmful drugs and dangerous cosmetics. Amendments in 1938 to the Pure Food and Drug Act of 1906 extended federal protection to buyers of cosmetics and therapeutic devices and made misleading advertising in the sale of these products an unfair trade practice. Government agencies also regulate some prices. The Interstate Commerce Commission has the power to regulate railroad rates; the Federal Power Commission, power rates; and the Federal Communications Commission, communications rates. These regulations afford the consumer some protection against monopoly prices. The Securities and Exchange Commission tries to protect the investor. The Federal Trade Commission makes an effort to protect the consumer against dishonest trade practices. The United States Bureau of Standards publishes lists of manufacturers who are willing to certify that their products comply with government specifications, but it cannot enforce compliance. The protection given by these various agencies is not complete or even adequate. For the most part, they are directed at extreme cases.

BUSINESS AGENCIES. Business organizations, supported by private business firms, seek to establish standards and discipline themselves. Better Business Bureaus and trade associations attempt to supervise selling methods. The United States Bureau of Standards co-operates with business in establishing standards. The American Standards Association serves as a clearing house for industrial, technical, and government groups in developing and co-ordinating standards and specifications. Individual firms standardize or brand merchandise in order to establish the character and quality of their goods, although a brand is no guarantee of quality.

INFORMATION FOR CONSUMERS. Consumers provide some protection for themselves by relating to others their experiences in buying and using certain commodities, by establishing their own co-operative stores, and by supporting their own research organizations (e.g., Consumers' Union). A number of courses in consumer problems are offered at many educational levels. Individually, consumers may improve their spending through

the use of household budgets and careful examinations of
various methods of payment (e.g., credit versus cash).

CONSUMERS' CO-OPERATIVES. The co-operative movement
in the United States has lagged behind that of England. *Co-operative credit* in the form of building and loan associations
and *co-operative marketing* in agriculture are quite common,
but *consumers' co-operatives* and *producers' co-operatives* are
of relatively minor importance. The retarded development in
the United States may be attributed to the individualistic nature of the population, to rapid expansion, to the size of the
country, and to the greater efficiency of the marketing system
(e.g., chain stores, etc.). British co-operatives, in 1944, had
about one-fourth of the total retail trade and had approximately
nine million members enrolled. In the United States, in 1944,
5076 farmers' and consumers' co-operatives secured only about
0.9 per cent of total retail sales. Recently there has been a
new stimulation to the growth of co-operatives. Government
support in the form of tax advantages and other aids, encouragement by the Departments of Agriculture and Labor and
many church authorities, and their own increased efficiency are
some of the reasons for the new spurt. On the other hand,
there has been marked opposition from other business enterprises.

Most co-operatives are based on the famous *Rochdale Plan,*
formed in 1844 by twenty-eight weavers. Under the Rochdale
system, a co-op is organized as a stock company. Each share
of stock has a very small par value and each shareholder has
one vote (to determine policy and elect officers) irrespective of
the number of his shares of stock. A moderate, fixed rate of
interest is paid on stock and for loans to the co-operative.
Goods are sold at market prices for cash to both members and
nonmembers. The surplus that is accumulated is distributed to
members on the basis of their purchases and not on the amount
of their investment in the organization, or the surplus may be
used for the social betterment of the group. Some of the co-
operatives engage in manufacturing, own land, and build houses
for their members. The success of the Rochdale Plan is due to
its conservative policy, the economy effected through quantity
purchases, and the avoidance of price competition. It is a business venture co-operatively owned.

Consumption—A Reward for Production. In their role as consumers, certain producers—namely, those who receive large money incomes—may influence adversely the consumption of others. They may demand an excessive amount of superluxuries or harmful goods and services as a reward for their efforts as producers. They set fashions in spending which others try to ape. When imitation becomes widespread, new freaks are developed in order to remain exclusive. Their consumption, then, tends to lessen the possibilities of large-scale production of necessities and comforts for the mass of consumers. In a system of free private enterprise attempts are made to justify such consumption on the grounds that it is difficult to determine what goods and services are undesirable for individuals, that the amount of such consumption is relatively small, and that such consumption is the best way to stimulate producers to maximum effort.

BALANCED CONSUMPTION AND PRODUCTION

Many problems emerge from the above discussion of the relationship of consumption and production. The more important ones are listed below, but will be discussed in subsequent chapters.

Maladjustment of Prices. In a capitalistic system based on private property and free enterprise, the maintenance of a balance between consumption and production is extremely difficult. Changes in consumers' demand are not easily anticipated. Since production requires time, mistakes cannot quickly be corrected. The efforts of producers to overcome these difficulties have created a more serious problem—the development of inflexible prices. By the use of informal price agreements, combinations, advertising, selling devices, etc., many producers have been able to avoid keen competition on a price and quality basis. If costs were reduced, the consumer received very little benefit in the form of lower prices.

Underconsumption. Because many inflexible prices are maintained at a high level relative to costs, the bulk of consumers whose incomes are small must consume less than under conditions where all prices are competitive. Lack of competition increases profits and tends to accentuate the unequal distribution of wealth and income. In the United States the bulk of savings available for investment is supplied by a small group of large income receivers. Opportunities to invest savings in production are lessened because the mass of consumers cannot buy the increased output at prevailing prices. Loan funds are partly diverted to speculative purposes, rather than to increasing production, employment, and wages, and to lowering prices. Under these conditions there is a chronic tendency for production capacity to exceed the capacity to consume. Idle men and machines and poverty in the midst of plenty are persistent ills of private capitalism.

Distribution—A Weakness of Private Capitalism. Inequality in the distribution of wealth and income, especially the latter, is a necessary incentive for production in a system of private capitalism. The existing inequalities in the United States, however, are difficult to justify. Saving, investment, and production depend in part on the level of incomes of the mass of consumers. Heavy taxes on the inheritance of wealth and moderately progressive taxes on personal incomes lessen the tax burden on the bulk of consumers and increase their ability to buy. Government intervention to enforce competition or to regulate inflexible prices aids materially, particularly if under these conditions the government provides loan funds to industry at very low rates of interest. Low interest rates on long-term investments stimulate production, increase employment, and increase incomes. The development of consumers' co-operatives is an aid in balancing production and consumption. Expansion of educational facilities, both to increase earning ability and to improve tastes and spending methods, is an important aid. In extreme cases of poverty and inability to obtain work, some payments on the basis of needs rather than ability to produce are essential (e.g., various types of social insurance and social services). The importance, however, of lessening the birth rate in impoverished families should not be overlooked in a program of assistance based on needs rather than ability to produce. Unless remedial measures, such as those mentioned above, are adequately applied, freedom of choice as it now exists is likely to be altered under some form of state control.

GENERAL REFERENCES

Chase, Stuart, *The Economy of Abundance.*
————, and F. S. Schlink, *Your Money's Worth.*
Childs, M. W., *Sweden, the Middle Way.*
Consumers' Union Reports, current issues.
Dameron, Kenneth, *Consumer Problems in Wartime.*
Dewhurst, J. Frederick, and Associates, *America's Needs and Resources.*
Gordon, L. J., *Economics for Consumers.*
Hoyt, E. C., *The Consumption of Wealth.*
Kyrk, Hazel, *Theory of Consumption.*
Lamb, Ruth de Forest, *American Chamber of Horrors.*
National Resources Committee, *The Structure of the American Economy.*
————, *Consumer Expenditures in the United States.*
Reid, M. G., *Consumers and the Market.*
Temporary National Economic Committee, *Consumer Standards.*
U. S. Dept. of Labor, *Family Spending and Saving in Wartime.*
Veblen, Thorstein, *The Theory of the Leisure Class.*
Waite, W. C., and Ralph Cassady, Jr., *The Consumer and the Economic Order.*
Warbasse, James P., *Co-operative Democracy.*

CHAPTER EIGHT

INDIVIDUAL PRICES: DEMAND AND SUPPLY

THE NATURE OF VALUE, PRICE, AND MARKETS

Since prices are the connecting links for all kinds of economic activity in a system of free private enterprise, an analysis of the price-making process is basic for most economic problems. At the outset the student is advised to watch carefully the distinctions and assumptions applied to various price situations and the consequent limitations of the price analysis. The first step in price analysis (or value theory) is to narrow and define the problem. In the present chapter the examination of the price-making process is confined mainly to individual prices for consumption goods. General changes in all prices which are connected with the changing value of money and the prices of the factors of production (cost to the firm) will be discussed later.

The relation between price and the various types of value is important. With regard to individual prices for consumption goods, the problem will be to explain how these prices are determined under various conditions. Individuals may estimate quite differently the worth to them (subjective value or utility) of certain commodities, but value in an economic sense is primarily connected with the outcome of these individual valuations in the process of exchanging goods—that is, with objective exchange value, market value, or price. Value, then, is expressed in the form of an exchange ratio. One pound of butter may be worth two pounds of lard or one pound of lard may be worth one-half pound of butter because farmers and dealers are trading on that basis. This value relationship exists when butter is selling for 60 cents and lard for 30 cents per pound, but it is stated in terms of a money price. Value is the quality possessed by any commodity which enables individuals to exchange it directly or indirectly (i.e., for money) for other commodities. Value, in an economic sense, and price express ratios of exchange. The first is a broader term which includes exchange ratios between any commodities; the second is a narrower term which includes only exchange ratios between one unit of a given commodity and money. There is nothing absolute or intrinsically fixed about value and price—they are relative. They depend on conditions of demand and supply. Since commodities today are usually exchanged in terms of money, an explanation of value resolves into an explanation of price.

From the standpoint of price analysis, markets are sometimes classified according to the number of buyers and sellers and to the nature of the commodity (all units the same or only similar). This classification attempts to indicate different degrees of competition. The prices, quality, and quantities of goods produced depend largely upon the type of market. In a free enterprise system the goal is pure and perfect competition because the relative quantities of different goods purchased by consumers are supplied usually at a minimum cost price under these conditions. In such markets the number of buyers and sellers is so large that no one of them can influence appreciably the price; the commodity consists of identical units; buyers and sellers are completely aware of market conditions; and firms may move freely in and out of the industry. This ideal type of market is never achieved, except perhaps in an approximate way by some of the organized markets for the buying and selling of graded raw materials.

For the most part, a free enterprise system which encourages inventions and innovations is one of imperfect, or monopolistic, competition. This type of market is typical of the retail trade in practically all kinds of consumers' goods. Although there is usually a large number of buyers and sellers for each commodity, the commodity consists of differentiated units. The differences are due to advertising of brands; to variations in quality, design, or color; to conditions of sale; and to legalized protection of innovations in the form of patents, trademarks, and copyrights. Each seller controls slightly the price of his product, and competition may center mainly on nonprice aspects of a sale.

Pure monopoly, or one seller of a commodity for which there is no substitute, is a rare type of market. Some of the industries classified by law as public utilities approximate this situation, and their prices are regulated by the government. Such monopolies avoid duplication of facilities and achieve low costs of large-scale production which would not be possible under competition. Two sellers of a commodity (duopoly) and especially fewness of sellers (oligopoly) are more common types of markets, particularly in manufacturing industries. (Monopsony is one buyer; oligopsony, fewness of buyers.)

In such situations the price and sale policy of one firm depends upon the anticipated reaction of its rivals. The market is unstable because of the possibility of intermittent price wars, elimination of rivals, collusion, and combinations. Instead of regulation of prices, the government may attempt to enforce competition by prosecutions based on antitrust laws.

COMPETITIVE PRICES

Competitive prices for consumption goods are explained mainly in terms of demand and supply for two different time periods—first, short-run market prices, and second, long-run normal prices. The important distinction between market price and normal price is that the first applies to a period so brief that producers can only vary supply from existing production facilities, whereas the second applies to a period long enough to enable producers to adjust their capacity to the market. In general, then, demand (utility) is a more active factor than supply (cost of production) in determining market price, but normal price is largely determined by cost of production in influencing supply. Of course, both demand and supply are indispensable to price making, but their immediate influence may be different. An explanation of these variations as well as the conditions which make up demand and supply are necessary for a complete explanation of competitive price. In general, a competitive market price may be simply described as a price which clears the market of offered goods. At some price for different brief intervals of time the amount demanded is equal to the amount supplied.

Analysis of Demand. For example, suppose a fixed tity of perishable vegetables (say 100 lbs.) is offered fo and buyers are willing to purchase on the following basis :

Price per lb.		Quantity demanded
14 2/7 cents	....	140 lbs.
16 2/3 "	....	120 "
20 "	....	100 "
25 "	....	80 "
33 1/3 "	....	60 "

If the sellers wish to dispose immediately of the entire quantity of 100 lbs., the price settles to 20 cents and the market is cleared. The sellers take what they can get. Since demand is the dominant factor in this case, an analysis of the complex elements which make up demand follows.

EFFECTIVE DEMAND. Demand means effective demand in a schedule sense (as above)—that is, buyers not only desire certain quantities at a series of assumed prices, but also have the ability to pay for them. Demand schedules may be individual (show prices and quantities demanded by one buyer) or collective (show prices and quantities demanded by several buyers as above). Demand prices are prices at which buyers are willing to purchase given quantities.

DEMAND AND PRICE. Buyers are usually willing to purchase more of a given commodity at low prices than at high prices—that is, the quantity of a commodity which buyers will purchase tends to vary inversely with the price. A demand schedule (e.g., the one above) graphically presented shows a demand curve sloping downward to the right which indicates the willingness of buyers to purchase larger quantities at low prices than at high prices.

DEMAND AND DIMINISHING UTILITY. Demand schedules and demand curves assume the above form, first, because individual incomes are limited, and second, because increased quantities of a given commodity at a given time yield diminishing utility to the consumer. Human wants in general are insatiable, but any particular one is satiable at a given time (excludes habit-forming over a period of time). The desirability of a given commodity tends to diminish as additional units are acquired (law of diminishing utility). Marginal utility is the utility of the last unit added to an individual's

The larger one's stock of a commodity, the lower will marginal utility—that is, any one unit (all are the same) ss desirable. Many commodities essential to human existence (e.g., bread) have a low value simply because they are not scarce relative to demand—that is, their marginal utility to

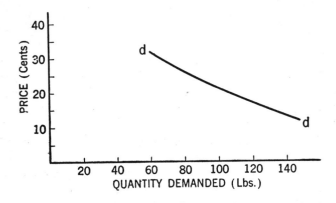

most consumers is small. Consumers tend to spend their incomes for different commodities and services in a way to obtain the greatest satisfaction, i.e., an individual's marginal utility for each of various purchases tends to be approximately equal, and marginal utilities are proportional to prices. In such a hypothetical equilibrium position the individual cannot improve his satisfaction by changing any of his expenditures for consumers' items or by changing the division of his income between spending and saving. Sometimes the same idea is expressed by saying that the marginal rates of substitution of one good for another tend to be proportional to prices.

ELASTICITY OF DEMAND. All demand tends to be elastic—that is, buyers are willing to purchase more at low prices than at high prices because of limited incomes and diminishing utility. The demand, however, for certain commodities (comforts and luxuries) tends to be very elastic, whereas for other commodities (necessities) it is much less elastic, or inelastic. To distinguish different degrees of elasticity of demand, a dividing line is established in the form of unitary elasticity of demand, which means that the quantity purchased by buyers varies inversely in exact proportion to different prices. Stated differently, buyers spend for a commodity at different prices exactly the same total sum; the quantity purchased is varied enough to equalize different prices. The demand schedule and curve cited above is an example of unitary elasticity. An elastic demand is one which is greater than unitary elasticity (total outlays by purchasers increase from high to low prices instead of remaining constant and decrease from low to high); an inelastic demand is one which is less than unitary elasticity (total outlays decrease from high to low prices instead of remaining constant and increase from low to high). Some demand schedules or curves may be elastic in one portion and inelastic in another.

CHANGES IN DEMAND. This means a new demand schedule or a shift in the demand curve. For instance, an increase in demand means that buyers are willing to purchase more at each of a series of prices than formerly (the demand curve is shifted to the right). A decrease in demand means just the opposite. (Sometimes a change in demand is used in the sense that a market price has shifted from one price in the demand schedule to another. For example, price falls because of the interaction of demand and supply, and more is purchased. Demand, however, in a schedule sense may not have increased; buyers may have been ready for some time to purchase more at that price and the explanation is an increase in supply.) It should be noted, however, that demand schedules are logical abstractions. An actual demand schedule for a given product has never been compiled. Consequently, the concept of elasticity of demand which is useful in a general way for certain explanations cannot be neatly separated from the concept of changes in demand in any study of price changes and total sales over a period of time.

Analysis of Supply. Market price is normally the result of more complex conditions than those cited above in which a given quantity of goods is dumped on the market by producers. Producers usually are able to withhold or reserve part of a stock of goods for a period of time. The supply of goods which they are willing to offer at a series of prices on a specific date may be less than the total stock of goods which they have. Effective supply, then, usually means supply in a schedule sense —namely, a series of quantities of some commodity which sellers at any given time are willing to sell at a series of prices (supply prices). For example, suppose dealers in the vegetable market mentioned above have more than 100 lbs. and are able to hold off the market for a day or two part of their stock. They are willing to sell on the following basis:

Quantity demanded	Price per lb.	Quantity supplied
140 lbs.	14 2/7 cents	40 lbs.
120 "	16 2/3 "	50 "
100 "	20 "	65 "
80 "	25 "	80 "
60 "	33 1/3 "	110 "

If the former demand schedule remains the same, market price is now 25 cents. At that price demand and supply are in equilibrium. Any other price would not satisfy certain buyers and sellers. Their competition would cause price to settle to 25 cents. For instance at 20 cents 65 lbs. are offered by dealers, but 100 lbs. are demanded by buyers. The competition of buyers would raise the price to 25 cents. Only one price would prevail. If the above demand and supply schedules are graphically presented, the demand and supply curves intersect at that price.

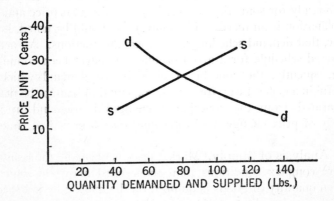

SUPPLY AND PRICE. Sellers are usually willing to sell more of a given commodity at high prices than at low prices— that is, the quantity which sellers will offer tends to vary directly with price (opposite of buyers). The supply curve slopes upward to the right which indicates the willingness of sellers to offer larger quantities at higher prices. The chief reasons for a supply schedule or curve showing the above tendency are: (1) sellers always gain more at a high price than at a low price for the same quantity; and (2) each seller or firm experiences within a range of practical operation rising marginal costs as output is increased from existing fixed capacity. For the expansion of output from any one firm under competitive conditions, rising marginal costs are due primarily to diminishing returns and not to higher prices paid for more units of the variable factors (e.g., labor and materials). Present storage costs, as well as anticipated future costs of offering a new supply, influence the action of sellers.

CHANGES IN SUPPLY. This usually means change in a schedule sense (similar to demand); the supply curve moves to the right for an increase and to the left for a decrease. Supply may be elastic or inelastic.

Market Price Equilibrium. Competitive market price, as described above, refers to an equilibrium of demand and supply at any given moment. Over a brief market period (say a day or two) changes in demand and supply may occur. If demand increases and supply remains the same, or if demand remains the same and supply decreases, price will increase. If just the opposite changes occur, price will decrease. If both demand and supply increase equally, or decrease equally, price will remain the same. If demand increases and supply decreases, price will increase (if vice versa, price will decrease). If they have large stocks, sellers may sometimes cut their supply prices, but for a time buyers may buy less rather than more in the expectation of a further price reduction—that is, a series of decreasing demands appear. If they have small stocks, sellers may raise their supply prices, but for a time buyers may buy more rather than less in the expectation of higher future prices. On the other hand, changes in demand may within narrow limits temporarily reverse the usual action of sellers by inducing the formation of new supply schedules. Market price in any brief interval of time which is insufficient for varying output from existing capacity may not be related to costs of production.

Short-run Market Price and Costs. Any increase or decrease in demand and price which persists for a period of

time sufficient to allow variation of output from existing capacity is likely to be offset in part by an increase or decrease in
supply. These adjustments tend to make the marginal costs of
each seller or firm equal to the price which prevails. The supply schedule or curve in the short run reflects the marginal
costs of suppliers. Total average unit costs of production,
however, are not closely related to price in the short-run period.

AVERAGE VARIABLE COSTS. Each firm would temporarily
suspend production unless the price is slightly higher than the
variable cost per unit of output. Although a price in excess
of variable costs may not be high enough to cover total unit
costs (variable and fixed including normal profit) of a given
output, the firm loses less by operating than by closing temporarily. Any excess above variable costs is a contribution
toward fixed costs which exist irrespective of output.

MARGINAL (VARIABLE) COSTS. Beyond this lower limit
of average variable cost, each firm expands output as long as
the cost of an additional unit (marginal cost) is less than the
price and ceases to expand when they are equal. Since under
competition each firm's relatively small output does not appreciably affect the price at a given level of total supply and
demand, price per unit for an individual firm is constant and is
the same as average receipts and marginal receipts per unit from
sales. Expansion of output stops, and the firm is in short-
run equilibrium (unable to improve its position by variation
of output) when marginal costs are equal to marginal receipts.
Additional output beyond this point adds more to costs than
to receipts, and hence, is less profitable. Each firm minimizes
losses or maximizes profits by equating marginal costs and
marginal receipts.

AVERAGE TOTAL UNIT COSTS. In the short-run period
firms may produce and sell at a price which is above or below
the total average unit cost of production and may experience
losses or more than normal profits. A competitive market,
however, forces each firm to make adjustments in the direction
of an output for which the price per unit is equal to the
minimum average total unit cost of production which includes
a normal profit. At this output marginal cost is equal to average total unit cost. In order to achieve this goal, sufficient
time is needed to change the total capacity of an industry.

Normal Price and Long-run Equilibrium. In the absence of all disturbances the firms in a competitive industry would eventually adjust both their output and capacity to a given demand and price so that minimum average total cost would be equal to receipts. If some firms are not making normal profits, perhaps receipts are only slightly in excess of variable costs, replacements are not made, and some capacity is finally scrapped. If some firms are making profits in excess of normal profits, new capacity is finally built. In long-run equilibrium each firm remaining in the industry would be operating at optimum capacity and minimum costs; each would have the same average total cost (including a normal profit, i.e., the cost of attracting and holding firms in the industry); and the price would be equal to the minimum average total unit cost.

The diagram which follows shows a firm under perfect competition in long-run equilibrium with capacity, output, and costs adjusted perfectly to price; it supplies 170 of the 80,000 units supplied by the industry at a price of 40 cents.

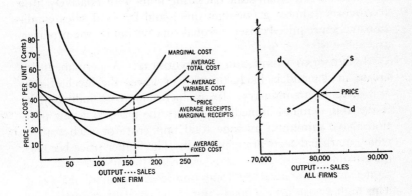

Some firms may have a larger capacity and output than others; some firms may have a lower proportion of variable costs and a higher proportion of fixed costs than others; and the normal profits included in fixed costs may be larger for some firms than for others. The total average unit cost of each, however, must be the same, must be at a minimum for a given total demand and output, and must be equal to the price; otherwise there is no long-run equilibrium with no further induce-ments for firms to improve their positions.

Competitive normal price is a hypothetical, minimum-cost price. In the long run total average costs of production are im-portant conditions of supply which determine a price for a given demand. Normal price, however, is an equilibrium price, and demand is important because changes in demand may change the level of costs in an industry.

CONSTANT COSTS FOR AN INDUSTRY. A permanent increase in demand in a constant cost industry does not in the long run raise the price of the output. The price will rise temporarily because of increased output and higher marginal costs, but eventually new firms with the same average costs as old firms enter the industry, and the price returns to its former level. In such a cost situation demand merely influences the amount of output and not the level of costs and prices. The capacity of the industry is enlarged by an increase in the number of firms and not by an increase in the size or scale of production of any firm. An industry which approximated constant costs would be characterized by small-scale operating units with relatively little fixed costs (almost a one-man unit) and by local sales condi-tions which required close, personal supervision by the producer and seller.

INCREASING COSTS FOR AN INDUSTRY. A permanent in-crease in demand is likely to raise or lower the level of cost and price in an industry. In an increasing-cost industry the increase in demand immediately raises the price to a new posi-tion above minimum average total unit cost for each firm at which marginal costs are equal to it. The higher price becomes permanent because new firms entering the industry have a higher minimum average total unit cost equal to the price. This higher cost level is due to the use of inferior resources and to the higher price of some scarce factors of production. In the new demand, price, and cost position the superior resources of the old firms have a higher earning power or value. These esti-mated higher values, or recapitalized earnings, especially for land resources, represent higher fixed costs. Unless these costs were covered by receipts, such superior resources would be sold or used for the production of some other product. In the long run, then, equilibrium is established when the higher level of minimum average total unit costs of all the firms in the industry are equal to the price. Nearly all mining industries and various types of agriculture may approximate at times conditions of long-run increasing costs. Of course, technological improvements (qualitative changes in the factors of production) may drop the cost and price level of a constant, increasing, or decreasing cost industry, but here the assumption is made that such disturbances are absent for a sufficient period of time to permit long-run equilibrium adjustments. Stability of the entire economy with no inflation or deflation of the general level of prices and costs is also assumed.

DECREASING COSTS FOR AN INDUSTRY. A permanent increase in demand for the product of a decreasing cost industry may temporarily raise its price, but new firms entering the industry and old firms expanding their scale of operation have lower minimum average total unit costs than formerly. This drop in the average total cost curve and competition forces a decline in price. The decrease in cost is due to economies of large-scale production (internal economics) which are made possible by the increase in demand and output. These changes make profitable the use of large, indivisible units of machinery, methods of production, and division of labor which are too costly relative to a small market and output—that is, they could not be fully utilized. As long as an increase in the size or scale of the production unit results in more effective use of the facilities and personnel, there is no long-run equilibrium under competitive conditions. The first firms to enlarge the scale of production have an advantage over the others in being able to sell at lower prices, and they are likely to retain the advantage by further expansions, lower levels of minimum average total unit costs, and lower prices. Some form of equilibrium may be achieved under monopolistic conditions, but no competitive long-run equilibrium is possible until the expansion results in diseconomies of large-scale production (mainly difficulties of managerial co-ordination) which more than offset the economies. Increasing costs for the industry then prevail as analyzed above. Industries which approximate decreasing cost conditions at times are those non-raw-material ones which have very large fixed facilities and fixed costs relative to variable costs, such as various types of manufacturing and some public utilities.

Applicability of Competitive Long-run Equilibrium Analysis.

DECREASING COSTS AND HISTORICAL DECLINES IN COSTS. As previously indicated, this type of competitive analysis does not apply to conditions of decreasing costs for an industry since these conditions involve monopolistic agreements or elimination of all rivals to a given firm as a basis of equilibrium. Moreover, long-run decreasing costs for an industry associated with an expansion of the scale of production and use of existing techniques are separated for analysis from historical declines in the level of costs for any type of industry which result from technological improvements. There is no basis for a long-run equilibrium analysis of an industry subject to frequent technological improvements. Under such conditions there is likely to be a fringe of losing firms using the older methods of production. They lose less by operating as long as receipts are in excess of variable costs than by scrapping plant facilities. The innovating firms with technological improvements and lower levels of average total unit costs than other firms enlarge their share of the market by selling at lower prices. The market is not perfectly competitive as defined previously, and the adjustments of costs and prices are short run, not long run. In the history of most industries a lowering of the level of cost and price has probably been a mixed process of change in scale of production and technological improvements which cannot be explained in terms of competitive long-run equilibrium of a static economy.

ALLOCATION OF JOINT COSTS AND FIXED COSTS. Not one but several products are frequently produced by the same plants and firms. Under conditions of joint supply and joint costs (whether constant, increasing, or decreasing for an industry), normal price for any one of the joint products is not directly related to costs. Demand determines the normal price of a joint product because no allocation of the joint cost to each product is possible. In the long run the combined prices and outputs of the joint products (total receipts) will tend to equal the total costs of the firms, but demand determines the price of each product. If demand for one product of a joint group increases, its price rises and more of it is produced. But the output of the other products of the joint cost group are also increased. Since the demand for them remains the same, their price falls.

Joint costs exist in an industry when two or more commodities are the inseparable results of one productive process (e.g., meat packing, petroleum refining, railway transportation, chemical manufacturing, cotton ginning). Joint costs include fixed and variable costs. In the later stages of production one product of a joint cost group may be separated from the original group (e.g., hog bristle in pork packing) for separate processing to make it usable. Without separate processing the hog bristle is discarded as waste. Demand, then, must be sufficient to fix a price for hog bristle which will at least cover the separate processing expenses, or the product will be discarded as waste.

When a manufacturing plant or store produces or makes available many products by using common fixed facilities, fixed costs resemble joint costs. The fixed costs must be allocated on an arbitrary basis among the products, but the variable costs of each are separate, and, hence, a partial adjustment of output on a cost basis to demand is possible. If the demand for one article in a group increases, its output is expanded until marginal costs equal marginal receipts for the one article. The production of other items may remain the same. In the long run, total receipts for the products of a plant and firm equal total costs, but the excess of receipts above average variable cost for each product may differ widely. Under such conditions fixed costs are allocated to each product largely on the basis of its excess of receipts over average variable cost—that is, on its ability to absorb them.

Commodities produced under conditions of joint supply and joint costs, as well as those produced in multi-product plants, are not amenable to detailed long-run, equilibrium analysis. There is no way of showing a precise relationship between the price of a given product and its minimum average total unit cost of production. In many instances, moreover, such products are probably sold under monopolistic conditions instead of competition.

CONTINUOUS FLUCTUATIONS IN COSTS. If alternating periods of prosperity and depression characterize the operation of the economic system, there is no long-run period for the application of equilibrium analysis. Periods of losses for many firms are succeeded by periods of very high profits, and the relation of a price to a minimum average total unit cost is obscure. If part of the labor force and plant capacity is unemployed, a permanent increase in demand for many commodities may temporarily have little influence on price. Output is expanded, but variable costs (average and marginal) may rise very little and fixed costs per unit decline with fuller utilization of capacity. Pseudo constant or decreasing costs appear. In the production of many agricultural products, changes in weather conditions and other difficulties in adjusting output to demand because of maturing periods for crops and animals result in fluctuating yearly average costs which are difficult to relate to a given price in the long run.

SIGNIFICANCE OF COMPETITIVE, LONG-RUN ANALYSIS. This type of analysis as indicated above has very limited application as an explanation of market adjustments. These adjustments are primarily of the short-run variety because of many disturbances, and, hence, the relation between the price of a given product and its average cost is often fluctuating and indefinite. Nevertheless, the analysis of a competitive normal price provides a useful standard for evaluating profits and allocations of goods and services. Statistical averages of prices, costs, and profits for a given industry over a period of years may be used as the basis of an excess profits tax. The conditions necessary for having a competitive normal price emphasize the monopolistic features of many markets and indicate that they are likely to remain monopolistic in an innovating system of private enterprise. In some cases of monopoly, however, governmental control is necessary, and the perfect allocation of a competitive market on the basis of price being equal to minimum average total unit cost is a guide to the control of price.

SEMICOMPETITIVE PRICES

Semicompetitive prices are prices which prevail under conditions of imperfect competition or monopolistic competition. Only the prices of highly standardized commodities which are bought and sold on well-organized markets conform closely to the above competitive price analysis, and many of these are subject to governmental control. Probably the major portion of consumers' goods are sold at prices which conform only loosely to the competitive price analysis. Buyers in the retail market (as noted in a previous chapter) frequently have a very inadequate knowledge of prices and quality. Sellers offer differentiated products; the units of a commodity class are similar, but not identical. In those cases, moreover, in which physical units are identical, commercially they may be only similar when different sellers furnish varied kinds of services as a part of a sale. A commodity, for example toilet soap, is a collection of items which are close substitutes for each other. Instead of one price for a homogeneous commodity at a given time and place, several prices may prevail even in the same store for a differentiated product or commodity. Several conditions which account for semicompetitive prices are listed below.

Custom and Competition. *Custom* is an important obstacle to free competition. If buyers and sellers become accustomed to a given price for some article, changes in demand and supply conditions slowly and imperfectly alter its price. Changed conditions may point to a higher price, but some dealers may prefer to sacrifice profit rather than to offend customers by raising their price. Other dealers may alter the quantity or quality of the article and retain the old price. On the other hand, changed demand and supply conditions may point to lower price, but dealers may be very slow to cut price. Consumers are accustomed to the present price, and price cuts may spoil the market—that is, consumers become interested in price comparison and delay buying in anticipation of further price cuts. Dealers may develop as a group the attitude that such price cuts are unwise and unfair and exert business and social pressure on dealers who cut prices. Many fees for personal services are maintained at customary levels because price cutting is frowned upon as unprofessional by groups of practitioners. Even if price cuts are made, they sometimes fail to lower dealers' prices to one level. Some dealers may have a clientele which remains with them regardless of the price cuts of other dealers. Routine characterizes much buying.

Unique Articles and Competition. The prices of *unique articles,* such as nonreproducible art objects, do not conform to the competitive price analysis. The individual seller takes what he can get; bargaining or higgling fixes price. The upper limit of the bargaining range is set by the highest subjective valuation of any possible buyer, the lower limit by the seller's subjective valuation, or the second highest valuation of a competing buyer (whichever is higher). Cost of production has little or no influence on the price; utility and demand are the determining factors. Since many reproducible articles have distinctive artistic features, the bargaining range within which price may be agreed upon by buyers and sellers is much wider than the range assumed under the previous discussion of competitive market price.

Location and Competition. Under competitive conditions different prices for the same product in different markets would reflect differences in transportation costs. In many markets sellers are not concentrated at a few points, and sales are made over a wide geographical area. The location, then, of a store is a shopping convenience which one seller may provide for a group of buyers, and another seller cannot easily duplicate it. Differences in the prices of two sellers may reflect buyers' estimates of the difference in shopping convenience.

Advertised Brands and Competition. The prices of particular *brands* of various commodities under the pressure of advertising and sales promotion are related but may differ greatly. Slight differences or alleged differences between two brands of a commodity are played up as selling features by each dealer to induce the consumer to buy without price comparisons. One particular brand seems unique even though it turns out to be common table salt. If substantial differences in quality do exist between two brands, the consumer cannot weigh accurately the quality difference and the price difference. Each brand of a given commodity within limits becomes a separate product sold by one dealer. Even the same product may be sold under different names at different prices by the same dealer in order to get a higher price from the more wealthy class of buyers. Although the prices of many quite similar products at any given time are diverse rather than uniform, the diversity may be partly compensated for in the form of extra services to the buyer.

Uncertain Relationship of Costs and Prices. Under semicompetitive conditions there are many possible adjustments of costs and prices. Although there is a large number of sellers of *similar* products, there is no composite or market supply schedule for an industry or group of sellers. Each seller supplies an individual market or group of customers. In a limited way each seller controls the price of his product or products by varying the amount offered for sale and the methods of selling or advertising. His control, however, is limited because of the possible changes in prices and advertising expenditures of rival sellers of similar products. The demand schedule, then, for the product of each seller is not an independent market demand, but is partly dependent on his own selling effort and the price and advertising policies of rival sellers.

From a short-run point of view aggressive price cutting and use of loss leaders to attract customers may develop at times, and the average variable costs of a product may be barely covered by receipts. Usually, however, nonprice competition characterizes such markets, and attempts are made to increase sales by means of advertising, special services, changes in quality, and other innovations. Selling costs, especially advertising costs, may be either fixed or variable depending upon their effects on sales. Because of the difficulty of allocating selling costs and other costs to specific products and because of the possible changes in demand, each seller or firm is not in a position to balance neatly marginal costs and marginal receipts as a guide to profits. An approximate average variable cost of a product can always be calculated, and to this cost a markup of a given per cent is added in order to formulate a price. The markup is an estimate, based partly on experience in a trade or industry, of a product's share of fixed cost including expected profit. Since many sellers of differentiated products are multi-product firms, the markup for each item may vary greatly depending upon estimates of what buyers are willing to pay. Receipts from some items may contribute more to fixed costs and profits than others. The average margin or excess of receipts for all products above variable costs is the important guide to profits.

In the long-run period several cost-price relations may prevail among groups of semicompetitive sellers. If new firms with differentiated products may freely and easily enter the field, a substantial fringe of losing firms may be normal. New firms may not be aware of the exact chances of profits and losses. Each one, moreover, enters with a slightly different product, cost, and price expectation and with individual ideas of successful selling. Under these heterogeneous conditions the existence of losing firms is no deterrent to new firms. There is chronic excess capacity and sales by some firms at prices less than average total costs. If entry by new firms is difficult because of large capital requirements, dominant position of existing firms, secret process and patents, and other obstacles, sales may continue at prices in excess of average total costs. These excess receipts or pure profits are not eliminated by competition of new firms or of existing firms. If product differentiation is very slight, the number of sellers large, and entry perfectly free, conditions almost approximate competition. Price for each seller will equal the average total unit cost of production, but not at the minimum cost output. This outcome, as indicated in the graph below, is due to the slight slope of the firm's average and marginal receipts curves. The average receipts per unit are the same as the price per unit and the demand curve for the firm's product. Its slope indicates that the firm can influence price by varying the amount sold. Marginal receipts which represent the difference in total receipts at any one output compared with the next additional output decline more sharply than average receipts.

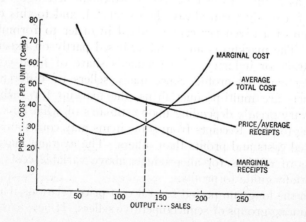

The long-run results of semicompetitive conditions are too varied for precise comparison with competitive markets. Nonprice competition which characterizes these conditions is qualitatively unlike price competition. It may be aggressive competition at times in terms of changes in quality, in special services given with a product, in trade-in allowances, and in advertising expenditures; or it may be highly monopolistic. Although operation of plants may be at less than the least-cost output and price higher than under competition, as indicated in the above diagram, the variation in products may be an offsetting advantage for many buyers. To please apparently the great diversity in tastes and preferences, an almost endless variety of similar products of all kinds is offered to consumers under all types of selling conditions. Selling costs, especially advertising costs, are an indispensable part of the production of nonstandardized products. In some instances these costs may be excessive and advertising may be misleading, but a complete evaluation of them includes many diverse factors, such as the effects of advertising on the satisfaction of wants, the scale of production, the expenditure of effort, the publication of newspapers and magazines, and the maintenance of radio programs.

MONOPOLY PRICES

Monopoly prices are prices fixed by one seller, or a group of sellers acting in unison, by means of control over the supply of a given commodity. There is no substitute for the commodity. As indicated previously, pure monopolies are not common. They exist in part because of decreasing costs of increased scale of production which reduce the number of sellers in a market to one, or a few who agree to avoid price competition. Sometimes in such cases a public franchise is granted to an industry to operate as a public utility. Patents are also the basis of many monopolies. In general, combination or agreements among sellers to restrict supply and raise prices are ancient monopoly devices. The demand schedule for the product of a monopoly is an ordinary market one, which may be influenced by advertising. The monopolist, however, primarily attempts to regulate the supply of a commodity in order to obtain a maximum profit.

Maximum Monopoly Profit. The *maximum net profit for a monopolist* depends on the quantity sold and the difference between cost and price per unit of output (i.e., the largest total obtained by multiplying the number of units sold by the profit per unit). Operation at the point of greatest difference between cost and price per unit of output may not yield the monopolist the highest total net profit because added sales beyond that point may more than offset the decline in profit per unit. Demand and costs of production form the basis for the monopolist's choice of output. In more precise terms profits are at a maximum when marginal costs are equal to marginal receipts. Under short-run conditions a monopolist may operate at a loss. However in the long run, a monopolist, as indicated in the graph below, operates at an output with a price above the average total cost of production (including a normal profit), and the excess represents a pure monopoly profit. Although a larger output might be produced at lower costs, the decrease in costs is more than offset by a decrease in receipts which lessens the monopoly profit.

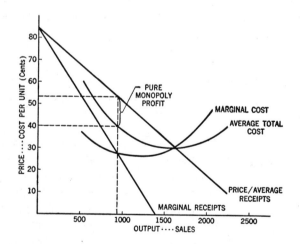

Monopoly Prices versus Competitive Prices. A *comparison of competitive prices and monopoly prices* is difficult. Some monopolies have a social justification, such as patent monopolies (encourage inventions), copyright monopolies (encourage art and research), public consumption monopolies (regulate consumption, e.g., liquor), and fiscal monopolies (source of revenue for the government). Other private monopolies are usually condemned because their prices are higher than competitive prices and because they tend to create scarcity rather than to overcome it.

MONOPOLY RESTRICTION OF SUPPLY. There is less incentive for a monopolist to organize his plant in the most efficient manner because profits may be greater than in competitive industries merely on the basis of restricting supply. Modernization of facilities, experimentation with lower prices and larger output, and managerial initiative may be retarded by lack of competition. In some instances the monopolist may be reluctant to experiment and expand even though greater profits were a probability.

MONOPOLY DIFFERENTIAL PRICES. Monopoly prices are frequently higher than competitive prices because the monopolists can more effectively charge different prices to different consumers. There are no competing dealers to whom the consumer may go in case of discrimination. If the monopolist divides his customers into classes on the basis of what they are willing to pay and charges each class a maximum profit price, a larger net profit will be made than under a uniform price. In general if the monopolist could estimate his marginal costs and receipts accurately, maximum profits with discriminatory prices would be made when marginal receipts from each group of buyers were equal and these were equal to marginal costs of the total output.

MONOPOLY AND DESTRUCTION OF COMMODITIES. Monopoly prices sometimes exceed competitive prices because the monopolist destroys part of a surplus stock in order to increase his profits. If demand decreases suddenly, a monopolist may maximize his profits by selling only a small part of his supply at a high price and by destroying the surplus to reduce carrying charges. Under competition the consumer would benefit from lower prices.

POTENTIAL EFFICIENCY OF MONOPOLY. Monopoly prices, however, in some cases may be as low or lower than competitive prices. For instance, in those cases in which the scale of production is much larger and the level of costs much lower than they would be under competition, there is the possibility of a monopoly price being lower than a competitive price. Further-more, greater long-run efficiency of production may sometimes be achieved under monopoly conditions when the economy is highly unstable. A monopoly can operate at a more uniform rate and carry stocks to even out changes in demand. Under competition firms must estimate demand and also the probable supply of competitors. The accumulation of stocks is risky, and consequently, many firms may operate beyond capacity at one time and much below capacity at another time. High prices induce overexpansion and result in very low prices. Very low prices may bankrupt many firms and result in very high prices. The average competitive price may exceed the mo-nopoly price.

LIMITS TO MONOPOLY EXTORTION. The extent of mo-nopoly price extortion is frequently exaggerated. Monopoly prices sometimes approximate competitive prices, and the mo-nopolists' power to control supply and raise price is limited. First, there is the possibility of substitution of other products for the monopolized product. If monopoly prices are excessive, consumers turn to less satisfactory, but cheaper, products. If no substitute exists (e.g., nitrates, camphor, etc.), a synthetic product may be developed. Second, there is the threat of poten-tial competition. High monopoly prices and profits encourage other producers to enter the field. Third, there is the fact that most monopolies are only partial monopolies. If one producer controls 80 per cent of the supply of a given commodity, he sets the price and the small producers follow. If the price is high and the profit per unit large, the small producers are tempted to expand their output and new producers will appear. Fourth, there is the fear of government intervention. If the monopoly is a "good" monopoly and charges reasonable prices, the gov-ernment is less likely to dissolve it or to control its prices. Regardless of whether monopoly prices are higher or lower than competitive prices, monopolies should be under govern-ment regulation. If monopoly is less efficient in a given in-dustry than competition and prices are higher, the monopoly should be abolished and competition enforced. If monopoly in a given industry is more efficient than competition and prices are lower, the monopoly should be regulated, output increased, and prices lowered until the rate of profit equals that in stable competitive industries. Greater stability in the entire economy would probably lessen monopoly extortion.

Taxes and Monopoly. The effect of taxes on a monopoly is important. If a fixed tax or a tax on net profits is imposed, there is no change in price to the consumer. The monopoly usually fixes a price which yields the highest net profit and the addition of the above tax does not alter his unit costs or the demand for his product. A unit tax on a monopoly, however, adds to the variable expenses and raises the price to the consumer. If less is produced, the costs of the monopolists are decreased and the price of the product is increased. In this case restriction of output maximizes net profit and part of the tax is paid by the consumer.

FIXED PRICES

Examples of Fixed Prices. Fixed prices determined by government agencies are an important subject in price analysis. The analysis of fixed prices, however, involves many factors and they will be examined later in their proper setting. Here are listed the more important examples. Government units own and operate important industries (e.g., the Post Office, canals, hydro-electric plants, etc.), and the price policy followed is largely the subject of public finance. If the industries make a profit, they are a source of revenue—if a loss, they are an object of expenditure. Government agencies (e.g., Interstate Commerce Commission, State Public Utility Commissions) regulate the prices charged by various public utility industries (monopolies of vital interest to the public, e.g., railroads, tramways, electric companies, telephone companies, etc.), but the problems of valuation, rate of return, and effective regulation require separate treatment. Changes in the value of money may change all prices, and consequently, the money and credit policy of the federal government and its fiscal agent, the Federal Reserve Banks, have an important influence on prices. The problems involved are discussed later under banking, business cycles, and price levels. Price fixing by government agencies in the form of minimum wages is discussed under labor problems. Federal tariff legislation affects prices. The Federal Trade Commission attempts to enforce fair competition. Its activities are discussed in connection with trust prosecutions.

An extensive program has been developed by the federal government to stabilize the prices of a few farm products. These activities are discussed in connection with problems of agriculture.

During World War II, as an emergency measure to prevent inflation and to promote the war effort, practically all prices were controlled by government agencies. The Office of Price Administration fixed prices and rents and rationed some vital consumers' goods. The War Labor Board adjusted wage rates. The War Production Board established priorities on all important materials which enabled producers of military equipment rather than of civilian goods to obtain them. Priorities and ration points rather than prices allocated goods to buyers. In the absence of these regulations the bidding-up of prices by the government in order to get war materials, the shortage of civilian goods, and the large income of the population would have resulted in tremendous price increases. Low income groups would have barely subsisted, and the war effort would have been impaired.

Difficulties in Fixing Competitive Prices. Many of the examples cited above involve the regulation of monopolistic prices. In general, government control of competitive commodity prices is a difficult task. Frequently there are numerous producers involved which makes close supervision a costly and complicated project. Production may require only small fixed investments, and hence, producers move about easily and escape regulation. Commodities which may be stored add a speculative problem. If expansion to meet a temporary demand demoralizes an industry, there is a tendency under political pressure to fix prices high enough to save all producers. Under conditions of usual demand a price high enough to save marginal producers retards the shift of production factors into other industries where they can be more advantageously used. Output is likely to increase rather than decrease. Either price must be fixed low enough to save only the bulk of producers, or production must be arbitrarily restricted under a permit or tax penalty system. Because of these difficulties, the government is reluctant to interfere with competitive prices except in times of grave emergency. Near the close of World War II, especially after V–J Day and until the end of practically all price controls in November, 1946, violations of price regulations became widespread. In the absence of war patriotism prices in excess of the legal ones were paid in order to obtain scarce goods. These black markets were largely responsible for the termination of price regulations.

Because of the Korean War, Congress passed in 1950 the Defense Production Act, which authorized the president to develop a program of defense production and economic stabilization. In the following year many features of the World War II mobilization concerning controlled materials, wages, and prices were re-established.

VALUATION PRICES

Valuation prices are important in determining the value of goods (especially production goods) not easily reproduced nor freely exchanged. One example, value of public utility property, will be discussed later. Since there is only infrequent and sporadic buying and selling, market price is no test of their value at any given time. Production goods which are freely reproduced and freely exchanged have a market price related to costs of production; the demand, however, differs from that for consumption goods. Production goods yield no utility to the user. They are desired because they produce goods which do yield direct satisfaction (i.e., production goods have derived utility). Usually producers acquire production goods and produce for a market rather than for their own use. The expected future income from the use of production goods is an important factor (demand factor) in determining their present value.

Capitalization is the process used to determine the present value of expected future income. If a production good is expected to yield enough for its perpetual maintenance and in addition $100 each year indefinitely, the income at 5 per cent (and hence, the goods which produced it) would be worth $2,000 ($100 ÷ .05). Stated differently, $2,000 invested in the production goods is expected to yield yearly $100 or a 5 per cent rate of return.

Capitalization of expected future incomes from production goods is a method of estimating value, and it influences present prices. However, it is not the sole explanation of value in production goods. Other factors, such as the cost of production or reproduction of the production goods, the interest rate, and the demand for the consumption goods made by the production goods are important in determining the value of production goods. If the production goods are freely reproducible and if the demand price of buyers based on a capitalization of expected future incomes is below the cost of producing them, less production goods are made. A smaller supply of production goods lessens the output of consumption goods and raises their price. A higher price for consumption goods increases the expected future income to be derived from production goods and brings their prices nearer to a cost of production basis.

GENERAL REFERENCES

Borden, N. H., *The Economic Effects of Advertising.*
Chamberlin, Edward H., *The Theory of Monopolistic Competition.*
Clark, J. M., *The Economics of Overhead Costs.*
Committee on Price Determination, *Cost Behavior and Price Policy.*
Commons, John R., *Institutional Economics.*
Hall, R. L., and C. J. Hitch, *Price Theory and Business Behavior.*
James, Clifford L., "Inflation and Price Control," *Americana Annual,* 1947.
Nelson, S., and W. Keim, *Price Behavior and Business Policy.*
Robinson, E. A. G., *Monopoly.*
———, *The Structure of Competitive Industry.*
Robinson, Joan, *Economics of Imperfect Competition.*
Schultz, Henry, *Statistical Laws of Supply and Demand.*
Stigler, George J., *The Theory of Price.*
Triffin, R., *Monopolistic Competition and General Equilibrium.*

Chapter Nine

MONEY

THE NATURE OF MONEY

Money is anything which is widely used as a means of payment—that is, it has general acceptability in exchange. It is a device which differs with the time and the place. Cattle, oil, wampum, tobacco, furs, precious metals, and pieces of paper have served as money. Money is a part of the general economic organization, and specific types of money are very closely related to the particular economic organization of the time. At all stages of economic development all types of money are in use to a certain extent and with varying emphasis. Money in the form of cash (bills and coins) is issued by the government and used for all kinds of payments. Checks, however, are now the most commonly used means of payment in the United States; 85 to 90 per cent of total annual payments (in terms of dollars) are made by check. Although checks have limited acceptability and bank deposits transferred by them are in a narrow sense a close substitute for money, the supply of money includes cash and bank deposits on which checks can be drawn.

Traditional Qualities of a Good Money. When coins were the predominant form of money and when gold was the favorite monetary material, the most satisfactory qualities of good money were those primarily related to the physical features of the precious metals. Gold and silver, bullion or coins, were durable, portable, divisible, and recognizable. The uniformity of these metals (degree of purity) could be easily maintained. But most important of all, these metals were always in demand for use in the arts and in industry. They were used widely for ornamentation and display. Their supply, moreover, in terms of an accumulated world stock was not likely to change suddenly. The risk of accepting money made of these metals was lessened because of their commodity or bullion value. As long as a commodity type of money was used, the precious metals, and especially gold, had the physical characteristics which made them a favorite monetary metal. The main functions of money, however, are performed in modern economic systems by noncommodity types of money.

Functions of Money.

MEDIUM OF EXCHANGE. Money is a medium of exchange which facilitates the flow of goods and services from producer to consumer. In the absence of some type of money, trading is reduced to cumbersome and restricted barter transactions. Barter depends on a double coincidence of wants; each party must want the particular commodity or service of the other.

STANDARD OF VALUE. Money is a common denominator for expressing exchange ratios. All commodities and services may be reduced to a common measure and expressed in terms of dollars. Such calculation has become a most important practice which directs production and consumption of goods and services. Without some unit of account and basis of calculation, complex operations in an economic system would be impossible.

STORE OF VALUE. When money is received, it is a store of value until spent or invested. Although the value of money may change over a period of time, money is an important store of value. It may be accumulated temporarily in order to meet uneven future expenditures. It may be hoarded (held in cash or idle bank deposits) in anticipation of a fall in prices instead of being spent on consumers' goods or invested in producers' goods.

Kinds of Money in the United States.

STANDARD MONEY. Standard money is an expression used to refer to standard coins which are coins having bullion value at least equal to their money value. Sometimes their bullion value is greater than their value as money, in which case the public will melt the coins and sell the bullion. Standard coins have been typically gold or silver, for which there are many uses. There are no standard coins in the United States now since a limited gold bullion standard prevails. The monetary unit of account, the dollar, is defined as being equivalent to

15⁵⁄₂₁ grains ⁹⁄₁₀ fine (standard) gold or 13¹⁵⁄₂₁ grains of pure gold (Gold Reserve Act of 1934), which means that the dollar will purchase this much gold.

Gold is not coined into dollars but is used in the form of bullion or bars. All monetary gold in 1934 became the property of the United States Treasury. All newly-mined gold is purchased by it. Industries buy gold bars under a license system from the Treasury. The Treasury now handles all shipments of gold in international transactions. Private holding of monetary gold and gold certificates is illegal. Except for use in industry and international trade, other money is not redeemable in gold. The gold clause in all federal and private obligations is cancelled (Joint Resolution of Congress, June, 1933, and Supreme Court Decision, February, 1935). Gold and gold certificates are not *legal tender*. All other kinds of money authorized by the government are full *legal tender*, i.e., must be accepted for payment of debts contracted in terms of money.

FIDUCIARY MONEY. The value of fiduciary money depends on the monetary traditions and habits of a community. Historically the gradual change from commodity money (commodities used directly for money) to fiduciary money corresponds approximately to the change from barbarism to stable national governments. Trust and confidence by a people in its government to maintain law and order and to issue money, which has little value as a commodity, in restricted amounts only, is the basis for the value of fiduciary money. Under these conditions individuals are willing to sell useful goods and services for small pieces of paper authorized by the government as money, because they find other individuals willing to accept the paper when they wish to buy useful goods and services. The money has value because the individual sells goods and services to obtain it and can buy goods and services with it. Paper money is more convenient to carry than a barrel of salt, but under primitive conditions the latter was used as money because the individual accepting it in a sale of goods or services could use it if others refused to accept it in a purchase. The individual protected himself against loss. In modern times, protection in the use of money, like protection of human life, is for the most part transferred from the individual to the government. Since most individuals, moreover, do not fill their own teeth or make their own jewelry, a government can maintain the value of its fiduciary money without redeeming it in gold for domestic circulation. From its own citizens a government can buy newly-mined gold at a fixed price and pay for it with authorized paper money. For industrial uses the government can sell gold to its citizens at the same fixed price and receive authorized paper money. Sales of goods and services abroad by its citizens for which gold is received can be purchased by the government with authorized paper money at the same fixed price. Purchase of goods and services abroad by its citizens, for which gold must be paid, can be sold by the government to them at the same fixed price in return for authorized paper money. Some international circulation of gold is still necessary because individuals and nations in their international transactions do not trust each other.

Paper money consists mainly of *Federal Reserve Notes, silver certificates,* and *United States Notes* (greenbacks). *Gold certificates* which are being retired can be held lawfully only by the Federal Reserve Banks and the United States Treasury. Although *National Bank Notes, Federal Reserve Bank Notes,* and *Treasury Notes of 1890* have been officially retired as forms of money, many of them continue to circulate. Prior to 1933, gold certificates and silver certificates were frequently classified as *representative money* since they were then virtually warehouse receipts for an equivalent amount of gold and silver held by the Treasury. Prior to 1933, the above notes of banks and the government were classified as *credit money,* i.e., promises to pay standard or lawful money to the bearer on demand without maintaining a full coverage of standard money, as in the case of gold and silver certificates. All of the above types of fiduciary paper money may now be classified as credit money. All paper money, except gold certificates, is full legal tender.

Silver dollars and *subsidiary coins* are types of fiduciary money and credit money (classified sometimes as *token coins*) because their value as bullion is less than their value as money. The silver dollar is illogically classified by law as standard money. Silver is now nationalized (Silver Purchase Act, June, 1934) by the government, and is regulated by the Treasury under a plan similar to that applied to gold. **Silver** dollars and subsidiary coins are now full legal tender. Their value is maintained by an indirect and restricted convertibility into gold (gold for industrial and international uses only).

In the United States, paper money, silver dollars, and subsidiary coins are maintained at par with the new gold dollar because of the trust and confidence of the people in the tangible and intangible assets back of them. Important tangible assets are as follows: approximately twenty billion dollars of gold bullion and more than two billion dollars of silver bullion held by the United States Treasury; commercial assets, banking assets, and government bonds used by Federal Reserve Banks as partial security for Federal Reserve Notes. Important intangible assets are as follows: the ability of industry and the government to settle for most of their purchases of goods and services abroad by means of the sale of goods and services abroad; the authority given to the government to curb unnecessary withdrawals of gold and silver by its own citizens or by foreign interests; the ability of the government over a period of years to pay off its debts by taxation without being forced to meet its obligations by a great increase in the quantity of paper money.

UNITED STATES MONETARY SYSTEM

The United States Monetary System is not a nice logical arrangement, but the result of legislation impelled by wars, by discoveries and improvements in gold and silver mining, and by conflicting group interests. Although the monetary legislation of the early thirties simplified the money system in part, it also added some new complications. Subsidiary coins which were formerly legal tender for only small payments are now inconveniently made legal tender for any payment. Nationalization of silver adds to the complexity of maintaining all forms of money at par with the gold dollar. One form of paper money, moreover, would be sufficient for the country—preferably Federal Reserve Notes. The present status and past history of the monetary system are discussed below.

Monetary Unit. The *monetary unit* is the dollar, the gold content of which is fixed by law at $15\frac{5}{21}$ grains of standard gold ($\frac{9}{10}$ gold, $\frac{1}{10}$ alloy), which is equivalent to $13\frac{15}{21}$ grains of pure gold. The former gold content was 25.8 grains of standard gold, or 23.22 grains of pure gold. The new gold content of the dollar amounts to 59.06 per cent of its former weight, or a devaluation of 40.94 per cent. The devaluation was accomplished by changing the price paid for gold by the government from $20.67 to $35.00 an ounce.

Brief Monetary History of the United States.

MINT ACT OF 1792. As early as 1652 "Land Banks" were issuing paper money in Massachusetts. Later colonial and revolutionary bills of credit (fiat money later redeemed at a small per cent of the face value) appeared. The Mint Act of 1792 made the dollar (either gold or silver) the monetary unit to take the place of this miscellaneous paper money and the English and Spanish coins in circulation. There was free coinage * of gold and silver, both were legal tender, and *bimetallism* was the legal monetary standard. The coinage ratio was 15 units of silver to 1 of gold. The market ratio was 15½ to 1; there was not enough silver in the silver dollar to equal the value of the gold dollar (by law silver was overvalued). Silver became the real standard since no one wished to pay debts in gold. The bright silver dollars, however, were desired by the Spanish-American countries in trade. Many silver dollars left the country and for this reason their coinage was stopped in 1804. Some gold was coined, and it also left the country to purchase imports. The United States relied upon paper money and foreign coins for its medium of exchange; certain foreign coins were even made legal tender.

ACT OF 1834. In 1834 Congress reduced the weight of the gold dollar. The mint ratio was now 16 to 1; the market ratio remained 15½ to 1. Silver was undervalued by the law. No one would pay debts in silver coin; it was melted down or hoarded; gold coins came into circulation and gold was the actual standard until 1862. Gold discoveries in California and Australia increased the discrepancy between the mint ratio and the market ratio.

---

* *Free coinage* does not mean without cost, but without limit as to quantity. When there is no charge for the minting process it is called *gratuitous coinage.* If the charge is just enough to cover the cost of minting and assaying, it is called *brassage.* If a charge is made to collect revenue, it is called *seigniorage* (such a charge is made in the United States for subsidiary coins less than one dollar).

During the period of the Civil War and afterwards (1862–1879) paper was temporarily the actual standard. The excessive issue of greenbacks depreciated their value and everyone preferred to pay his debts in paper. Neither gold nor silver was in circulation. When the redemption of the greenbacks in gold began in 1879, the United States was again on an actual gold standard and continued so until 1933.

DEMONETIZATION OF THE SILVER DOLLAR. The end of bimetallism in the United States was marked in 1873 by the dropping of the silver dollar from the list of coins minted (little or no silver had been brought to the mint for coinage into silver dollars for some time). The effect was gold monometallism. Silver dollars circulated as standard money and were legal tender, yet they were worth less than face value and free coinage was stopped. Silver was called the "limping standard."

In 1876 the world's silver supply was greatly increased by the opening of rich mines in Colorado. In addition, India and several European countries began to use less silver. Silver prices, which had been almost stationary for years, declined sharply. The value of gold itself rose. The market ratio between the two metals began to rise (in 1878 it was 18 to 1). The demonetization of silver was now resented and termed the "crime of 1873." People demanded cheap money to pay their debts. Congress enacted two compromise measures:

The *Bland-Allison Act,* 1878, required the Secretary of the Treasury to purchase each month not less than two million dollars' or more than four million dollars' worth of silver bullion and to coin it into dollars.

The *Sherman-Silver-Puchase Act* of 1890 increased the amount to four and a half million ounces of silver each month to be paid for in Treasury Notes which were redeemable in gold as well as silver. The Secretary of the Treasury was required to keep the two metals on a parity with each other. Cheap silver dollars flooded the country. Gold disappeared from circulation and was exported to other countries. To stop the inflation of silver, the act was repealed in 1893.

GOLD STANDARD ACT, 1900. This act officially established gold as the monetary standard. Actually gold had been the standard since 1879 under the system of bimetallism. It made the gold dollar (25.8 grains of gold %₀ fine) the monetary unit. It provided for an unrestricted gold market ($20.67 per ounce), free coinage of gold only, legal tender of gold, and convertibility of paper money and coin into gold.

PITTMAN ACT, 1918. The Pittman bill authorized the Treasury to melt down and sell a part (up to 350 million dollars) of the large stock of silver on hand because the British and Indian governments were in the market for silver. Federal Reserve Bank Notes replaced the silver certificates. Recoinage started again in 1921, and by 1928 all the silver dollars melted had been recoined.

ABANDONMENT OF THE GOLD STANDARD, 1933. Because of a grave banking emergency, the President by executive proclamation (March 6, 1933) closed all banks in the United States. The proclamation also placed an embargo on gold and silver exports, except under special license, and prohibited banks and the Treasury from paying out gold or silver. An *Emergency Banking Act* (March 9, 1933) confirmed these measures and authorized the president to prohibit all private hoarding of gold and to require that all gold coin, bullion, and gold certificates be exchanged for other kinds of money. The *Thomas Amendment* (Emergency Farm Relief Act, May, 1933) authorized the president to reduce the gold content of the dollar up to 50 per cent; to establish a bimetallic system of gold and silver; and to issue three billion dollars of United States Notes (greenbacks). Only the first authority enumerated has been exercised (devaluation of 40.94 per cent). By joint resolution (June, 1933), Congress cancelled the gold clause in all federal and private obligations.

GOLD RESERVE ACT AND PROCLAMATION OF JANUARY, 1934. These measures placed the United States on an international gold bullion standard (restricted gold standard). Gold was nationalized and the entire monetary stock was taken over by the Treasury. For industrial uses or international transactions gold bullion is obtained in return for other money. Hoarded gold became subject to confiscation with a 100 per cent penalty. The Secretary of the Treasury was authorized for three years to deal in gold, foreign exchange, and other necessary instruments in order to stabilize the exchange value of the dollar and to maintain the parity of other kinds of money. For this purpose, an exchange *stabilization fund* of two billion dollars was authorized, to be taken from the government profit made by devaluation (about two and three quarter billion dollars).

SILVER PURCHASE ACT, JUNE, 1934. This act and a subsequent executive order (August, 1934) nationalized silver bullion. The Secretary of the Treasury was directed to buy silver bullion at a price not above $1.29 per fine ounce (statutory price since 1837), except for silver bullion in the United States prior to May, 1934, for which the price was not to exceed 50 cents, and to sell silver bullion whenever its market price was above its statutory price or whenever the proportion of silver to gold in the government's monetary stock exceeded 25 per cent. Purchases of silver were to be paid for by the issuance of silver certificates. Domestic trade and international trade in refined silver bullion were to be regulated by the government. Silver dollars and coins were allowed to circulate because no devaluation of silver was involved. The effect of the silver program has been to increase vastly the silver stocks of the country and to raise the price of silver bullion. It is not bimetallism. Higher silver prices aided domestic producers of silver, increased the profits of foreign speculators in silver, and disturbed the monetary systems of several countries (particularly China and Mexico). Economically there was very slight justification for the silver legislation. Politically it enabled the government to satisfy in part the demands for inflation either in the form of free coinage of silver or in the form of new paper money, without losing control of the monetary system.

MONETARY STANDARDS

Gold Standard. The *gold standard* (in its most complete form) is characterized by having gold as the standard metal; the monetary unit stated in terms of gold; other forms of money maintained at par with gold; free coinage of gold; full legal tender of gold; and a free and unhampered gold market. Before 1914 practically all the industrialized countries of the world were on the gold standard. World War I caused nearly all countries except the United States to abandon the gold standard. During the postwar period these countries returned to the gold standard, but the depression of 1929–1933 caused many of them to abandon it again. Although gold fulfills more than any other metal the requirements of a good monetary standard, its use in a monetary system demands careful administration. (See chapter on price levels.)

Gold Bullion Standard. The *gold bullion standard* is sometimes used in order to conserve gold or to serve as a transitional stage prior to a full gold standard. Domestic currencies are convertible into gold bars of a prescribed weight, and gold coinage and redeemability in gold coin are stopped. England had such a standard from December 31, 1925, to September 21, 1931. The United States now has a restricted gold bullion standard.

Gold Exchange Standard. The *gold exchange standard* is sometimes used in a country where the local coin is silver. The local money is made redeemable in bills of exchange (bank drafts) payable in gold in a gold standard country. The effect is to provide the stabilizing influence of a gold standard without the cost of maintaining a complete gold standard. International trade is also facilitated. Many countries adopted it after World War I pending the restoration of a full gold standard.

Silver Standard. The *silver standard* is governed by the same principles applying to the gold standard—namely, expression of the unit of value in terms of a fixed weight of silver, free coinage of silver, full legal tender of silver coins, redemption of paper money in silver coins, and the maintenance of a free domestic and foreign silver market. No country is on a complete silver standard today. Even China abandoned the silver standard as of 1935 and established a paper money managed currency system.

Bimetallic Standard. The *bimetallic standard* exists when the standard unit of money is expressed in terms of two metals, usually gold and silver, at a fixed weight proportionate to each other; when there is free coinage of both metals; and when both metals are full legal tender. (Bimetallism legally existed in the United States from 1792 to 1873.) If the two metals are gold and silver, the ratio between the weight of pure silver in the silver unit and the weight of pure gold in the gold unit is called the *mint ratio,* the *coinage ratio,* or the *legal ratio.* The *market ratio* is the ratio between the value of a given amount of gold and the value of the same amount of silver on the open market. The market ratio, then, is determined not by law but by supply (mines and mining methods) and demand (industrial and monetary) of the two metals. The difficulty with bimetallism is to make the mint ratio and the market ratio correspond. If they are *equal,* either metal will be coined and bimetallism truly exists. If the market ratio (say 15 ounces of silver to 1 of gold) is *less* than the mint ratio (say 16 to 1), then gold is overvalued at the mint. Gold will be used to pay debts; silver will be melted down and exchanged for gold; and only gold will be coined. If the market ratio (say 17 to 1) is *greater* than the mint ratio (say 16 to 1), then silver is overvalued at the mint. Debts will be paid in silver; gold will be melted down; and only silver will be coined. If both the market and mint ratios are 16 to 1 for a given country, but if other countries establish different ratios, only coin of one metal tends to circulate in each country. In these cases actual monometallism has been substituted for theoretical bimetallism; the metal which is overvalued will usually drive the other out of circulation.

GRESHAM'S LAW. The above process is known as *Gresham's Law* which can be popularly stated as—cheaper money drives dearer money out of circulation (out of the country), or bad money drives out good money. (Gresham's Law is effective only when there is free coinage, free melting, and full legal tender.)

FAILURE OF THE COMPENSATORY PRINCIPLE. Those who favor bimetallism contend that there is a tendency for the discrepancy between the two ratios to be corrected—i.e., when the supply of silver increases (silver would then be overvalued at the mint), demand will shift from gold to silver; the demand for gold being decreased, its value will fall; the demand for silver being increased, its value will rise (no longer overvalued at the mint); and the market and mint ratios will be equal again. This compensatory principle might operate over a long period of time, but monetary problems usually require immediate changes. At present no country is on a bimetallic standard. Many European countries operated on a bimetallic standard until the gold standard supplanted it in the 19th century.

Paper Standard. The *paper standard* is generally adopted involuntarily. Because of an emergency, such as a war, paper money is issued to pay extraordinary expenses. If the quantity is excessive (and this temptation is great), purchasing power falls, and confidence in redeemability is lost. The paper money becomes *fiat money* or *printing press money*. The paper standard is always expressed in terms of the specie standard which existed prior to the inflation, but the paper has displaced the specie as the medium of exchange and the standard of value. The United States during the Civil War (greenbacks) and many European nations during the World Wars were on a paper standard.

Commodity Standard. The *commodity standard* uses the prices of a series of commodities in the form of an index number as a guide to monetary and credit policy. One type is the *managed currency* plan. The value of money is maintained by limiting the amount issued, by government operations in foreign exchange and control of international trade, and by the confidence of the people in the ability of the government to manage the currency. The plan eliminates the holding of costly stocks of idle gold and enables the government to control its money internationally as well as domestically. This control, however, sometimes involves a severe restriction of imports in order to maintain the international value of a country's currency. The commodity standard will be discussed further under price levels.

THE CHANGING ROLE OF MONEY

One of the outstanding changes in the nature of money is the widespread substitution of paper money and checks for specie in business transactions. Money is now made of cheap materials; it is no longer a commodity type of money. There is, moreover, a tendency among governments to make no further commitments as to the redeemability of their paper money. In most advanced countries specie or hard money is used only in making change and for international business transactions. The International Monetary Fund may lessen greatly the use of gold in the settlement of international accounts. Since checks require a banking system to offset debits and credits, banking assumes a dominant role in our monetary system. Bank deposits, as stated previously, are an important part of the total supply of money. This aspect of the monetary system is examined in the following chapter.

GENERAL REFERENCES

Bradford, F. A., *Money and Banking.*

Chandler, Lester V., *An Introduction to Monetary Theory.*

Dewey, D. R., *Financial History of the United States.*

Hawtrey, R. G., *Currency and Credit.*

Halm, George N., *Monetary Theory.*

Keynes, J. M., *A Treatise on Money.*

Laughlin, J. Lawrence, *History of Bimetallism in the United States.*

———, *A New Exposition of Money, Credit, and Prices.*

Mitchell, W. C., *History of the Greenbacks.*

Prather, C. L., *Money and Banking.*

Robertson, D. H., *Money.*

Thomas, Rollen G., *Our Modern Banking and Monetary System.*

Westerfield, R. B., *Our Silver Debacle.*

CHAPTER TEN

CREDIT AND BANKING

DEPOSIT CURRENCY, CREDIT, AND CREDIT INSTRUMENTS

Deposit currency, as already indicated, constitutes the main means of payment and supply of money. Such deposits (checkbook money) are handled primarily by commercial banks. These deposit operations of commercial banks usually involve credit transactions and credit instruments.

Credit Transactions. *Credit transactions* are the purchase or loan of goods, services, or money in the present with a promise to pay in the future. By the use of credit, more exchanges are possible, and actual money transfer is eliminated through the banking system by cancellation of debits and credits. Bank credit is elastic and varies with the volume of trade. Loans and deposits increase when business is expanding; when business declines, old loans are paid off faster than new loans are made, and credit contracts. Banks also attract surplus savings and make them available to industry. Intermittent seasonal activity is replaced by more uniform production throughout the year.

Personal credit which is an individual's promise to pay has limited acceptability. *Bank credit,* which is the bank's promise to pay, has general acceptability. Personal credit (promissory note) is exchanged for bank credit (deposit subject to check) so it may have wide circulation. *Commercial credit,* the promise of a manufacturer, wholesaler, or retailer to pay, was very important in early industry.

Credit Instruments.

THE CHECK. It is written by a depositor who orders his bank to pay a certain amount of money to some person, firm, or organization, to the bearer, or to himself. The bank debits the amount from the deposit and gives the payee cash, or credits the sum to his deposit account. A check rarely serves for more than one transaction. Frequently payment by check is the equivalent of a cash transaction. It is a deferred payment or credit transaction if cash is needed immediately.

THE PROMISSORY NOTE. This one-name paper is a simple promise to pay signed by the debtor. It may be made out to an individual or to a bank. It may be unsecured or secured by collateral, usually stocks or bonds, which the creditor may sell if the note is not paid. The promissory note becomes a "two-name paper" when the creditor, rather than wait for it to mature, endorses it (which makes him liable if the debtor does not pay) and has it discounted at his bank. In this event the bank holds the note until it matures and the debtor pays the bank or has the note renewed.

THE BILL OF EXCHANGE OR DRAFT. This is an order to pay drawn up by the creditor. When the debtor signs it and writes "accepted" on the bill, it becomes *an acceptance*. If the debtor's bank accepts the bill, it becomes a *banker's acceptance* or *banker's bill*.

CLASSES OF BANKS AND FUNCTIONS

Commercial Banks. *Commercial banks* are organized in very much the same way as any corporation. The balance sheet shows both assets and liabilities; in a solvent bank these are always equal. State banks are chartered under state laws; national banks and Federal Reserve Banks are chartered under federal law. There are a few private, unincorporated (partnership or individual) commercial banks.

The traditional function of all commercial banks has been to supply industry with circulating capital in the form of short-term, self-liquidating loans. Incidental functions may include a savings department, a trust department, an investment department, a foreign exchange department, and a safe deposit department.

LOANS. These are made by taking a borrower's promissory note and giving him the privilege to receive money on demand from the bank—i.e., establishing a deposit, or by giving him money. If the note is drawn with *interest,* the borrower agrees to pay the principal plus the interest at maturity. (On a loan

of $100 at 6 per cent interest the borrower would pay $106 at
the end of the year.) If the note is *discounted,* the interest is
deducted from the principal in advance. (The borrower would
receive $94 but would pay back $100 at the end of the year.
The $6 is called the *discount,* and $94 is called the *proceeds.*)
Discounting is slightly more expensive for the borrower because interest is calculated on the amount asked for ($100)
and not on the amount actually received ($94). In general
discount and interest rates for similar loans are identical.

Commercial banks increase their assets when they make
loans and discounts, and at the same time they are adding to
their liabilities in the form of deposits. If cash is loaned, the
assets are increased by the amount of the promissory note, decreased by subtracting the proceeds from the reserve, and the
discount is added to the liabilities in the form of undivided
profits. Loans may be repaid in cash, by a check on the borrower's deposit in this bank, or by a check on his deposit in
another bank. Loans and discounts and deposits tend to rise
and fall together. Credit extension is limited by the volume of
the bank's legal reserves which can be increased, as indicated
later, in a number of ways.

DEPOSITS. A depositor has the right to demand money from
a bank; a deposit is the obligation of the bank to pay money on
demand. Time deposits usually require a thirty-day notice of
withdrawal. Deposits are *primary* when actual cash, checks,
or drafts on other banks are deposited. Deposits are *derivative*
when they are created by a loan or are accumulated in anticipation of repayment of a loan. Deposits, liabilities of the bank,
should not be confused with the reserve, an asset of the bank.
Deposit liabilities are secured in a general way by the bank's
cash reserve; its claims against other banks; the personal credit
and collateral security behind its loans and discounts; and its
investment in bonds and property. In national banks and some
state banks the depositor is afforded additional security by
the Federal Deposit Insurance program.

RESERVES. Working reserves consist of the actual cash on
hand with which the bank pays off depositors or gives cash
when it is requested in a loan. *Secondary reserves* are the
securities held by the bank which can be quickly converted into
cash. The ratio between the reserves and liabilities is fixed

by law (see below). As a bank's business (loans and discounts) increases, the reserve ratio is lowered and the bank becomes less safe. The amount of reserve above the legal minimum which a bank may keep and be safe depends on the state of public confidence, the stability of industry, and the number and nature of its deposits. Bank reserves seldom exceed one quarter of the demand liabilities, because a simultaneous demand for cash from all the bank's creditors would be most unusual. The reserve ratio is increased by selling securities, by rediscounting commercial paper, and by discouraging borrowing. It is reduced when borrowing is made attractive and loans result, and when securities are bought. In the United States the legal reserve to be held against deposits of a member bank of the Federal Reserve System consists of its deposits with the Federal Reserve Bank of its district. Nonmember banks' legal reserves are defined by state laws and are not uniform.

CLEARANCE. This is a system of interbank bookkeeping whereby debits and credits of various banks are balanced and canceled. In cities a *clearing house* is established by the banks. Each bank sends in all the checks on other banks which it has received. The total claims of each bank are checked off against the total claims of all other banks against it. Each bank then pays to or receives from the clearing house only the net balance which is due. A bank outside the association may clear through a member bank. Out of town checks are sent through the mail. The Federal Reserve Bank in each district acts as a clearing house for that district by making on its books the proper entries of debits and credits in member banks' reserves. The *Gold Settlement Fund* in Washington makes the necessary adjustments in the gold certificate reserves carried by each Federal Reserve Bank and is used as a clearing house for the whole Federal Reserve System. The interbank transfer of money is eliminated.

NOTE ISSUE. This is a privilege (with legal restriction as to amount, denomination, and forms of security) of the Treasury and the Federal Reserve Banks. Bank notes (paper money) are promises of banks to pay money on demand. Bank notes, like deposits, are liabilities of the bank issuing them. In nearly all countries the central bank is the only bank which now has the privilege of issuing bank notes. Commercial banks' extension of credit in the form of checking accounts has replaced their former issuance of bank notes when making a loan.

MODERN TENDENCIES. In commercial banking one tendency is toward *consolidation* and *concentration,* with large banks assuming many diverse functions as integrated units. Another tendency is toward *specialization* in banking. Branch banking, permitted by the McFadden Act of 1927 and liberalized by the Banking Act of 1933, is now quite common within many states, but nation-wide branch banking has not yet developed. In some states chain or group banking, with control centered in a holding company, is extensive. More efficient management, more profitable use of deposits, and opportunity for loan diversification are some of the advantages of chain banking. In addition to these advantages of chain banking, branch banking offers other advantages: greater economy in reserves, greater uniformity in interest rates, and greater geographical mobility of funds.

Investment Banks. *Investment banks* provide industry with huge long-term loans. These funds are used for permanent capital equipment. The bonds and stocks of a corporation may be taken over by the investment bankers who attempt to sell them to the investing public at a profit. The most prominent investment banks are large private enterprises.

Mortgage banks and *agricultural credit institutions* (such as the Federal Farm Loan system which will be discussed in another chapter) are investment banks of a special kind.

Trust Companies. Although trust companies perform most of the functions of commercial and investment banking, they are chiefly concerned with the duties of trustee, administrator, and executive. They hold property, funds, and estates in trust; act as guardians for minors; execute commissions, etc. The kinds of investment open to trust companies are limited by law.

Savings Banks. These banks gather together small savings and invest them in long-term securities. Since safety rather than profit is the aim of savings banks, resources are invested in conservative securities. Savings deposits are not transferable by check, and notice of withdrawal is often required. Savings banks are of many kinds—Stock, Mutual, Postal Savings, School Savings, and Insurance companies.

Miscellaneous Financial Enterprises.

NOTEBROKERS. Notebrokers deal in commercial paper for a commission and endeavor to bring buyers and sellers of such paper together.

COMMERCIAL PAPER HOUSES. Commercial paper houses buy commercial paper directly and sell to banks, insurance companies, and investors for a higher price. Such houses provide a wider and cheaper market for the businessman's notes and a variety of commercial paper for banks which would otherwise be confined to local investments.

BUILDING AND LOAN ASSOCIATIONS. These organizations deal in mortgages and assist people in building or buying homes.

MORRIS PLAN BANKS AND CO-OPERATIVE CREDIT UNIONS. These firms provide consumers and small producers with loans based on the kind of security a small borrower is able to offer.

PROFESSIONAL MONEYLENDERS OR "LOAN SHARKS." *Pawnbrokers, chattel loan* and *salary loan brokers* extend credit at exorbitant rates of interest and often refuse to allow partial payments on the principal. The fact that these extortive lenders exist may be evidence of a defect in our loan system— borrowers were unable to secure credit elsewhere.

BANKING SYSTEMS IN THE UNITED STATES

Banking before the Civil War. Prior to the Civil War the national government had no direct control over the banks of the country. The early colonial banks had issued notes freely with little security. The United States Bank (1791–1811) and the Second Bank of the United States (1816–1836) were conservative, ably-managed institutions which performed their functions well. Political opposition, however, prevented the establishment of another central bank in the United States, and the government established (1840) an independent treasury for the government funds.

Banking laws and practices in the various states differed widely and were loosely supervised. Local banks, except in conservative New England, were often reckless and unsound.

Note issue was chaotic, unsafe, and nonuniform. Reserves were inadequate and money panics were frequent. Counterfeiting and "wildcat" banking in the frontier regions caused widespread loss. Such was the situation in 1863 when Congress was faced with the problem of financing the Civil War.

The National Banking System.

LEGAL REQUIREMENTS. The banking laws of 1863–1864 created national banks under the supervision of the federal government. Note issue and capitalization were based on the purchase of government bonds. A 10 per cent tax was put on the note issue of state banks which gave the national banks a virtual monopoly. The banking law in 1900 was as follows: to organize a national bank, stockholders must have a minimum capital which varied from $25,000 in towns less than 3000 to $200,000 for cities of more than 50,000 population. Note issue was not to exceed the amount of capital stock of the bank; as security, United States government bonds equal to the amount of the notes issued and lawful money equal to 5 per cent of the notes issued were deposited with the United States Treasury. The ratio of reserves to deposits was as follows: for country banks, 15 per cent; for reserve city banks, 25 per cent; for central reserve city banks (St. Louis, Chicago, and New York), 25 per cent. Only a part of the reserves except for the last group needed to be kept in the banks' own vault. Uniformity and safety were now established. The system, however, was too rigid since banks were prohibited from extending credit when the reserve fell below the above minimum requirements.

DEFECTS OF THE REQUIREMENTS. The *defects* of the system centered around the note issue and the peculiar reserve requirements. *Notes,* although safe, had inverted elasticity due to the nature of the collateral backing them (government bonds with the circulation privilege). It was natural for bankers, impelled by the profit motive, to sell their collateral in periods of business recession when the price for government bonds rose (and thus contract the currency). This accentuated the recession. The opposite was true during prosperous periods. Since banks were permitted to count as legal reserves their deposits in other banks, all surplus reserves were immediately deposited to draw a small rate of interest and most of them found their way to New York. Such pyramiding led to *inadequate reserves* for the country as a whole. When panics occurred in one part of the country, other banks would not co-operate. The New York banks were often tempted to use their reserves to extend credit to stock market speculators, and the whole country was affected by any financial disturbance in New York. There was no unified management of the entire banking system.

The Federal Reserve System. Money panics and numerous business failures made a new banking system imperative. The Aldrich-Vreeland Act, 1908, permitted National Banks to issue notes, under heavy tax, on security other than government bonds. In 1913 the Federal Reserve System was adopted. It improved the banking system, but many defects appeared during the boom years 1927–1929 and subsequent depression, such as lack of central control over an excessive number of small independent banks, continued concentration of loan funds in New York banks for speculative purposes, and the largest number of bank failures on record. The Banking Acts of 1933 and 1935, and other supplementary legislation designed to eliminate these defects, have made fundamental changes in the system.

ORGANIZATION OF THE FEDERAL RESERVE SYSTEM.

Board of Governors. This board of seven members, appointed by the president with the consent of the Senate for a term of fourteen years, represents the government and centralizes control over the entire banking system. The Board has the following important powers: (1) to compel one Federal Reserve Bank to loan to another (rediscount its commercial paper); (2) to control open-market operations of the Federal Reserve Banks; (3) to alter the reserve requirements of member banks (double statutory requirements if deemed necessary); (4) to review and determine the discount rates of the Federal Reserve Banks; (5) to issue or withhold supplies of Federal Reserve Notes from a Reserve Bank; (6) to control completely the rediscounting of commercial paper (types and amount) by a member bank; (7) to regulate the payment of interest on time and saving deposits by member banks (payment of interest on demand deposits is prohibited); (8) to control credit used in margin accounts for security speculation (Securities Exchange Act, 1934) and to regulate generally the speculative use of credit.

Federal Open-market Committee. This committee consists of the Board of Governors and five representatives of the twelve Reserve Banks. The committee formulates regulations for open-market operations and directs the actual transactions. It centralizes control over an important central banking function and eliminates the former dominance of the Federal Reserve Bank of New York.

The Twelve Federal Reserve Districts. These districts divide the country into sections with a bank in each city named. The district numbers and cities are as follows: 1, Boston; 2, New York; 3, Philadelphia; 4, Cleveland; 5, Richmond; 6, Atlanta; 7, Chicago; 8, St. Louis; 9, Minneapolis; 10, Kansas City; 11, Dallas; 12, San Francisco. Besides the twelve Federal Reserve Banks there are twenty-four branches.

Federal Reserve Banks. Each bank is a corporation owned by the *member banks* in its district. National banks are required to become members and to subscribe 6 per cent of their capital and surplus to the stock of the Federal Reserve Bank. The minimum capital for national banks is now $50,000 (more for those in larger cities) and the same requirement for membership applies to state banks. All national banks are required to build up their surplus out of earnings to a level of 100 per cent of their stock. Membership is optional for state banks, mutual saving banks, and trust companies. Although slightly less than half the banks are now members of the Federal Reserve System, they dominate the commercial banking system. Member banks account for about three-fourths of the total deposits, loans, and investments.

Directors of Federal Reserve Banks. A board of directors (nine members for three year terms) determines the policy and manages each Federal Reserve Bank subject to the control of the Board of Governors of the Federal Reserve System. The directors are divided into three groups: Class A, three elected by member banks as their representatives; Class B, three elected by member banks to represent commerce, agriculture, and industry; Class C, three appointed by the Board of Governors of the Federal Reserve System. The directors appoint a president (five-year term) subject to the approval of the Board of Governors.

FUNCTIONS OF THE FEDERAL RESERVE BANKS. Federal Reserve Banks are bankers' banks and most of their business is with member banks, with each other, and with the government.

Centralization of Reserves. Since 1917 the only reserves *required* of member banks are *deposit credits* in the Federal Reserve Banks. Till money (about 5 per cent of demand deposits) is, of course, kept on hand. The minimum per cent of *demand deposits* required as reserve varies—7, 10, or 13 per cent depending on the size of the city in which the member bank is located. All *time* deposits require a 3 per cent reserve. The Board of Governors may alter these requirements with a maximum limit of 14, 20, and 26 per cent in order to control credit expansion or contraction; any changes apply generally and not to an individual bank in the system. Federal Reserve Banks are also required to hold certain reserves. Back of their deposits each must maintain a 25 per cent reserve in gold certificates, and against outstanding Federal Reserve Notes a 25 per cent reserve in gold certificates. *Adequate funds* are now available in all parts of the country. In case one district has greater need for cash at a certain season, it can call on Federal Reserve Banks in other districts to come to its aid.

Rediscounting, Borrowing, and *Open-market Transactions.* Federal Reserve Banks may rediscount certain commercial paper—notes, drafts and bills of exchange which are of short duration—and meet other safety requirements for their members. Member banks may also borrow on their own promissory notes, provided they are backed by government securities or other collateral satisfactory to the Federal Reserve Bank. Thus a member bank may quickly increase its funds or add to its deposits in the Federal Reserve Bank and continue to extend credit in times of unexpected demands. When different parts of the country are in need of funds, the Federal Reserve Banks may discount commercial paper for each other. Federal Reserve Banks, with the consent of the Board of Governors, are permitted to raise or lower their discount rate. When the discount rate is *raised,* borrowing is made less attractive and credit is restricted; when the rate is *lowered,* borrowing is more attractive and credit is expanded. Federal Reserve Banks may buy or sell certain investments (primarily bankers' acceptances and government securities) on the open market. Such transactions along with the manipulation of the discount rate have a stabilizing effect upon the money market. To *ease* the market, the Federal Reserve Banks would *buy* securities and put funds into circulation; to *tighten* the market, they would *sell* securities and contract the funds. This important function is controlled by the Board of Governors.

Note Issue. Federal Reserve Banks issue *Federal Reserve Notes* which are secured by a minimum 25 per cent gold certificate reserve and enough commercial paper and government bonds to make up 100 per cent. About three-fourths of the money in circulation (excluding demand deposits) consists of Federal Reserve Notes. National Bank Notes were officially retired in 1935, and Federal Reserve Bank Notes are being retired. Note issue has become (properly) a public monopoly.

Elasticity in note circulation has at last been established. Member banks may withdraw parts of their checking accounts at the Federal Reserve Banks of their district in the form of Federal Reserve Notes when there is a demand for currency. Thus Federal Reserve Notes get into circulation. Sometimes new funds enter the market when businessmen ask for loans and put up commercial paper as collateral; member banks sell the paper to Federal Reserve Banks; a Federal Reserve Bank discounts the paper and gives the bank Federal Reserve Notes; the member bank now has increased funds with which to extend credit to businessmen. The circulation of Federal Reserve Notes contracts in the following manner: businessmen pay off their notes to banks; banks send their surplus reserves to the Federal Reserve Banks; Federal Reserve Banks sort out their notes and release the gold certificates, commercial paper, and government bonds which have been set aside as security. At any time bankers may send their surplus cash to the Federal Reserve (and much of it will be in form of Federal Reserve Notes). When Federal Reserve Notes are deposited at the Federal Reserve Banks of the district, they become a source of legal reserve for the member bank in that they increase the member bank's checking account (or legal reserve) at the Federal Reserve. Federal Reserve Notes are quickly retired because member banks are not allowed to count the notes themselves as part of their legal reserves and because Reserve Banks when they receive a note of another Reserve Bank must ship it home.

Miscellaneous Functions and Changes. The Federal Reserve System acts as a *clearing house* for the banks of the country and provides a *par collection system* for bank checks. It serves in part as a fiscal agent for the government (subtreasuries were abandoned in 1920). In order to prevent member banks from using commercial deposits as the basis for large investment loans, security affiliates and investment loans are closely regulated. Holding companies which control other banks are subject to strict regulation.

EFFECTIVENESS. The Federal Reserve System has succeeded in eliminating local panics and seasonal money shortages. During World War I it assisted the government in the sale of bonds and provided a controlled inflation. But it failed to check (in spite of warnings and raised discount rates), the speculative expansion of 1929. It failed to stimulate borrowing in the depression that followed although the discount rate in New York dropped as low as $1\frac{1}{2}$ per cent and extensive open market transactions were undertaken. The recent changes in the system, however, have for the most part greatly improved it. The control of credit is now sufficiently centralized in the Board of Governors to prevent a repetition of the speculative expansion of 1929. Credit control alone, however, is likely to prove ineffective in breaking the grip of a general business depression. To meet such an emergency a fundamental change from *qualitative* to *quantitative* credit control has been made. Formerly only certain types of commercial paper (short-term and highly liquid) were eligible for rediscounting at Federal Reserve Banks. The volume of such commercial transactions tended to regulate automatically the volume of note issue. Under the present system other collateral (less liquid than 90-day commercial paper) and government bonds may be used as the basis for note issue. Elasticity of note issue, or the quantity of notes and credit to be made available, is no longer restricted (qualitatively) to the amount of certain types of commercial paper arising from business transactions, but is regulated by the Board of Governors of the Federal Reserve System. This change in the elasticity of note issue and liquidity of loans is viewed unfavorably by some experts. Effective control of credit and business activity, however, requires two fundamental conditions: first, complete centralization of banking authority over the issue of notes; and second, the authority of the central banking system to deal in long-term as well as short-term private and government obligations. Recent changes in the Federal Reserve System have contributed much to the development of an effective central bank system for the United States. Shortly before World War II, however, it became obvious that central banking policy alone is not sufficient as a tool to mitigate business fluctuations. Fiscal policy in conjunction with monetary policy must be used. For example, the time of imposition of taxes and varied rates of certain taxes must be used along with monetary policy in an attempt to offset fluctuations in general business conditions. Complete government ownership and operation of banks may be necessary to control effectively money and credit. Bank failures have been a serious problem among the approximately 14,500 banks of the country. Nearly 6000 banks failed during the period 1921–1929; nearly 9000 during the period 1930–1933. About 1000 in the first period and over 2000 in the second period were member banks of the Federal Reserve System.

Other Important Changes in the Banking System.

FEDERAL DEPOSIT INSURANCE CORPORATION. This corporation, managed by three directors (two appointed by the president and the Comptroller of the Currency), is authorized to purchase, hold, and liquidate the assets of closed national and state banks and to insure in part the deposits of eligible banks. The capital was provided by the sale of stock to the Treasury ($150,000,000) and to the Federal Reserve Banks (each subscribed half of its surplus, approximate total $140,000,000). All Federal Reserve member banks are required to insure deposits and any nonmember state bank may participate on the approval of the corporation. An insurance fund is created by assessing each insured bank at the rate of $\frac{1}{12}$ of 1 per cent per year of its total deposits. Individual deposits in the insured bank are insured up to $10,000. Payment of inter-test on demand deposits is prohibited and interest rates on time and saving deposits are regulated by the corporation (for insured banks are not members of the Federal Reserve System). Practically all banks are now insured and most depositors (a large depositor may have accounts in several banks) have full coverage.

The prohibition of interest payments on demand deposits is a constructive measure designed to prevent excessive competition among banks for deposits. If the FDIC supervises carefully the operations of its members, small depositors will be protected against loss.

RECONSTRUCTION FINANCE CORPORATION. This corporation was an emergency bank created by Congress in 1932 to furnish loans primarily to financial institutions which in turn would be enabled to lend more freely to business enterprises. Its initial capital and subsequent additions were provided by the government. It was also authorized to borrow funds. During the depression of the 1930's it assisted many financial institutions to remain solvent. During World War II it provided billions of dollars (loans and investments) for financial institutions, railroads, industrial and commercial enterprises, and other government agencies. Because of certain lax lending practices, particularly in the early postwar period, its operations were terminated in 1953–1954.

FEDERAL HOME LOAN PROGRAM. In 1932 a system of twelve Federal Home Loan Banks (later eleven with two branches) was created. Their capital is supplied by the government and by home financing institutions which become members of the system. Federal Savings and Loan Associations (private, mutual associations under federal charter) are members of the Home Loan Bank System. A Board of three members, appointed by the President with the approval of the Senate, supervises the system. The Federal Savings and Loan Insurance Corporation (1934) insures all investors in Federal Savings and Loan Associations against loss up to $10,000. Insurance is optional for other building and loan associations. The Home Loan Banks lend primarily to their members which provides a financial reserve for the latter's operations in lending to homeowners.

All federal credit agencies involved in housing and home finance are consolidated for administrative purposes in the Housing and Home Finance Agency (1954). It includes, in addition to those agencies mentioned above, the Federal Housing Administration (1934) which provides government insurance for mortgages and property improvement loans made by approved lending institutions. Also, the Federal National Mortgage Association furnishes supplementary assistance to the secondary market for FHA-insured and Veterans Administration-guaranteed home mortgages. The Public Housing Administration makes loans to local housing authorities to build low-rent housing for low-income families, and manages public defense housing. (The Home Owners' Loan Corporation, which was created in 1933 to refinance mortgage loans of distressed homeowners during the depression, was terminated in 1951.)

FARM CREDIT ADMINISTRATION. Various agricultural credit agencies have been consolidated. Their organization and function will be discussed in the chapter on agricultural problems.

OTHER BANKING SYSTEMS

The Bank of England is the great central bank which heads the highly centralized British banking system. Under it are several (five dominate) large joint stock banks with thousands of branches and a few private banks. None of the banks succumbed in the depression. The Bank of England has recently been nationalized. It receives deposits from the joint stock banks; it fixes the discount rate; it issues notes and manages the currency; it is fiscal agent for the government; and it is primarily a banker's bank. Funds of the entire country are concentrated in London, and the Bank of England holds the bulk of them.

The Bank of France heads the French banking system and it, too, has been recently nationalized. For the most part the Bank of France is a banker's bank although it has some dealings with the public. It has the exclusive right to issue notes. This is very important since deposit banking is undeveloped. Banking facilities are furnished by a few large banks in the cities with branches scattered over the country.

The Bank of Canada, established in 1935, is the central bank for the Canadian banking system. Over a period of fifteen years it has acquired a monopoly of note issue. The bank took over Dominion notes not legally retired and may issue more notes as needed by the country or by the chartered banks. In 1940 the 25 per cent gold-reserve requirement for the bank's notes and deposit obligations was suspended. Most of the banking is carried on by an excellent system of large chartered banks (ten since 1928) and their numerous nation-wide branches. All banks must keep an 8 to 12 per cent reserve in the form of a deposit in the central bank or in its notes as determined by the Bank of Canada. Since January, 1950, chartered banks may maintain their own note issue only outside the Dominion and in an amount not to exceed 10 per cent of their unimpaired capital. Their lending is primarily for short-term needs and is protected by a first lien on the borrower's goods which is used as collateral. No bank has failed since 1923.

GENERAL REFERENCES

Board of Governors of the Federal Reserve System, *Banking Studies.*

————, *The Federal Reserve System: Its Purposes and Functions.*

————, *Federal Reserve Bulletins.*

Einzig, Paul, *How Money Is Managed.*

Harris, Seymour E., *Twenty Years of Federal Reserve Policy.*

Mueller, F. W., *Money and Banking.*

New York Federal Reserve Bank, *Money: Master or Servant.*

————, *The Treasury and the Money Market.*

Shaw, Edward S., *Money, Income and Monetary Policy.*

Steiner, W. H., and E. Shapiro, *Money and Banking.*

Thomas, Rollen G., *Our Modern Banking and Monetary System.*

Westerfield, R. B., *Banking Principles and Practices.*

Whittlesey, C. R., *Principles and Practices of Money and Banking.*

CHAPTER ELEVEN

PRICE LEVELS: CHANGING VALUE OF MONEY

THE RELATION OF MONEY AND PRICES

In a previous chapter changes in the price of individual commodities were analyzed on the basis of demand and supply for a given commodity. The assumption was made that the value of money remained constant. A commodity (gold or silver, or both), however, is usually selected as standard money, and other types of money and credit are completely or partially based upon it. Although the government may fix by law the price of $13^{15}\!/_{21}$ grains of pure gold at one dollar ($35 per ounce), the value of gold and the money based upon it fluctuates with changes in its supply and demand. Since the demand for money arises because of its general acceptance in exchange for goods and services, its value or purchasing power is measured in terms of the amount of various goods and services for which it exchanges. All prices are stated in terms of money, and a general change in prices indicates a change in the value of money. If the general price level rises, the purchasing power, or value, of the dollar falls. Under the play of demand and supply individual prices fluctuate about a general price level, but the general price level changes and carries with it individual prices. Changes in the general price level and the purchasing power of money are indicated by index numbers.

INDEX NUMBERS

Index numbers are calculated to represent the general price level for any given year or time period as compared with the general price level of a given base year which is represented by 100. To compare directly the multitude of prices from year to year would be an impossible task. During a ten year period, moreover, a few prices might be rising while the remainder were falling and a comparison of each actual price change would give a confusing picture. Even changes in a few prices over a period of time are indicated more clearly by relative prices rather than by actual prices. For example, consider the average wholesale price changes of the following commodities:

Year	Wheat	Milk	Coal
1913	$0.91 per bu.	$0.044 per qt.	$2.34 per ton
1914	1.04 per bu.	.042 per qt.	2.39 per ton
1915	1.34 per bu.	.04 per qt.	2.48 per ton

To compare quickly these price changes, the year 1913 may be taken as the base year (represented by 100), and each price for each commodity may then be expressed as a percentage of its price in the base year (for wheat, $1.04 \div .91 = 114$ per cent; $1.34 \div .91 = 147$ per cent, etc.).

Year	Wheat	Milk	Coal
1913	100	100	100
1914	114	95	102
1915	147	91	106

These price relations show readily the percentage changes in the price of each commodity from the base year. For instance, the price of wheat in 1915 relative to the price in 1913 was 47 per cent higher. In order to show general price changes from year to year, the price relatives of all commodities for each year are combined in the form of an average or index number for each year. Here, for simple illustration, only three commodities are used. The number and kinds of commodities selected for making an index number depend upon the purpose of the index. If an improper sample of commodities is used or if the collection of price and quantity data is inaccurate, the index is erroneous regardless of the mathematical methods used. The selection of the base year is also important; its selection depends upon the purpose of the index. There are many types of average index numbers.

Simple Arithmetic Average. A simple arithmetic average of price relatives is sometimes used to formulate an index number. For example, in the above illustration the average for 1913 is 100, for 1914 the average is 104 $\left(\dfrac{114 + 95 + 102}{3} \right)$, for 1915 the average is 115. The simple average index has two defects. First, it has an upward mathematical bias—that is, it exaggerates price increases and understates price decreases because increases in percentages can be infinite whereas decreases are limited to 100. Second, it gives equal importance or weight to changes in the price of different commodities when their relative importance is usually quite different. For instance, in the above example, wheat may be twice as important as milk (i.e., the total value of wheat exchanged in a given year may have been twice the value of milk) ; hence, its increase in price should be given twice as much weight as the decrease in the price of milk. Because of these defects, some expert statisticians advocate the abandonment of the simple arithmetic average index number. Since it is easily calculated and readily understood, its practical use may be valuable—that is, if a 5 to 10 per cent margin of error is allowed.

Weighted Arithmetic Average. A weighted arithmetic average corrects the defect of treating all price changes as equally important. For example, by multiplying the price relatives of each commodity by a weight based on its importance and by dividing the results by the sum of the weights, a weighted average index is obtained (e.g., in 1914 the above index becomes $\frac{(114 \times 2) + (95 \times 1) + (102 \times 1)}{4} = 106$). Various methods of weighting may be used, and the choice of methods depends upon the purpose of the index. Weighting, of course, introduces bias into index numbers, but usually the results are more representative than those obtained from an unweighted average index. (More elaborate index numbers, such as Fisher's ideal formula, eliminate some of the bias introduced by weighting.)

Weighted Geometric Average. A weighted geometric average index of price relatives corrects both defects of the simple arithmetic average index. It has no mathematical bias either upward or downward, and gives less weight than the arithmetic average to extremely small and extremely large items. A simple geometric average of price relatives is obtained by taking the nth root of the product of n relatives (e.g., in 1914 the above index becomes $\sqrt[3]{114 \times 95 \times 102} = 103$). If the geometric average is weighted, the root becomes the sum of the weights and the weights are exponents of the price relatives (e.g., in 1914 the above index becomes $\sqrt{114^2 \times 95 \times 102} = 106$). (If many items are involved, the number, of course, is computed with logarithms.)

Median Average Index. A median average index of price relatives is more accurate than the simple arithmetic average and is usually as accurate as the simple geometric average. It is easy to calculate; the price relatives for a given year are arranged in order from the lowest to the highest, and the middlemost number is taken as the index for the year (e.g., in 1914 the above index becomes 102). If data for weights are not available, the simple median and simple geometric average are preferred to the simple arithmetic average.

Weighted Aggregative Index. A weighted aggregative index avoids the mathematical bias of the arithmetic average of relative prices and avoids the calculation of price relatives for each commodity. A simple aggregative index is calculated directly from the sum total of actual prices for a given year compared on a percentage basis with the sum total of prices in the base year. For example, if the original price figures cited above are added for each year, the result is $3.294 for 1913, $3.472 for 1914, and $3.86 for 1915. The simple aggregative index number for 1914 is 105 (i.e., the year 1913 is the base and $3.294 becomes 100 which makes $3.472 for 1914 on a percentage basis 105 or $3.472 ÷ $3.294). Aggregative index numbers should be weighted. The weighting is accomplished by multiplying the actual quantities of commodities exchanged in a selected year, or years, by the average prices of the commodities in different years. The total value of all commodities for a given year is then compared on a percentage basis with the total value in the base year. The index numbers most generally used in the United States—those published by the United States Bureau of Labor Statistics—are of the aggregative type (present series). The revised series uses 1926 as the base year, includes almost nine hundred commodities (wholesale prices), and is weighted according to the values exchanged in 1923, 1924, and 1925. Since 1926 is no longer a very suitable base period, there is a trend toward shifting to a 1935–1939 base. The Bureau of Labor Statistics is using the latter period as a base year for its cost of living index number.

The purpose of index numbers is quite varied. There are index numbers of the cost of living, retail prices, security prices, business cycles, national income, etc. They may be presented in tabular or graphic form. In this chapter index numbers are of interest as measuring devices to show changes in the general price level which reflects changes in the purchasing power or value of money. For example, if the index of prices is 127, the value of the dollar (called 100 for the base year) is inversely proportional, and the reciprocal is 79. As compared with the base year the purchasing power, or value, of the (wholesale) dollar fell 21 per cent.

SECULAR PRICE TRENDS

General changes in the price level usually extend over periods of ten to twenty-five years. These long-run rising or falling price movements are referred to as secular price trends. Superimposed upon these long-run secular price trends are short-run fluctuations of prices which are referred to as the business cycle. The nature of the business cycle and its relation to secular price trends will be discussed in the next chapter. A brief statement of the major secular price trends in the United States and their effects upon different income groups is given below.

Price Trends in the United States. Wholesale prices in the United States for the period 1720–1947 were extremely high five different times—during the Revolutionary War, the War of 1812, the Civil War, World War I, and World War II. The cardinal lesson of price history is that war produces inflation and maladjustment of prices. War produces an abrupt rise in general prices (inflation) because the vast needs of the government are usually financed by credit in the form of bond issues or paper money issues. Increased taxation to finance wars would largely eliminate inflation since total purchasing power is not greatly increased, but merely transferred from the taxpayers to the government. Some prices (war materials) would rise, but general prices would not increase greatly. Since taxes would be heavily increased and working cash reduced, businessmen might borrow more from the banks to carry on trade and thus bid up general prices slightly. Increased taxation, however, for war purposes is impractical because the returns are neither prompt enough nor large enough. If bond issues for war purposes were purchased largely out of current income, the amount of inflation would be slight—purchasing power would be merely transferred. Huge bond issues, however, cannot be quickly sold unless bankers are willing to purchase large quantities and to extend credit to individuals for the purchase of bonds which increases total purchasing power. Paper money issues for war financing enable the government to buy goods and services immediately, total purchasing power is increased, and general prices rise. Some of the paper money may be used in bank reserves for the extension of additional credit. As prices rise, government expenditures increase, and more bank credit or paper money is needed; inflation is cumulative. The inflationary spiral begins slowly in its early stages but gains momentum very rapidly in the later phases.

Prior to the Revolutionary War there was an irregular, but gradual rise in wholesale prices. From 1790 to 1814 the secular price movement was upward, from 1814 to 1849 downward, from 1849 to 1865 upward, from 1865 to 1897 downward, from 1897 to 1920 upward, from 1920 to 1933 downward, and in the World War II period upward. Wholesale prices in England followed trends similar to those in the United States. Since England was not engaged in war during the United States Civil War period, English wholesale prices of that period rose much less than those in the United States, and the downward trend did not appear in England until 1873. The interrelation of price levels in different countries is important and will be discussed in a later chapter.

Effects of General Price Changes. The effect of general price changes upon different income groups constitutes a most devastating factor in modern economic life. Many forms of economic activity are regulated by contracts extending over a period of years. Either a high or a low price level is satisfactory when contractual economic relations have become adjusted to it. But a change from one to the other disrupts the entire economic system. For example, if the secular price trend is downward (say the deflation period of 1865–1897) and the purchasing power of money is increasing, the creditor class gains and the debtor class loses. Farmers who borrow money to purchase land are heavy losers. Wholesale prices decline more rapidly than retail prices and farmers sell at wholesale prices and buy at retail prices. Suppose an older brother sold a farm in 1865 for $5,000 in cash and a $10,000 mortgage to a younger brother and then retired to a nearby town. During the next fifteen years the younger brother agreed to pay interest at 6 per cent and the principal of the mortgage. But the wholesale prices of farm products declined to a point in 1879 which was less than half as high as in 1865. At these prices the younger brother would have needed more than twice the usual output from the farm to meet his payments. (Frequently the more efficient farmers lose more in a deflation period than the less efficient farmers because they incur greater costs in order to increase their output.) Probably by 1879 he had paid the interest and $2,500 on the principal. Apparently the younger brother now had a half interest in the farm, but the fall in prices reduced the value of the farm to half its former purchase price. His equity disappeared, and he decided to quit farming. The older brother received $7,500 plus interest and still owned the farm which he now sold for only $7,000 in cash because many other farms were being sold for debts. (The political protest of farmers during this period appeared in the form of the greenback, populist, and silver movements.) If the same transaction had occurred during a period of rising prices (say 1897 to 1913), the younger brother could easily have paid for the farm and the older brother could have purchased much less with the $15,000 which he received for the farm. As long as the general price level fluctuates, the date of one's birth is an important item in determining one's success or failure in business.

Any class which receives a contractual or fixed income (including creditors) gains from a falling price level and loses on a rising price level. Rents, wages, and salaries are slowly adjusted upward or downward to a new price level. During the transition to a higher price level, those receiving a fixed number of dollars in the form of rents, wages, and salaries, have their real income temporarily reduced. If the transition is to a lower price level, their real income is temporarily increased.

(During a price decline many workers may be unemployed, and hence, the gain of the working class may be partly offset.) Some of the injustice created by fluctuations in the general price level is alleviated by the fact that many individuals are both creditors and debtors; they lose in one capacity but gain in the other. Nevertheless, a change in the price level may transfer billions of dollars worth of property from one class to another and dispossess countless individuals of their property, savings, and livelihood under a legal system based on the "due process of law." Under these conditions much economic activity becomes a grand gamble on the price level.

EXPLANATION OF GENERAL PRICE CHANGES

The theory or explanation of changes in the general price level and the purchasing power of money is still in the stage of hypothesis. It is complicated by the relation of short-run fluctuations in prices (the business cycle) to the long-run secular price trends. A statement and criticism of a widely accepted theory, the quantity theory of money, is given below.

The Quantity Theory of Money. The basic principle of this theory is that general prices vary directly (not necessarily in exact proportion) with the quantity of money in circulation and inversely with the total volume of goods sold. If the quantity of money in circulation is doubled, other things remaining the same, the general price level will double and the purchasing power of money will fall to one-half its former value (i.e., the value of money varies inversely with the quantity of money and prices). If the volume of trade is halved, other things remaining the same, the general price level will double. The relation of money to commodities and general prices is usually expressed in the form of an equation of exchange as follows: $MV + M'V' = PT$ (i.e., amount of cash in circulation during a given period $\times$ average turnover of each cash dollar $+$ amount of credit in circulation $\times$ average turnover of each credit dollar $=$ average price at which goods are sold during the same period $\times$ total quantity of goods sold). The equation of exchange is a mathematical truism. It merely shows that the total supply of all kinds of money actually spent (not total stock of money) for goods during a given period equals the total demand for money—that is, the total value of all goods purchased during the same period.

The equation of exchange, however, is made the basis of the quantity theory of money in which the analysis of cause and effect becomes a debatable issue. Stated differently, the equation is used to indicate that the price level, and hence the value of money, is the resultant of two primary causes—namely, the relationship between changes in the quantity of all kinds of money and changes in the volume of goods sold (i.e., $P = \dfrac{MV + M'V'}{T}$). Some economists, however, maintain that the price level (P) is not the result, but the cause, of the changes in money and trade. The question of causal relationship also involves other items in the equation.

Criticism of the Quantity Theory. In a critical analysis of the quantity theory explanation of changes in general prices, the distinction between long-run and short-run changes is important. The conclusion is that over long periods of time the quantity of money and credit in circulation is the most important factor causing general prices to rise or fall; that changes in prices are likely to be only approximately proportional to changes in the quantity of money; and that over short periods of time there is a complex interaction among the various items in the equation of exchange in which the changes of the business cycle dominate the supply of money and credit in circulation. No conclusive statistical verification of the conclusion exists, but statistical studies of secular price trends conform more closely to the quantity theory explanation than to any other hypothesis. Rigid quantity theorists do not admit that price level changes are affected by every element in the equation of exchange. They ignore demand which is an important factor because it causes changes in V and V'. Velocity declines before the volume of M declines. Also, P in the equation is so comprehensive that it lacks significance. A series of significant qualifications and interpretations of the quantity theory is given below.

RELATION OF MONEY AND CREDIT. Money and credit (M and M') over a long period tend to increase or decrease together. Over a period of a few years, however, the stock of money may increase without increasing the amount of credit in circulation. When the stock of money has increased, central banks may for a time discourage, by means of open market transactions and manipulation of discount rates, an extension of credit. The use of credit, moreover, in the short run largely depends on the price changes of the business cycle. Businessmen may be reluctant to borrow because of low prices (and thus fail to bid up prices) even though the stock of money and potential credit have increased. In time, an increase in the stock of money in the form of bank reserves lowers discount rates because bankers make no profits from idle funds. Lower loan rates gradually encourage borrowing, and increased purchases cause prices to rise. Changes, then, in the stock of money and the potential credit based upon it, affect prices only as money and credit go into circulation over a long period of time.*

INCOMES AND PRICE CHANGES. The nature of price changes produced by an increased supply of money and credit in circulation depends upon the source and use of the additional purchasing power. If the funds are available in bank reserves and are mainly used by businessmen, the process of price change will be slow. On the other hand, if the additional purchasing power is released by the government (e.g., public works, relief aids, etc.) partly to businessmen and partly to masses of workers and consumers, prices are likely to move upward more quickly. Changes in the incomes of different groups affect prices differently.

VELOCITY OF MONEY AND CREDIT. Changes in the velocity of circulation of money and credit (V and V') may temporarily neutralize the effects of changes in the supply of money and credit upon prices. For example, an increase in the supply of money may temporarily not affect prices because most of the additional money is hoarded, or an increase in money and credit may temporarily not affect prices because each unit circulates more slowly. In both cases the price changes of the business cycle largely determine the short-run velocity of circulation

---

* The 41 per cent reduction in the gold content of the dollar, for example, had little immediate effect upon domestic prices. The theory upon which it was based (Warren's gold bullion theory) was an extreme form of the quantity theory of money.

because they are the forces determining individual or business choices as to the average size of cash balances that will be held. In the long run, however, velocity of circulation depends upon population density, transportation development, and banking facilities. Over long periods the monetary habits of a given country are likely to remain fairly constant, and hence, an increase in money and credit will ultimately increase prices.

PRODUCTION AND PRICES. Changes in the quantity of money and credit in circulation may temporarily increase the volume of trade and not affect prices. Over short periods of time production capacity may not be fully utilized and an increase in money and credit may temporarily increase the volume of trade without affecting prices. In the long run, however, the volume of trade depends mainly upon the technique of production, and hence, a steady increase in the supply of money and credit would finally raise general prices.

GOLD PRODUCTION AND PRICES. In a money and credit system based upon gold reserves, a long-run discrepancy between the average rate of increase in gold production and commodity production results in an upward or downward secular price trend. The trend may be corrected by changes in the monetary stock of gold or by changes in the laws which regulate bank reserves. If the rate of gold production is exceeded by commodity production, the supply of money and credit (without changes in the legal bank reserves) is relatively reduced, and a downward general price trend is generated. (Although credit becomes relatively scarce for most business enterprises and precipitates a fall in prices, interest rates on the average during the period may be low because cyclical depressions are prolonged and funds for preferred investments accumulate.) A fall in prices, however, over a period of years tends to increase the monetary stock of gold—first, because gold mining costs are lowered and gold production is profitably increased; second, because the industrial use of gold is less profitable; and third, because lower prices are likely to reduce gold hoarding, particularly in oriental countries. (The movement of gold in international trade is discussed later.) The corrective process is slow partly because large increases in gold ouput depend upon the discovery of new gold deposits and partly because the increase in monetary gold affects prices only gradually through larger bank reserves and more liberal loan policy.

IRREDEEMABLE CURRENCY AND PRICES. Under conditions of irredeemable paper currency, changes in the quantity of money and credit usually affect prices quickly. Governments are likely to use irredeemable currency only in a time of great financial need, and hence, the amount of money in circulation is immediately increased. Since gold, if in circulation, is hoarded under these conditions, prices are not affected until more than enough currency is issued to replace the hoarded gold. If the irredeemable currency issue is closely controlled, prices may rise more slowly.

REMEDIES FOR SECULAR PRICE CHANGES

Remedial measures designed to eliminate secular price changes are numerous. All of them are subject to various criticisms. A criticism common to most of them is the difficulty of constructing an index number which will adequately reveal general price changes. General policy, moreover, with regard to long-run price stabilization is controversial. Should the long-run trend of general prices be held approximately constant, or be allowed to rise *moderately,* or to fall *moderately?* With improvements in the efficiency of production, producers would probably benefit most in the first case; producers and possibly wage earners in the second (government debt burden also lessened); and consumers and creditors in the third case. Because of the devastating effects of *extreme* general price changes, many economists favor the trial of some remedial plan based upon existing index numbers. The value of money would then be related not to one commodity (gold), but to all the commodities included in the index number. Some of these plans are set forth below.

Contracts in Terms of Purchasing Power. Since contractual relations stated in terms of money (e.g., leases, insurance, savings accounts, investments, salaries, etc.) appreciate or depreciate with changes in the price level, some injustice could be prevented by writing contracts in terms of the purchasing power of the dollar. If the price level rose as measured by an index number agreed upon in the contract, dollar payments would be proportionally increased to maintain the same purchasing power as originally agreed upon. The merit of this plan is that it would not require legislative enactment and could be voluntarily tried in a limited number of suitable transactions. Its piecemeal character, however, is also a source of weakness. Since general prices would continue to fluctuate, a few protected contracts would be difficult to maintain, and their widespread use would be checked. The successful introduction would probably first require government adoption.

International Control of Gold Production. Since gold production has been a basic factor in determining the trend of general prices, one plan of price level control involves establishing an international monopoly to regulate the output of gold. Several objections appear. First, various gold mining countries would probably not agree to an occasional forced reduction of their output and the resulting unemployment of their workers. Second, the plan provides only indirect control over bank credit and no control over the issue of paper money. Third, to increase gold output, costly subsidies would be necessary.

The Stabilized Gold Dollar. The plan of "the stabilized dollar" proposes to maintain a constant purchasing power for both money and credit dollars by varying the amount of gold in the gold dollar. Gold coins, of course, would be withdrawn from circulation and replaced with gold certificates which would be redeemable in gold dollars of varying weights. Variations in weight would be based on changes in a carefully constructed index number. In order to prevent excessive speculative profits in gold, variations in weight (not more than one every two months) could be limited to 1 per cent and the government would always buy gold at a price 1 per cent less than the price at which it would sell.

International trade and finance relations present the greatest obstacles to this plan. First of all, it would mean that the dollar would sell at varying prices in terms of foreign currencies. American exporters and importers would sometimes gain and sometimes lose on their transactions because of changes, or anticipated changes, in the gold weight of the dollar. Hedging transactions would in part eliminate such gains or losses. In the second place, sharp changes in prices (cyclical changes) under this plan would enable foreign bankers to profit in American money and would accentuate domestic booms and depressions. For instance, if prices fell sharply, a series of decreases in the weight of the dollar (say 1 per cent every two months for eight months) would accumulate. Foreign bankers would borrow funds in New York where interest rates were low as a result of falling prices, and would convert these funds into gold for shipment abroad where interest rates were higher. Later the loans would be repaid in New York in terms of the decreased gold content of the American dollar. The foreign banker would gain both on the interest rates and on the decreases in the gold content of the dollar. At the same time the withdrawal of gold from New York would tend to restrict credit and to accentuate the domestic depression. The active co-operation of the Federal Reserve Banks would be necessary under this plan to offset in part by credit expansion or contraction the movements of gold.

Managed Currency. This plan which seems to be most feasible at the present time, is discussed briefly in the chapter on money.

International Monetary Co-operation. Since price levels in different countries are interdependent, any effective plan to control secular price trends must be based in part at least on international action. If the leading central banks of the world co-operated in the management of money or credit either on a metal basis (gold or silver, or both) or on a paper basis, major changes in general prices would be largely eliminated. The difficulties, however, which block the way toward effective international control of general prices are formidable. Rising prices might be successfully checked by means of international agreements among nations with regard to central bank discount rates and open market transactions. Falling prices, on the other hand, might require additional co-operation in the form of pooled gold reserves, an internationally guaranteed paper currency, a concerted public works program, and a tariff truce. National differences of a political and social character are grave obstacles to a high degree of international co-operation. But effective co-operation to control general prices would, from time to time, require various nations to sacrifice their economic advantages in international trade and finance (Chapter Twenty) in order to promote the general welfare of all nations—a sacrifice which some nations are unwilling to make. The International Monetary Fund established in 1945 by more than forty nations to stabilize international monetary relations may, if supported by trade and employment co-operation, succeed in achieving international monetary stability.

GENERAL REFERENCES

Angell, J. W., *The Behavior of Money*.

Chandler, L. V., *Inflation in the United States 1940–1948*.

Fisher, I., *Stable Money*.

Halm, G. N., *International Monetary Cooperation*.

Hansen, Alvin H., *America's Role in the World Economy*.

———, *Economic Stabilization in an Unbalanced World*.

Hardy, C. O., *Is There Enough Gold?*

Hart, A. S., *Defense Without Inflation*.

Hawtrey, R. G., *The Art of Central Banking*.

Keynes, J. M., *Indian Currency and Finance*.

———, *A Treatise on Money*.

King, Wilford I., *Index Numbers Elucidated*.

League of Nations Publications, *Final Reports of the Gold Delegation*, 1932.

Robertson, D. H., *Money*.

Spahr, W. E., *The Monetary Theories of Warren and Pearson*.

Warren, George F., and Frank A. Pearson, *Gold and Prices*.

———, *Prices*.

Wright, Quincey (ed.), *Gold and Monetary Stabilization*.

CHAPTER TWELVE

BUSINESS CYCLES

IMPORTANCE

Short-run fluctuations (roughly from two to five years) in general prices which are characterized by business prosperity, recession, depression, and recovery are termed business cycles. As early as 1819 a Swiss economist, Sismondi, recognized and systematically investigated these short-run changes in general business activity. Although many able economists since that time have made extensive statistical studies of business cycles, no conclusive findings with regard to causes and remedies have been developed. Since business cycles during the last century have become increasingly severe with the increased complexity of economic activity, their analysis and control has become one of the most important problems in economics. Mass unemployment of workers in recurring periods of depression is an intolerable condition.

BUSINESS CYCLE INVESTIGATION

Correction for Secular Trend. A more concise concept of business cycles is obtained from a brief reference to the statistical methods of investigation. Various noncyclical price movements are distinguished and eliminated by statistical devices from studies of business cycles. Secular trends in price movements over long periods of time form a base from which the cyclical fluctuations are usually measured. For example, if the secular price trend is upward, it may be statistically eliminated by making each month, from the index numbers of general prices, a deduction equal to the average monthly increment of increase.

Correction for Seasonal Variation. Seasonal variations in business activity which occur because of seasonal changes in the weather, annual holidays, differences in the length of months, etc., are characteristic of many industries. Since these changes occur regularly, they are usually eliminated from statistical studies of business cycles by dividing into the monthly index of general prices a number which is calculated to represent the average seasonal variation.

Key Industries. Index numbers of general prices, corrected for secular trend and seasonal variation, show only price changes which are greater or less than the long time trend or the usual seasonal change—that is, they show the cyclical and accidental price movements. The accidental price movements are irregular and may be the result of wars, strikes, earthquakes, etc. The cyclical movements exhibit some regularity and tend to appear in all major industries about the same time. Agriculture, because its output cannot be quickly changed and depends in part on the weather, is an exception. Although cyclical price movements in various industries differ somewhat, there is enough uniformity to justify the construction of index numbers based upon key industries which are then used to indicate cyclical movements in general business activity.

Regularity of Business Cycles. The degree of regularity in cyclical price movements is an unsettled point among economists. Since the duration of the cycle, or any part of it, varies from time to time, many economists contend that any prediction of price movements for more than a few months in the future is a mere guess. Recent experience seems to support this point of view. Therefore, there are disadvantages involved in the use of the term "business cycle" since it implies regularity as to frequency of occurrence and amplitude of fluctuations. Business cycles, however, do recur and economists hope that forecasting methods will be improved enough as experience accumulates to make estimates of future price movements correct in more than half the cases. At present professional forecasters rely upon the analysis of business barometers such as bank clearings; railway gross earnings; imports and exports; output of coal, copper, iron, and steel; shipments of grain, cotton, and livestock; government crop reports; and transactions of the New York Stock Exchange.

PHASES AND EFFECTS OF BUSINESS FLUCTUATIONS

Prosperity. The phases of business fluctuations overlap and are dynamic. A description of the phases and effects of business fluctuations serves well as an introduction to a discussion of causes and remedies. The *prosperity phase* of a business cycle is characterized by rising commodity prices (particularly wholesale prices). Since wages, rents, and interest rates rise more slowly than commodity prices, profits increase in most industries. Rising prices and profits stimulate speculative buying of securities and commodities. Sales improve greatly, production is increased (old plants are fully utilized and new ones built), and employment is provided for most workers. The eager demand for credit gradually forces up money rates. The general scramble to produce, sell, and manipulate commodities tends to discourage increased efficiency in production.

Recession. The *recession phase* of a business cycle is frequently precipitated by a spectacular crash of security prices and the failure of a few large banks heavily involved in the financing of security and commodity speculators. The speculative buying of securities and commodities finally reaches a limit. Increased sales resistance and higher costs stop the rise of prices and profits. Bank loans become more costly and more difficult to obtain. Securities and commodities, purchased on the basis of anticipated future increases in prices and profits, are offered for sale, and a general selling movement at lower prices develops. A feeling of uncertainty permeates business activity.

Depression. Once the selling movement at lower prices develops, the *depression phase* of the business cycle quickly ensues. Lenders refuse new loans and attempt to collect outstanding loans. Borrowers in a desperate effort to remain solvent force sales at even lower prices. Efforts to lower costs of production usually appear first in the form of pay-roll cuts and salary reductions. Production is curtailed, and unemployment increases. Financial and commercial bankruptcies become widespread. Real estate mortgage foreclosures become general, and construction ceases. Wages, rents, and money rates gradually decline in the wake of falling commodity prices. Consumer purchasing power declines, and accumulated stocks of commodities are slowly disposed of at prices greatly below their cost of production. The pessimistic outlook for profits discourages investment; short-term money rates become low in relation to long-term rates. The hoarding of money may assume large proportions.

Recovery. The *recovery phase* of a business cycle develops when costs have become adjusted to the lower price level and when accumulated stocks have been largely consumed. Banks which weathered the storm accumulate large reserves, and credit is available on favorable terms. Lower wages and rents, however, as well as new improvements in production, encourage businessmen to borrow and to increase production as soon as depleted stocks improve prices. The liquidation of real estate ceases and the apparent surplus of houses disappears. The construction industry resumes activity, unemployment decreases, purchasing power increases, and a gradual rise of prices and profits develops.

Effects. The devastating effects of cyclical fluctuations in business need no elaboration. Boom periods encourage wasteful methods of production and speculative manipulation of securities. Periods of depression result in huge wastes in the form of idle men and idle capital equipment. Friction between employer and employee becomes intense. Debtors, and sometimes creditors, suffer severe hardships. In general, cyclical changes increase the gambling element in business; speculative buying and selling, clever extension of credit, and favorable financial connections become almost as important as efficient production.

CAUSES OF BUSINESS CYCLES

From the above description of a business cycle there emerges the idea that business cycles are self-generating—one phase develops conditions which produce the next stage and so on indefinitely. But what are the factors which produce the initial instability and continue the fluctuating momentum? The number and diversity of answers to this question are likely to confuse most students. The diverse answers, however, of many able economists suggest that there is no specific factor which may be labelled as the cause of business cycles, but rather that a group of factors interact under a general impulse to produce cyclical fluctuations in business activity. The general impulse is the *profit motive*. The interacting factors are listed below.

Producers and the Profit Motive. *Producers* in a dynamic, competitive system must act quickly to utilize profit opportunities. The initial opportunity may arise because of external factors, such as the outbreak of a war, variations in agricultural output in different years, changes in the trade and finance policies of governments; or because of internal factors, such as improvement in the technique of production, business consolidations, and more effective sales promotion. Over a brief period of time the pressure to make profits is likely to find some outlet which results in a headlong rush on the part of producers somewhat similar to the movement of sightseers on an excursion boat. Producers in a few industries, or in several industries, see the same opportunities and attempt to exploit them. Since production is roundabout and output cannot be greatly increased at short notice, no single producer can gauge the future total output of all producers in a given industry. The demand for capital equipment and raw materials mounts rapidly, and other industries are involved in the scramble for profits. A spirit of optimism spreads rapidly through the business community. Over-production in certain industries or misdirected production is the inevitable result of a cumulative uncoordinated process of production. Competition to sell accumulating stocks of goods to consumers who have purchased all they desire of certain commodities, or who lack the purchasing power to buy, finally results in price cuts. A price decline initiates a cumulative process of liquidation because of financial commitments made on the basis of anticipated profit opportunities.

Bankers and the Profit Motive. *Bankers* and other moneylenders compete in the loan market to make profits. Since production and the financing of production is usually closely interrelated, creditors may assume either a passive or active role in the misdirection and overexpansion of certain industries. If financial interests dominate certain industries, they may lead the way in the exploitation of profit opportunities. Their role is also an active one when they buy and sell foreign and domestic securities for a profitable commission. On the other hand, bankers may be passive agents in providing short-term credit for commercial transactions—passive in the sense that under a competitive system of banking one banker is likely to lose profitable business to competitor banks unless he is willing to lend credit on equally favorable terms. Creditors, as well as producers, are unable to estimate the total output of competitive efforts in certain industries and are subject to the same competitive enthusiasms. Although interest rates rise, loans continue until reserve limits are reached. Only a very powerful central bank with the co-operation of foreign central banks would be able to control credit under these conditions. Many loans are made on the basis of new capitalizations and high-priced inventories. Output increases, sales resistance stiffens, pressure develops to restrict and recall loans, and a cumulative process of liquidation ensues.

Lag in Purchasing Power and the Profit Motive. As a boom period develops under the collective efforts of producers and creditors to make profits, a third factor emerges which combines with misdirected production and limited credit to force liquidation—namely, the *lag in purchasing power,* particularly among wage-earning groups and farmers. Price studies of boom periods indicate that some prices are more flexible than others—i.e., that prices are a mixture of competitive, semicompetitive, and monopoly prices. Since agricultural prices are highly competitive, they tend over a period of years to follow changes in costs. They may rise moderately during a boom period (or fall if costs decline), but the rise is less relative to many industrial and retail prices. The farm population, therefore, becomes progressively and relatively a poorer market as the boom develops. Urban wages (especially industrial wages) and some salaries tend to rise during a boom period, but the rise is slower and relatively less as compared with most industrial and retail prices and profits. Since the rise in nearly all costs tends to lag behind the rise in many industrial and retail prices, the profits of many enterprises, particularly those enjoying a semicompetitive or monopoly position, are greatly increased.

During the early part of a boom these changes cause no apparent difficulties. Some income groups (especially profit receivers) are better off than other groups, but the increase in employment spreads prosperity through the entire economic system. Total income increases, spending and saving increase, and the opportunities for investment are abundant and attractive. Income not spent for consumption goods is spent for capital goods which later will increase output of consumption goods. Expenditures for capital goods entail large wage disbursements for their manufacture. Consequently total consumers' purchasing power tends to increase more rapidly than consumption goods, and their prices rise. Additional investment is stimulated, and a rate of expansion is generated which cannot be maintained. During this early part of a boom, there is a *lead* rather than a *lag* in total consumers' purchasing power. Apparently the process could continue until there was full employment of men and resources and a permanent state of prosperity.

The lag in consumers' purchasing power, which finally develops and precipitates a crisis, is the result of a cumulative series of maladjustments. Production in many of the large-scale industries supplying articles for mass consumption slows up because selling becomes more difficult. Technological bottlenecks in some industries may result in sharp increases in costs and prices without any appreciable increase in output. Some of the increased output intended for farm consumers and other groups cannot continue to be sold at the prices maintained because their incomes have not increased sufficiently. Other income groups do not wish to increase further their consumption of these articles. Speculative accumulation of stocks, rather than price reductions or shifts in production, is the expedient adopted.

Hoarding and the Profit Motive. When general income increases, moreover, spending on consumption goods increases, but (largely because of the great inequalities in the distribution of wealth and income and inflexible prices) the increased spending is proportionately less. Saving by the group of large income receivers increases greatly. Attractive investment opportunities in industry for these savings are soon exhausted because markets appear less favorable. There seems to be general overproduction. Some income groups cannot buy more at the prevailing prices, and other groups do not choose to buy more. Price reductions for the products, the costs of which were being lowered, would quickly dispel the mirage of general overproduction, but such reductions would lessen the accumulation of profits for the large income receivers. If a few enterprises, moreover, made price reductions, they would tend to lose relative to enterprises which maintained prices. A shift in production from articles for mass consumption to superluxuries for the large income receivers would provide investment opportunities if the large income receivers were willing to spend more and save less. Lavish expenditures, however, by this group would lessen their accumulation of capital and are usually not undertaken.

During the latter part, therefore, of a boom period, savings or loan funds are diverted from long-term investment in production equipment to short-term speculation in securities, commodities, and real estate. Some income may be saved and hoarded in the form of cash and idle bank deposits in anticipation of lower prices. For the most part, the savings and loan funds used in this manner reduce total income because neither are they spent for consumption goods which would improve the opportunities for investment in industry, nor are they invested in a manner to increase the production of capital goods which would increase employment, wage disbursements, and consumption. Hoarding and the subsequent shrinkage of total income soon force a decline in some prices. The speculative use of loan funds for holding commodities and real estate continues until higher interest rates and the pressure of creditors force some liquidations. In the security markets prices are bid up until the available loan funds and credit are employed and a substantial group of speculators decide the game has reached its limit and unload their holdings on the market. Sporadic liquidation under these conditions quickly develops into a severe spiral of deflation and a depression. Investment practically ceases and unemployment, especially in the capital goods industries, becomes widespread.

REMEDIES FOR CYCLICAL FLUCTUATIONS

Since cyclical fluctuations seem to arise because of the way in which the profit motive operates and since the profit motive is the prime mover in the present economic system, the elimination of severe fluctuations is a difficult and serious problem. Individuals and groups strongly enough entrenched financially to weather these fluctuations frequently argue for noninterference —they say that depressions will cure themselves. Liquidation, if allowed to continue, will finally end, but the argument contains no suggestion of how to care for millions unemployed during the process. Money wage reductions at the beginning of a depression are also suggested as a way of quickly ending the depression. Wages are costs and lower costs ease the transition to a lower price level. The suggestion has merit if not only wages but also other costs (interest, rent) and inflexible prices are reduced in a manner to prevent unemployment. Shorter hours and more leisure is a helpful suggestion if output and incomes are not reduced. But more leisure and less real income are inappropriate when a substantial portion of the population cannot maintain a healthful level of consumption. Constructive remedies for control of cyclical fluctuations try to solve the basic problem of unemployment, either by government regulation of the present economic system or by fundamentally changing the entire system.

Government controls are aimed at preventing and offsetting serious business fluctuations. The crux of the problem is that of maintaining or increasing the flow of income in order to maintain a high level of employment. If output and employment lag, both consumers' expenditures and investments may require expansion. If the savings planned by private individuals are greater than private investment plans—that is, hoarding is involved—government expenditures may be used to offset and compensate for the decrease of private investment. The upper limit to an expansion is the point at which investments and spending upon consumers' goods absorb the total output with full employment of all available labor. Full employment is an optimum relation between consumption and investment. After full employment is reached, however, attempts to increase investment further will result in an unlimited rise in prices— pure inflation.

Control of Money and Credit. Effective control of money and credit in a highly centralized banking system (discussed in previous chapters) alleviates greatly cyclical fluctuations. In the United States, Treasury and Federal Reserve policy affect the volume of money and credit. The Treasury Department exercises its influence through such activities as the sale of bonds to banks, the issue of new money, or the withdrawal of Treasury deposits in the commercial banks and the transfer of these deposits to the Federal Reserve Banks. Federal Reserve policy is concerned with changes in discount rates, alteration of the rate on advances and variation of the degree of stringency in requirements as to collateral for advances, open-market operations, raising and lowering of the legal reserve ratio, changes in margin requirements, control of the volume of member bank security collateral loans, and control of installment credit. International co-operation by governments and central banks to control secular price trends would make the plan more effective. Upward secular price movements tend to accentuate boom periods of business cycles and downward secular price movements tend to accentuate depressions. Effective control of money and credit may curb speculation during a boom and lessen the severity of a depression, but it does not meet squarely the problem of unemployment. It may even check the increase in employment during prosperous years. To curb, moreover, savings and loan funds from entering short-term speculative investments is not likely to force them into long-term investments in production equipment as long as consumers' purchasing power, spending habits, and inflexible prices make long-term investments unattractive. Curbing short-term speculative investments would encourage hoarding, rather than increase long-term investment and employment. If the control of money and credit included the provision of loan funds for long-term investments at very low interest rates by the government or its agencies, the effectiveness of the plan would be greatly increased. Investment, employment, and incomes would increase, but spending habits and inflexible prices would remain as an obstacle to full employment.

Taxation and Public Works. There is a close connection between monetary and fiscal policy—i.e., between the control of money and credit and taxation, government borrowing, and government spending. In recent years there has been much discussion concerning the possibility of using taxes with fluctuating rates as offsets to booms and depressions. Proper timing would be involved. Conspicuous examples of taxes that lend themselves to this type of treatment are sales and payroll taxes.

Heavy inheritance taxes and moderately progressive personal income taxes would lessen the great inequalities in the distribution of wealth and income. Taxes on low income receivers would be lessened. This group would then be able and willing to spend more on consumption goods. Opportunities to invest savings in productive enterprises would be improved, and employment would increase. If direct investments by the government, or public works, were combined with the tax plan, greater effectiveness would be achieved. Public debts, incurred for public works in order to increase employment during slack periods, would be paid off by heavy inheritance taxes and progressive income taxes during prosperous times. A program of government investment and public works broad enough to provide competition for industries enjoying a semi-competitive or monopoly position, would eliminate one of the important obstacles to full employment. A unified program which included control of money and credit, as well as the remedies here discussed under taxation and public works, would constitute an effective attack on the problem of cyclical fluctuations and unemployment.

Other Aids for the Maintenance of Employment. *Unemployment insurance,* by maintaining purchasing power, eases the price maladjustments caused by technological changes. When part of the insurance is collected from employers, greater effort is made to regularize employment and to maintain high wages. *Old age pensions* and *insurance* maintain the purchasing power of a large group whose productive capacity has declined or disappeared. An effective application, however, of the above unified program would render unemployment insurance and old age pensions and insurance of minor significance. *Government labor exchanges* facilitate the shifting of labor and reduce the loss of income during the job-seeking period. More adequate *free educational facilities* would improve the earning and spending abilities in the low income groups. And finally, government policy and action with regard to agricultural subsidies, rate control of public utilities, and international trade and finance could be developed to reinforce a high level of employment.

Drastic Remedies. More drastic remedies will probably be necessary if the above plans are not effectively applied, or if their effective application fails to reduce materially cyclical fluctuations and unemployment. Their effective administration would be extremely difficult because it involves the development of a system in which private industry and vested interests would surrender to the government many of their present privileges and profit opportunities. To overcome these difficulties, government ownership and operation of the banking system and some basic agencies of production, transportation, and distribution may be necessary.

Although the United States does not have a comprehensive program to stabilize the economy at a high level of employment, a step in the proper direction was taken with the enactment of the Employment Act of 1946. This act, approved by a majority of both political parties, provides for an annual report of the nation's economic condition and an annual program to achieve the declared policy of continuous maximum employment and production. Under the act, the Joint Congressional Committee on the Economic Report and the Council of Economic Advisers to the President, who prepare the report, have been established, and those charged with responsibility are enjoined to consult with industry, agriculture, labor, and consumers. From year to year any positive program, of course, requires approval by Congress and authorization by it of funds for any expenditures.

GENERAL REFERENCES

Beveridge, W. H., *Full Employment in a Free Society.*
Clark, J. M., *Strategic Factors in Business Cycles.*
Habeler, G. von, *Prosperity and Depression.*
Hansen, A. H., *Business Cycles and National Income.*
———, *Economic Policy and Full Employment.*
———, *Fiscal Policy and Business Cycles.*

Keynes, J. M., *The General Theory of Employment, Interest, and Money.*

Leven, M., H. G. Moulton, and C. Warburton, *America's Capacity to Consume.*

Mitchell, W. C., *Business Cycles and Their Causes.*

———, *Business Cycles, the Problem and Its Setting.*

Nourse, E. G., *America's Capacity to Produce.*

———, *Price Making in a Democracy.*

Pigou, A. C., *Industrial Fluctuations.*

Robbins, L., *The Great Depression.*

Schumpeter, J. A., *Business Cycles.*

Slichter, S. H., *Toward Stability.*

Snyder, Carl, *Business Cycles and Business Measurements.*

Tinbergen, Jan, and J. J. Polak, *The Dynamics of Business Cycles.*

Wright, D. M., *The Economics of Disturbance.*

CHAPTER THIRTEEN

DISTRIBUTION OF INCOME

RELATION OF FUNCTIONAL AND PERSONAL DISTRIBUTION

An analysis of the distribution of income involves two problems—first, the functional distribution, which is an explanation of how the factors of production obtain a money income in the form of rents, interest, wages, and profits, and second, personal distribution of income, which is largely a statistical analysis showing the size and types of incomes received by individuals and families. The two problems are closely related but are not identical. Functional distribution analysis attempts to explain the price paid for the use of land, capital funds, labor services, and entrepreneurial ability in production. Personal distribution analysis attempts to explore inequalities in the distribution of income among individuals. For labor, functional and personal distribution tend to approximate each other—that is, an individual laborer's personal income is usually entirely made up of wages. A small shopkeeper, however, may receive part of his income in the form of rent from the ownership of land, a part as interest from the ownership of capital used in his business, and a part in wages and profit.

FUNCTIONAL DISTRIBUTION

Functional distribution of money income is a price or value problem, and its analysis is similar to the analysis of the price of consumption goods. The demand for and the supply of the factors of production determine their market price (short-run) and their share of income. The demand of entrepreneurs, however, for the factors of production is not based on their utility to entrepreneurs, but on the present and prospective selling price of the products which the factors co-operatively produce (i.e., on derived utility). The supply of the factors of production, on the other hand, does not conform closely to a cost of production analysis; costs affect the supply of factors only in the form of disutility costs or opportunity costs. The price of entrepreneurial ability (profits), moreover, is adaptable only in a broad social sense to a supply and demand analysis. Under competitive conditions, minimum profits are a kind of wage of management or supply price for entrepreneurs.

The market prices of the factors of production fluctuate greatly with the changes in conditions of demand and supply. Their competitive normal prices (long-run) are determined theoretically by the marginal productivity of each factor of production. Such a normal price for the factors of production is a hypothetical price which would prevail in the long run under conditions of perfect competition and perfect mobility of the factors of production. *The analysis assumes that each factor of production is homogeneous and can be varied separately to determine its marginal output.* Under these conditions entrepreneurs would vary their use of different factors to achieve a least-cost combination which would make the selling price of the increment of product attributable to the marginal unit of each factor equal to its price. In other words each factor would be treated as a variable and increased in a firm until marginal cost was equal to marginal receipts. There would exist a perfect allocation of the factors among firms and industries—that is, there would be no cost or profit inducement to substitute or to transfer factors of production.

The marginal productivity explanation of the normal price of the factors of production shows the combined influence of demand and supply. If the demand for a given factor increases (i.e., if the selling price of the increment of product attributable to the marginal unit of the factor is higher), its marginal productivity and price increase. If the supply of a given factor increases (i.e., if the increment of product attributable to the marginal unit of the factor becomes less and is worth less on the market), its marginal productivity and price decrease. Since the price of consumption goods influences marginal productivity, and hence, the price of the factors of production, costs of production (i.e., the prices of the factors) are related to the price of consumption goods both as cause and effect. All prices are interrelated, and no one group can be isolated as a sole cause or final determinant of another group.

Marginal productivity in functional distribution does not refer to physical productivity but to the value productivity (marginal receipts) which may be imputed to a given factor under special conditions by using more or less of it in combination with other factors in a business enterprise. To say, moreover, that the normal price of the factors equals their marginal productivity is not to justify their returns, because the productivity of any one depends upon the general productivity of the combined factors.

The separate analysis of the price of each factor of production which follows deals mainly with the demand and supply conditions peculiar to each factor (market price). The relation of the market price to the normal price (marginal productivity) is uncertain. Market price deviates from normal price because of imperfect competition, monopoly in the sale of factors and monopsony in their purchase, the practical impossibility in most instances of accounting separately for the marginal cost of one more unit of a factor and for its marginal product, and the constant stream of dynamic changes in the economy.

LAND RENT

In an economic sense, rent is the price paid for the use of land, including permanent improvements (e.g., cleared land) and natural resources (waterfalls, mineral deposits, virgin timber, etc.). The so-called "rent" of buildings and the return from other man-made capital equipment and improvements which are readily reproducible, in an economic sense, are earnings closely related to interest rates. The distinction, however, between land and man-made capital equipment is one of degree which some economists do not consider sufficient to justify separate analysis. Loan funds may be borrowed and invested primarily in more land or in more capital equipment on the same basis—namely, until expected net marginal receipts are equal to the rate of interest. Land is here treated separately because of the social importance attached to the fact that the fixed supply of land and natural resources limits population and because certain qualities of land, such as location, cannot be duplicated. Land can be produced in the sense of making it available for use; the fertility may be restored to exhausted land; swamps may be drained, and deserts irrigated. But land made available has little influence on the total supply. The production of capital equipment, on the other hand, may be varied greatly if the rate of return as compared with interest rates increases or decreases. Those types of capital equipment which are infrequently produced and are highly durable (e.g., hydro-electric plant, skyscraper, steel mill) resemble land and the return is similar to land rent. The return depends more on changes in demand than supply and is sometimes termed quasi rent.

The Supply of Land. The supply actually used is less than the total physical supply of land. The supply differs greatly with regard to fertility and location. Fertility is important for agricultural land, but distance from markets (location) also affects its value-productivity. Location is more important for urban land (attractive for residential use or large volume of business for commercial use), but the quality of the land is not negligible (building foundations are better in some places than in others). Both agricultural land and urban land are used extensively and intensively—that is, the amount of other factors of production combined with land depends in part upon the principle of nonproportional returns.

For agricultural land, viewed as a fixed factor but not homogeneous, the use of the other factors of production in combination with it is increased until an additional application adds to the total product an increment which (when sold) equals the cost of the additional application (margin of cultivation or utilization). On good land, more of the other factors of production can be used before the margin of cultivation is reached (intensive margin). On poor land less of the other factors of production can be used before the margin of cultivation is reached (extensive margin). Mixed types of land somewhat blur this distinction.

To urban land the same principle also applies, and land is used both extensively and intensively. If a given location attracts a large volume of business, more of the other factors of production can be combined with it before the margin of utilization is reached (intensive margin). Higher buildings, for example, will be erected on a small plot of land. But additional stories require stronger foundations, more elevators, and larger ventilation systems. The intensive margin is reached when the estimated cost of an additional story is equal to the estimated return from it.

There are many kinds and grades of land, and they frequently can be put to more than one use. From this point of view the supply of land for a given use is not fixed, and the firm can usually vary the amount of land which it combines with other factors.

The Demand for Land. This demand arises because of its use with the other factors in the production of commodities and services of all kinds. The demand for land is of social significance. If the techniques of production remained the same over a period of time while population (labor) increased greatly, the increased demand for consumption goods would raise their prices because of diminishing productivity. To obtain a larger output, good land would have to be used more intensively and poor land formerly unused would have to be cultivated. But more of the factors of production would not be used on the good land or the poor land until the selling price of the diminishing additional output obtained rose enough to cover the cost of the increased use of the other factors. The diminishing additional output obtained from land with the use of more labor would lower wages, but the total output from land would increase and would sell at higher prices. The owners of land would benefit, but the money wages as well as the real wages of labor would be reduced. The imminent danger of a land famine and a subsistence level of consumption for the labor class was stressed by early English economists (Malthus and Ricardo), but technological improvements in the use of land and the other factors combined with land and the slowing up of population growth make the danger less imminent today. Shifts in demand for the products and services of land are the important aspects in modern times. Adjustments, for example, in agriculture to changes in demand are extremely difficult. In the urban utilization of land, zoning laws and planning programs are developed to direct and stabilize the demand for land in certain areas and uses.

Determination of Land Rent. Rents are based on contracts for a varying period of time. As indicated above, many commercial rents include a return on capital improvements which is an interest return. In general rents are the result of a bargaining process between owners and users of land. The markets are frequently imperfect and monopolistic. The market price paid for the use of a given plot of land (contract price) may be only loosely related, if at all, to its marginal productivity. Entrepreneurs in some instances may be able to vary separately the amount of land which they use with the other factors of production. The variation may indicate the marginal productivity of the land used in the combination and the rent which can be paid for an additional unit. The rent of that unit times the number of units used equals the total rent which could be paid for the land employed in the combination. Since entrepreneurs bid for land on the basis of its present and prospective marginal productivity in various enterprises, rentals, and especially the purchase price of land, are subject to speculative movements.

The relation of rent as a cost of production to the price of consumption goods is one of both cause and effect. If the total supply of land in a given country is viewed as a fixed factor in the process of production, rent appears as an effect of prices. An increase in the supply of the other factors increases the demand for the products and services of land. The higher prices of these products and services make it profitable to use more of the other factors of production partly on good land, and partly on poor land formerly unused, until the additional return equals the additional expense of the increased factors. With land viewed as a fixed factor, demand (i.e., prices of products and services from land) determines the margin of intensive and extensive land utilization. The greater the demand, the lower the margin of utilization, and the higher rents become. On the basis of this analysis, the rent for any given plot of land (rural or urban) devoted to a specific use represents its differential productivity as compared with other plots. Two retail drug stores, for example, on the same street may sell similar items at the same prices, although one pays more rent than the other because one location attracts a larger volume of business (i.e., differential productivity). The two stores treat rent as a cost from an accounting point of view and attempt to make a gross return which will cover that cost, but the rent cost does not cause prices to be higher in the one store.

If land, however, is viewed as a variable factor when combined with the other factors of production, rent appears as a cause of certain prices. Entrepreneurs may be able to vary the use of land with regard to the amount and manner of use. Rent, then, becomes a price which determines the development and location of various enterprises. If the amount of land combined with the other factors is increased, the increase stops when an added unit yields a return which equals the rent paid. High rents, then, restrict the use of land for enterprises which need large amounts of land with the other factors of production (e.g., agricultural industries), lessen the number and output of these industries, and hence, raise the price of their products. When land becomes a scarce factor in any country, the development of enterprises which use relatively small amounts of land in combination with the other factors of production is stimulated, and the prices of their products decline (e.g., various manufacturing industries). In this way, as stated previously, the diminishing productivity of land is offset and prices are lower than they otherwise would be. The development of transportation facilities raises rents in some regions and lowers them in others. The consequent change in rents influences the location and number of various industries and affects the price of their products. Over a period of time the shifting of certain types of enterprises from the high rent sections of a city to the lower rent sections, or to rural sections, influences the price of their products.

To say that the price of finished products determines the margin of land utilization and the various uses of land (i.e., prices determine rents) is true on the basis of the assumption that land is always a fixed factor in the production process. But land may be either a fixed or a variable factor and in the process of varying its use with the other factors of production, rents influence the industrial structure of a country and prices. Prices react on rents, and rents react on prices.

Price or Value of Land. The purchase price or value of land is calculated by capitalizing rent. If an entrepreneur wishes to buy rather than to lease land, he estimates a price which will make the rent represent the average rate of return on that type of investment (i.e., if the rent is $500 per year and the average rate of return on that type of investment is 5 per cent, the price or value is $500 ÷ .05 or $10,000). The gross return, then, of a farmer who owns his own land and capital equipment is a mixed return of land rent, interest and depreciation on capital equipment, wages of management, and possibly some profits.

Land Values and Taxation. Increases in land values present a problem which involves the personal distribution of wealth and income—namely, the possibility of unearned increment received by landowners. Since land rents and values reflect the general growth and development of a country, the owners of land may receive a return for which they perform no service. Land improvements made by owners, and their services as managers are paid for in the form of interest, wages, and profits. Land rent is a payment for the productivity of land and is received by the owner under a system of private property. Because of this fact many reformers (Henry George and other single taxers) have advocated a tax to absorb all land rents. A tax which would absorb all land rents would of course confiscate private ownership in land. The tax paid to the government would represent land rent, and land would probably be leased from the government.

UNEARNED INCREMENT. Although land rents are not always earned by the owners of land, any plan to confiscate them raises the question of government ownership versus private ownership of all kinds of property. Interest and profits, as well as wages, may be unearned under certain conditions (i.e., the price paid for certain types of labor, some capital funds, and entrepreneurial ability could probably be less without changing the quantity or quality of the supply). If private property in general is considered desirable, then the discriminatory taxation and confiscation of ownership in land is not justified. Marked increases in the value of certain plots of land over a period of time may not exceed a compound interest rate on the investment. Extreme changes, moreover, in the general price level cause *decrements* as well as increments in land values to appear. To distinguish between land rents and the return for improvements on land is difficult. If taxes encroached on the latter return, improvements would be discouraged. To tax only future increases in land values would partly confiscate private property in land because land is purchased on the basis of its prospective, as well as present, marginal productivity (cf., English land tax 1909–1910). From a fiscal point of view a single tax on land with no other taxes would provide an inelastic source of revenue.

CAPITALIZATION OF LAND TAXES. Special land taxation is also advocated because purchasers of land apparently buy free of taxes. In the example of capitalization of land rent cited above, the purchaser would pay less than $10,000 for the land if subject to taxation. For example, if the yearly tax were $100, the net income from the land would be reduced to $400. This capitalized at 5 per cent would make the price $8,000. If other types of investments, however, are taxed, the purchaser deducts only the excess of the land tax over similar taxes on other investments. Purchasers of land, then, do not escape the general burden of taxation, but any special discriminatory tax on land would fall on the present owners of land.

Under perfect competition and a perfect tax system, ad valorem taxes on land (i.e., taxes levied according to value) are not shifted to tenants or consumers. Since taxes based on land values under the above assumptions would not be levied on marginal land, the supply of land in use and the products obtained would remain unchanged. With no change in the supply of products, their price to consumers would remain the same, and tenants could not afford to pay higher rents. But competition is imperfect, and in the bargaining process between owners and tenants part of the tax may be shifted in some cases, the tenants making less in the form of wages and profits. Moreover, if taxes based on land values are improperly applied —that is, levied on marginal land (land with no rent and hence, no value)—land will revert to the state in lieu of tax payments. The decrease in the supply of land and products will then shift some of the tax to consumers in the form of higher prices.

INTEREST RATES, LOAN FUNDS, AND CAPITAL

Interest is the price paid for the use of loan funds. It is usually stated as a percentage of the sum borrowed for a year—that is, $3.00 paid for the use of $100 for a year is a 3 per cent rate of interest. At any given time different market prices or rates of interest are paid for the use of loan funds largely because of the different estimated risks involved with regard to defaults and losses on loan transactions. The type of borrower (government, financial institution, or individual), the borrower's payment record or credit standing, the collateral security, and the length of the period specified before repayment of the loan are some important conditions which account for different risk premiums on loans and different rates of interest. The following analysis of interest deals primarily with market rates for short- and long-term loans and their relation to a risk-free rate of interest equal to the marginal productivity of capital goods and equipment.

Supply of Loan Funds. The *supply of loan funds* depends partly upon saving and partly upon the creation of loan funds by commercial banks. If all income were spent for consumption goods by the people receiving it, an important source of loan funds would disappear. Many individuals spend only part of their income for consumption goods. The remainder of their income is saved. It is usually placed in a savings account with some financial institution, in life insurance, in securities, or in some instances it may be hoarded (i.e., held as cash or idle bank deposits). Entrepreneurs may obtain these savings (they may also save part of their money income) by borrowing them directly or by selling securities. The process of saving is disagreeable for many individuals because it involves a postponement of consumption. The future is uncertain, and many individuals prefer a given amount of consumption goods now rather than at a future date—that is, they have a time preference for present goods as compared to future goods. To induce many individuals to abstain from some consumption in the present and to wait for goods in the future, one must offer them the possibility of a larger amount of consumption goods in the future. If an individual, for example, lends $100 for a year, he is unable to buy that amount of consumption goods for a year. But the promise of $106 (6 per cent interest) at the end of the year offers the possibility of more consumption goods later. The disagreeableness involved in foregoing the use of consumption goods now for consumption goods in the future is an important condition which affects the supply of loan funds. In part some interest is paid to induce postponement of consumption—a kind of cost of waiting.

Under modern conditions, however, the cost of waiting or saving varies greatly. It depends upon the source of the savings. Stated differently, variations in the rate of interest may not in some instances appreciably and directly affect the amount of saving.

INDIVIDUAL SAVING. It is largely determined by habit and the size of incomes (also age, sex, race, profession, marital status, etc.). Many individuals wish to provide for the future when their earning power becomes less, and hence, if their present incomes are more than sufficient to maintain them at their customary level of consumption, part of their incomes would be saved without any inducement in the form of interest. If they are saving for a fixed money income in the future (annuity savers), a high rate of interest would make less saving necessary. Some individuals would probably save even if a penalty were placed on saving (negative interest)—that is, their time preference or desire for consumption goods in the future would be so great that they would be willing to pay someone for the service of safeguarding their savings. The bulk of individuals' savings, moreover, is furnished by a small group of large income receivers, and their saving is not likely to be a painful postponement of consumption. The difficulty of spending large incomes for consumption goods, habits of accumulation, and the prestige of amassing large fortunes are factors which eliminate the cost of waiting or saving for some individuals. The first thousand or fifty thousand saved (not inherited) may involve the painful postponement of present consumption, but not the second million.

CORPORATION SAVING. This is usually the most important source for the accumulation of loan funds for investment. A large portion of the saving done by large corporations would probably continue without any interest inducement. If profits are sufficient, the directors may build up a large surplus which they partly invest in plant extensions. The stockholder receives a modest rate of dividend and may be unaware of the fact that if less were saved, larger dividends could be paid. The accumulation of a corporate surplus will increase the selling price of his stock in the future. The disagreeableness of waiting or the cost of saving tends to disappear. But it does not entirely disappear because stockholders may sell their stock if they are not satisfied with the rate of dividends paid and wish to have their share of the accumulated surplus for immediate consumption. If corporations and entrepreneurs save and supply their own capital, interest equal to the rate paid on similar investments (implicit interest) should be charged as an expense or cost. Otherwise interest appears as a profit, and the entrepreneur may be making less than he would make by lending his capital and hiring out as a manager.

FINANCIAL INSTITUTIONS. Institutions, such as banks, insurance companies, and building and loan associations, facilitate individual saving. They increase the opportunity to save, promote the idea of saving, and reduce the risk of losing loan funds. Savings banks, for example, accept loans (deposits) sometimes in very small amounts, and pay a relatively low rate of interest because the funds may be withdrawn at short notice. Since new deposits over a long period of time tend to offset withdrawals, savings banks can relend part of their funds for relatively long periods to different types of borrowers at a higher rate of interest. Financial institutions also accumulate savings of their own which are similar to the corporation savings discussed above.

Commercial banks expand credit and supply loans by providing a system in which nonliquid assets, already saved, can be mobilized in liquid form for use in production. Savings invested in raw materials, finished goods, securities, and other tangible assets become collateral security and are partially transformed into cash or deposit loans. Intangible assets (e.g., prospective earning capacity) also become in part the basis for loans. Instead of postponing present consumption in order to obtain additional savings for immediate use, the borrower is enabled to use savings already accumulated but held in a nonliquid form. The commercial banks under existing legislation and practice can extend loans for equity financing over a period as long as twenty years. These loans are used by the borrower to start small businesses or to buy and operate farms. The creation of such loans on the part of the commercial banks may at times expand greatly the total supply of deposit money. The increased demand for producers' goods and indirectly for consumers' goods raises at least temporarily their prices. As a result some individuals are able to buy less than before, and an involuntary postponement of consumption occurs (forced saving). By controlling deposit credit, the commercial banks and the government's central bank can influence the supply of loan funds and interest rates in an important way.

Demand for Loan Funds. The demand for loan funds depends mainly upon the productivity of capital. The above discussion of the supply of loan funds explains why some interest payment is necessary. It does not explain how it is possible to pay interest. The possibility of paying interest depends largely upon the productivity of capital. Since many individuals prefer present consumption goods to consumption goods in the future, labor would be applied almost entirely to the direct production of consumption goods without capital equipment unless the indirect or roundabout capitalistic production yielded a sufficient product to compensate for the delay. Labor applied indirectly (i.e., to make tools which labor then uses to produce consumption goods) is more productive than labor applied directly because natural forces, such as falling water, air currents, steam pressure, and electricity are brought under control to aid labor in production; because capital equipment enables labor to perform tasks impossible for unaided labor; and because the use of capital equipment improves the productivity of the other factors of production, especially by increased specialization and enlarged scale of operation.

Indirect production is not productive merely because it is roundabout, but it is roundabout because it is more productive than direct methods. Productivity may sometimes be increased by shortening the production process. On the other hand, some products improve with age (e.g., wine and timber), but the chemical changes which occur during the aging process must contribute enough to their productivity to pay for the cost of waiting. The demand, then, for loan funds (savings) is based partly on their productivity in the purchase of capital equipment. The main sources of demand for loan funds are cited below.

ENTREPRENEURS' DEMAND. In general entrepreneurs increase the use of capital equipment in various enterprises as long as its marginal productivity (i.e., the sales value of the product obtained from the last increment of capital) is sufficient to pay depreciation charges for its replacement plus the interest payments necessary to induce individuals to supply loan funds. Diminishing productivity determines the amount of capital needed. In some industries the margin of utilization will be reached when only small amounts of capital equipment are used, in others when large amounts are used. If the productivity of capital in some industries is not sufficient to meet these payments, it is shifted to other uses. Some capital, however, is designed for one special use and the shifting requires time—that is, enterprises continue to operate at a loss as long as returns are sufficient to pay direct expenses plus some contribution to fixed expenses. Gradually part of the funds invested in capital equipment are retrieved, the worn out machine is sold for scrap, and the funds realized are then available for investment elsewhere. Some specialized capital equipment may never be shifted when its productivity suddenly declines. The enterprise is reorganized and the investment decapitalized— that is, the capital equipment is given a lower value which makes the returns sufficient for maintenance and interest. The loss, however, suffered by the investors discourages new capital from entering the industry. Shifting occurs by using new capital in more productive industries.

Entrepreneurs' demand, then, for loan funds is based on the present and prospective net marginal productivity of capital goods. Such productivity can be roughly estimated when separate variations of capital are possible. Their borrowing ceases when the net marginal productivity of capital equals the prevailing interest rate. Substantial changes in the demand for loan funds may occur because of changes in expectations with regard to the net marginal productivity of capital. The demand for the bulk of loan funds comes from this source.

The demand for loan funds by various financial institutions, as indicated above, is partly the result of entrepreneurs' demand. Financial institutions act as financial middlemen. They accept small savings from many individuals and pool these savings for the use of business enterprises. Since many small savers are unable to invest their funds satisfactorily (i.e., are unable to diversify investments and lessen risks), they are willing to pay for the service of financial institutions by accepting a lower rate of interest than the rates paid by entrepreneurs to financial institutions for the use of their savings.

GOVERNMENT'S DEMAND. This demand for loan funds is not closely related to the net marginal productivity of capital. Many government investments of capital yield an intangible return which cannot be measured in monetary terms (e.g., they may promote the general welfare). If a government enterprise does produce tangible goods and services for which a money charge is made, the charge may be only sufficient to maintain the enterprise without providing an interest return. Funds, moreover, may be borrowed for war operations in which capital is destroyed rather than maintained and increased. The general tax burden which is made necessary in order to repay funds borrowed by the government is related to the total productivity of the country. The productivity of capital equipment, however, is an important item in the total productivity. To obtain loan funds the government offers a rate of interest which is largely determined by the rates paid by entrepreneurs. Since loans to some governments are less risky than loans to individuals or business enterprises, the rate of interest paid is usually less than for ordinary business loans. Indirectly, then, government borrowing is related to the net marginal productivity of capital.

CONSUMERS' DEMAND. This demand for loan funds is not closely related to the net marginal productivity of capital. Since the funds are spent for consumption goods and not for production goods, the possibility of repaying the loan with interest is less. The ability for repayment is not based on the productivity of capital acquired with the loan, but on the present and prospective income of the borrower. Prior to the widespread development of commerce and industry in the 15th and 16th centuries, many loans were for consumption purposes. The difficulty of repayment provoked opposition on the part of church and civil authorities to all interest payments for loans.

Although the great increase in loans for the purchase of production goods later eliminated objections to interest payments, many states still have usury laws to prevent interest extortion.

Not all consumption loans are spendthrift loans (i.e., loans for consumption goods which are used immediately without contributing to the borrower's ability to repay). Funds may be borrowed for educational purposes which increase the borrower's future income and make possible the repayment of the loan with interest. Durable consumption goods, such as houses, autos, and house furnishings, may be purchased with loan funds. Gradual repayment of the loan with interest means that the borrower saves and pays for the consumption goods as they are being used up. Since the risk element for consumption loans is greater than for production loans, the interest paid is usually higher.

Determination of Interest Rates.

NORMAL RATE OF INTEREST. The normal rate of interest is a hypothetical rate (or pure interest rate) which would prevail over a long period of time if risk were eliminated from loans, if the value of money remained constant, if competition and the mobility of capital were perfect, and if all loans were used to increase capital equipment. The normal rate of interest would be a price paid for the use of loan funds which would equate the marginal cost of waiting or saving and the net marginal productivity of capital equipment. Many loans, however, are not made to increase capital equipment; old loans or existing investments are large relative to new loans and new investments in a current period, and the changing monetary situation is subject to some control by government and its centralized banking system. Because of cyclical fluctuations in trade, a heavy demand for loan funds frequently develops for speculative uses. As long as the speculative transactions are profitable, interest rates for the loan funds used rise with little regard to marginal productivity of capital equipment. For these reasons and others, market rates of interest, especially short-term rates, have little or no relation to a normal rate of interest.

MARKET RATES OF INTEREST. If individuals expect prices to fall, they will prefer to hold money rather than commodities or bonds and other investments. Their liquidity preference increases. The movement to sell bonds and other investments is likely to lower their price and raise the rate of yield or interest return obtainable from such investment (i.e., a $100 bond with interest fixed at 3 per cent yields more than 3 per cent when purchased at less than $100). The higher interest return is an inducement primarily for individuals to part with liquidity (not hoard) and invest, rather than an inducement to save. Conversely, an expectation of a rise in prices and a decrease in liquidity preference will result in higher prices for bonds and other investments and in a lower interest return. The short-term rate of interest is largely the result of liquidity preference (demand for money) and the supply of money (cash and demand deposits). The rate of interest tends to rise or fall in order to equalize changes in these demand and supply conditions.

The supply of money, especially demand deposits, can be varied, as indicated in a previous chapter, by the monetary authorities and the commercial banks. They may, for example, force down the rate of interest by having the banks lower their interest and discount rates and offer more loans to borrowers. The Federal Reserve Banks can buy securities at favorable prices which keeps down their rate of yield, satisfies the liquidity preference of some sellers, and enables other sellers to lend money if they wish. The government itself may borrow large sums, especially during a war, and at the same time maintain or lower interest rates. Bank credit is expanded, and the banks increase their purchase of government securities. These purchases maintain or raise the price of securities which maintain or lower the rate of interest. If the liquidity preference of individuals remains the same, the increase in the supply of money will make them willing to purchase securities.

The long-term rate of interest, as indicated by the yield on long-dated government bonds, is closely related, as explained above, to short-term rates. It tends on the average to exceed short-term rates by a risk-premium for possible changes in bond prices. It may, however, not always respond completely to changes in the supply of money and bank credit. As bank credit is expanded and securities are purchased by the Federal Reserve Banks, the liquidity preference of individuals may increase because of expected lower prices in the future. They will then hoard the additional cash and demand deposits and wait for a fall in the price of securities and a rise in the rate of interest. In a similar way if the expected net marginal productivity of capital improved greatly and new investment expanded until full employment was achieved, an attempt by the monetary authorities to maintain a low long-term rate of interest leads to inflation. Rising prices and decreased liquidity preference may end in a general refusal to accept and to use money with a rapidly depreciating value. Under such conditions a higher rate of interest is needed to encourage saving and to check investment. In terms of broad limits and long periods of time, the rate of interest may equalize in a rough way the marginal cost of saving and the marginal productivity of capital. Within these limits, however, the short-term rate of interest is largely the result of changes in liquidity preference and the money and credit policy enforced by the monetary authorities.

Spending, Saving, and Investing. In a modern industrial system spending, saving, and investing are interdependent vital processes. The formation of capital and the expansion of production capacity depend on all three processes. They also depend on technological improvements which raise the general level of spending, saving, and investing. When individuals hoard or save and invest in existing assets for highly speculative purposes, total income available for buying consumption good is decreased, and some savings already invested are lost. If everyone decided to save for an unspecified time all of h income except enough to support a bread and water existenc the savings, as well as existing investments, would be almo worthless because there would be no market for the output industry. The decline, moreover, in output, employment, a incomes would reduce to a low level the ability to save. On other hand, assuming no technological improvements and p duction at full employment, more saving, voluntary or forced, is necessary in order to expand total investment. Less consumers' goods are purchased, and labor is shifted to making more producers' goods. When production is below full employment as in a depression, governmental expenditures for public works, expansion of bank credit, and low interest rates may increase employment and the amount of both consumers' and producers' goods.

LABOR AND WAGE RATES

Wages are prices paid for the services of labor. Labor includes all wage and salary workers employed by entrepreneurs in the process of production. The returns received by entrepreneurs in the form of profits may closely approximate wages (i.e., wages of management), but not all profits are wages, and hence, profits are treated separately. Wages are a main part of the costs of production and a major share in the total distribution of income. There are many different market rates of wages for different kinds of labor. An explanation of these differences is given largely in terms of conditions of supply and demand. The marginal productivity of labor influences the market rates of wages and the average level of real wages.

Supply of Labor. The supply of labor is not homogeneous. Because of biological traits and environmental influences, there are many grades of labor skill. Occupations also differ with regard to the attractiveness and the complexity of the work required of labor. Throughout industry there are roughly four or five classes of labor (noncompeting groups)—unskilled manual labor, semiskilled workers (machine tenders, clerks, etc.), skilled workers (machinists, carpenters, bookkeepers, etc.), professional groups (lawyers, physicians, business managers, accountants, etc.), and entrepreneurs (outstanding business promoters and organizers). Although these classes are not distinct, individuals within each group compete mainly for jobs within the group rather than for jobs in another group. Some workers may rise to a higher group (i.e., acquire a new skill or become entrepreneurs in their former trade); some may drop to a lower group (i.e., cease to be entrepreneurs or skilled workers). Young workers entering industry often follow their fathers' occupations. The number of workers, however, in each group relative to the demand differs enough because of ability, training, and attractiveness to make wage rates differ among the various noncompeting groups. Labor unions which have very restrictive rules for apprentices learning a trade may also affect the supply of workers in a given group. Labor in a given non-competing group tends to be homogeneous and tends to receive a uniform wage, but the level of wages varies from group to group. There is no general wage rate, but rather several wage levels corresponding to the various noncompeting groups.

NONCOMPETING GROUPS AND COSTS. The wage differences among noncompeting groups tend to equal the cost of transferring from one group to another. If arduous study and expensive training are necessary for entrance into a given group, fewer individuals enter it, and the higher wages received because of higher marginal productivity tend to compensate for the cost of transferring. If the wages are not high enough to compensate for the cost of transferring, the number entering the group tends to decline, and marginal productivity and wages rise until they equal the cost of transferring. Some occupations are especially attractive because of the agreeableness of the work and the social prestige attached to them, because of the ease and cheapness of learning them, and because of the greater probability of moderate success in them. These occupations attract many individuals, and hence, marginal productivity and wages tend to be low.

If individuals were born with equal ability, and were given equal opportunity to enter different occupations, wages would offset the real costs (disagreeableness or disutility) of entering different occupations. The most disagreeable work would then command the highest pay. But individuals are born with unequal ability, and opportunity is restricted by the financial position of parents. Some very attractive occupations, therefore, may pay wages greatly in excess of the real costs and the money costs of entering them simply because that type of ability is scarce relative to the demand for it. Individuals, therefore, who possess rare ability receive a return similar to land rent— the rent of ability (i.e., it is not closely related to any cost of production). On the other hand, the supply of the least efficient workers, either because of the initial lack of ability or the failure to receive proper training, is large relative to the demand, and their remuneration is low even in the most disagreeable occupations. Since their remuneration is low, they are frequently unable to improve their ability in order to enter a more remunerative occupation.

TOTAL SUPPLY OF LABOR AND COST. The total supply of labor depends on the size and structure of a given population group. Since most wage-earners are males between the ages of fifteen and sixty-five, the proportion of males of that age group in any population is important with regard to the total supply of labor. In prosperous times the total supply of labor is not fully employed. If the demand for labor suddenly increases (say in time of war), some additional workers may be recruited from that portion of the population which is usually not working for wages (housewives, retired individuals, etc.), and hours of work may be lengthened. In some instances a higher wage rate increases very little or decreases the supply of labor. Fewer members of a family need to work in order to maintain a customary level of living, or those employed can work for fewer hours. The total supply of labor, unlike the supply for any given occupational group, tends to be inelastic. To offset a permanent increase in the demand for labor would require at least fifteen years for new workers to mature. Malthus and other English economists thought that the total supply of labor was elastic (i.e., if demand increased and wages rose, the birth rate among the laboring class increased until wages fell to a subsistence level—the "iron law of wages"). Wages according to this analysis tended to equal the cost of producing or maintaining labor. Population in many countries did increase with increasing productivity, but the rate of increase did not prevent a rise in real wages. The growth of population today in most advanced industrial countries does not conform to the Malthusian analysis. Population in these countries increases slowly, and changes in its structure do not conform closely to the demand for labor. Higher wages for labor and better educational opportunities tend to restrict rather than to increase the birth rate. The supply of labor, therefore, is not closely related to its cost of production.

Demand for Labor. The demand for labor in industry and trade arises because of its use with the other factors of production. Theoretically, entrepreneurs bid for labor on the basis of its estimated present and prospective marginal productivity. Entrepreneurs can profitably add labor to the other factors of production until the additional product obtained yields, when sold, barely enough to cover the cost of the additional labor or unit of labor. Marginal costs composed entirely of wages equal marginal receipts. Labor, like land and capital, is used in varying amounts by entrepreneurs, and diminishing productivity affects its use. In a given industry lower time rates and piece rates would be offered if more and more workers were employed because the output per worker would decrease and the price per unit of the output would fall.

In many instances, however, estimates of marginal productivity are practically impossible to make because labor is not varied separately and the process of production is too complex to calculate marginal product for each kind of labor. In other employment, such as by government and service organizations, there is no specific product for sale. Monopoly conditions in the sale of the product or in the purchase of labor services lessen the demand for labor. Output is restricted and less labor hired in order to raise the price of the product and to depress the wage rate.

Determination of Wage Rates.

Wages are based on contracts for varying periods of time. They are largely the result of a bargaining process between entrepreneurs and labor. In many basic industries labor is organized in unions for collective bargaining. The market rate of wages (short-run) in any given group of laborers depends upon supply and demand conditions. The normal rate (hypothetical long-run rate which assumes conditions of full employment) for any given labor group equals its marginal productivity. The market rate of wages is not likely to approximate closely the normal rate because of cyclical fluctuations, imperfect competition among employers of labor, difficulties in calculating marginal product, monopolistic labor organizations, and imperfect mobility of labor. There is a wide bargaining range in the determination of wages.

BARGAINING POSITION OF LABOR. Unorganized laborers are in a weak bargaining position in modern industry. Their specialized skill reduces their ability to shift quickly from one occupation to another when wages within their trade become unsatisfactory. The localization of industries, moreover, in certain regions makes more important the geographical mobility of labor. If industries decline in one section of the country, wages in those industries fall below the wage level in similar industries elsewhere unless some labor shifts to other industries. Family ties, meager financial resources, and lack of labor market information frequently reduce the geographical mobility of labor and weaken its bargaining power. Modern industry also places a premium on labor skill during the prime years of a laborer's life. His services are perishable, and consequently, to withhold them in order to obtain better wages may result in a serious loss.

Labor organizations improve the bargaining power of labor. Experienced negotiators can be hired to sell collectively the services of labor in various industries. Collective bargaining offsets the pressure exerted by employers to reduce wages or to maintain a customary wage level. Since the wage bill for many industries is large compared to other costs, any small increase in wages may, at least temporarily, greatly reduce profits and dividends. Unless labor is well organized, a reduction in costs to improve profits when adverse conditions appear is likely to mean wage reductions because the short-term contracts with laborers can be more easily changed than those involving rent and interest payments. The measurement, moreover, of individual labor performance in any given enterprise in which thousands of tasks are minutely specialized is difficult, and in the absence of keen competition among employers for labor (employers may informally agree in some industries or cities not to spoil the labor market by paying higher wages), organized labor may improve its wages. Monopoly conditions in the sale of labor services offset similar conditions on the buying side of the labor market. If a piecework system based on time and motion studies is used, organized labor may be able to prevent unfair cuts in rates on jobs when output is increased, to prevent managers from becoming lax in supplying materials for piecework jobs, and to prevent excessive speeding up of work. In general if the efficiency of labor improves and its marginal productivity increases, wages tend to rise slowly (depending upon the competition of employers for labor) unless labor is well organized to press its demands. To be effective a labor union must include the majority of workers in a given occupation. Its effectiveness is increased by means of closed shop agreements, peaceful picketing, and apprenticeship rules which aid in preventing nonunion workers from breaking up strikes.

LIMITS TO WAGE BARGAINING. The limits to the bargaining range for wages are determined by the profits of employers and the customary level of consumption of organized laborers. Under competitive conditions if wages for one group of laborers are forced above an estimated marginal productivity level, profits are reduced (rent and interest payments may also be affected), and the demand for labor is likely to decrease. Some firms may be bankrupt; others may employ less labor. The market rate of wages then declines to the normal rate based on marginal productivity. In some cases, however, the higher wages may improve the efficiency of labor (higher wages may also slow up labor efficiency) and stimulate management to increase its effectiveness with the result that the marginal productivity of labor rises to the new wage level. Under these conditions employment may remain approximately the same. If the effectiveness of management remained unchanged, other less well-organized groups of laborers in the same industry may suffer from unemployment and lower wages because of the higher wages obtained by the well-organized group (i.e., management economizes by cutting the wages of the less well-organized group and discharging some workers). On the basis of relative bargaining power as discussed above, the market rate of wages may frequently be below the normal rate, and hence, labor organizations may often obtain an increase in wages without causing unemployment or without injuring other labor groups. This situation exists when all firms in an industry are making substantial monopolistic profits. Output remains about the same, and the higher money wages result in higher real wages. If under monopoly conditions union wage increases are largely passed on in higher prices, unorganized workers experience a loss in real wages. General wage increases without a corresponding increase in output raise prices and leave real wages unchanged. If employment and output expand, however, in anticipation of improved business, real wages may increase (i.e., wages may increase more than prices).

The lower limit to the bargaining range for wages is fixed by the customary level of consumption in various labor groups.

In extreme cases where labor is unorganized, the lower limit may be a subsistence level. If wages fall below a subsistence level, the supply of labor is gradually lessened (i.e., because of ill health, premature death, etc.). Organized labor usually resists, by strikes if necessary, wage reductions below their customary level of consumption. Rising prices for consumers' goods and an appreciable higher cost of living which reduce real wages are usually the basis for demands for higher wages. Organized labor by pooling its resources is in a position to stop work for a relatively long period of time. Since many industries have large fixed expenses, a prolonged strike causes employers serious losses. The settlement of wage disputes between organized labor and employers on the basis of a customary level of consumption is a fairly satisfactory one. It offers a more definite standard than marginal productivity which would be extremely difficult or impossible to calculate. To avoid wage settlements based on a customary level of consumption, which seem to show no improvement with increases in general productivity, organized labor frequently insists on a "saving wage" instead of a "living wage" (i.e., a wage which maintains the customary level of consumption and enables the workers to save for future needs).

Technological Unemployment. Such unemployment indicates the difficulty of shifting labor from one employment to another. The introduction of improved machines in a given industry is likely to result in unemployment for many skilled workers, especially when the demand for the product is inelastic. The lowered production costs may lower the prices of the product and increase the profits of the entrepreneur. The demand of entrepreneurs and consumers for other goods, as well as the demand of the industry making the new machinery, in time provides employment for these workers in other industries. But the shifting process may require the workers to learn new skills and to move to other industrial centers. In the meantime the buying power of the displaced workers is lost. In modern industry improvements are continuous, and hence, technological unemployment tends to be chronic. In the absence of unemployment insurance and effective labor exchanges which would assist displaced workers to maintain their buying power and to obtain new employment, organized labor's only defense is a restriction of output (i.e., they work slower on jobs so that more workers will be employed). Restriction of output in the long run lowers real wages, but it pools the burden for all labor instead of concentrating it upon displaced workers. *Cyclical unemployment,* a more serious problem than technological unemployment, is discussed in Chapter Twelve.

Minimum Wage Legislation. Such legislation presents the problem of adjusting wages to an approximate marginal productivity level. In some industries wages may be abnormally low. Women workers, for example, frequently receive very low wages in some industries as compared to similar work done by men. Their low wages are partly the result of low productivity. But other conditions may result in wages below the marginal productivity of their work (e.g., the majority of women are not permanent workers, and hence are usually unorganized; they have less opportunity to enter many occupations, etc.). A minimum wage for an exploited group of this kind tends to raise wages to the marginal productivity level for that general grade of labor. Because of competition, the exploitation may have lowered prices to the consumer instead of increasing profits. (If profits are abnormally high, no change in employment or prices will occur.) If profits are low, marginal enterprises will be unable to pay the minimum wage, output will decrease, and prices will increase. Some laborers and entrepreneurs will be forced into other industries which increases their output and lowers slightly the marginal productivity of labor in those industries. The consumers pay more for the product formerly produced by exploited labor, but less for the products of other industries. A better adjustment of production results. If minimum wages are fixed too low or too high, they are ineffective. In the former instance they do not help the low income worker; in the latter instance they result in some unemployment and affect adversely non-wage-receiving groups. In these groups there are low-income receivers who need legislative protection and assistance.

Labor Organizations. As indicated by the foregoing discussion, labor organizations improve wages mainly by forcing wages to a marginal productivity level. Early English economists (e.g., J. S. Mill) opposed labor organizations (Mill later recanted) because they believed that in any given year a definite fund (in the form of real wages) was destined for the payment of all labor, and consequently if one organized group received more, another group would receive less. Each year there is a total supply of consumption goods available which can be increased only over a period of time because of the round-about organization of industry. But the wage fund (i.e., the portion of total consumption goods which laborers can buy during the year with their money wages) may be increased if wages are below the marginal productivity level in some industries without injury to other groups of labor (i.e., excessive profits are reduced in those industries). If labor organizations, however, force wages above the marginal productivity level in some industries in which the efficiency of management and labor cannot be improved, organized groups gain at the expense of the less well-organized groups.

. Other methods for improving the position of wage earners include immigration restriction, birth control, vocational guidance, increased educational opportunities, and free income in the form of public recreational facilities and public health service. The development and present status of labor organizations are discussed in Chapter Sixteen.

NATURE OF PROFITS

Profit is the compensation which the entrepreneur may receive for his services as owner and manager of a business enterprise. The compensation is not contractual, but depends upon a gross income from an enterprise in excess of the actual or contractual expenses. The entrepreneur, then, may incur a loss; he may receive a net income which includes wages for his services as manager (minimum profit), and interest and rent for his ownership of capital and land used in the enterprise; or he may receive a net income which exceeds his implicit wages, interest, and rent—this excess above minimum profits is called pure profits. Pure profits are the result of dynamic conditions; minimum profits, the result of long-run (static), competitive conditions.

Minimum Profits. The items included in profits depend upon the form of business organization. In an individual proprietorship or in a partnership, the owner or owners usually manage the enterprise and furnish most of the money capital. Under these conditions profits would include wages of management (i.e., minimum profits or the amount which they could earn if they hired out as managers, or the amount which they would need to pay for satisfactory managers), as well as interest and rent from their ownership of capital and land (i.e., the amount which they could receive if their capital were lent and their land leased, or the amount which they would need to pay for the use of capital and land). In many corporations the stockholders (owners) furnish part of the money capital; some capital is borrowed (bondholders), and the directors (mainly large stockholders) hire a president or general manager. Ownership and management are partially separated. The board of directors may assume responsibility for decisions with regard to general policy, but many of the stockholders usually have very little interest in the choice of management or in the formulation of general policies. The president or manager receives a salary, but his compensation may partly depend on the net income of the corporation—that is, unless the net income is large enough to satisfy the directors, his salary may be reduced or he may be discharged. Sometimes the president or manager receives in addition to his salary a special bonus for exceptional performance, or a percentage of the net income. Under these conditions any net income above expenses, such as interest on bonds, rent, and salary of the manager, is available for dividends to stockholders. This net income or profit includes fewer items than those listed above for a proprietorship. Income available for dividends (some may be retained in the corporation) is in part an interest return on capital invested by the stockholders. Any of this income in excess of an interest return on lending capital is compensation for the partial managerial function of stockholders, especially those serving as directors of the corporation. Under competitive conditions wages of management, or minimum profits, for a corporate type of business consist of the compensation of the manager and that portion of income available for dividends which is a managerial compensation for stockholders.

Minimum profits, then, require no special explanation. Entrepreneurship is usually a mixture of special labor ability and the ownership of capital and land. Minimum profits are indirectly related to the marginal productivity of labor, capital, and land. Unless entrepreneurs receive on the average (losses included) a compensation which approximately equals the amount which they could obtain by hiring out as managers, leasing their land, and lending their capital, they cease to be entrepreneurs. Under conditions of perfect competition, perfect mobility of the factors of production, and a stable price level, different enterprises would make different average minimum profit rates. If implicit interest and rent returns were deducted, the remaining differential returns would represent wages of management for different grades of entrepreneurial ability. Average minimum profit rates, then, are normal profit rates (i.e., rates which would prevail in the long run under the above assumed conditions). Although minimum profits are treated from an accounting point of view as a residual sum or surplus, they are, from an economic point of view, part of the cost of production and affect the prices of consumption goods.

Profits may approximate a minimum level occasionally in some industries and trades, but perfect competition, perfect mobility of the factors of production, and a stable price level do not exist. Technological changes, differentiation of products, and other innovations make pure profits appear at least temporarily in many lines of production. Entrepreneurs in some industries may receive pure profits over a long period of time; in others, losses may persist.

Causes of Pure Profits.

UNIQUE ABILITY AND INNOVATIONS. Entrepreneurs assume certain noncalculable risks. They contract to pay interest, rent, and wages, but their compensation depends upon uncertain future market conditions. Laborers, creditors, and landowners also assume risk in the process of production, but decisions with regard to production for future markets is the function of the entrepreneur—a function of assuming noninsurable risks and severe losses. Exceptional ability to anticipate future demand and to cope with economic uncertainty may result in high minimum profits (wages of management) for some entrepreneurs. Exceptional ability, however, may sometimes be unique. A few individuals with unique ability may be able to earn more as entrepreneurs than as managers because employers fail to recognize the merit of their ideas and are unwilling to allow them to experiment. These individuals as entrepreneurs may exploit new inventions, introduce new methods of production, develop new marketing technique, and carry out other innovations. They receive more for a period of years than they would have received as managers. The excess returns represent one type of pure profits.

Luck. To distinguish between pure profits which arise because of unique ability and innovations and those which arise because of mere chance is difficult. However, because of luck, many entrepreneurs may receive large windfall gains during a few years (e.g., during a war or other price level changes) which make their average profits exceed a minimum rate over a long period of time. The excess gains constitute another type of pure profits.

Imperfect Mobility and Monopoly. Because of the immobility of the factors of production, especially labor, entrepreneurs in some industries may be able to obtain over a long period of time certain factors at prices below their marginal productivity. This situation is often linked with various degrees of monopoly in the purchase of factors (monopsony) and in the sale of products. These monopoly gains, as indicated in a previous chapter, frequently exceed a competitive rate of return. The excess represents a third type of pure profits.

Causes for Persistent Losses. On the other hand entrepreneurs in some industries may receive over long periods of time returns below the minimum profit level. Industries which are characterized by small operating units and small fixed investments are likely to be overcrowded (e.g., farming, repairing, retailing, etc.). Wage and salary workers can easily become entrepreneurs. Because of the social prestige of being in the entrepreneur class, the satisfaction of being one's own boss, and the security against an arbitrary discharge, many individuals are willing to accept lower returns as entrepreneurs than they would receive if they hired out as workers and lent their capital. Even in industries which require relatively large amounts of capital, many entrepreneurs may receive over long periods of time returns below minimum profits. Many individuals who become entrepreneurs overestimate their ability and opportunities. They judge their future success on the basis of entrepreneurs who have succeeded in a given industry, and not on the basis of the number of entrepreneurs who have failed. The entrance of new optimistic entrepreneurs into a given industry from year to year lowers profit rates for many enterprises below a minimum level. If an industry is dying out, profits for most entrepreneurs are likely to be below the minimum level for a period of years.

Pure Profits and Costs. For the most part, pure profits are not a necessary cost of production. They represent a form of unearned increment. Pure profits and the number of enterprises receiving them over a long period are probably small. The existence of pure profits is likely to attract entrepreneurs into a given industry, and competition causes them to disappear. The possibility of making pure profits is not essential in order to induce entrepreneurs to exercise their ability and to assume risk. Minimum profits (wages of management), plus the prestige, freedom of action, and security against arbitrary discharge which go with entrepreneurship, are sufficient to stimulate initiative and to attract entrepreneurs.

Taxation of Pure Profits. The taxation of pure profits like the taxation of unearned increment from land is impracticable. To separate pure profits from minimum profits is a qualitative rather than a quantitative problem. The manner of making profits, not the size of profits, is the point of distinction. Nearly all enterprises in a given industry may make profits in excess of a theoretical minimum for a few years, but these may be offset by subsequent losses. If the profits and losses of a given industry were averaged over a period of years, any attempt to tax profits in excess of the average would place a penalty on entrepreneurs with superior ability. Over a period of years each enterprise, rather than a given industry, has a minimum profit rate. To calculate these rates and to apply a tax on pure profit is an impossible task. An excess profits tax is justifiable only as an emergency measure to raise revenue (e.g., during a war).

The Profit Motive and Production. From a social point of view pure profits and some minimum profits are difficult to justify. Hired managers are usually carefully selected, but in many industries anyone can plunge in as an entrepreneur. The unregulated selection of entrepreneurs is likely to result in over-expansion of certain industries, or in the multiplication of small units of production. If production were concentrated in the hands of the more capable entrepreneurs, the marginal productivity of labor would be higher, and the increase in large-scale production would lower prices to the consumer. Production for profit, moreover, does not always guarantee the quality of products. Since consumers are not expert buyers, the producers of harmful and inferior products make profits. Monopoly profits based on restricted output represent an economic loss. The wasteful exploitation of natural resources is another example of the injurious social effects of the profit motive.

Although profits are an imperfect guide to production and investment and an imperfect incentive for efficiency in a social sense, the profit system (or system of free enterprise) must be credited with remarkable achievements. Capital equipment has been multiplied and perfected, an intricate system of finance has been developed, production has been increased, and the level of consumption raised. The difficult problem, moreover, of planning the total production of a country, of selecting capable managers, of fixing wage rates, of pleasing the majority of consumers (e.g., under a system of state socialism) lessens the significance of the above disadvantage of a system of free enterprise. In a practical way the pursuit of profits has accomplished a rough allocation of scarce means of production and has increased those means. But a system of free enterprise needs careful regulation, and the difficulties of enforcing fair competition, of protecting labor and the consumer, of controlling price levels, and of supervising monopolies may prove to be a costly and impossible task. The disadvantages of a system of free enterprise may be viewed as necessary costs to obtain its advantages.

PERSONAL INCOME AND PERSONAL DISTRIBUTION

The Gross National Product. Estimates of the dollar value of production and income are collected by the Department of Commerce and provide a statistical summary of the distribution of income. The *gross national product* is the estimated dollar value of all goods and services produced in a given year. When certain deductions are made from the gross national product (see Table I), the remainder is called the *national income*. It represents the payments to the factors of production (functional distribution). By making certain deductions from and additions to the national income, we can find the *personal income* or the income payments to individuals.

Table I. Gross National Product, National Income, and Personal Income in 1953.[1]

Gross National Product	$364.5 billion
Less:	
Capital consumption allowances	27.8
Indirect business tax and nontax liabilities	30.1
Business transfer payments	1.2
Statistical discrepancy	1.4
Plus:	
Subsidies less current surplus of government enterprises (−)0.4	
Equals: *National Income*	$303.6 billion
Less:	
Undistributed corporate profits	7.7
Corporate profit tax liability	21.3
Corporate inventory valuation adjustment .... (−)1.1	
Contributions for social insurance	8.7
Plus:	
Net interest paid by government	5.0
Government transfer payments	12.8
Business transfer payments	1.2
Equals: *Personal Income*	$286.0 billion

The distribution of national income on a functional basis as analyzed previously can be presented only in an approximate form. Rent, interest, and profits are frequently merged in an income (e.g., small proprietor) and they cannot be shown separately. Wages and salaries, the largest item, usually represent about two-thirds of the total. The factoral distribution is as follows:

Compensation of employees	$209.2 billion
Proprietors' and rental income	48.4
Corporate profits and inventory valuation adjustments	37.2
Net interest	8.8
National Income	$303.6 billion

[1] For a detailed explanation of these items, see *Survey of Current Business*, July, 1955; and special supplement to the *Survey* entitled, "National Income and Product Statistics of the United States, 1929–1951," (1954 edition).

If from the personal income the personal tax and nontax payments are subtracted, the result is the *disposable personal income* or the amount individuals have to spend. Then, in turn, if from the disposable personal income the amount of personal consumption expenditures is subtracted, the difference represents the amount of personal savings. In 1953 personal income was $286.0 billions; personal tax and nontax payments, $35.8 billions; and disposable personal income, $250.2 billions. Expenditures on personal consumption were $230.5 billions which left $19.7 billions in personal savings.

These figures show the aggregate purchasing power of the entire economy. The higher the gross national product, the greater will be the personal income, although differences in taxes may make the amount of disposable personal income proportionally less. An increase, however, in dollar income does not necessarily measure the real purchasing power since prices may vary with changes in income.

Personal Distribution. The personal distribution of income indicates how the income is divided among spending units, that is, single consumers and families (all persons living in the same dwelling and belonging to the same family who pool their income to meet their major expenses). The concentration of income is decreasing slightly. In the highest income groups two-fifths of the spending units in 1935–1936 received about 74 per cent of the total money income; in 1953, only 67 per cent. Since some income in kind (e.g., food and fuel produced and consumed on farms) is not included, the inequality is overstated by a small amount. The inequality is also lessened if income after deduction of federal income tax is considered.

During World War II, there was a general shifting of spending units from lower to higher income groups. About one-half of all spending units received incomes under $1,000 in 1935–1936, about one-third in 1941, and about one-seventeenth in 1953. These increases do not mean that the spending units increased their purchasing power accordingly. Higher prices and taxes offset part of these gains.

Inequalities of Income. In spite of these shifts, the distribution of income is still markedly unequal. The top 10 per cent receives a third of the income, and 90 per cent the other two-thirds. The bottom 30 per cent of the spending units received only 10 per cent of the money income in 1953 or less than $3,000 per spending unit. Such inequalities have many political and economic consequences. Probably the most important consequence is the difficulty experienced by the masses of consumers to purchase, over a period of time, the goods which are produced for them. Over a period when incomes are increasing, there is the possibility that the savings and investment of the high-income groups expand too rapidly relative to spending, especially among the low-income groups. The readjustment in terms of falling prices, contracting savings and investment, and reduced income and employment may take the form of a major depression. The low-income group are unable to save and acquire property which maintains and perhaps increases the inequality in the distribution of income. In 1949 about 60 per cent of spending units had net savings, about 35 per cent had expenditures in excess of income, and the remainder about broke even. The first group saved about 23 billion dollars and the second group had a deficit of 14 billion dollars.

Causes of Inequality.

DIFFERENCES IN ABILITY. Individuals are not born with equal ability. Many individuals lack the physical energy and mental alertness essential to a high degree of productivity. To the extent that economic inequalities are the result of unequal abilities, society gains by rewarding the more capable individuals so that they will work with maximum efficiency. If individuals were given equal opportunity to develop their abilities, economic inequalities would probably be lessened, but great differences would still appear. Ability may or may not be inherited, but wealth and opportunity are inherited, and consequently some economic inequalities are not based on differences in ability. These differences in ability, however, are frequently difficult to ascertain.

NATURE OF INSTITUTIONS. The institutions of private property, inheritance, and free enterprise foster inequality in wealth and income distribution. Huge fortunes have been established and increased through the years because of unequal privileges or mere chance. Piracy and slave holding were the foundations for some of the first American fortunes. Real estate speculators, exploiters of mineral resources, patent holders, and producers of materials for the armies during the Civil and World Wars have built up huge fortunes. Most modern fortunes are made from large-scale production under corporate management in which the control of ownership is concentrated in the hands of a few individuals. Inheritance is a cumulative force which increases the already existing inequalities. The heirs of a large estate, which may have been built up because of exceptional ability, may be totally unfit to manage it, but under a capable and well-paid trustee their incomes may be maintained and even increased.

ECONOMIC FACTORS. The distribution of income may be affected by many economic factors. Unequal bargaining relations between employer and employees, between manufacturers and the sellers of raw materials, indeed, any inequalities arising from monopoly elements or imperfections in the market will influence the distribution of income. Changes in the price level may favor creditors or debtors depending on the direction of change. Tax policies may favor one income level against another. Tariff policies may affect adversely one section of the country as compared with another and thus influence the income received by that section.

Amelioration of Inequalities. Inequality may be lessened by modifying the amount of accumulated wealth, by decreasing large incomes especially from property, and by raising incomes in the lower income groups. The principle of inheritance is useful in a system of free enterprise as long as the family remains an important social unit—the provision for dependents stimulates initiative and thrift. Moderate inheritance taxes, however, do not interfere with initiative and capital accumulation, and they tend to lessen economic inequalities. Income taxes with moderately graduated rates perform the same function. Control of monopoly and the prevention of unfair competition are also important aids. Low income groups may be benefited by an increase in public health, recreation, and educational facilities. Minimum wage laws, social insurance, and restriction of immigration may aid this group. Birth control in defective and indigent families would tend to eliminate the unfit and inefficient.

NERAL REFERENCES

Bain, J⌿ *istribution and Employment.*

Bye, C *ent and Issues in the Theory of Rent.*

Dalto⌿ *Aspects of the Inequality of Incomes.*

Dobb⌿ *ges.*

Doug⌿ *eal Wages in the United States.*

—— *ory of Wages* (1934).

Dur⌿ *Wage Determination under Trade Unions.*

Ec⌿ *port of the President and the Annual Economic Review, 1951.*

Fi⌿ ng, *The Theory of Interest.*

G⌿ enry, *Progress and Poverty.*

G⌿ R. A., *Business Leadership in the Large Corporation.*

F⌿ ⌿. R., A. G. Hart, and J. W. Ford, *The Social Framework of the* ⌿erican Economy (2nd edition).

⌿n, J. A., *The Economics of Distribution.*

⌿s, J. M., *The General Theory of Employment, Interest, and Money.*

⌿ets, Simon, *National Income: A Summary of Findings.*

⌿s, Harry, and Emily C. Brown, *From the Wagner Act to Taft-Hartley.*

⌿lton, H. G., *Income and Economic Progress.*

⌿ional Bureau of Economic Research, *Studies in Income and Wealth.*

⌿ynolds, L. G., *The Structure of Labor Markets.*

⌿ggles, Richard, *An Introduction to National Income and Income Analysis.*

⌿rvey of Current Business, March, 1955, "Income Distribution in the United States."

Tawney, R. H., *Equality.*

Triffin, R., *Monopolistic Competition and General Equilibrium Theory.*

Wright, D. M., *A Key to Modern Economics.*

CHAPTER FOURTEEN

POPULATION PROBLEMS

IMPORTANCE OF POPULATION

The population of any country is an important economic factor because it is both the object for which goods are produced and the chief agent in producing them. Population changes necessarily lead to new economic problems and social adjustments. Both quantitative and qualitative considerations are involved in the economics of population. The former were the first to be studied historically because of the rather definite relationship between the labor supply and the size of the population. In recent years the qualitative aspects have been emphasized.

QUANTITATIVE ASPECTS OF POPULATION

The Concept of Optimum Population. The size of a country's population has meaning only when considered in relation to its other resources. Absolute numbers are of little importance unless related to natural resources and to the acquired skills and technology of the people. Britain with a population of 45 million is a wealthier and more productive nation than China with 450 million. A densely populated area like Puerto Rico may be considered "overpopulated" because of the poverty of its soil and the backwardness of its people. Another densely populated area like Belgium may not be considered "overpopulated" because of its high degree of industrialization and the advanced culture of its people.

The ratio of natural resources (those which man is able to utilize) to a given population determines how far the population can develop. There is a direct relationship between population and the principle of nonproportional returns. For each country there is a theoretical optimum population. The optimum may be defined as follows: for a given stage of the arts (technique of production) the optimum population for any given area is that which, when combined with the available resources, will yield the highest per capita production. Any increase in population beyond the optimum will cause a decrease in per capita output and a lower standard of living. A population lower than the optimum would mean that some natural resources could not be properly developed. Since an optimum size for any given population group varies with changes in the technique of production and other factors, such as the distribution of wealth and income, tariff policy, and age and sex distribution, no close approximation to an optimum population is attainable. A stationary population at the optimum is the ideal goal.

The Malthusian Theory of Population. The first serious quantitative analysis of population problems was that of Thomas Malthus, an English clergyman-economist, who published his "Essay on Population" in 1798. Malthus was writing in the early days of the Industrial Revolution when the population of England was increasing very rapidly and when the working and living conditions of the people were still extremely bad. His gloomy views simply reflected the depressing atmosphere of the times.

SUMMARY OF THE MALTHUSIAN THEORY. Malthus said that population was necessarily limited by the means of subsistence. The natural tendency was for population to increase at a faster rate than the means of subsistence, which meant that people were doomed to a marginal standard of living since any increase in the means of subsistence (principally food) would be absorbed by an increase in the population. (Population increased in a geometric ratio and subsistence in an arithmetic ratio according to Malthus.)

The checks which prevented population from increasing beyond subsistence, according to Malthus, were:

1) Preventive checks which operate to prevent new life from being born, e.g., moral restraint, late marriage, celibacy, or vice;

2) Positive checks which operate to eliminate life already in existence, e.g., famine, wars, disease, and extreme poverty.

EVALUATION OF THE MALTHUSIAN THEORY. Malthus' dire predictions have not been borne out by subsequent events so far as the Western World is concerned. The history of the past hundred years has shown that Malthus overestimated man's willingness to reproduce himself and that he underestimated man's ability to produce the means of subsistence. Since, in western countries, the means of subsistence has actually increased faster than the population, the standard of living, far from being constantly depressed to a minimum, has actually gone up. Malthus did not realize that the opening-up of new agricultural lands in the Western Hemisphere in the 19th century and the development of new agricultural techniques including the use of fertilizers and the application of agricul tural machinery, would lead to a vast expansion of food pr duction. Nor did he realize that preventive checks to popu tion increase would turn out to be so important. As standard of living of western countries has risen, the b rate has tended to fall for reasons that will be explained r in this chapter.

Although it is fashionable in some circles to consider M us outdated, his theory is nevertheless valid at the presen me as far as the Orient is concerned. In India and Chi for instance, the population has been increasing faster t the means of subsistence, and this increase is resulting in reme poverty among the people. In these countries there s not been the improvement in the arts of production whic iabled Western Europe and America to increase the mear f subsistence, nor have the preventive checks been o ing to reduce the birth rate. In the Orient Malthus' pos checks have unhappily been mainly responsible for elin ing the "surplus" population. In summary, therefore, it be said that Malthus' analysis is correct if one assumes progress in the arts of production and no development society's culture of the preventive checks to reproduction

Population Trends in Recent Times. Dv the Middle Ages the population of Europe increased rather slowly. Both birth and death rates were high. However, the gradual improvement in the techniques of industry and agriculture which began in the 17th century permitted a considerable increase in numbers. As a result of the Industrial Revolution, Europe's population more than doubled during the 19th century. The birth rate remained high at first while the death rate was reduced as a result of improved standards of living and advances in medical knowledge and public health. This widened gap between the birth and death rates was primarily responsible for the great natural increase in the size of the population. After the middle of the 19th century, however, the birth rate started to fall in all civilized countries, and the gap between it and the death rate has been progressively narrowed with the result that today the population of some countries, notably France, is stationary, whereas that of other countries, including the United States and Britain, is increasing only at a decreasing rate. The population of the Soviet Union is still increasing rather rapidly as a result of a high birth rate and a falling death rate. In Asia the birth and death rates are both very high, and the population is pressing on the means of subsistence.

There has been a remarkable increase in the population of the United States which is attributable partly to natural causes and partly to the high rate of immigration before World War I. In 1790, when the first census was taken, the population of the United States was 3,929,214; in 1860 it was 31,443,321; in 1900 it was 75,994,575; and in 1950 it was 151,700,000.

The rise in the birth rate following World War II was spectacular, but the long-run trend in the United States is toward a stationary population of about 250,000,000 which is expected to be reached before the end of the 20th century. The density of the population of the United States varies considerably from approximately 2 persons per square mile in Nevada to 650 persons per square mile in Rhode Island.

Net Changes in Population. Data dealing with changes in population are usually known as *vital statistics.* Changes in a given population may be effected by any one of the following factors or by any combination of them—births, deaths, immigration, or emigration.

BIRTH RATE. The crude birth rate is defined as the number of births per year per thousand of the population. Adjusted or corrected birth rates are defined as the number of births per thousand of the women of the population, or better, the number of births per year per thousand of the women of childbearing ages of the population. The birth rate in all civilized countries has shown a decline since the middle of the 19th century.

In the United States the birth rate stood at 17.9 per 1000 of the population in 1940, having fallen from 23.7 in 1920. There was a rise to 23.3 in 1946, but there is reason to believe that this was due to the abnormalities of the war and postwar periods and only a temporary interruption of the long-term trend. The birth rate in 1950 was 23.5.

Principal Causes of the Declining Birth Rate. There is a close relationship between the standard of living and the birth rate. As the standard of living in an area rises, the birth rate tends to fall. More and more families "plan" the size of their families to fit their incomes and to permit them to enjoy the material advantages of a society with a high level of production. This is made possible not only by the higher intelligence of the people which comes from improved education but also by the spread of knowledge regarding the use of contraceptives. Old taboos regarding birth control have been broken down in most civilized countries.

In countries with a high standard of living, women have been emancipated, and their desire for a career or at least for more social freedom has reduced their desire for children. The economic burden of rearing children has become increasingly heavy—the result of child labor laws, compulsory school attendance, and the pronounced shift in the United States from agriculture to industry.

The Differential Birth Rate. This is a system by which the birth rate is broken down on the basis of income groups, racial groups, occupational groups, etc. The differential birth rate thus presents a more detailed picture than the crude rate. In the United States, for instance, it shows that immigrant stock from south and eastern Europe have a higher birth rate than native-born, Anglo-Saxon stock, that rural families are larger than urban ones, and that lower income groups tend to have a higher birth rate than upper income groups.

THE DEATH RATE. The crude death rate is the number of deaths per year per thousand of the population. This disregards age groups, and a more accurate figure is obtained by finding the number of deaths per thousand of the population by different age groups. A series of such rates will show the higher rates to be in the very young and the very old groups.

The crude death rate stood at 10.8 per 1000 of the population in 1940, 9.6 in 1950, having fallen from 13.1 in 1920.

Infant Mortality. In western Europe and in the United States the death rate has been greatly lowered in the past hundred years. The greatest reduction has been in the rate of infant mortality. A high infant mortality rate frequently accompanies a high birth rate because both result from poverty, ignorance, and a low standard of living. Each reduction in the birth rate is accompanied by a decline in the infant mortality rate. It is higher in the lower income groups and probably lowest among the professional classes. The infant mortality rate in the United States (children under one year) has fallen from 85.8 deaths per 1000 live births in 1920 to 29.2 in 1950.

Adult Mortality. There has been no decline in the adult mortality rate comparable to that in the infant mortality rate. There has been, however, a remarkable reduction in the rate of adult mortality because of improved sanitation, lessening of industrial accidents, higher living standards, and improved medical practice. This reduction is very narrowly limited because after a certain point each additional reduction is made at greater cost and effort.

RATE OF NATURAL INCREASE. The net increase of population—that is, the survival rate—is the ratio of total births to deaths (total births minus total deaths). The survival rate has been increasing in spite of the declining birth rate, because while the birth rate has been falling, the rate of infant mortality has been falling still more sharply. It is evident that this cannot proceed much farther because as the birth rate continues to fall there will be fewer and fewer people in the lower age groups, and more and more in the higher age groups. Assuming that the average length of life cannot be extended much farther, the death rate will inevitably increase as the people in the middle age groups grow older and enter the higher age groups.

Experts estimate that 29 per cent of the population of the United States in 1975 will be over fifty years of age and 43.2 per cent under thirty as compared with 21.4 per cent over fifty now and 50.3 per cent under thirty now. In 1920 only 16 per cent of the population was over fifty and 58 per cent under thirty. This shift in age distribution will give rise to serious problems in connection with old age pension programs and will also cause shifts in the nature of the demand for goods (e.g., fewer bicycles and school buildings and more wheel chairs and eyeglasses).

QUALITATIVE POPULATION PROBLEMS

The Importance of Quality. Qualitative population problems were not considered important in a general way until the publication of Darwin's *Origin of Species* in 1859. In recent years, the fact that the masses of the population (who are still in the lower income groups) are continuing to expand in numbers while the higher income groups with better opportunities are decreasing, has drawn attention to the problem of quality.

RACIAL STOCK. Most sociologists are agreed that there are no inherent racial differences, but instead merely varying cultural characteristics acquired as a result of differences in economic and social status and opportunity. Nevertheless, in the popular mind the quality of the population is often associated with a desire to increase the birth rate among the "superior" groups (actually superior with regard to economic and social conditions) and to reduce it among the so-called "inferior" groups. Attitudes of this kind lay behind the discriminatory measures against immigrants of Latin and Slavic origin which were introduced in the Immigration Acts of 1920 and 1924.

RACE SUICIDE. Some writers believe that the continuous decline in the birth rate among the superior groups will lead to eventual race suicide. Other authorities say that this process has been going on for centuries and need cause no alarm. They argue that it stimulates the ambitions of the abler members of the lower classes to attain the top level. As the birth rate declines rapidly in the upper levels, there is room for some of those in the lower levels to move toward the top. Social heredity rather than personal heredity is stressed.

Eugenics. Sir Francis Galton in his work on heredity emphasized the qualitative aspects of the population problem and was the first to use the term *eugenics*. At the present time the term refers to the movement for attempting to improve the quality of the population by increasing the birth rate of superior groups and decreasing that of inferior groups. Eugenics may be either positive or negative.

POSITIVE EUGENICS. This program is based on the following assumptions:

1) Classes with the lowest birth rates are biologically the best. (This is not necessarily the case.)

2) Exceptional capacity is a family trait rather than an individual variation.

Positive eugenics often fails to distinguish cultural from biological characteristics—a biological improvement in the race would not necessarily result in social and cultural advance. If the distinction were possible, the problem of knowing what characteristics to develop is not easily solved.

The Hitler regime in Germany took some experimental steps in the direction of developing a Nordic "master race" which would dominate the "inferior" Jewish, Negro, Slav, and Latin peoples. While the Nazis were quite successful in rearing healthy young storm-troopers, it can hardly be said that social and cultural advances resulted.

NEGATIVE EUGENICS. The aim of negative eugenics is to stop, as far as possible, the increase of the biologically unfit, especially when it can be shown that the defect is hereditary. The methods include segregation, sterilization, and prohibitions of marriages among certain groups. Danger of bias is the greatest weakness of negative eugenics. To decide scientifically what characteristics should be regarded as hereditary and what practical plan should be adopted is difficult.

IMMIGRATION: A QUALITATIVE AND QUANTITATIVE PROBLEM

Immigration is the most recent form of the historical tendency of people to migrate from one region of the earth to another with the hope of raising their standard of living. Migration has taken the form of invasion, conquest, colonization, and immigration—the last two being characteristics of modern history. Migration has invariably been away from overpopulated areas toward newly-opened, underpopulated regions, from low-standard-of-living countries to those with higher standards of living.

Immigration has been particularly important in American history, the United States having received more immigrants in the space of one century than any other country in history. Immigration policy is therefore extremely important, dealing as it does not only with the total number of persons admitted as immigrants but also with their race, nationality, religion, economic status, etc.

Nature of Immigration into the United States.

From 1776 until 1820 only about 250,000 immigrants arrived in the United States. This small figure may be attributed partly to the lack of adequate transportation and partly to the various wars in Europe and the bans on emigration imposed by many countries there. Between 1820 and the virtual cessation of immigration around 1930, however, no less than thirty-seven million persons arrived in the United States. The peak of this vast movement of people was reached just before World War I when more than one million immigrants were being admitted to this country each year.

THE "OLD" IMMIGRATION. Until the middle 1880's the bulk of the immigrants came from the British Isles, Scandinavia, and Germany. These people pushed the frontier westward and developed agriculture. A large proportion of them were farmers and craftsmen.

THE "NEW" IMMIGRATION. From the end of the 1880's until the 1920's, when the gates were closed to mass immigration, the majority of the new arrivals came from southern and eastern Europe—principally Italy, the Balkans, Poland, and Russia. These persons were mainly unskilled workers who went to work in the factories and the mines. The frontier had been closed when they arrived, and agriculture relative to industry was declining in importance.

RECENT TRENDS. In recent decades only a trickle of immigrants has been admitted—mostly professional persons and intellectuals fleeing from totalitarian oppression. Since World War II the problem of nearly one million "displaced persons" in Europe has arisen. By special legislation (Displaced Persons Act of 1948 and amended in 1950) approximately 200,000 refugees have been admitted into the United States. A 1952 law brought together various restrictions of previous laws.

Immigration Policies of the United States. In the earlier period, when the United States was undeveloped and sparsely populated, the policy was to encourage immigration. The promise of political equality and economic opportunity was held out to all. With the exception of laws excluding Asiatics, contract labor, criminals, diseased persons, etc., passed towards the end of the 19th century, there were no serious restrictions on immigration into the United States until after World War I. The literacy test established in 1917 imposed only a mild qualitative restriction.

REASONS FOR ADOPTION OF IMMIGRATION RESTRICTIONS. The reasons for the reversal after World War I of the traditional free immigration policy were several and reflected the point of view of widely assorted groups. Labor unions saw in a continued influx of foreign labor ready to work for low wages a threat to their attempts to raise wages. A severe depression was experienced in 1920–1921 and many people thought that unemployed should not be subjected to the competition of immigrants in their search for jobs. Many felt that the "Anglo-Saxon" nature of the American "race" had already been "diluted" by the flood of Slavic and Latin peoples and that this "dilution" should be stopped. In addition the United States was just embarking on a decade to be characterized by isolationism.

NATURE OF THE RESTRICTIONS. Immigration restrictions were imposed through the quota system established by the acts of 1921 and 1924. The latter, with minor variations prior to 1929, limits total immigration per year to 150,000 with each country receiving an annual quota of immigrants calculated with reference to the number of persons of that national origin in the United States in 1920. The act does not apply to the independent countries of the Americas; Asiatics are excluded by other measures. The act provides large quotas for the countries of northwest Europe, whose citizens are not interested in coming to the United States in large numbers; but relatively small quotas are given to countries of southern and eastern Europe whose citizens were eager to come. The British have an annual quota of 65,721 although in 1939, for instance, only 2,828 Britons migrated to the United States. Hungary, on the other hand, receives an annual quota of only 869 and Greece of only 307. Since one country's unused quotas cannot be transferred to another country, the total number of immigrants has never reached the maximum permitted by law.

When the depression came in 1929, the quota system was reinforced by administrative restrictionism under which an immigration visa would not be granted, even if a quota number were obtained, unless the immigrant could show that he would not become a public charge in the United States. This form of restriction can be applied against citizens of Western Hemisphere countries who are not subject to the quota law. So stringently were the laws applied that in 1932, for the first time in American history, emigration actually exceeded immigration. Since 1924 the number of nonquota immigrants was almost as large as the number of quota immigrants.

The days of mass immigration into the United States are gone forever. There are still possibilities of migration from densely populated European areas to South American countries and to Australia; such population movements will probably have to be financed and organized by the governments concerned.

GENERAL REFERENCES

Bowen, Ian, *Population.*

Cook, R. C., *Human Fertility: The Modern Dilemma.*

Davis, Kingsley, *The Pattern of World Urbanization.*

Field, J. A., *Essays on Population and Other Papers.*

Isaac, Julius, *Economics of Migration.*

Jenks, J. W., and W. J. Lauck, *The Immigration Problem.*

Landis, P. H., and P. K. Hatt, *Population Problems* (2nd edition).

Lorimer, F., and F. Osborn, *Dynamics of Population.*

Malthus, T. R., *An Essay on the Principle of Population* (6th edition).

Smith, Thomas L., *Population Analysis.*

Thompson, W. S., *Population Problems.*

Willcox, Walter F., ed., *International Migrations.*

Wright, H., *Population.*

CHAPTER FIFTEEN

AGRICULTURAL PROBLEMS

THE IMPORTANCE OF AGRICULTURE

The products of agriculture feed the nation and supply its industry with raw materials. Farmers and their families constitute an important minority of the population. Unless the farmer receives an income comparable to that of nonfarm workers, his buying power is curtailed. This reduces the market for industrial products and can result in serious depression. The prosperity of the nation depends upon the maintenance of a balanced relationship between agriculture on the one hand and industry and other urban pursuits on the other. The absence of such a balance is an indication that the factors of production of the nation are not being directed into their most productive channels. The "agricultural problem" arises principally from the fact that, for the past thirty years, there has been a serious lack of balance between the supply of agricultural products and the demand for them.

THE POSITION OF AGRICULTURE IN THE ECONOMY

The Relation of Farm Income to General Income. The vast majority of farmers receive very low incomes, both in absolute terms and in relation to those of nonfarm workers. In the mid-thirties, for instance, no less than 75 per cent of the six million farmers not on relief received incomes of $1,500 a year or less, and six hundred thousand farm families were actually on relief. Although many farm families do receive some nonmonetary income in the form of foodstuffs produced at home, this is not true, for instance, of cotton-growing sharecroppers in the South. Also farm families tend to be larger than urban families, a fact which further emphasizes the income disparity. Farm incomes tend to fall very low in times of depression because of the inelastic demand for many agricultural products and the fact that the fall in prices does not usually result in any significant decrease in output. Farmers have traditionally been in favor of "easy money" policies since such policies tend to raise farm prices. The Populist movement in the late 19th century and the support given by farmers to more recent legislation for the purchase of silver to increase the monetary supply are evidence of this attitude.

The Relation of Agricultural Population to Nonfarm Population. The agricultural population in general suffers from inferior medical and educational facilities and poor housing. The latter is characterized by a noticeable lack of such conveniences as electricity, bathtubs, and indoor toilets. The majority of the farm population is not covered by the social security legislation enjoyed by urban dwellers, such as minimum wage laws, workmen's compensation, old age pensions, and unemployment insurance. Although there has been a general drift of farm dwellers to the cities, this relative decline in the number of farm workers has not resulted in a decrease in production since it has been offset by increased mechanization and other improvements in technology. In times of depression, rural distress is often aggravated by the development of a counter-drift from the city to the country. It may be said, therefore, that the high degrees of inelasticity in the supply of agricultural labor hinders the downward adjustment of agricultural production in the face of declining demand.

The Land Factor. Land, of course, is one of the most important factors of production in agriculture. There are few other uses to which farm land can be put, so its withdrawal from production in the face of a declining demand is slow. Since the supply of land is inelastic, agricultural depressions have been characterized in the past by a collapse, and booms by an inflation, of land values. These fluctuations have helped make agriculture an unstable industry.

The Importance of Fixed Costs. A large part of a farmer's costs of production are relatively fixed and nonpostponable, such as interest on mortgage debt and property taxes. These costs become a heavy burden when farm income falls during a depression. Production is continued during a depression because such fixed costs must be covered in order to avoid loss of ownership. Often, production is actually increased in order that the same total income may be received even though prices have fallen. This expansion, of course, only leads to a further fall in prices.

The Relationship between Agricultural Prices and Industrial Prices.

Industry and the urban population are the principal markets for agricultural produce, and the instability of farm prices is in part due to the changes in demand brought about by business fluctuations. Instability is due in part also to two other factors: (1) fluctuations in yield which are brought about principally by changes in weather conditions and which can cause considerable changes in supply even though acreage does not change and (2) the time lag in the response of production to changes in demand. The latter is caused by the length of the production period in agriculture and the seasonal nature of production.

The ratio of farm prices to the prices of other commodities represents the real purchasing power of the farmer's dollar. During the past thirty years this real purchasing power has tended to decline. Actually, however, parity of income rather than parity of prices is the significant index of farm prosperity since prices without quantities sold tell nothing about gross income. The growing spread between the level of farm prices and the level of other prices during the interwar period may be partly attributed to the prevalence of semicompetitive and monopolistic prices in industry.

Government measures to improve the relative position of farmers in the economy have to take the form of various kinds of subsidies paid either by consumers or by taxpayers. They can be justified on the grounds that all persons in low income groups should be helped regardless of their occupation, or on the grounds that special aid is accorded to other groups (e.g., tariffs to help industry, minimum wage laws to help labor) and therefore farmers merit aid too, or on the grounds that the very nature of farming makes it an erratic, insecure industry worthy of help, or on the sociological grounds that a healthy prosperous farm population is essential to the nation. At all events, farmers have demanded and got in recent years a high degree of government assistance.

The Importance of International Trade to Farmers. Normally a large part of the annual production of important farm products, such as wheat, cotton, and tobacco, has to be sold in foreign markets. Experience has shown that farm surpluses tend to accumulate unless a healthy flow of international trade is maintained. The loss of foreign markets reduces farm incomes, which in turn reduces farmers' purchasing power in domestic markets. The establishment of the Food and Agriculture Organization of the United Nations and the continuation of the Reciprocal Trade Agreement Program are evidence of a growing realization that American farm problems cannot be solved by domestic measures alone but only within the framework of a world economy. American farmers producing commodities for export have traditionally been in favor of low tariffs; others, producing such things as fruits and dairy produce, which are more subject to the competition of imports, have been more in favor of protection.

THE AGRICULTURAL DEPRESSION, 1920–1940

Agriculture never really prospered between 1920 and 1940. Even during the prosperity period of the 1920's, farmers were dissatisfied and were demanding government aid. The causes may be found in an analysis of long-run factors to which must be added the effects of catastrophes, such as World War I and the Great Depression.

Long-run Supply and Demand. The supply of agricultural products in the United States has for some time tended to increase at a faster rate than the demand for them.

The slowing-down in demand may be attributed partly to the declining rate of population increase and partly to the failure of industrial output to expand as rapidly as formerly. The population of the United States increased by 21 per cent between 1900 and 1910 but only by 7 per cent between 1930 and 1940. Industrial output increased by 150 per cent between 1895 and 1915 but only by 50 per cent between 1919 and 1939. In addition, as the national income has risen, a relatively smaller portion of it has been spent on necessities like bread and cotton clothing and a larger portion has been devoted to luxuries and savings. Demand for American farm products has also been reduced by the expansion of production in other countries which in many instances has been assisted by subsidies and tariffs.

The supply of agricultural products has been increased by improved technology, especially the development of new farm machinery; by the progress made in developing new types of crops; and by other improvements resulting in a greater yield per acre. In addition, irrigation projects and soil conservation measures have succeeded in opening up new areas for cultivation.

The tendency for increases in supply to outstrip increase in demand has produced a downward pressure on farm prices and incomes and an accumulation of agricultural surpluses. At the same time, as already stated, the relative immobility of the factors of production used in agriculture has made an adjustment to the situation by reallocation of the factors extremely difficult. The farm population of the United States was only a little over one million less in 1939 than it had been in 1920.

The Effect of World War I. There is evidence that before 1914 American agriculture was adjusting itself to a less important position in the economy. World War I, however, generated an artificial inflation of demand for American agricultural products which forced prices up to record heights and produced a corresponding expansion of output. The demands, however, of European allies and the U. S. armed forces during the war and of foreign relief for devastated areas afterwards was only temporary, and disappeared after 1920 leaving American farmers with an inflated capacity to produce. Farm prices fell catastrophically. Farmers found themselves not only deprived of markets but also burdened with heavy mortgage debts contracted during the boom. The fact that the rest of the nation was prospering during the 1920's tended to obscure the seriousness of the farmers' position.

The Great Depression. The Great Depression, which began in 1929, naturally reduced the demand for farm products. The national income of the United States was not brought back to its 1929 level again until the defense boom of 1941. It is not surprising, therefore, that the 1930's were characterized by huge farm surpluses and low prices.

Tariffs and International Trade. The interwar period was one of growing economic nationalism, and American farmers were among the worst sufferers from this trend. Tariffs, quotas, and other barriers to international trade imposed by other nations deprived the farmer of his foreign markets, whereas the rising American tariff lessened his real income by increasing his costs of production and his living expenses. The foreign markets for American farm products were also decreased because the purchasing power of other countries was lessened by their inability to sell to the United States.

Growth of Industrial Monopoly. The further growth of monopoly in American business between World Wars I and II resulted in a growing inflexibility in industrial prices and often in their maintenance at higher levels than would have prevailed in competitive markets. This reduced the real purchasing power of the farmer's dollar. When the depression came in 1929, the disparity between farm and industrial prices was intensified, for industrial prices fell much less than farm prices. In addition, competing farmers often found themselves dealing with monopolies or semimonopolies in the field of processing and distribution. Milk marketing is a good example.

Freight Rates. Freight rates were increased after World War I at a time when farm prices were falling. Since transportation is an important item in the cost of marketing, this had a deleterious effect on farmers.

Changes in Dietary Habits. Changes in dietary habits have taken place in recent years. Nutrition experts now place less emphasis on basic starch foods, such as wheat and potatoes, and more on protective foods, such as dairy produce, fruits, and vegetables. This shift necessitates a corresponding shift in the pattern of production which has, however, tended to lag, thus causing an imbalance between the supply and demand for individual commodities.

Development of Substitutes. The development of synthetic materials has tended to reduce the demand for certain agricultural products. Cotton, for instance, is being replaced in part by rayon and nylon.

THE GOVERNMENT AND AGRICULTURE

Before the Great Depression, government intervention in the field of agriculture was limited to such things as the provision of cheap farm credit and the operation of agricultural experiment stations and the extension service. Since 1933, however, large-scale intervention has taken place for broader purposes which include supporting prices, supplementing farm incomes, planning production acreage, and disposing of surpluses. Although farmers are among the most individualistic of citizens, government participation in the industry is not likely to be reduced.

Farm Credit and Finance.

FARM CREDIT ADMINISTRATION. In order to handle farm loans more effectively, all federal agricultural credit agencies were consolidated in 1933 into a single agency known as the Farm Credit Administration. These included the Twelve Federal Land Banks (organized in 1916), which are owned by about 3200 co-operative national farm loan associations and which supply long-term mortgage loans (five to forty years) to association members, and the Twelve Federal Intermediate Credit Banks (established in 1923), which supply loans ranging from one to three years. In addition, twelve production credit corporations were established and supplied with government funds to be loaned to local production credit associations. Finally, a Central Bank for co-operatives and twelve regional banks lend to co-operatives for aid in orderly marketing.

FARM SECURITY ADMINISTRATION. The FSA, an outgrowth of the emergency Resettlement Administration, was established in 1937 for the specific purpose of helping low income and underprivileged farmers. Its activities have been numerous and have included such things as the granting of long-term rehabilitation loans to sharecroppers, the provision of community services in backward rural areas, caring for migrant farm workers, and education in better farming methods. It has performed particularly useful work in the South. In 1946 the FSA and the Emergency Crop and Feed Loan Division of the FCA were combined to form the Farmers' Home Administration.

FEDERAL FARM MORTGAGE CORPORATION. This agency was established in 1934 at a time when a wave of mortgage foreclosures and evictions was sweeping the country. It was authorized to use its two hundred million dollar capital supplied by the government and its maximum bond issue of two billion dollars guaranteed by the government for the purpose of refinancing farm mortgages and preventing foreclosures and evictions by private citizens.

Federal Farm Board, 1929–1933. The main purpose of the Agricultural Marketing Act of 1929 was to promote co-operative marketing and bring about orderly production and distribution of farm products. Actually, the stabilization operations of the Federal Farm Board, which it established, turned out to be of greater importance. This Board, through loans to co-operatives and also through special buying operations of its own in wheat and cotton, attempted to correct temporary fluctuations in price by holding surpluses off the market until better times. Since no controls were exercised over production, supply not only did not decrease; it actually increased! Prices fell to even lower levels. The Federal Farm Board was liquidated in 1933 with an estimated loss of $350,000,000.

Production Controls.

FIRST AGRICULTURAL ADJUSTMENT PROGRAM, 1933–1936. As a result of the failure of the Federal Farm Board, the first Roosevelt administration decided that production controls were necessary to eliminate surpluses. The first Agricultural Adjustment Act of 1933 therefore established a program of production restriction to be achieved by paying farmers to reduce output. This restriction in supply was intended to raise the prices of basic farm commodities (cotton, wheat, corn, hogs, rice, tobacco, milk, cattle, and sugar) until they reached "parity," which was described as being that level which would give the farmer's dollar the same real purchasing power in terms of nonfarm products as it had had in the years 1909–1914. (To calculate "parity" the index numbers for both farm and nonfarm prices in the base period, 1909–1914, are assumed to be 100. Thus if nonfarm prices should rise by 20 per cent, making the nonfarm price index 120, farm prices would also have to be raised until their index reached 120, if parity was to be maintained. If the government decided to support farm prices at only 90 per cent of parity, however, farm prices would only have to be raised until their index was 108.) The money needed to finance this program was raised by a tax levied on the first processors of the commodities covered. Because of this method of financing, the Supreme Court declared the act unconstitutional in 1936.

An evaluation of the first AAA is difficult. Prices did rise and farm incomes were increased during the period of its operation, but how far this was due to the act and how far to the disastrous droughts which reduced supply is difficult to say. From an emergency point of view and taking into account the lack of experience in agricultural planning at the time, the first AAA was justifiable in the short run. But from a long-run point of view the creation of artificial scarcity in the face of widespread human need, as evidenced by the killing of little pigs and the plowing under of every third row of cotton, is both economically and morally indefensible.

SOIL CONSERVATION ACT, 1936. This act attempted to continue production control under the guise of soil conservation, which was certainly much needed. The government might pay bonuses (not to exceed five hundred million dollars a year) to farmers who grew specified crops considered favorable to soil conservation. Since this usually involved an extension of grass acreage at the expense of basic crops, production control was continued in a disguised form. This was essentially a stopgap measure.

THE SECOND AGRICULTURAL ADJUSTMENT PROGRAM, 1938– . The second AAA continued the idea of production control. The Secretary of Agriculture was authorized to fix acreage allotments for basic crops each year in order to regulate supply in accordance with the needs of the "ever-normal granary." This program was to take care of yearly needs plus adequate reserve stocks in the event of shortages. Reinforcing this were marketing quotas which were to be enforced if two-thirds of the producers of a particular crop voted for their establishment. After the entry of the United States into World War II, stimulation of production took the place of restriction, but the power of control still exists.

Commodity Loans and Parity Payments.

COMMODITY LOANS. The Commodity Credit Corporation was established in 1933 for the purposes of bringing about a rise in agricultural prices over the years and stabilizing those prices against undue variations in supply and demand. The assumption was that it would be more successful than the Federal Farm Board in this respect since its activities were backed up by the AAA's production control. The method used took the form of nonrecourse loans to farmers who pledged their crops as security. If the market price fell below the level established in the loan (the level was gradually raised to 90 per cent of parity in 1942 for most crops and even higher for cotton), the farmer simply turned his crop over to the CCC which bore the loss. If the market price rose above the loan level, the farmer repaid the loan and kept the extra amount as profit. The system thus in effect established a floor under farm prices but no ceiling over them. In this way the CCC accumulated huge stocks of basic commodities which the war demand liquidated.

PARITY PAYMENTS. Direct payments to supplement farmers' incomes when they are below parity were authorized by Congress. The largest amount appropriated was $253,694,000 in 1943. In general, the support program of 1938 was used to lessen sharp declines in prices, not to prevent declines when surpluses persisted. The supports were low and flexible, 52 to 75 per cent of parity. The larger the crop-surplus, the lower were the supports in order to discourage planting. The losses during the first three years' operation of the 1938 act were less than $50 million—a modest amount by recent standards.

Development of Foreign Markets.

RECIPROCAL TRADE AGREEMENT PROGRAM. Since 1934 the State Department has pursued a policy of trying to expand the market for American exports, particularly farm products, by negotiating trade agreements with foreign countries which involve a mutual reduction of tariff barriers. There is evidence that American farmers have derived considerable benefit from this policy even though the Department of Agriculture's policy of trying to raise farm prices has hardly been in accord with the State Department's desire to develop foreign markets.

EXPORT SUBSIDIES. After spending a great deal of money to raise domestic farm prices, the Department of Agriculture found it necessary on several occasions to subsidize exports of wheat and cotton in order to bring down their sale price in foreign markets. Export subsidies are uneconomic and a fertile source of international friction.

INTERNATIONAL ORGANIZATIONS. The United States took the lead in establishing the Food and Agriculture Organization at the Hot Springs Conference in 1943. This organization is trying to co-ordinate the policies of agricultural producers and consumers and to develop an orderly world marketing system for agricultural commodities. Its aim is to avoid a recurrence of the situation in the 1930's when surpluses persisted in some countries while the people of others went hungry. The United States is also trying to expand the program of reciprocal trade agreements which will reduce the barriers to world trade. American farmers can benefit from both the FAO and the reciprocal trade agreements.

Other Government Action. The federal government operates agricultural experiment stations and an extension service which makes the fruits of scientific research freely available to all farmers. Since 1939 it has operated a crop insurance plan to protect farmers against the vagaries of the weather. During the 1930's the Federal Surplus Commodities Corporation disposed of some food surpluses by direct relief grants to needy families and by establishment of the "food-stamp" plan, which enabled needy families to buy with special stamps certain surplus commodities from private stores. The stamps were issued to supplement relief grants and were redeemed from the stores by the government. For once surpluses were dumped at home instead of abroad.

AGRICULTURE IN WORLD WAR II AND AFTER

The defense boom, the lend-lease program, and finally the entry of the United States into a global war once again generated a tremendous demand for agricultural products. The whole government program of the 1930's was thrown into reverse and every effort was made not to restrict but to stimulate production. The CCC's accumulated stocks, with the exception of cotton, were disposed of, and eventually food rationing and a priorities system had to be introduced because of shortages even though overall production was expanded to a point about one-third above the prewar level. Price ceilings were established to prevent a repetition of the inflation of World War I.

The Steagall Amendment. In May, 1941, price-support was extended to the so-called "Steagall commodities" (which included milk, potatoes, soybeans, peanuts, etc.), and in October, 1942, the production of essential commodities for the war effort was encouraged by the raising of the parity loan rate to 90 per cent. In order to prevent a letdown in prices after the war, the support of both basic crops and "Steagall commodities" was guaranteed until the end of a two-year period beginning on the January 1 following the end of hostilities. This period expired on December 31, 1948, but Congress extended it and provided additional provisions in 1949. Wages paid by the farmer for hired labor were included with other farm "buying prices" in the parity formula and the latter was based on a ten-year sliding average instead of on the years 1909–1914. Flexible price supports on basic commodities (except tobacco at 90) were adopted (75 to 90 per cent of parity). But Congress reconsidered and continued the 90 per cent.

Postwar Inflation. During the early years of the postwar period the demand for farm products continued high, stimulated by full employment at home and relief and reconstruction demands abroad. Later, increasing farm productivity, slackening demand abroad, rigidity of supports, and the CCC's acquisition of record-stocks induced Congress (1954) to fix 82.5 to 90 per cent of parity (5 basic crops) for 1955 and 75 to 90 thereafter.

Careful planning will be necessary in order to avoid another agricultural depression. Among other things, full employment will have to be maintained at home; trade barriers will have to be reduced and international planning of production and consumption through the FAO will have to be resorted to; and domestic price support, acreage allotments, and stabilization schemes will have to be continued. Co-operative marketing along the lines of the California Fruit Growers' Exchange should be encouraged among farmers. Government planning is necessary in agriculture in order that a stable framework may be established within which private enterprise may operate. In this case, at least, government planning and private enterprise are complementary rather than competitive.

GENERAL REFERENCES

Baird, Frieda, and Claude L. Benner, *Ten Years of Federal Intermediate Credits.*

Black, J. D., *Agricultural Reform in the United States.*

———, *The Dairy Industry and the AAA.*

Davis, H. A., *Wheat and the AAA.*

Dowell, A. A., and O. B. Jenness, *The American Farmer and the Export Market.*

Johnson, D. Gale, *Trade and Agriculture.*

Nourse, Edwin G., *American Agriculture and the European Market.*

Robertson, C. J., *World Sugar Production and Consumption.*

Rowe, H. B., *Tobacco under the AAA.*

Schultz, Theodore W., *Agriculture in an Unstable Economy.*

———, *Production and Welfare of Agriculture.*

Shepherd, Geoffrey S., *Agricultural Price Control.*

Temporary National Economic Committee, Monograph No. 23, *Agriculture and the National Economy.*

Timoshenko, V. P., *World Agriculture and the Depression.*

Warren, G. F., and F. A. Pearson, *The Agricultural Situation.*

CHAPTER SIXTEEN

LABOR PROBLEMS

THE LABOR MOVEMENT

Growth of Labor Organization. Trade-unionism originated in Britain—an inevitable concomitant of the modern industrial system. Beginning in the 18th century, the Industrial Revolution took individuals from agriculture and home industries and concentrated them in large numbers in cities where they worked in factories. A new social class of propertyless workers was created—men and women who sold their labor services to employers who owned the new machines and other means of production. Low wages, abominable working and living conditions, and social distress were general in industrial areas in the 19th century. Since an individual worker was in no position to bargain with his employer, workers in different trades gradually established organizations for the purpose of taking collective action to improve their lot. In all walks of life men with common interests organize for the purpose of furthering those interests. This is true of businessmen (National Association of Manufacturers, Chambers of Commerce, trade associations), veterans (American Legion), farmers (the Grange, National Farmers Union), doctors (American Medical Association), and economists (American Economic Association) to mention only a few. Similarly, workers in different crafts and industries have formed labor unions. Through organization labor has the strength of concerted action, and the result has been to raise the level of consumption and promote industrial democracy.

Although labor unions were at first regarded as criminal conspiracies (prior to 1825 in Britain) and were subjected to various legal restrictions, these obstacles were gradually removed, and by World War I European labor unions were powerful forces in politics. The British Labor Party was formed as the political organ of the British labor movement and receives its greatest support from the Trades Union Congress. It has also gained the support of socialists in other walks of life and in 1945 won an overwhelming victory in the general election, after which it became engaged in an ambitious program of nationalization of basic industries. In 1947 nearly all advanced countries, with the exception of the United States and Canada, had left-wing (semisocialistic) governments, drawing their main support from the labor movement. They included France, Italy, Sweden, Belgium, Australia, New Zealand, and Japan. Even in the United States the labor unions were a powerful force in politics.

Late Development of Unions in the United States. The labor movement was relatively late in developing in the United States. This may be attributed in part to the fact that for the greater part of the 19th century agriculture was more important than industry. The United States was a young expanding country in which opportunities for the individual were almost limitless. The general social and economic situation did not favor collective action. In addition, the continuous influx of immigrants, many of them not speaking English and anxious to take any job, made organization of workers difficult. There were numerous legal obstacles in the way of labor organization; labor unions were legal, but many of their activities were not formally sanctioned, e.g., collective bargaining; the courts were unsympathetic; and soldiers were often used to break strikes. In the famous Danbury Hatters' case (1908), labor unions were held subject to an act which had been passed in 1890 to deal with monopolies in business—the Sherman Antitrust Act which prohibited "conspiracies and contracts in restraint of trade."

Finally, employers had a whole arsenal of legal and nonlegal weapons at their disposal to prevent unions from achieving their goals. These included the *blacklist*—that is, lists of union sympathizers which were circulated among employers who would then refuse such persons employment; the *yellow-dog contract,* under which an employee was compelled by his employer to agree not to join a union as a condition of getting a job; the *injunction,* a court order obtained by the employer which restrained the union from a wide range of activities considered necessary for the successful operation of a strike; the *lockout,* in which the employer closed his plant and tried to starve the workers into submission; and *physical force,* union members and sympathizers being beaten up and terrorized by hired thugs and professional strikebreakers.

Growth of Labor Unions since 1932. The greatest period of growth in the history of the American labor movement came after 1932. This was a result of the favorable legislation passed in the '30's, the friendly attitude of the New Deal Administration, and the public's readiness (because of the depression) for economic change. In 1947 labor unions had a total membership of fifteen to sixteen million workers.

NORRIS-LAGUARDIA ACT, 1932. This act drastically limited the ability of employers to get court injunctions against union activities. Unions were thus enabled to plan and organize strikes, picketing, and other activities without fear of being enjoined to cease and desist by the courts. The act also outlawed the yellow-dog contract and thus removed another obstacle in the way of organization.

NATIONAL LABOR RELATIONS (WAGNER) ACT, 1935. This act, passed after the invalidation of the National Industrial Recovery Act, which had contained a clause guaranteeing the right of collective bargaining, was a landmark in labor history. It has been called labor's "Magna Carta" and has been responsible for a tremendous expansion of union membership. Briefly, the Wagner Act compelled an employer under pain of severe penalties to bargain in good faith with a union when it was certified as a bargaining unit representing the workers by the National Labor Relations Board. The NLRB, the administrative unit established under the act, was empowered to conduct plant elections to determine which union, if any, the workers wished to represent them. Employers were also prohibited from a number of so-called "unfair labor practices," such as interfering with the organization of a union and discriminating against union sympathizers in hiring or promotional policies. The NLRB also acted as judge and jury in that it could hear complaints about alleged violations of the act and issue judgments which could be upheld in federal courts. For instance, the NLRB could order the reinstatement of a worker wrongfully fired for union activities. Important features of the Wagner Act have been changed by the Labor-Management Relations Act of 1947 (the Taft-Hartley Act).

ATTITUDE OF ADMINISTRATION AND COURTS. During the New Deal, labor leaders had considerable influence in the government at Washington. The Roosevelt Administration made no secret of its sympathetic policy toward labor organizations as an offset to powerful business interests. The Supreme Court, too, after its "liberalization" in the late '30's, delivered many decisions favorable to organized labor. After World War II labor began to lose its influence in the national government, but by that time unions had become a great political and economic power in the land.

Organizational Features of the American Labor Movement.

In the 1870's and 1880's the Knights of Labor attempted and failed to unite the whole mass of workers, regardless of their trade, into a great industrial union. The main development of local and national labor organizations on a permanent basis was in the form of craft or trade unions. Unionism among unskilled workers, or a combination of unskilled and skilled workers, developed slowly.

AMERICAN FEDERATION OF LABOR. The AF of L was founded in 1881 and is the oldest of the big labor organizations in the United States. It is primarily a loose federation of national craft unions, organizations of skilled workers in a single trade or several closely related trades, who unite on the basis of their common skill regardless of the industry. Local craft unions are federated into city councils and state and national organizations, the national organizations belonging to the AF of L. Each craft union has control over its own policies and problems affecting all members. AF of L unions are mainly in the building trades, local transport services, the printing trades, and coal mining. The AF of L is a relatively conservative organization. It does not support any political party in national affairs, but operates on an economic level supporting labor's friends in Congress and opposing its enemies. Since 1933 the AF of L has more than doubled its size and by 1947 had over seven million members.

CONGRESS OF INDUSTRIAL ORGANIZATIONS. The CIO originated as the Committee for Industrial Organization formed within the AF of L by a group of labor leaders who were dissatisfied with the practices and policies of the AF of L. They wished to organize industrial unions—that is, organizations of all workers in a particular industry, skilled or unskilled, and regardless of craft. In 1936 these "rebels," including John L. Lewis and David Dubinsky, were expelled from the AF of L and formed the CIO. Lewis and the United Mine Workers returned to the AF of L in 1946. They withdrew again in December, 1947, when the organization refused to support Lewis' defiance of noncommunist affidavits required by the Taft-Hartley Act. The CIO has organized mass production industries, such as steel, automobile, glass, and rubber. In 1950 its total membership of about six million was considerably reduced through expulsion of six left-wing unions.

THE RAILROAD BROTHERHOODS. The railroad workers of America have their own powerful unions which have never affiliated with either of the two major groups. The railroad unions include the Brotherhood of Railway Trainmen and the Brotherhood of Locomotive Engineers. Total membership of all the operating and nonoperating railway unions is approximately half a million. The railroad workers not only have their own unions but also have their own pension plan under the Railroad Retirement Board and their own government machinery for the settlement of labor-management disputes. The latter was established by the Railway Labor Act of 1926.

There are a few other independent unions which have not affiliated with either the AF of L or the CIO, e.g., the telephone workers' union and the watchmakers' union. Company unions are now presumably independent. In 1947 probably one and a half million workers belonged to independent labor organizations.

COMPANY UNIONS. Company unions are composed of workers employed by a single plant or company. Formerly they were often dominated by management, but the Wagner Act prevented a company union from being used by management to exclude a truly independent union. The employee's organization of Standard Oil of New Jersey is an example of a successful company union not dominated by management.

OTHER LABOR GROUPS. There are some smaller labor groups, such as the Industrial Workers of the World, famous a generation ago as the "Wobblies" and who are associated with radical utopianism. A substantial majority of American employees, however, belong to no union. This is particularly true of workers in agriculture, domestic service, and clerical occupations.

Aims and Accomplishments of Labor Unions in the United States.

MEMBERSHIP AND UNION SECURITY. The primary aim of any union is to acquire members, achieve recognition, and establish as complete a monopoly as possible over the supply of labor to employers. Membership drives and union recognition, formerly difficult to carry out and achieve, have been encouraged and facilitated since 1935 by the Wagner Act machinery. Membership in unions has increased more than fourfold since that date—that is, from approximately three and a half million to about fifteen million.

Closed Shop. The most complete form of union security is the agreement for a closed shop under which only union men may be hired by an employer. Over 3,350,000 workers were covered by closed shop agreements in 1947. If the union is an open one and new members may join without restrictions, then certain advantages may result from a closed shop. The main ones are the stability in contractual relationships between labor and management and the inability of nonunion members to take advantages of concessions won by the union for its members without sharing the sacrifices. If, however, the union is a closed union and limits its membership by enforcing long apprenticeship or by charging high initiation fees, then a closed shop can result in an undesirable labor monopoly. Until the passing of the Labor-Management Relations Act which put an outright ban on the closed shop, thirteen states (not including any important industrial state) had laws specifically banning the closed shop.

Union Shop. In a union shop, the employer may hire anyone he pleases, but the new worker must join the union within a certain specified time. The Labor-Management Relations Act permits a union shop only when the majority of workers in a plant vote for one. In 1947 over four million workers were covered by union shop agreements.

Maintenance of Membership. This was a type of union security introduced during World War II as a compromise so that the closed shop issue could be held in abeyance during hostilities. After the signing of a contract between the union and management, the worker was allowed a certain period of time (usually fifteen days) to make up his mind about his membership in the union. If he did not quit the union during the period of grace, he had to maintain his membership for the full period of the contract. If he did quit the union, he could still keep his job. Almost 3,700,000 workers were covered by this type of arrangement in 1947.

HIGHER WAGES. Higher wages are sought by unions, and the degree of success usually depends on the degree of monopoly over the supply of labor and the financial strength of the union if a strike is called on the pay-issue. Unions have been very successful in the last ten years in getting more money for their members. The average earnings of a coal miner, for instance, for a forty-hour week have risen from $39.14 in May, 1941, to $52.14 in May, 1947; those of an automobile worker from $39.16 to $59.56; and those of a worker in the women's clothing industry from $21.56 to $51.88. In recent years, wage increases have tended to follow national patterns laid down by the leading unions and corporations. For instance, the 1946-wage-increase pattern of 18½ cents an hour in hourly rates was set by the General Motors-United Automobile Workers agreement although only after a costly strike. In 1947 the wage pattern of 15 cents an hour increase was set by the United Steel Workers-U. S. Steel Corporation agreement. Recently the question of an annual wage has begun to assume some importance—that is, some unions are seeking a guarantee from employers of a minimum amount of work and wages per year.

UNION DUES CHECK-OFF. One way in which the union can keep control over its members and assure itself of funds is through an agreement for the compulsory check-off of union dues. Under such an agreement the employer deducts the workers' dues from their paychecks and hands them over to the union treasury before the workers receive their pay. This has been a very common procedure. The Labor-Management

Relations Act, however, permits the check-off of a worker's
union dues only if the worker himself gives permission in
writing.

HOURS OF WORK. Unions are anxious to see that part of
the gains of increased productivity are handed on to workers
in the form of shorter working hours. These have been con-
sistently lessened as a result of union activity. One hundred
years ago many Americans worked seventy hours a week; now
the forty-hour week is the rule. Excessive hours of work lead to
deadly monotony, fatigue, and an increased number of accidents.
With an eight-hour day the workers have had more leisure for
rest, recreation, and self-expression and their productive efficiency has usually increased.

WORKING CONDITIONS AND WORKERS' WELFARE. Important subjects for union-management negotiation have been
grievance procedures, the question of holidays with pay, promotional policies, the provision of adequate toilet facilities, sickness insurance schemes, retirement plans, and many other things
affecting the personal happiness and security of the worker.
So-called "health and welfare funds" have been set up in some
industries to which employers contribute in order that money
may be available for sick or retired workers or their dependents.
One of the largest of these is that of the United Mine Workers,
financed out of a levy on each ton of coal mined. The Labor-
Management Relations Act forbids employer contributions to
health and welfare funds unless the employer has some voice
in the control of it.

CO-OPERATIVE SCHEMES. In order to enlist the loyalty
and interest of workers—to "give labor a stake in capitalism"
as one prominent businessman has put it—and thus increase
output and induce harmonious labor-management relations, co-
operative schemes have been developed by some unions and
employers. Union representation on councils affecting labor
welfare, profit-sharing, joint management and personnel administration are a few of the plans. Many prominent American
companies have profit-sharing plans for employees. This incentive for superior performance by employees is very successful
in certain kinds of enterprises (e.g., where majority of workers
are highly skilled technicians). Joint management arrangements, however, which provide for a junior board of directors

elected by employees are occasionally very effective, but such multimanagement is uncommon. It seems to operate most effectively in some small, single plant, family-owned companies, and results in reduced labor turnover and increased productivity.

POLITICAL AIMS. In recent years labor unions have played an important role in national politics. The Political Action Committee of the CIO has held public meetings, organized "write-your-congressman" campaigns, lobbied vigorously in Congress and in state legislatures, and in many cases has been a powerful factor in the defeat or victory of candidates for public office. Although labor unions have not yet sponsored their own political party as in England, nevertheless they have become a power in the land politically. The Labor-Management Relations Act of 1947 bans expenditures by unions for political purposes.

Weakness of the American Labor Movement.

DIVISION BETWEEN THE CIO AND THE AF OF L. The division of the American labor movement into two major groups means that the power of labor on a national basis is weakened. The split between the AF of L and the CIO over basic principles has been aggravated by the fact that the leaders of the two groups do not co-operate well on a personal basis. John L. Lewis, first president of the CIO, resigned his position after the 1940 election in which he backed the candidacy of Wendell L. Willkie, and then withdrew the United Mine Workers from the CIO. In 1946 he took the UMW back into the AF of L, but he withdrew again in December, 1947. Recent talks between AF of L and CIO leaders on the subject of unification have at last been successful. Union occurred at the end of 1955.

INTERNAL CONFLICT WITHIN UNIONS. Some unions, particularly those in the CIO, were weakened by internal rifts between different factions, and the division was very often over the issue of communism. In the 1940's the United Automobile Workers had two factions: the "right-wing" group of Walter Reuther and the "left-wing" group of R. J. Thomas. In the National Maritime Union, President Joseph Curran was engaged in conflicts with left-wing elements suspected of being "fellow travelers." While the extent of communist influence in labor unions is often exaggerated by those seeking to "smear" labor, there is no doubt that communists or persons with communist sympathies have succeeded in penetrating into positions of influence in some unions. The Labor-Management Relations Act of 1947 refuses NLRB recognition of a union as a bargaining unit if any of its officers are communists.

CLOSED UNIONS, RESTRICTIONS, "FEATHERBEDDING." Some unions maintain an unfair monopoly by restricting unreasonably the entry of new men into the craft. In many of the craft unions also there are "make-work" rules, such as limiting the size of a paintbrush a painter may use or the number of bricks a bricklayer may lay. The American Federation of Musicians has received unfavorable publicity in recent years because of its policy of often compelling theaters and radio stations to hire musicians they do not need. The Labor-Management Relations Act of 1947 makes "featherbedding" of this kind an unfair labor practice. Although such policies are indefensible from an economic point of view, they spring from the fundamental feeling of insecurity experienced by workers under capitalism. Since a worker feels he may be out of a job if a depression develops, he wishes to make his existing job last as long as possible. One way to improve the situation is by preventing depressions, extending social insurance to cover all important risks and groups of workers, and thus reducing the degree of economic insecurity.

"PARALYSIS" STRIKES. Traditionally a strike has been considered a test of economic strength between a union and management. In recent years, however, some strikes have affected principally the public. Strikes in the railroad and coal industries during 1946, for instance, brought the whole economic life of the United States to a standstill. Regardless of the real issue in the strike the fact that a single union can, if it wishes, paralyze all economic activity in the country is a matter of vital national importance. The Labor-Management Relations Act of 1947 permits the government to obtain an injunction to hold up for eighty days a strike which threatens the national health or welfare.

JURISDICTIONAL STRIKES. These occur when two unions both claim jurisdiction over a particular job and one strikes to enforce its claim over the other. One phase of work is then stopped, and other work in a process of production is thereby disrupted. Jurisdictional strikes are particularly frustrating for the employer who endures a strike without being able to do anything about it. The Labor-Management Relations Act outlaws such strikes.

SECONDARY BOYCOTTS. These occur when union members refuse to handle goods produced by another firm where a strike is in progress or where substandard labor conditions exist. They have been outlawed by the Labor-Management Relations Act.

VIOLENCE IN STRIKES. In recent years there has been an unfortunate tendency for strikes to result in violence, particularly on the picket line when massed pickets try to prevent nonstrikers from entering a plant. Under the Labor-Management Relations Act such action is now condemned as an unfair labor practice. Regardless of the issues involved, violence as a means of settling disputes cannot be tolerated in the United States.

SETTLEMENT OF LABOR-MANAGEMENT DISPUTES

Collective Bargaining. Collective bargaining between union and management representatives is the normal way of settling problems of common interest. Strikes make spectacular front-page news, but actually the vast bulk of problems are settled through free discussion on a give-and-take basis. Free collective bargaining is most successful where there is not too great a disparity in the economic strength of the bargainers. The purpose of the Wagner Act was to develop the bargaining power of labor at a time when unions were the weaker party. The sponsors of the Labor-Management Relations Act of 1947 claimed that this piece of legislation was necessary in order to redress the balance once more after twelve years in which labor had gained great power.

Mediation. If collective bargaining fails to produce agreement, mediation may be resorted to. Here a third party, an impartial person who has the confidence of both sides, intervenes and tries to effect a compromise. The mediator makes suggestions but has no authority to enforce an agreement. The Conciliation Service of the U. S. Department of Labor provides federal mediators who have succeeded in settling many disputes.

Voluntary Arbitration. Under voluntary arbitration the two parties to a dispute, failing to reach an agreement, decide to hand over the whole matter to an impartial judge or arbitrator by whose decision they agree to abide. Arbitration of this kind is only resorted to when both parties agree to it voluntarily. Many states provide for certain public officials or boards to act as arbitrators, or the governor may appoint them from a list of representatives presented by each side, or an arbitrator may be named by prior agreement between the two parties. The latter method is only possible in a highly organized industry like the New York garment industry which has a noteworthy record of success in the field of settling disputes by resort to arbitration.

Compulsory Arbitration. This requires submission of disputes to arbitration by government decree, and the award is enforced by government power. Australia and New Zealand have experimented with this method, but it is opposed in the United States by both labor and management. During World War II, compulsory arbitration was resorted to under the War Labor Board although the Montgomery Ward case in 1943, in which a corporation defied the government, proved that enforcement of a decision was difficult.

Fact-finding. Fact-finding commissions have long been used in disputes involving railroad workers, and they achieved a sudden and spectacular popularity in 1946 in the steel, automobile, and other strikes. Since big strikes involve heavy barrages of propaganda by both sides in the press and radio, a fact-finding commission of prominent impartial citizens may sometimes elucidate the real "facts" in the dispute. Once the facts were clear, the weight of public opinion would compel a solution on terms recommended by the committee. One criticism of this procedure in 1946 was that the government threw its weight on the scales in favor of labor, thus making free collective bargaining impossible.

"Cooling-off" Periods. These are periods of varying length during which a strike is illegal. The purpose is to gain time for further discussion, mediation, and investigation. A peaceful settlement is more likely to be reached if strikes cannot be called on the spur of the moment. Under the Railway Labor Act of 1926 a strike can be postponed for as long as sixty days while mediation boards and fact-finding commissions go to work. Under the Smith-Connally War Labor Disputes Act of 1943, a wartime measure now expired, a thirty-day strike notice had to be filed by the union. Critics of "cooling-off" periods say that they often turn out to be "heating-up" periods during which both sides maneuver for position and public support, and that they can be evaded anyway by the union filing a strike notice well in advance of negotiations. The Labor-Management Relations Act requires a sixty-day period of negotiations before a strike can be called in a wage or contract dispute, followed by a secret vote of the workers on the employer's last offer. A premature strike would deprive the workers of NLRB protection, and the employer could fire them.

The Railway Labor Act, 1926. The Railway Labor Act established special machinery for labor disputes in the railroad industry including a National Mediation Board, special presidential-appointed emergency fact-finding commissions, and "cooling-off" periods. Although considered successful for many years, this machinery failed to prevent the great rail strike of 1946.

Strikes. A strike is a last resort in labor-management disputes. Contrary to the impression often given, workers do not like to strike. It involves them in serious economic losses which can often be made up only by years of work. If a strike does start, it becomes an endurance test between the two parties. In such a test of strength, the union is at a grave disadvantage because of its more meager resources, and union treasuries have often been seriously depleted by long strikes. The whole purpose of establishing machinery to settle disputes is to avoid this ultimate and mutually ruinous test of strength.

LABOR LEGISLATION

Norris-LaGuardia and Wagner Acts. These important pieces of legislation have already been discussed. They were primarily responsible for labor's rise to power.

Child Labor Laws. Most states have passed child labor laws to prevent the economic exploitation of young persons.

The laws vary in different states, but nearly all of them set the minimum age limit at fourteen years. The hours of work per day range from eight to eleven. The laws are often loosely enforced, and employers in states with strict enforcement sometimes find themselves at a competitive disadvantage. Federal laws attempting to regulate child labor and to make uniform requirements were passed in 1916 and 1922 but were declared unconstitutional. A constitutional amendment to permit federal child-labor legislation has not yet been ratified by three-fourths of the state legislatures. In 1938, however, the Fair Labor Standards Act, containing a child-labor clause, was passed and its constitutionality later upheld. A large proportion of the children employed in the United States at the present time are farmers' children working on their parents' farms.

Labor Laws for Women. Labor laws regulating working conditions, hours, and night work for women in manufacturing, mechanical, and mercantile trades are enforced in most of the states. Because of their weaker bargaining position (unorganized and not always self-supporting), women are underpaid as compared with men, and special legislation has been found necessary to prevent their exploitation.

Labor Laws for Men. Most states have passed laws regulating the hours and working conditions of men, particularly in hazardous industries. The eight-hour day has become a general rule for most public employees. Recently some states, including New York and Ohio (in 1947), have passed laws banning strikes by public employees, including teachers. The penalty is automatic discharge.

Factory Acts. To prevent accidents and occupational diseases, factory acts have been passed by the states under their police power. Factory inspection, however, is not always as efficient as it might be. Certain requirements in connection with ventilation, fire escapes, sanitation, etc., are almost universal.

Wages and Hours Legislation. For many years state efforts to pass minimum wage and maximum hour legislation were blocked by the question of their constitutionality. In March, 1937, however, the Supreme Court reversed its negation of the New York law and upheld the Washington minimum-wage law. In 1938 the federal Fair Labor Standards Act was passed which fixed a minimum wage of twenty-five cents an hour in industries engaged in interstate commerce, later raised to forty cents an hour, and set the working week at forty hours with all overtime to be paid at time and one-half rate and double time on Sundays and holidays. Because of the rises in prices and wages during and after World War II, the minimum wage was raised in 1950 to 75¢ and in 1956 to $1.00.

State Legislation. In recent years more and more states have passed legislation imposing restrictions of various kinds on unions. By June, 1947, thirteen states had banned the closed shop and several more were submitting constitutional amendments to the voters to achieve such a ban. Public utility employees are forbidden to strike in New Jersey, Wisconsin, and Virginia; check-off of union dues is forbidden in Colorado, Arkansas, and Tennessee. Altogether more than half of the states have passed regulatory labor union legislation.

Labor-Management Relations Act, 1947. In June, 1947, the first comprehensive piece of labor legislation since 1935 was passed by Congress and became law in spite of a presidential veto. Bitterly denounced by labor leaders, the Labor-Management Relations Act bans the closed shop and permits the union shop only when a majority of the workers vote in favor of it. It permits the government to halt by injunction for eighty days any strike threatening the public health and welfare. It repeats the Wagner Act ban on unfair labor practices by employers, but adds to this a list of unfair practices forbidden to unions. These include coercion of workers to join a union, failure to bargain with employer in good faith, jurisdictional strikes, secondary boycotts, and "featherbedding." The NLRB is empowered to attack these outlawed practices by injunction. The act also refuses recognition to foremen's unions and to unions which have communists in official positions. It permits unions to be sued in federal courts for breach of contract and enforces a sixty-day cooling-off period in disputes involving wages and new contracts. It bans political contributions by unions, imposes restrictions on health and welfare funds and the check-off system, and separates the judicial and prosecuting functions of the NLRB, placing the latter in the hands of a general counsel whose nomination by the president must be confirmed by the Senate. This act reflected the swing of the pendulum from a prolabor attitude in the '30's to a rather antilabor attitude after World War II as a result of the great growth of union power and particularly of the wave of strikes in 1946.

UNEMPLOYMENT

Unemployment is perhaps the most difficult economic problem with which modern society must deal. Substantial and prolonged unemployment not only is wasteful and productive of human suffering but also breeds political discontent and is a real threat to democracy. In the late '40's the United States enjoyed virtually "full employment" with almost sixty million at work. At the depth of the depression in the early '30's, however, approximately fifteen million persons or almost one out of three of the working population were unemployed, and even in 1940 the unemployed numbered eight million. In mid-1950 the Bureau of the Census reported about three million unemployed, including a normal "float" of two million in seasonal, technological, and frictional unemployment.

Seasonal Unemployment. In certain industries, such as building, coal mining, and agriculture, seasonal fluctuations cause unemployment. In seasonal industries a labor reserve exists which is in excess of the number of laborers who could be hired if the industry were stable. Although daily wages are high, which attracts a large labor supply, yearly wages are actually less because they must be spread over the idle period.

Technological Unemployment. This is unemployment created by the introduction of new laborsaving devices or new inventions. In the short run this is a serious economic loss for those losing their jobs. In the long run the productivity of the nation as a whole is increased. Saddle makers and horse dealers lost their jobs when automobiles were invented, but many times their number found new jobs in automobile manufacturing, service-station operation, oil production, and highway construction. Unemployment compensation schemes and retraining facilities can smooth over the readjustment period for such displaced workers.

Frictional Unemployment. There will always be some workers who happen to be between jobs when the "count" is taken. There will be those who are moving from a contracting industry to an expanding one. Unemployment compensation can alleviate this situation. The operation of an efficient nation-wide system of employment agencies, like the United States Employment Service, is also helpful.

Cyclical and Stagnation Unemployment. This is the most serious type of unemployment and refers to the situation which exists when a large number of workers, able and willing to work, are unable to find jobs because the economic system is functioning so badly that there are no jobs for them. Unemployment compensation is inadequate to take care of such a situation. The only cure for it lies in sound economic policies designed to prevent depressions. (See Chapter Twelve.)

SOCIAL SECURITY

Social security is a broad term used to refer to plans devised to protect the population against various economic risks, such as unemployment, old age, industrial accidents, and sickness, which can deprive persons of the chance to earn an income and support themselves. The most important one of these schemes in the United States today involves the insurance principle under which premiums are paid either by workers or the employers or both to various state or federal agencies or funds and then benefit payments are made if the worker succumbs to one of the risks. This is social insurance and such schemes exist for unemployment, old age, and industrial accidents. Another way of providing social security is for the state or federal government to make outright grants to assist the aged, blind, and other less fortunate groups.

Philosophy of Social Security. Social security is based on a growing realization that many of the economic misfortunes that overcome persons today do not result from personal vices. Unemployment usually results not because people are lazy and do not want to work but because the economic system operates in such a way that there are not always enough jobs. Old people are unable to support themselves not so much because they were extravagant but because their incomes were too small to permit saving. Industrial accidents occur not so much because people are careless but because they live in a complicated machine age where a certain number of accidents are inevitable. In short, a personal explanation of economic misfortunes is not adequate. And since economic risks are inherent in a modern industrial society, it is only proper that society should organize public schemes to combat them. This is the justification for social security legislation.

Social Security Act, 1935. The Social Security Act passed in August, 1935, marked the first attempt by the federal government to provide social insurance. The act is administered by the Social Security Board whose three members are appointed by the president with the consent of the Senate. The act deals principally with three types of social security— unemployment compensation, a contributory old-age pension scheme, and noncontributory assistance plans for needy groups.

UNEMPLOYMENT INSURANCE. Under the terms of the Social Security Act, unemployment insurance was to be provided by the passage of state laws. Inducement to pass such legislation was provided by federal grants for administration and by a so-called "tax-offset" plan. A payroll tax of 3 per cent is levied on employers (of 8 or more persons—4 since 1955—the tax after 1940 levied on the first $3,000 earned in any year from any one employer) by the federal government but 90 per cent of the tax is credited to the employer's account providing his state has a satisfactory unemployment insurance scheme. Since the employers have to pay a tax anyway, they might as well have a state scheme and get something for their tax money. Every state now has an insurance scheme.

A great deal of freedom is allowed as to the type of law the states may pass. The *compulsory unemployment reserves plan* (the *Wisconsin* or *individual reserve*) requires payments to be made into a state fund. No employer is forced to pay out in benefits more than he pays in, nor does he pay benefits to any but his own employees. After an employer has built up a certain reserve, his contributions are reduced, depending on his employment record, to a minimum. According to the *pooled fund* type of unemployment insurance, payments are made into a single pooled fund, without separate account being kept of individual employers' contributions. The individual reserve plan is considered to be an incentive to employers to stabilize employment; the pooled fund plan is based on the principle that the causes of unemployment are beyond the control of the individual employer. It attempts to provide greater security to the workers by broadening the base over which the unemployment risk is spread. Merit rating (i.e., reducing contributions of those employers who have a good employment record), however, may be used with either type of unemployment insurance. Merit rating, when combined with the pooled fund system, simply involves keeping separate records for each employer, but all contributions are pooled and all disbursements for unemployment come from the same general fund. Federal credits are granted regardless of any reduction in contribution because of merit rating.

A *Federal Unemployment Trust Fund* was created by the act to serve as a depository for the state reserves. The Secretary of the Treasury must invest the fund in securities issued or guaranteed by the federal government. Withdrawals are to be only for the purpose of benefit payments. The amount and duration of such payments are left to the discretion of the states, but they must be paid through public employment offices or other agencies designated by the Social Security Board. Benefits may not be withheld if employment is offered but refused because of labor disputes or because of conditions less favorable than in similar work in the same locality.

OLD AGE INSURANCE. Prior to the enactment of the Social Security Act, several systems of old age insurance were being used successfully in the United States, most of them covering railroad and public employees. The Social Security Act provided for a federal system of old age insurance covering all employees except casual or agricultural labor, domestic servants, federal or state employees, and employees of charitable or educational institutions. The 1935 law levied a tax on the employee's income and an excise on the employer's payroll. No tax was payable on the portion of wages over $3,000 earned by an individual. The tax started in 1937, the employer and the employee each paying 1 per cent. The amount was to have risen every three years until each paid 3 per cent in 1949 and thereafter, but for many years Congress froze the rate at 1 per cent. This policy was followed because of the deflationary effect of higher taxes and also because huge reserves were being built up. The Act of 1935 provided that a beneficiary had to be sixty-four or over and must have contributed for a minimum period.

Congress amended the old age and survivors insurance several times to include more kinds of employment, to liberalize benefits, and to increase tax contributions for the reserves held by the Treasury. In 1950 coverage was extended to the majority of regularly employed domestic servants and farm workers, to government employees not covered by retirement systems, and to some self-employed groups. Benefit payments and tax contributions were increased. Similar changes were made in 1954. As of 1955, about 9 in 10 of the nation's jobs were covered; 70 million persons were fully insured; the average benefit paid to a retired worker was $61 a month (legal minimum $30, maximum $108) and to an aged widow or widower $47. The tax rates for the worker and his employer (2% each) and for the self-employed (3%) were based on taxable earnings up to a maximum of $4,200. Amendments of 1956 extended coverage to additional kinds of employment; made totally disabled workers eligible for pensions at age 50 and women eligible for benefits at age 62; and raised the tax rates for the worker and his employer (2¼% each) and for the self-employed (3⅜%).

ASSISTANCE PLANS FOR NEEDY GROUPS. State governments have long made grants to needy persons. The Social Security Act provided a system of federal grants-in-aid to states for the purpose of supplementing state payments. In general, the principle was that of the matched grant, i.e., the federal government would give so much if the state would also give so much. The act provided that the federal government would match state payments to indigent aged persons up to $15 monthly, thus raising the total payment to $30.* The act also

---

* Amendments at different times have increased the federal share for payments to needy persons who are aged, blind, or disabled, and to dependent children. In 1956 it was set for needy persons at four-fifths of $30 plus one-half the balance up to a maximum of $60 monthly.

provided for federal grants-in-aid to the states for the purpose of caring for the blind, for extending and improving local maternal and child health programs, for extending rehabilitation programs for the physically disabled, and for extending assistance programs for crippled, homeless, and delinquent children. Several times (most recently in 1956) Congress has passed bills liberalizing payments to the states for such purposes.

Workmen's Compensation. These plans are operated entirely by the various states at the present time. Accidents and industrial diseases are important costs of modern industry. To minimize this cost the number of injuries must be reduced and for those that are sustained the worker must be rehabilitated as soon as possible. The old common law doctrine of responsibility for an injury was wholly inadequate as a protection to workers. Only about 10 per cent of those injured received any compensation in court actions. Contributory negligence, fellow-servant negligence, and assumption of risk provided the employer with easy arguments for evading liability. Loss fell on the worker who could least afford it. Workmen's compensation laws constitute the earliest form of social insurance attempted by government units in the United States. Between 1911 and 1949 all states enacted some form of compensation laws. The laws make no attempt to place the blame for accidents on either employer or worker, but charge it to the cost of production in a modern machine age. Most states require the employer to insure in some public or private company, and often the premiums are determined by the accident rate, which is an inducement for the employer to start safety campaigns. Some states set aside funds for retraining injured men. Although laws make compensation more certain, it is often insufficient to cover the worker's loss and care for his dependent family.

Evaluation of Social Security in the U. S. The principal criticisms that may be levied at social insurance programs in the United States are that they do not cover enough people, that the payments made are often inadequate to take care of the need, and that they do not cover all risks. Important groups of workers are excluded from state unemployment and workmen's compensation laws and from the federal old-age pension scheme. Payments under some state laws are very small. It was partly the inadequacy of payments under workmen's compensation laws that caused John L. Lewis to demand a "health and welfare" fund for the members of the United Mine Workers union. The greatest gap in existing programs, however, is the total absence of any plan to take care of medical expenses and loss of income because of sickness. Although such schemes have operated successfully in many countries for a long time, they are still attacked in the United States as "socialized medicine." The president has on several occasions requested that Congress establish a sickness insurance plan and a system of prepaid medical care. Two states, California and Rhode Island, now interpret their unemployment insurance laws in such a way as to make an individual eligible for compensation if he cannot work because he is sick. A final criticism that may be made of the U. S. programs is that they are complicated to administer and result in much overlapping and duplication as far as taxing is concerned.

GENERAL REFERENCES

Abbott, Grace, *From Relief to Social Security.*

Bachman, G. W., and Lewis Meriam, *The Issue of Compulsory Health Insurance.*

Burns, Eveline M., *The American Social Security System.*

Commons, J. R., and J. B. Andrews, *Principles of Labor Legislation.*

Cummins, E. E., *The Labor Problem in the United States.*

Daugherty, C. R., *Labor Problems in American Industry.*

Douglas, P. H., *Social Security in the United States.*

———, and Aaron Director, *The Problem of Unemployment.*

Epstein, A., *Insecurity: A Challenge to America.*

Frankfurter, Felix, and Nathan Green, *The Labor Injunction.*

Harris, Seymour, *Economics of Social Security.*

Metz, Harold W., *Labor Policy of the Federal Government.*

Millis, Harry A., and Royal E. Montgomery, *The Economics of Labor*—
    Vol. 1, *Labor's Progress and Some Basic Labor Problems;*
    Vol. 2, *Labor's Risks and Social Insurance;*
    Vol. 3, *Organized Labor.*

Perlman, Selig, *A History of Trade Unionism in the United States.*

Prentice-Hall Labor Course.

Slichter, Sumner, *Union Policies and Industrial Management.*

CHAPTER SEVENTEEN

INDUSTRIAL CONCENTRATION AND GOVERNMENT CONTROL

NATURE OF MONOPOLISTIC POWER

A pure monopoly exists when there is only one seller in a market (see Chapter Eight). He controls the supply and is thus able to maintain complete control over the price of the commodity in question. A purely monopolistic market is the other extreme of a perfectly competitive one in which there are so many sellers that no one of them is able by himself to influence the price, which is in fact determined by the impersonal forces of supply and demand. Actually, however, these extremes of absolute monopoly and perfect competition are both rather rare in the United States. The typical market falls somewhere between the two and is characterized by elements of both competition and monopoly.

In some markets competition may be very keen and the element of monopoly very slight as, for example, in the market for canned peas where the sellers are numerous, price competition is quite strong, and the element of monopoly arises chiefly because of the ability of individual producers to "differentiate" their product by means of brand names and successful advertising. To the extent that this product differentiation is successful, the individual seller has a limited degree of control over the price of this product. In other markets, however, the element of competition may be very weak and the element of monopoly very strong as, for example, in the case of cigarettes or typewriters where there are only four or five producers who have succeeded in virtually eliminating price competition altogether and who compete with one another chiefly through extensive advertising. In such cases, the price of the product, while not absolutely controlled by one producer, is usually maintained at a higher level than would prevail if there were true competition. Fewness of producers (oligopoly) in a given industry or industrial concentration is the characteristic of many branches of manufacturing. Industrial concentration, however, is only a partial measure of monopoly power. A few large producers may sometimes engage in more aggressive competition than many small producers who may agree to follow certain practices.

Since the Civil War there has been a steady growth of industrial concentration and monopoly power in the United States, and the consequences are undesirable from at least two points of view. First, the growth of monopoly is a threat to the capitalistic system which is based on open markets and free competition. In a competitive market the interests of producers and of consumers coincide because the way to larger profits for the former is through greater efficiency, price reductions, and increased volume of sales, all of which naturally benefit the latter too. In a monopolistic market, however, profits may be maximized at the expense of the consumer by selling a smaller quantity of goods at a higher price than under competition. The existence of monopoly also means that the spur to efficiency and technical progress, which competition provides, is lacking. Monopoly can result not only in exploitation of the consumer but also in an inefficient use of the factors of production and in the growth of unfair business practices designed to eliminate possible competitors.

Secondly, from a noneconomic point of view, the growth of monopoly is a threat to democracy. By tolerating political competition and more than one political party a democracy protects itself against the concentration of political power in a few hands. Concentration of economic power, however, is likely to promote concentration of political power. In the United States economic power has already become concentrated in the hands of a relatively small number of persons who control the largest corporations. About two hundred large corporations control nearly one-half of the nation's corporate wealth, and control of most of these corporations is now vested in the hands of a minority group. From the point of view then, of both economic efficiency and the social welfare, government action of some kind with regard to monopolies is necessary in the public interest.

REASONS FOR GROWTH OF MONOPOLY

The size of the business unit has tended to increase and the number of firms to decrease in many industries during the last eighty years. The decline of competition, which has been a natural result of these developments, may be attributed to several factors.

Advantages of Large-scale Production. Many efficiencies result from the large-scale operation of business enterprise. As indicated previously, greater specialization, mechanization, and utilization of certain factors can be attained under such conditions. Overhead costs can be spread over a large output, a low unit cost thereby resulting. These economies are the secret of the mass production practiced so successfully in the United States and encouraged by an abundance of natural resources and a huge home market. Smaller business units might result in higher unit costs in many industries, and hence the answer to the problem of monopoly is not necessarily the breaking-up of big firms. The so-called "natural monopolies," such as public utility undertakings, are a case in point, and government regulation or ownership would seem to be the only way in which the benefits of the greater efficiency of monopoly can be obtained for consumers.

Desire for Monopoly Profits. The desire for monopoly profits, which are obtained by eliminating or restricting competition, has always been an important factor in the combination movement (e.g., mergers, price agreements). However, new improvements to obtain monopoly profits may lower costs and prices more than competition of many firms.

The Tariff. Successive tariff laws have afforded an undue amount of protection to some industries in the United States. High import duties frequently excluded foreign competition and permitted American firms to build up monopoly power in this country.

CONCENTRATION OF ECONOMIC POWER IN AMERICAN BUSINESS

Extent of Concentration. Detailed studies made by the Temporary National Economic Committee just before World

War II show that concentration of economic power in the United States has developed to such an extent that traditional terms like "competition" and "free enterprise" almost cease to have any significance. The TNEC found, for instance, on the eve of the war many basic indicators of monopolistic power.

1) One-tenth of one per cent of all corporations owned 52 per cent of all corporate assets and earned 50 per cent of total corporate income.

2) One-tenth of one per cent of all corporations employed five hundred or more workers but accounted for 40 per cent of all nonagricultural employment.

3) Fewer than 4 per cent of the corporations engaged in manufacturing earned 84 per cent of the total net profits of all such corporations.

4) One-third of the value of all manufactured goods was produced under conditions where the four largest producers of a commodity accounted for over 75 per cent of the total U. S. output of that commodity. In the plate-glass industry, for example, two producers controlled 95 per cent of the total output; in typewriters, four producers controlled 95 per cent.

The conclusion drawn is that the economic life of the United States is dominated by about two hundred nonfinancial and fifty financial corporations, which control billions of dollars worth of assets and employ millions of workers, and whose policies regarding prices, production, and wages affect almost every citizen in the land. Since the activities of these giant corporations affect the public interest so deeply, the idea that they have public responsibilities has developed.

Monopolistic Devices. Competition has actually declined even more than the above figures suggest since monopolistic collusion, resulting in price fixing and the allocation of markets, has been found to exist in markets where several apparently independent firms operate. Some of the devices used to eliminate competition are indicated below.

PRICE LEADERSHIP. In some industries there are a relatively small number of firms, and one dominates the market by virtue of its size and economic power (e.g., U. S. Steel Corporation in the steel industry). The dominant firm acts as price leader, and the others follow similar policies either because of the fear of the consequences if they do not or because of the benefit from price stability. The result is an absence of price competition and often higher prices than would prevail in a competitive market.

PRICE AGREEMENTS. It is illegal for firms to conspire to restrain competition by means of price-fixing agreements, but new cases are constantly being unearthed by the Federal Trade Commission. In 1940, four typewriter companies, accounting for 95 per cent of total U. S. output, were charged with fixing uniform prices, discounts, and allowances. A similar situation was found to exist in the market for eyeglasses where three corporations controlled 75 per cent of total output.

DELIVERED-PRICE SYSTEM. In the case of bulky commodities, such as steel, transportation costs are important and could result in differences in delivered prices even though agreement had already been reached on f.o.b. prices. To avoid this, the so-called basing-point system has been used under which all freight rates are calculated from one point regardless of the actual origin of the goods, thus preventing any price differences from arising because of transportation costs. The most famous example of this was the so-called "Pittsburgh plus" system in the steel industry under which quotation prices included freight rates from Pittsburgh regardless of actual origin. It was ruled illegal in 1924 and replaced by a complicated multiple basing-point system that was to be ruled illegal in 1948.

PATENT CONTROL. In order to stimulate invention, patents are granted by the government which give exclusive control over articles and processes for seventeen years. These legal grants of monopoly privilege have been used to establish and maintain a monopolistic position. Patent rights are property and can be rented with certain conditions of use specified. They have thus formed the basis of agreements to maintain prices, allocate markets, and restrict production. An example of this was the Ethyl Gasoline Corporation, jointly owned by Standard Oil of New Jersey and General Motors (in turn controlled by duPont), which held the patent on tetra-ethyl, "antiknock" gasoline. It licensed all refiners and eleven thousand independent retail distributors, forcing them to agree to maintain a price differential over ordinary gasoline and to follow the big oil companies' price policies, as a condition to making and using tetra-ethyl. The practice was stopped by the Department of Justice in 1940. Other firms using patent rights to maintain monopoly power have been the United Shoe Machinery Company and the Aluminum Company of America.

INTERCORPORATE RELATIONS. Sometimes apparently independent firms are linked with others by means of such devices as interlocking directorates, holding companies, or one firm owning a controlling interest in another. This can result in monopolistic collusion. For instance, the duPont Company owns a controlling interest in General Motors and in the United States Rubber Company. Approximately four hundred men hold one-third of the 3544 directorships in the 250 largest corporations. With these connections some apparently independent firms collaborate rather than compete. A holding company is a corporation which holds in its own name a controlling interest in a number of other companies, thus enabling the holding company to dictate the policy of all and to channel the profits of the operating companies up to its owners. This form of business organization has developed particularly in the field of public utilities in order to control operating companies as well as equipment and service companies supplying them.

MARKET SHARING. Dominant firms in an industry often agree not to compete in one another's markets. For instance, investment banking houses usually refrain from competitive bidding in the security underwriting business, and the big meat packers usually avoid competing with one another in buying livestock.

TRADE ASSOCIATIONS. Trade associations are organizations formed for the benefit of members of the same trade in order to promote joint advertising, carry out market surveys, publish trade journals, develop common cost accounting methods, exchange technical information, and so on. There were over eight thousand of them in 1940, of which two thousand were nation-wide in scope. Among the most important are the American Iron and Steel Institute, the Wool Institute, and the National Retail Dry Goods Association. While the above-mentioned activities are harmless enough, trade associations have sometimes been used to fix prices (as in the case of the Metal Windows Institute), allocate production and sales on a quota basis, and divide up markets. This has often been done through so-called "codes of fair competition" and other such devices. Trade associations are also very active in lobbying for federal and state legislation favorable to their members.

BUSINESS PRACTICES OF DOMINANT FIRMS. Powerful firms often impose special conditions on distributors. Automobile and agricultural machinery companies, for instance, compel dealers to carry all lines of products and parts and not handle those of competitors. Eight moving-picture companies were convicted of tying up most movie theaters, compelling their owners to accept "block-booking" of first- and second-rate movies and denying independent exhibitors first-run movies until several weeks later.

MERGERS. Mergers, where two or more firms combine, occurred at a tremendous rate during the 1920's and the same thing has happened since World War II. In 1950 a Clayton Act amendment illegalized mergers by purchase of assets which lessen competition.

Separation of Ownership and Control. Not only competition *between* companies has declined but also the power of control *within* corporations has become concentrated in fewer hands. This trend has resulted principally from the increased dispersion of stock ownership which has enabled a well-organized minority, or in many cases simply the managers, to control the firm and wield economic power even though legal ownership (and theoretically control too) rests in the hands of the stockholders.

In many corporations, no single stockholder owns as much as 1 per cent of the stock. In such cases control of the business usually rests in the hands of the managers who solicit the voting rights of stockholders. In other cases, a small minority of stockholders can control enough proxies to achieve their ends. In no case is there any guarantee that those in control will always use their immense power to benefit the public or even the majority of the stockholders. On the eve of World War II, 50 per cent of all the corporate stock in the country was held by seventy-five thousand people (0.06 per cent of the population), and half of all corporate dividends went to sixty-one thousand persons.

ANTITRUST LEGISLATION

In contrast to most other countries, some effort has been made in the United States to curb the worst abuses of monopoly by legislation.

State Laws. Various state laws were passed in the late 19th century to check monopolies, which were arousing the increasing resentment of farmers and small businessmen. The original Standard Oil trust was driven out of Ohio as a result of action by the State Attorney-General. State laws were not very effective, however, since they did not cover interstate commerce. New Jersey, Delaware, and West Virginia did not at first impose any restrictions with the result that many corporations registered in these states even though they operated elsewhere. Even today Delaware is the home of an abnormally large number of corporations attracted there by its lenient corporation laws. As a result of the inadequacy of state laws, federal legislation was finally passed.

The Sherman Act, 1890. The Sherman Antitrust Act (1890) was the first attempt to control monopoly by federal legislation. It declared that any contract, combination, or conspiracy in restraint of trade was illegal and that any person who attempted to restrain trade was guilty of a misdemeanor. This act was ineffective for several years because of a court ruling in the E. C. Knight case (1895) that the American Sugar Refining Co. was engaged in "manufacturing" rather than "commerce" and therefore the Sherman Act could not be applied to it. Under the administration of Theodore Roosevelt, however, the so-called "trust-busting" era started, and the law was applied vigorously. In a series of cases, the Supreme Court held that holding companies (Northern Securities case, 1904), price fixing (Swift and Co., 1905), and outright mergers (American Tobacco Co., 1911) were all violations of the Sherman Act when they resulted in "restraint of trade." The most famous case involved the Standard Oil Co., which was found guilty of violating the Sherman Act in 1911. It was this case which established the so-called "rule of reason," i.e., a line was drawn between what was reasonable and what was unreasonable in restraint of trade, and the latter was illegal.

The Federal Trade Commission. The Federal Trade Commission was established as a permanent commission in 1914 to investigate and report on business practices, to interpret and enforce the antitrust laws, and to prevent unfair competition. Its job is thus to police business activity in the United States. The FTC may investigate on its own initiative and also hear complaints from injured parties. Hearings are held and "cease-and-desist" orders may be issued which are enforceable through the Circuit Court of Appeals. Publicity is given to unfair business practices, and the commission's restraining orders tend to raise the level of competition. The FTC was later given control over false advertising in the sale of foods, drugs, and cosmetics.

The Clayton Act, 1914. The Clayton Act tried to tighten up the Sherman Act by specifying what unfair business practices and "restraint of trade" are. For instance, it stated that interlocking directorates which substantially lessen competition are illegal. It also exempted labor unions from the antitrust laws. In the famous Danbury Hatters' case (1908) a labor union had been convicted of "restraint of trade" when it organized an interstate boycott. Perhaps the most important precedent established since 1914 has been the "bigness-is-not-badness" doctrine. In the U. S. Steel Corp. case (1920), the Supreme Court held that it was not size alone that made a corporation bad, even though it was a monopoly, but only the abuse of power, i.e., engaging in unfair business practices and restraint of trade. Under this doctrine the Aluminum Company of America was acquitted in an antitrust suit in 1940 even though it was at the time an absolute monopoly.

The Robinson-Patman Act, 1936. It expanded the prohibitions against discriminatory pricing. The act forbids discrimination between buyers where the effect is to limit competition, either at the seller's stage in distribution, or at the buyer's stage, or both. Different prices to different buyers must be related to differences in the costs of serving them. One aim was to prevent large stores from buying at prices below ordinary quantity discounts—that is, at prices below those justified by lower costs of filling large orders—and thus from obtaining an unfair advantage over small stores in the sale of goods.

Evaluation of Antitrust Legislation. The antitrust laws are based on the belief that competition is an effective regulator of most markets and, with a few exceptions, that monopolistic practices can be stopped by enforcing competition. These beliefs run counter to the basic trend of industrial development in the last seventy years. The weakness of the program may be traced to several factors. During much of the time since 1890 there has been no real enthusiasm for enforcement. At one time (1933–1934) there was an actual reversal of the program, the Codes of Fair Competition adopted by many industries under the National Industrial Recovery Act permitting cooperation on prices and other matters that had formerly been illegal. In addition, some exceptions to the law appear. Export associations (Webb-Pomerene Act, 1916), agricultural cooperatives (Capper-Volstead Act, 1920), and rate-making associations (Reed-Bulwinkle Act, 1948) are partially exempted from the federal antitrust laws. Federal resale-price-maintenance legislation (Miller-Tydings Act, 1937), which supplements state "fair trade" laws, permits a manufacturer to fix the retail price of his product when such action is authorized by the state in which the product is sold.* Nearly all states have such laws which affect primarily drugs and cosmetics. The use of "loss leaders" and other deep price cutting account in part for the legislation.

Although Presidents Theodore Roosevelt, Taft, and Wilson pushed enforcement of the law, there were times (in the 1890's, 1920's, and early 1930's) when practically nothing at all was done. The most vigorous enforcement came between 1938 and 1940 when Thurman Arnold was Assistant Attorney-General in charge of antitrust activities, but his work was cut short by World War II. The courts have often been hostile to the idea of prosecuting business because of monopolistic practices. The most serious weakness in the program has probably been the fact that the enforcement agencies have been inadequately supplied with funds and personnel.

The conclusion is that a vigorous, consistent, and con-

---

* A Supreme Court decision in 1951 held that nonsigners of suppliers' price-fixing contracts could not be enjoined from reducing their selling prices below the minimum set in such contracts as provided by state "fair trade" laws.

tinuous program of curbing flagrant monopolistic practices which is backed up by adequate funds and personnel would be socially desirable. In general, however, "big business" is now so well entrenched that spectacular results cannot be expected. Moreover, the inventions and innovations of a vigorous private enterprise system are likely to result in a constant stream of monopolistic developments. The major part of the solution lies perhaps more in the direction of government ownership of monopolistic industrial enterprises of vital interest to the public, or at least in their operation as public utilities—that is, semipublic institutions with public responsibilities.

EFFECTS OF WORLD WAR II ON MONOPOLY

The problems of industrial concentration and monopoly power in the United States were accentuated by developments during and immediately after World War II. Big corporations emerged from the conflict in a much stronger position; small business was seriously weakened. This was a result of several developments including the way in which war contracts were granted, the way in which government-built war plants and property were disposed of, and the way in which federal research contracts were granted.

Prime Contracts. Between June, 1940, and September, 1944, prime supply contracts to the amount of about $175,-000,000,000 were granted by government departments and agencies. These were instruments of economic power which guaranteed their holders markets and sizable profits, brought them priorities on parts and raw materials, and gave them the right to take advantage of favorable depreciation and tax carry-back provisions. In addition, prime contractors were the recipients of most of the government-built war plants. Over half of these contracts (in value) went to thirty-three large corporations and no less than two-thirds to one hundred corporations.

Subcontracts. Prime contractors let out 34 per cent of their work in subcontracts, but three-quarters of the subcontracts went to other large firms. It is estimated that small business (firms with fewer than five hundred employees) got only 29.7 per cent of the supply program. Many small firms eliminated their purchasing and sales staffs and virtually lost their independent status while they worked on subcontracts for big companies.

Materials. From 1943 onward, the Controlled Materials Plan gave most prime contractors the power to allocate raw materials among subcontractors. When the end of the war approached and contract termination began, the prime contractors were often able to "pull in" on subcontracts and use the raw materials themselves.

New Production Facilities. The productive capacity of American industry was increased by about 50 per cent as a result of new plant and equipment construction during the war. For example, aluminum capacity was increased fivefold; magnesium nineteen-fold; steel by 50 per cent; basic chemicals threefold; the number of machine tools almost doubled. Two-thirds of this expansion was financed by federal government funds and one-third privately. An estimated 70 per cent of the publicly financed new plants has been taken over since the war by the two hundred largest corporations. Over half of the privately financed expansion was done by one hundred big corporations.

Research. During the war the federal government spent about $600,000,000 a year on industrial research (not including atomic energy). Over one-third of all research and development contracts went to ten big corporations and two-thirds went to sixty-eight big corporations. Although the government got royalty-free licenses to use the results of this research, in 90 per cent of the cases the patents reverted to the corporation concerned after the war. Thus the hold of big business on new techniques and processes was strengthened.

Working Capital. Big corporations were able to increase their working capital during the war and were thus in a strong position after the war to purchase government-owned plants, start new sales campaigns, and buy out small competitors. In the first decade of the postwar period mergers were numerous and substantial. Concentration increased appreciably in some industries. However, it decreased in others (e.g., aluminum) and no general lessening of competition seemed to occur.

COMBINATIONS IN EUROPE

The monopoly problem has appeared in all industrial countries, especially in the chemical, metal, and electrical equipment industries. In Germany, the government actively encouraged the growth of cartels and other monopolistic forms of business. Among the biggest were I. G. Farbenindustrie and the Rhenish-Westphalian Coal Syndicate. Eventually, these big business interests were instrumental in supporting Hitler's rise to power. Monopoly in Germany led to fascism and ultimately to war.

In England, nothing was done before World War II to check the growth of monopoly, which was encouraged by the tariffs of 1931 and 1932. Later, however, the Labor Government engaged in a program of nationalization of basic industries. Some de-nationalization occurred subsequently, but a moderate antimonopoly law was enacted.

Perhaps the worst aspect of the monopoly problem before the war was the collusion that existed between giant firms in different countries through the medium of international cartels which restricted production, maintained prices, and allocated markets on a world-wide scale. There is evidence that the defense program of the United States was hampered in 1940 and 1941 by the restrictive agreements concluded between certain American and German firms. The war disrupted many cartels; later, they declined in importance. International monopolies created only minor difficulties.

GENERAL REFERENCES

Arnold, Thurman W., *The Bottlenecks of Business.*

Berle, A. A., and G. C. Means, *The Modern Corporation and Private Property.*

Blair, John M., *et al., Economic Concentration and World War II.*

Edwards, Corwin D., *Maintaining Competition.*

Federal Trade Commission, *Annual and Special Reports* (Corporate Mergers).

Fetter, F. A., *The Masquerade of Monopoly.*

Handler, Milton, *A Study of the Construction and Enforcement of the Federal Antitrust Laws,* TNEC Monograph No. 38.

Holt, W. S., *The Federal Trade Commission.*

James, Clifford L., *Industrial Concentration and Tariffs,* TNEC Monograph No. 10.

Kaplan, A. D. H., *Big Enterprise in the Competitive System.*

Leifmann, Robert, *International Cartels, Combines, and Trusts.*

Lynch, David, *The Concentration of Economic Power.*

Lyon, L. S., and Associates, *The National Recovery Administration.*

Mason, E. S., *Controlling World Trade.*

Purdy, H. L., M. L. Lindahl, and W. A. Carter, *Corporate Concentration and Public Policy.*

Ware, C. F., and G. C. Means, *The Modern Economy in Action.*

Watkins, M. W., *Industrial Combinations and Public Policy.*

Weissman, Rudolph L., *Small Business and Venture Capital.*

Wilcox, Clair, *Competition and Monopoly in American Industry,* TNEC Monograph No. 21.

CHAPTER EIGHTEEN

PUBLIC UTILITIES

NATURE AND NUMBER

Public utilities are semipublic industries. They are privately owned and operated, but government agencies attempt to regulate their operations, particularly with regard to rates and earnings. Industries publicly owned and operated by government units are public industries. Many industries, such as banking, food-packing companies, restaurants, hotels, and taxicab companies which are subject to government regulation, are not public utilities—that is, rates and earnings are not regulated. The kind and number of public utility industries depend upon the enactment of state and federal laws, as well as court interpretations of the laws. Legislators prompted by the wish of voters, may enact a law which subjects a given industry to public utility regulation, but the courts may declare the law unconstitutional. To regulate a given industry as a public utility infringes on the constitutional property rights of the owners, and hence, the courts hold as constitutional only those infringements in which the public welfare is vitally affected. The kind and number of public utility industries, therefore, vary with time and place, as well as with changes in judicial opinion with regard to the necessary degree of public interest needed to justify public utility legislation. The most important public utilities in the United States are the railroads. Other important public utilities include electric, gas, water, telephone, telegraph, street railway, air transport, motor transport, pipe line, express, and pullman companies.

Characteristics of industries affected with a vital public interest and regulated as public utilities are rather definite. First, there is a pronounced tendency toward monopoly control of a given market because of a high fixed investment and decreasing costs. Competition and price-cutting to obtain more business and lower costs become so severe that only a few firms survive in a given market. Second, to enforce competition is unsatisfactory because the amount of capital needed restricts the number of competitors and because duplication of service in a given market is costly and less valuable (e.g., several telephone systems in a city instead of one). Third, the demand for the product is usually inelastic. It is a necessity for which there is no satisfactory substitute available and a necessity which the consumer cannot forego without serious discomfort or possible impairment of health. Fourth, public utility enterprises must obtain public permission to begin operation or to cease operation, and their rates and services are regulated by public agencies.

PUBLIC UTILITY REGULATION

The development of public utility regulation in the United States occurred mainly after 1878. Prior to that time the various states passed special laws and granted special charters for public utility companies, but rates were usually unregulated. In the seventies the agricultural states of the Middle West began to limit freight rates and to curtail railroad rate discriminations ("Granger Laws"). Since most of the commerce was interstate, state legislation was ineffective. Competition remained the principal regulator of rates.

In 1876 the United States Supreme Court (Munn *v.* Illinois) declared constitutional a law of the Illinois legislature which regulated the rates and practices of grain elevators. Thereafter state public utility laws and advisory public utility commissions developed rapidly. Eleven years later the federal government created the Interstate Commerce Commission for the purpose of preventing rate discriminations and monopoly rate agreements among the railroads.

The problem of valuation of public utilities as a basis for rate making and effective regulation of earnings became an issue near the close of the 19th century. During a period of falling prices, the public utility companies favored and the public opposed valuations based on the original cost of the investment; during rising price periods the two parties reversed their position. The United States Supreme Court in the case of Smythe *v.* Ames (1898) declared that the public utilities were entitled to a "fair return" on a fair valuation, but no specific valuation method was designated. Although several subsequent court decisions (Minnesota Rate cases in 1913; McCardle *v.* Indianapolis Water Company in 1926; O'Fallon Railway Company case in 1929) stressed the reproduction cost method of valuation, no definite rule of valuation (e.g., Southwestern Bell Telephone Company in 1923) has been established to serve as a guide for public utility commissions.

Regulation of the Railroads. State regulation of railroads proved ineffective, and since 1887 the federal government has exercised an increasing amount of control over the operation of this form of transportation.

INTERSTATE COMMERCE ACT, 1887. The Interstate Commerce Act declared that railway rates should be "reasonable and just" and that there should be no discrimination between customers. Pooling and division of freight earnings was forbidden. A federal regulatory agency, the Interstate Commerce Commission, was established to enforce the act. The ICC required annual reports and uniform accounting methods of the railroads and compelled them to give ten days' notice of any advance in rates. It could inquire into railroad management and hear complaints about alleged violations of the act.

HEPBURN ACT, 1906. This act gave the ICC the power to fix maximum railroad rates and also tightened up the administration of controls. The railroads now had to give thirty days' notice of either a reduction or an advance in rates.

MANN-ELKINS ACT, 1910. This act gave the ICC power to suspend changes in rates or classifications for 120 days pending investigation of the reasonableness of the change and to impose a further suspension of six months if necessary, in order to give the shipper time to protest.

TRANSPORTATION ACT OF 1920. During World War I the railroads were operated by the government. This act returned them to their private owners. The ICC was to fix rates which would yield a "fair return on a fair valuation" of the property. This was stated to be 6 per cent (lowered to 5¾ per cent in 1922), and, under the so-called recapture clause, any earning in excess of this amount would be surrendered, half going to the government and half into a reserve fund. The ban on pooling, imposed in 1887, was lifted in cases where a division of traffic or earnings would not restrain competition but would benefit the public. The ICC now received the power to fix not only maximum rates but minimum ones and actual rates too. The commission also received power to regulate new railroad construction and the dismantling of old lines and to control security issues in order to prevent malpractice in the field of railroad stocks and bonds.

EMERGENCY TRANSPORTATION ACT, 1933. This act repealed the fixed per cent of return and the recapture provision of the 1920 act. Rates now were to be just and reasonable—high enough to give the railroads a reasonable profit but not so high that the consumer would be exploited. A Federal Coordinator of Transportation was appointed to make economies in railroad operation although he was not allowed to effect any economies that would reduce employment. These changes were the result of the depression.

RECENT DEVELOPMENTS. During the depression many railroads had to be supported by government loans from the Reconstruction Finance Corporation. They have suffered increasingly from the competition of motor transport and more recently from aircraft transport. During World War II earnings of the railroads improved greatly as a result of huge shipments of war materials and troops but since the end of the war they have experienced declining revenues again. The most recent development in the field of regulation is the Reed-Bulwinkle Act of 1948, which basically gives the ICC power to prescribe and supervise the way in which the nation's common carriers may decide jointly rate changes to be filed with the ICC.

Motor Transport. The Motor Carrier Act of 1935 gave the ICC control over motor carriers engaged in interstate commerce. It regulates the right to operate, rates, security issues, mergers, and accounts. Federal safety regulations are also enforced. In addition the various states have many regulations affecting this form of transport.

Inland Waterways. The Transportation Act of 1940 gave the ICC control over inland waterways which had formerly operated under the jurisdiction of the Maritime Commission. The ICC has the same power over inland water transport as it does over motor carriers.

Merchant Shipping. Since 1950 (when the Maritime Commission created by the Merchant Marine Act of 1936 was presidentially reorganized) American shipping on the high seas has been regulated by the Federal Maritime Board and Maritime Administration in the Department of Commerce. Shipping rates are filed with the Board, which has power to fix maximum and minimum levels and which also is in charge of a governmental subsidy program to encourage American merchant shipping.

Air Transportation. After 1918 the government exercised an indirect control over air routes flown and the type of plane used through the granting of conditional air-mail contracts. The Ail Mail Acts of 1934 and 1935 gave the Postmaster-General power to regulate schedule frequencies, departure times, stops, speed, load capacity, maximum flying hours of pilots, etc., while the ICC got the power to regulate accounts. Finally, under the Civil Aeronautics Act of 1938, the Civil Aeronautics Authority was established with power to grant or withhold certificates and permits for operation, fix rates and tariffs, control accounts, and regulate consolidations. The Civil Aeronautics Board investigates safety requirements and other conditions.

Power. State public utility commissions regulate electric power generated and used within state borders, but since World War I power lines have begun to cross state lines in increasing numbers. In 1920 the Federal Power Commission was established with authority to issue permits or licenses for private and public power projects involving interstate commerce. In 1935, by which time about 18 per cent of all electric power generated entered into interstate commerce, the authority of the FPC was extended to cover regulation of rates, earnings, financial transactions, and accounting practices. In 1938 control over the interstate transmission of natural gas was placed under the FPC which also obtained planning control over all river basins.

Communications and Radio. The Mann-Elkins Act of 1910 gave the ICC regulatory power over telephone and telegraph companies. This authority was transferred in 1934 to the newly established Federal Communications Commission which determines whether rates charged are just and reasonable. The FCC also grants licenses to radio stations, assigns them frequencies, fixes their hours of operation, prevents interference between stations, and in general supervises the entire industry including television.

Public Utility Holding Company Act, 1935. Many public utility companies formerly escaped regulation because of the development of interstate utility business and of holding companies. Both operating and holding companies carried on interstate business over which neither state commissions nor any federal agency had control. The evils of holding companies were many and became particularly apparent in the electric power and light industry at the time of the Insull Scandals. An equipment company owned by a holding company could sell materials and services at exorbitant prices to operating companies owned by the same holding company. These inflated expenses were used to obtain higher rates or to conceal profits from state authorities. The pyramiding of holding companies on top of one another resulted in a great concentration of power in the hands of the promoters at the top and in the channeling of profits from the operating companies to the top holding company. In order to prevent this, the Public Utility Holding Company Act of 1935 was passed by Congress. This act, enforced by the Securities and Exchange Commission, ordered the dissolution of all holding companies beyond the second degree and compelled those remaining to confine their holdings to a single geographically integrated system. The constitutionality of this so-called "death sentence" clause was finally established by the Supreme Court in 1946 which upheld a decree by SEC ordering the giant North American Company to divest itself of all its properties except those in the St. Louis area. This holding company at the time controlled eighty companies. operated in seventeen states and the District of Columbia, and had over two billion dollars in assets and three million customers.

PUBLIC OWNERSHIP OF UTILITIES

There are many persons who believe that the whole machinery for regulating public utilities in the public interest is so complicated and unwieldy that the only thing to do is to socialize them all. Actually important sections of the public utility business in the United States are already either socialized or closely supervised. Some public ownership, however, in crucial areas of the industry may be sufficient to keep rates and service at a reasonable level on the part of nearly all private companies.

Rural Electrification. Before 1935 rural areas were inadequately supplied with electric power. Private companies "skimmed the cream" of the best markets, but, because of high costs, they did not find it profitable to supply electricity to most rural districts. In 1925 only 4 per cent of the farms of the nation were served by private electric companies; in 1935 the figure had risen to only 11 per cent. Needy farmers went without, and those that did receive service were very often the victims of monopolistic exploitation. Some parts of the country (e.g., California, Utah, New England) were served better than others. Most inadequately supplied were the South and the Middle West.

In 1935 the Rural Electrification Administration was established to finance and administer a rural electrification program. It was primarily a lending agency whose principal purpose was to make loans to nonprofit borrowers. Most loans have gone to rural co-operatives for the purpose of extending electric power service. The REA supervises the construction of power facilities, audits the construction costs, sets up an accounting system, and in general acts as administrator and adviser.

In ten years the number of electrified farms rose from 11 per cent to 45 per cent, and the REA financed construction of 425,000 miles of electric lines, supplied 1,300,000 new customers, and allotted $600,000,000 dollars of federal funds. In addition, the competition has stimulated private companies to lower rates and to improve efficiency.

Regional Power Projects. The federal government has gone into the electric power business in many parts of the country. The Hoover Dam on the Colorado River in Nevada, the Shasta Dam in the Central Valley of California, the Grand Coulee and Bonneville Dams on the Columbia River, and the series of dams on the Tennessee River are examples of this development. These projects comprise not only flood control (in the Tennessee Valley), irrigation (in California and the Pacific Northwest), and the generation of electric power but also improved navigation, soil conservation, and the general rehabilitation of the region. The Tennessee Valley Authority, established in 1933, has been particularly successful in this respect and in many ways is a model for future developments along the same lines in the Missouri, Arkansas, and Ohio valleys.

Municipal and State Ownership. Many cities and towns own their own streetcar and subway systems, gas and electricity plants, and waterworks. This type of public ownership is so common that it no longer excites much controversy. The principal example of local government ownership is Nebraska where all electric power facilities are owned by local government authorities. A few state governments own some public utilities, but the bulk of government ownership is either federal or local.

RATE–MAKING

Rate-making for public utility services involves two problems: first, the *determination of specific rates* for different services; and second, the *determination of the general level of rates*. The latter problem deals with the rate of return which public utilities are to be allowed on their investment. This is primarily a valuation problem and is discussed in the next section. The first problem deals mainly with the fairness of different rates to different customers—that is, with differential rates.

Problems of Differential Rates.

RAILROAD RATES. These for the most part are fixed according to the principle of what the traffic will bear (value of service principle) because of lower costs obtained from more complete utilization of facilities and because of the difficulties of allocating overhead costs and joint costs to specific services.

In order to accommodate future traffic many railroads were overbuilt. Huge investments, moreover, in tracks, terminals, and rolling stock made the fixed costs of many railroads amount to as much as one-half or two-thirds of their usual total expenses. Even the operating or variable costs (salaries, wages, maintenance, fuel, etc.) do not change proportionally with decreases or increases in traffic. Any rate, then, which attracts more business and is high enough to pay for slightly more than the additional variable expense incurred is profitable to the railroads because it helps to defray overhead costs. During the early railroad rate wars even a lower rate was profitable for some roads because traffic temporarily carried at a loss would bankrupt competitors and higher rates could be charged later.

Value of Service Principle: Advantages. Rates based on the value of service (what the traffic will bear) are discriminatory. Within certain limits they are justifiable. If cheap bulky freight is given a low rate, traffic is increased and the heavy fixed costs are spread over a larger volume of traffic. The shipper of expensive compact commodities may benefit either from lower rates in the future, or from the fact that the railroad might have to discontinue operations if the cheap, bulky freight trade were lost. Rates based on the value of service not only ignore the weight and size of commodities, but also the distance which they are carried. Long-haul shipments are given low rates as compared to short-haul shipments on the same line. Low rates on long hauls increase traffic and decrease unit costs. Without the additional traffic from the long hauls, rates for short hauls would be even higher, or perhaps the entire line would be discontinued. If rates could be based approximately on costs (weight, size, and distance), railroad facilities would be only partially utilized, some lines would be discontinued, and many essential commodities would have higher prices while many luxuries would have lower prices.

Value of Service Principle: Disadvantages. There are limits, however, to the application of the value of service principle in railroad rate-making. Its unrestrained application results in secret rebates to large shippers, in the uneconomical overlapping of markets, in subsidies to poorly located plants and mines, in low rates to compensate shippers for the delay involved in wasteful long hauls by circuitous routes, and in the transportation of commodities at rates which fail to pay for the additional direct expense incurred. On the other hand, this principle in rate-making frequently results in monopoly price extortion. Rates based on the value of service principle may be either too high or too low.

Cost of Service Principle. The Interstate Commerce Commission has the power to fix either maximum or minimum rates —that is, rates submitted to it may be rejected either because they are too high or too low. If rates are too high, they decrease shipments and injure both the railroads and industry; if they are too low, some railroads and industries are given an unfair and uneconomical advantage as compared to other railroads and industries. Value of service determines maximum rates; cost of service, minimum rates. The rates for any shipment should not fail to pay for the additional direct cost incurred plus some portion of the fixed costs for which the additional service is responsible. Rates for a long haul are not permitted to be lower than for a short haul which is included in the long haul on the same line and in the same direction except when permission is granted by the ICC (e.g., when there is water transport competition). The economic justification for this exception is doubtful. Rebates to large shippers are illegal. There are about fifty million individual rates on various kinds of freight between different points in the United States. In the eastern part of the United States rates are proportional to distance; in the South and the West basing points are used; blanket rates cover freight from the Pacific Coast to points east of the Rocky Mountains, or from the East to points west of the Mississippi River. Simplification of rates and greater emphasis on the cost of service principle in making rates seem desirable.

ELECTRIC RATES. *Electric light* and *power rate-making* presents about the same differential rate problem as railroad rates. The use of electricity varies with the time of day. Electric plants are constructed to provide adequate service at the peak of use. Both plant and lines, moreover, are built to accommodate future increases in business. Large plants with large generating units tend to have lower unit costs than smaller plants. Fixed costs form a high percentage of total costs, and hence, unit costs decrease with increased plant utilization. Economical operation, then, depends upon an even volume of business, as well as a large volume of business.

Value of Service. Since the cost of different kinds of service is extremely difficult to determine (overhead cost allocation uncertain), rates are based on the value of service. Large industrial users of electricity are granted much lower rates than residential users. Large industrial users increase the volume of business; they may provide a more even volume of business (use power mainly at off-peak periods during the day or night); and finally, they may produce their own power unless the rates are made attractive. Without the large industrial users, residential rates would be even higher and some service might be discontinued.

Residential rates are usually arranged in schedules—the greater the amount of electricity used, the lower the rate. A minimum rate or service charge may be imposed which the consumer pays although no electricity is used. Service for small, infrequent users of electricity is possible only because of other consumers, and hence, a minimum rate or service charge lowers the rate for those who make the service possible. Special low power rates for residential users, as well as the above rates, tend to increase the volume of business. (A power meter for household appliances may be installed in addition to a light meter.) Large residential users benefit directly; other consumers benefit indirectly.

Cost of Service. Electric rates based on the value of the service are in the main satisfactory, but cost of service should not be entirely ignored by state commissions when utilities present their schedules. Any rate should at least pay for slightly more than the extra direct expense incurred in providing a given service. Some large industrial consumers may use more peak-power than off-peak-power which necessitates an expansion in utility equipment. Low industrial rates and high residential rates in such cases may result in a subsidy to the industrial consumer and discourage mass consumption by residential users.

Problem of General Rate Levels. The general level of rates involves the problem of a fair return on a fair valuation (i.e., should all rates for a given utility company be higher or lower in order to allow the utility a fair profit?). To determine a fair valuation, and to a lesser extent a fair return, is a difficult task for the commissions. The value of a competitive business enterprise is mainly determined by capitalizing its present and prospective net income. The rates of public utilities, however, are regulated, their net income and their capitalized value thus being limited. Consequently, in order to determine the fairness of general rates and income for public utilities, the value of the investment must first be determined (rate base), and then rates can be altered until the net earnings represent a fair return on the investment.

RATE BASE. The *rate base* in recent years has usually been determined by the reproduction cost method—that is, a ten-year-old plant is given a value equal to the cost of replacing it at prevailing prices minus depreciation (spot valuation). Less emphasis has been placed on valuations based on the original construction cost. Utilities have favored the reproduction cost method because of rising prices which have inflated the rate base; and courts have generally favored it because to deny public utilities the increase in property value from rising prices seems to take property without due process of law. However, two Supreme Court decisions (Natural Gas Pipeline Company, 1942, and Hope Natural Gas Company, 1944) indicate that regulatory commissions may use any method of valuation provided that the end result is reasonable. Regulatory commissions and consumers have preferred the original cost method of valuation.

Reproduction Cost: Disadvantages. The *reproduction cost* minus depreciation (spot valuation) method of valuation is less satisfactory than the original cost method in the determination of a rate base. Public utilities are not competitive industries, and hence, are not entitled to increases in property value because of rising prices (the stockholders, not the bondholders, gain from increases in property values). The hypothetical reproduction cost, moreover, of a new plant which duplicates the old one is not valid even on a competitive basis, because a new plant, if actually built, would use different equipment (more modern) and the cost might be greater or less, but the efficiency of production would be improved. The use of the reproduction cost method when prices are falling would bankrupt many utilities. After the price decline of 1929, some utilities objected to its use. The service rendered would likely deteriorate, and although the consumer paid lower rates, he would receive less service. And finally, if the rate base determined by the reproduction cost method of valuation is revised with changes in the price level, valuations become expensive and frequent changes in the rate base complicate the work of regulatory commissions.

Original Cost: Advantages. The *original cost* method of valuation, or prudent historical cost method, is easier to determine and administer, and the consumer pays only for the capital actually provided. The regulatory commission would take from the accounting records of a given utility figures of the actual money outlay for the original plant and subsequent equipment. If early records were incomplete, estimates would be used. To encourage prudent management, careless outlays would not be included or would be included at a proper figure. Organization expenses (interest during construction and early losses) would be included as part of the investment. No deduction would be made for depreciation. Stockholders, as well as bondholders, would receive a fixed money return. The real income of both groups would decrease with rising prices, but increase with falling prices. Standards of service could be formulated in order that efficient utilities would not be penalized by low rates. And finally, the rate of return, rather than the cumbersome rate base, could be changed to encourage or discourage investment in public utilities. A fair valuation, or fair rate base then, should mean an original cost valuation.

RATE OF RETURN. The rate of return for public utilities should usually be less than the rate of return for highly competitive industries. Their monopoly position and public regulation gives them greater stability of income. In recent years many utilities have been allowed a return of 6 to 8 per cent on their investment. The reproduction cost rate bases, however, made the actual return much higher. If the rate base is determined by the original cost method of valuation, a fair return is one which attracts sufficient capital into utilities to maintain satisfactory services.

TRENDS IN PUBLIC UTILITY REGULATION

The future of public utility regulation is uncertain. Unregulated public utilities mean monopoly price extortion. Past regulation, however, by state commissions has been ineffective and costly. In the field of federal regulation, the ICC has been criticised as a tool of the railroads and as a weak control mechanism. Part of the regulatory weakness is due to the shifting decisions of the courts in rate cases. The most promising developments in recent years have been in the field of public ownership. The Tennessee Valley Authority and the public ownership of electric power facilities in Nebraska have been successful. These projects are likely to be expanded, and they may set a pattern for rates and services for private utilities which would make less difficult the problem of regulation. In the meantime, the policy of regulation by a multiplicity of commissions and agencies becomes more and more difficult to carry out.

GENERAL REFERENCES

Bauer, John, *Transforming Public Utility Regulation.*

Clemens, Eli W., *Economics and Public Utilities.*

Daggett, Stuart, *Principles of Inland Transportation.*

Dearing, Charles L., and Wilfred Owen, *National Transportation Policy.*

Glaeser, M. G., *Outlines of Public Utility Economics.*

Jones, Eliot, *Principles of Railway Transportation.*

Lilienthal, David, *TVA—Democracy on the March.*

Lloyd, E. M. H., *Experiments in State Control.*

Mosher, W. E., and F. G. Crawford, *Public Utility Regulation.*

Moulton, H. G., and Associates, *The American Transportation Problem.*

Ruggles, C. O., *Problems in Public Utility Economics and Management.*

Sharfman, I. L., *The Interstate Commerce Commission.*

Taft, Charles A., *Commercial Motor Transportation.*

Thompson, C. W., and W. R. Smith, *Public Utility Economics.*

Troxel, Emery, *Economics of Public Utilities.*

Wilson, G. Lloyd, and L. A. Bryan, *Air Transportation.*

Wiprud, Arne, *Justice in Transportation.*

CHAPTER NINETEEN

PUBLIC FINANCE

NATURE OF PUBLIC FINANCE

Public finance is a critical study of the spending activities of governments (federal, state, and local), of the methods used by governments to procure funds, and of the administration of government funds. The major divisions, then, of public finance are public expenditures, public revenues (including public borrowing), and financial administration (budgeting, auditing, and custody of public funds). Public finance is part of economics because it deals with one method (collective method) of satisfying certain human wants and because it affects the personal production, distribution, and consumption of wealth.

Public economy differs from private economy because the state has the sovereign power to compel individuals to make financial contributions and to accept certain services. Another difference is the nonmaterial and general welfare character of most government activities. Unlike private business they are not always expected to yield financial returns. If financial returns are anticipated from a given state activity, the returns need not be immediate (e.g., reforestation) and may be adjusted to a cost basis rather than a profit basis. An apparent difference between public and private economy arises because the state may spend and then adjust its income to fit the expenditures, whereas individuals adjust spending to their income. In most countries, however, the increase in expenditures compels an adjustment of state outgo to income.

PUBLIC EXPENDITURES

Increase of Expenditures. The increase of public expenditures in the United States is indicated by the changing percentage of national income spent by federal, state, and local governments. Public expenditures in 1890 constituted slightly more than 7 per cent of the national income, but in 1926 approximately 15 per cent. In 1932, when private incomes had been drastically reduced by the depression, they had risen to about 36 per cent. In 1941 after incomes had been greatly increased by the war, the ratio of public expenditure had fallen to 26 per cent. In 1949 it was about 28 per cent, but because of the defense program further increases were expected for subsequent years.

FEDERAL EXPENDITURES. War costs, past and prospective, account for 75 to 80 per cent of the federal expenditures. These costs include maintenance of the Department of National Defense, military pensions and compensation, and debt redemption and interest for loans contracted for war purposes. Civil expenses (executive, legislative, judicial, and administrative) account for the remainder of federal expenditures. A history of federal expenses indicates that war expenses have always been a large portion of federal government costs. Not only are war expenses large, but each war tends to increase permanently the cost of the civil branches of government (i.e., the expansion of organization during a war is not quickly curtailed after the war). Federal expenditures, of course, vary with general economic conditions. Beginning with the depression of the 30's, the federal government assumed greater responsibility than formerly for various types of relief and recovery expenditures.

STATE EXPENDITURES. The amount of various expenditures made by the states changes from year to year, but usually the largest expense items are for education, highways, and health and welfare (i.e., charities, hospitals, correction, etc.). They constitute about 75 per cent of the total state expenditures. Other state expenditures include those for general government, protection for life and property, interest on debt, outlays for permanent public improvements, etc.

LOCAL EXPENDITURES. The expenditures of local government units (municipalities, counties, school districts) resemble those of state governments. Municipal expenditures (for cities of 30,000 population or more) usually account for more than half of the local expenditures. The largest expenditures of these municipalities are outlays for education, protection of persons and property, highways, and general welfare. Prior to World War I local government expenditures represented approximately two-thirds of all government expenditures. In the future the proportion is likely to be substantially less than one-half.

Causes of Increasing Expenditures. In all civilized countries during the past century public expenditures have increased more rapidly than population and perhaps more rapidly than wealth and income. The cause of the increase, therefore, cannot be attributed to any special type of government (democratic or otherwise), nor can it be entirely explained by war and militarism. Increased government ownership does not explain it because most public service enterprises impose no net financial burden upon the community. Government inefficiency and extravagance may account for part of the increase in some countries.

NATIONALISM AND WARS. These are important causes of the increase in public expenditures, especially for national governments.

CONCENTRATION OF BUSINESS. The development of large business units has brought about problems for the government to solve. These problems require regulation with regard to labor relations, consumer protection, labor protection, monopoly, and unemployment.

SOCIAL WELFARE. This is still another important cause of the increase in public expenditures. Many needs which formerly a few individuals supplied for themselves are now supplied through public co-operation. Education, for example, was formerly almost entirely provided by private schools and tutors. Public co-operation enables all individuals to receive a limited amount of education. Police protection, sanitation, highways, etc., can be provided more advantageously by means of public co-operation. The increase in population (especially urban) and the growing complexity of modern industrial civilization multiply social needs. The severity of the recent depression necessitated a great increase in expenditures, especially federal, for welfare services (poor relief, public works projects, etc.).

Control of Public Expenditures. Control of public expenditures implies some scrutiny of total expenditures and careful evaluation, as well as administration, of specific expenditures. The limit to total expenditures depends upon the willingness of a given population to pay taxes or carry debt. Willingness to pay taxes or to borrow varies with the wealth and income of a given population, with its traditions, and with emergency conditions (e.g., war or program of expansion). In Great Britain, for example, public expenditures constitute a larger proportion of the national income than in the United States. There is no proper proportion between the total income of a country and its public expenditures, but the rapid increase of public expenditures invites study.

SIGNIFICANCE OF INCREASING EXPENDITURES. There is the possibility that the tax burden may reduce incomes until capital accumulation is retarded. The increase of public expenditures, however, increases the tax base and thus lessens the difficulty of collecting taxes. Many taxes are satisfactory when the rates are moderate, but become highly unsatisfactory at higher rates. Reform of the tax system, then, depends in part upon the amount of public expenditures. Since expenditures for war and welfare activities constitute the major portion of public expenditures, public policy with regard to these activities will determine future trends in total expenditures.

EVALUATION AND ADMINISTRATION OF EXPENDITURES. In order to develop intelligent public policy with regard to public expenditures and to execute effectively that policy, several conditions are indispensable.

Classification of Expenditures. Proper classification of expenditures by different government units is an important aid to public policy. If ordinary public expenditures are listed as extraordinary (i.e., nonrecurring over short periods of time) and are financed by an increase in public debt, current costs of government are understated. For the federal government a statement of ordinary expenditures should distinguish between military and civil expenditures. Nominal expenditures, such as bookkeeping transfers of funds from one department to another, or from one government unit to another, should be stated separately in order to show the real status of total expenditures. Commercial enterprises operated by government units should have a separate budget and any deficit would then appear as an expenditure for that type of activity—any surplus as a revenue. To combine the total expenses of government commercial enterprises with ordinary expenditures and the total receipts with revenues, obscures the real status of that particular type of government activity. Ordinary government expenditures are not expected to yield any tangible return (i.e., they promote the general welfare and productivity of the country), but expenditures for government commercial undertakings are expected to yield, as any business enterprise (except that the returns may be less immediate), some tangible returns.

Budget System. A budget system may be effectively used where expenditures are properly classified by different government units. Budget estimates of public needs will then permit intelligent judgment as to the proper distribution of expenditures to various activities. Proper classification and effective budget-making provide a superior type of control over expenditures as compared to the usual mechanical checks (e.g., tax rate and debt limitations) which are applied to local government units. They also enable taxpayers' associations to exert a more intelligent influence with regard to expenditures.

Centralization of Administration. Centralization of administrative authority in different government units increases the effectiveness of a budget system and lowers government costs. It facilitates the introduction of uniform accounting systems and improves auditing. The federal government is reorganizing some of its conflicting and competing administrative agencies. The new Department of National Defense includes the former Departments of War and Navy. A few state governments have eliminated numerous boards and commissions and have concentrated administrative duties in a few departments. Municipal administration in many cities is effectively centralized under the city manager plan. The manager plan might also be applied to counties in which there is a rather large and wealthy population.

Effective centralization of administrative authority in order to control expenditures also involves a proper distribution of activities among the various government units. There is no definite principle of functional distribution. In some cases the federal or state governments may perform certain functions more efficiently than local units. Sometimes the local units may surpass the state government in the performance of certain tasks. In general the state and federal governments must assume certain functions which the local units because of inadequate resources, constitutional restriction, or lack of adequate jurisdiction cannot perform (e.g., administration and maintenance of the metropolitan drainage district around Boston, of the Erie and Panama canals, etc.). The state must also assume functions which the local units can perform but are unwilling to perform adequately enough to protect the common interests of other communities (e.g., public health activity, highway construction, etc.). The same principle applies to the distribution of functions between the federal government and the state governments.

Subsidies or grants-in-aid are frequently made by the federal government to the states (e.g., for highway construction) and by the state governments to local government units (e.g., for educational facilities). The subsidy system fosters local autonomy which frequently results in wasteful expenditures. In some cases subsidies may be justifiable, but they should be subject to close supervision by some central authority to determine the use of the subsidy, standards of efficiency, etc. In some cases the government unit granting the subsidy should take over the activity performed by local units with the aid of the subsidy. In other cases a regrouping of local subdivisions (e.g., consolidation of school districts, county governments, etc.) would eliminate the need for a subsidy and would lower the cost of government.

PUBLIC REVENUES

Various government units support their program of expenditure by means of revenues. Government revenues or income may be classified as follows: (1) commercial revenues (i.e., receipts from government business enterprises); (2) administrative revenues (i.e., fees, licenses, fines, escheats, profits on coinage, and special assessments which arise directly or indirectly because of the exercise of strictly governmental functions); (3) tax revenues; (4) public loans; and (5) bookkeeping transfers. Revenue from taxation furnishes the bulk of government income for most units of government. Government borrowing (public loans) is a means of anticipating future revenues. These two sources of government income are the main subjects for the analysis which follows. Bookkeeping transfers were briefly discussed under expenditures. They are expenditures for the government making the transfers and are revenues for the units which receive them.

Commercial Revenues. The accounts of government enterprises, as mentioned previously, should be classified separately in order to determine whether they add to the net tax burden. If government enterprises yield a net profit, they are a source of revenue.

PUBLIC DOMAIN : LAND, FORESTS, MINERALS. The federal government has received most of its revenue from this source. Net returns including sales, rentals, and royalties totaled about one hundred million dollars in 1928. The return is small in comparison with the rich territory which the federal government once possessed. Most of the land was given away as an inducement to settlement. Huge grants of land were made to the states for the purpose of aiding public education, but the states' record with regard to managing and disposing of public land was not always creditable either. The federal government also used the public domain wastefully to subsidize railroads. Western settlement of the United States is an epic of heroic achievement, but it is also a sordid tale of public laxness, private graft, and exploitation. The pressure of private interests to obtain timber and water-power resources in the national parks illustrates the modern trend. The present federal conservation policy, however, is opening a new era in the history of public domain.

PUBLIC INDUSTRIES. In the United States public industries are usually municipal industries. The state governments maintain few enterprises of a commercial character. The post office is the chief federal industry. The postal savings system is a form of federal investment banking. The post office not only transmits official and private communications, but also acts as fiscal agent for individuals (money orders) and for the government (postal savings) and serves as a common carrier (parcel post). The post office is operated on a cost of service basis rather than as a state fiscal monopoly. Consequently deficits frequently appear. Criticism of the postal system is not based on these deficits, but on the lack of efficient business methods, low wage policy, and rate discrepancy. The low rates, for example, on second class mail which contain large amounts of advertising do not cover the cost of handling it, and hence, this service is subsidized by the employees and taxpayers. The Tennessee Valley Authority was created in 1933 to build dams on the Tennessee River in order to control floods, to improve navigation, and to manufacture nitrates for the purpose of national defense. For the latter purpose, the TVA has authority to construct hydro-electric plants and to sell surplus electrical energy. The United States Printing Office is the largest printing establishment in the world. The federal government is sponsoring many public housing projects. There are also a number of government corporations besides the TVA—corporations such as the Federal Deposit Insurance Corporation, the Reconstruction Finance Corporation, the Home Owners' Loan Corporation, the Inland Waterways Corporation, and the Panama Railroad Company. In the United States the public corporation is becoming increasingly popular as a form of business organization for public enterprise. Its advantage lies chiefly in its flexibility as compared to the ordinary government agency or bureau within a department.

Municipal industries in the United States are mainly enterprises which supply water, electricity, gas, and street railway service. Other municipal enterprises are docks, wharves, public markets, public halls, etc. Criticism of municipal industries is based largely on faulty accounting methods. Their accounts are frequently merged with those of the municipality; they may or may not be credited with the full amount of their revenues or debited with all the expenses which they incur. Current expenses are frequently charged to capital accounts and inadequate provisions are made for depreciation. Municipal industries are also usually exempted from taxes. A tax charge should be included as a cost of operation in order to diffuse the tax burden, to avoid subsidizing the users of these services, and to permit an easy comparison of their operation with the operation of similar private industries. Cities differ widely as to how much revenue they raise through public enterprise. For example, Tacoma and Jacksonville receive twice as much revenue from operating public enterprises as they do from tax collections, whereas Gary, Indiana, relies almost entirely on tax receipts.

In general no definite conclusion can be stated for or against government enterprises in the United States because their accounting records do not reveal their actual status. European government enterprises are more numerous and appear more successful, but European political conditions differ from those in the United States. The management of many American government enterprises has been only moderately successful, but that is also true of many important private enterprises. Government ownership of industries in the United States is still in the experimental stage. The most important need at present is to obtain a clear-cut record of the experiment.

Administrative Revenues. These revenues are not of great fiscal importance. The increasing burden of general taxation, however, suggests the possibility of extending the use of these revenues in order to make some government departments more nearly self-sustaining. The most important administrative revenues are fines, fees, licenses, and special assessments.

Fines. They are charges imposed on individuals because of the infraction of laws. They are a by-product of law enforcement and are not intended to be made a primary source of revenue, the most obvious exception being the "speed traps" of municipalities.

Fees. They are charges made for a special service rendered to individuals by some essential government agency or institution, such as a university. Formerly many public officials were allowed to retain fees as part of their compensation. The system produced excessive diligence on the part of officials and provoked excessive competition for the more lucrative offices. Consular and passport fees collected by the State Department formerly enabled the department to be self-supporting, and substantial sums are still being collected. License fees are very common. The service rendered is usually in the form of a privilege or permission for individuals to engage in some activity—the regulative element is a distinctive feature. The most important licenses at present are those imposed upon motor vehicles and alcoholic beverage dealers.

Special Assessments. These charges are usually imposed for a specific improvement to property. They resemble taxes because the levy is compulsory upon the owners of the property benefited by the improvement, but the benefits are special rather than general.

Revenues from Taxation. Taxes are compulsory charges imposed upon individuals for the support of government services. Since taxes are usually paid for the general services of government and not for any special service rendered to the individual taxpayer, the distribution of the tax burden presents difficult theoretical and practical problems. The relatively large proportion of total revenues raised by means of taxation and the growing burden of taxation imposed by increasing expenditures, add to the importance of the tax distribution problem. Every tax redistributes income because revenue is collected from the taxpayer and is rarely, if ever, returned to the same taxpayer in like amount.

PRINCIPLES OR TESTS OF A SOUND TAX SYSTEM.

Fiscal Adequacy. Taxes should be productive of sufficient revenue to meet general public needs. Old taxes are sometimes preferable to new ones, because their fiscal adequacy has been tested. If taxes encroach severely upon incomes and retard capital accumulation, their revenue yield in the future will likely become inadequate. To obtain fiscal adequacy in any tax system a *diversity* of taxes is necessary. Since all taxes in any sound tax system are ultimately paid out of individual incomes, a single tax on incomes appears to offer an easy solution of the tax problem. A single tax on incomes, however, would be fiscally inadequate during a severe business depression— that is, a tax system to be fiscally adequate must have some *elasticity.* A rigid tax system (i.e., one provided by constitutional law rather than statutory law) over a long period is likely to become fiscally inadequate. *Flexibility* of a tax system is an aid to fiscal adequacy. Taxes which are *economical* to collect and to administer promote fiscal adequacy.

Convenience. All taxation is burdensome, but a sound tax system will include taxes which are least vexatious to pay. Complicated tax laws which require an elaborate administrative organization as well as intricate tax returns are obnoxious, partly because the cost of compliance is high. This is one disadvantage of the federal income tax law. The payment of some taxes in installments or by withholding adds to the convenience of the taxpayers.

Certainty. There are two types of certainty which are important for a sound tax system. First, legal certainty refers to the formulation of tax laws and the possibility of avoiding tax payment. Unless tax laws are carefully stated, tax dodgers, or legal experts employed by them, find loopholes which enable them to avoid or to reduce their tax payments. Recent senate investigations of income tax evasions indicate the importance of legal certainty in taxation. The general property tax is another excellent example. The administrative provisions of a tax law should make the time and amount of tax payments certain (e.g., under the federal income tax law the final audit and determination of the tax has occurred several years after the income was received).

Second, economic certainty refers to the possibility of having the individual who pays a given tax shift the burden to other individuals. The shifting of a tax may or may not be desirable. The important point is to determine with a reasonable degree of certainty whether a given tax is, or is not, shifted, and if it is shifted, to determine upon what group, or groups, of individuals the burden finally rests.

Direct and Indirect Taxes. The terms "direct" and "indirect" are frequently applied to the incidence of taxes. Their meaning varies, but a direct tax is usually a tax which is difficult to shift and which is therefore ordinarily borne by the persons on whom it is levied, whereas an indirect tax is one that is easy to shift. The intended results, however, may not always be realized. The incidence of any tax varies with economic conditions. To say that some taxes are always shifted (i.e., are indirect) whereas others are never shifted (i.e., are direct) may overlook important exceptional conditions.

Incidence of Taxes. The person who pays the government bears the impact of a tax, but he may move the burden of the tax to some other individual. The other individual bears the incidence of the tax. Taxes can be shifted forward to the consumer through the raising of prices or backward to the worker (by cutting wages) or to the seller of raw materials (by paying less for the raw materials). These methods of shifting are not alternatives but instead may be used in various combinations with a partial absorption of the tax by the one who initially pays it. Thus the burden of the tax may be widely diffused. A further complicating feature is that business groups tend to anticipate the levying of business taxes and to act immediately to protect themselves, in which case there may be no price changes after the levying of a tax. Hence to all appearances no shifting has occurred.

Under competitive conditions taxes which affect the marginal supply of goods are in part shifted. A tax on houses, for example, tends to be shifted to tenants and to buyers of houses because owners of capital seek a higher return elsewhere until the shortage of houses increases the rental and selling price. The amount of the tax shifted and the speed of the shift depend upon the mobility of capital and the exclusiveness of the tax. In a rapidly growing community the shortage of houses would develop quickly, and the shifting might be quickly accomplished; in a stationary community, the shifting would occur slowly (i.e., when old houses needed replacement). If investments other than houses were about equally taxed, capital might not be shifted from house building and less of the tax shifted. If all capital investments are heavily taxed, the supply of capital may be reduced and then some shifting of taxes on all capital goods will occur. The shifting, then, affects laborers, landowners, and entrepreneurs, as well as consumers. The time element is important. The gasoline tax, for example, may not be shifted over a short period of time because of the immobility of capital. Over a long period of time it is likely to be shifted partly to consumers. Demand, as well as supply, is important in the shifting of taxes. A general sales tax or an excise may be shifted more quickly on commodities for which the demand is inelastic and less quickly on other commodities (i.e., with an elastic demand or a customary price). Taxes on increasing cost industries are likely over a period of time to be shifted, but the increase in price is less than the amount of the tax. For a decreasing cost industry, the increase in price is more than the amount of the tax.

Taxes which affect surplus returns rather than marginal returns are not likely to be shifted. The federal tax on personal incomes is for the most part not shifted because of the exemption of small incomes and the use of moderately progressive rates on larger incomes. The federal corporation tax, taxes on business profits, inheritance taxes, and taxes on land are not likely to be shifted. A percentage tax on monopoly profits is not shifted, but a unit tax on a monopoly is partly shifted (i.e., the amount of shifting depends on supply and demand conditions) to consumers. If part of an industry is taxed more in one district than in another, part of the extra burden in the high tax district is likely to be borne by the entrepreneurs in that district. Profits are not necessarily reduced, because management may be stimulated to greater efficiency.

Justice. When a group of taxes are combined into a tax system for a given government unit, the problem of a just or equitable distribution of the total tax burden arises. Unless the taxes are fiscally adequate, convenient, and certain, there is little to be gained from an attempt to test the equity or justice of the tax system. There are two main principles with regard to just taxation.

Benefit Principle. This principle means that individuals should be taxed according to the benefits which they receive from various government services (i.e., the cost of various services would be apportioned on this basis). In most cases, however, the benefits derived by an individual from government services cannot be practically determined. If the total tax burden, moreover, could be practically adjusted to a benefit basis, the poor would be taxed much more heavily than the rich because they are more dependent on government assistance and protection. Nevertheless, there are some cases, particularly in local finance, in which benefits can be approximately determined and in which taxation according to benefits is the only practical basis.

Ability Principle. This principle means that individuals should be taxed according to their ability to pay taxes for the support of government services. To determine the ability of different individuals to pay taxes is a difficult task. Some economists have suggested "equality of sacrifice" or "minimum sacrifice" as a test of ability. But a subjective test to determine how badly tax payments hurt each individual is impracticable. The test of ability or faculty to pay taxes in colonial times was the possession of property. But the development of diverse kinds of property and property rights makes the money valuation of legal property an inequitable test of ability to pay taxes. Income, rather than property, is the usual test or measure of ability to pay taxes. But income is difficult to determine. The period of time in which the income was made is important. The type of income (i.e., a funded income derived from property, or a precarious income derived from individual effort, etc.) is also important in a test of ability to pay taxes. Because of these difficulties and other practical limitations, it is impossible to base an entire tax system on the ability principle.

Combination of Benefit and Ability. For fiscal adequacy any tax system requires a diversity of taxes, and some combination of the benefit and ability principles is the most feasible solution. For fiscal reasons some taxes (e.g., income and inheritance taxes) should have *progressive* rates—that is, the tax rate should increase as the amount assessed increases. For fiscal reasons some taxes (e.g., excise taxes and custom duties for revenue purposes) may be used which have a *regressive* effect—that is, the amount of the tax paid in proportion to income will decrease with increases in the size of incomes. For fiscal reasons some taxes (e.g., property tax) may be used with *proportional* rates—that is, the tax rate will be the same for all amounts—flat or uniform rates. If the use of some taxes with progressive rates offsets the regressive effects of other taxes, a rough proportionality of the total tax burden may be obtained, which is about the only practical justice to be expected from any tax system. For nonfiscal reasons the use of income and inheritance taxes to reduce great inequalities in the distribution of wealth and income may be justifiable from a general economic and social point of view.

FEDERAL TAX SYSTEM. The most important federal taxes from a revenue standpoint are the personal income tax, the corporation income tax, and the consumption taxes (e.g., customs duties, excises, and sales taxes). The federal estate tax is important, but not as a revenue producer.

Customs Duties. Prior to the Civil War most of the ordinary federal revenue was derived from customs duties. From the Civil War to World War I, customs duties usually produced about half of the federal revenue. Since World War I the yield is much less. The use of customs duties in the United States for protective rather than revenue purposes makes them a cumbersome and fiscally inadequate source of revenue. Usually when revenue is needed, their yield declines. The bulk of revenue is collected from relatively few classes of commodities.

Excise Duties and Special Sales Taxes. There is a tendency to multiply the use of such taxes. The taxation of a few commodities, such as alcoholic beverages, tobacco products, playing cards, etc., which are nonessentials of widespread consumption yield a substantial revenue. If the taxes are collected from manufacturers or wholesalers rather than from retailers, they are economical and easy to administer. Either a sales tax on many commodities or a general sales tax is difficult to justify. The expense of administration would be greatly increased and the total tax burden might become regressive.

Personal Income Tax. The federal government levied a tax on personal incomes during the Civil War and postwar period (1862–1872). Another income tax was enacted in 1894, but it did not become operative because the United States Supreme Court declared it unconstitutional. The court had upheld the constitutionality of the first income tax law on the grounds that it was an indirect tax. In 1894 the income tax was declared by the court to be a direct tax, and hence, unconstitutional because it was not apportioned to the states on the basis of population. The Sixteenth Amendment (1913) legalized direct taxes of the federal government without apportionment among the states on the basis of population.

The personal income tax forms an indispensable part of the tax system. Although the determination of net taxable income has not been satisfactorily solved, experience will add improvements. The tax is assessed partly by declaration and partly by withholding, both methods being supplemented by information at source. With moderately progressive rates the inducement to avoid the tax payment is less and administration is more effective. There is no good reason for the use of normal and surtax rates—one scale of rates was adopted (1954) to simplify the tax and furnish adequate progression.

Federal Corporation Income Tax. The federal government in 1909 levied a tax on corporation net incomes. The constitutionality of the law was upheld because it was designated as a special excise tax on the privilege of conducting business under the corporate form of organization. In 1913 it was replaced by an income tax on corporations. In 1936 a new tax law, repealed in 1939, taxed undistributed net income of corporations at graduated rates, forcing distribution of earnings to stockholders. The former tax system encouraged the accumulation of huge corporate surpluses. Before 1936 corporate dividends were exempt from the normal tax but not the surtax. Thus individuals with small incomes, mainly in dividends, may have been taxed very little under the personal income tax, but very heavily under the corporation income tax. Since 1936 dividends have been subject to the normal tax as well as the surtax. To tax profits under the corporation income tax and the dividends paid out of these profits under the normal rates of the personal income tax does not constitute unfair double taxation, since the corporation has a tax-paying ability separate from that of individual stockholders and since the government is aware that it is taxing twice and has fixed both sets of rates accordingly. In 1951 Congress re-established an excess profits tax (similar to one of World War II) but repealed it beginning with 1953. Nearly all corporate income (over $25,000) is now taxed at 52 per cent.

Federal Estate Tax. Since 1916 the federal government has taxed the transfer of the net estate of deceased persons. (Inheritance taxes impose duties upon the distributive shares of an estate.) The tax yields a small revenue, but it prevents inequality among states in the use of inheritance taxes. The federal estate tax provides a liberal tax offset if the estate has already paid a state inheritance tax. The tendency of some states to exclude inheritance taxes to attract wealthy people is checked. Although the yield is small, the tax, both federal and state, conforms to the ability principle and lessens the burden of ordinary property taxes. A federal gift tax is imposed to stop the leaks in the estate tax.

STATE AND LOCAL TAXATION. The most important state and local taxes from a revenue standpoint are property taxes, consumption taxes (mainly gasoline and sales taxes), business taxes (licenses), income taxes, and inheritance taxes.

Property Taxes. These taxes supply over one-half of the total state and local revenues. A common type is the general property tax. Under this tax all kinds of taxable property are assessed (either by assessors or by residents who submit sworn lists of property values to assessors) at some money value, and a uniform or a classified rate structure is then applied to all property. The rate is varied by the state and local governments according to fiscal needs.

Defects of General Property Tax. Since the development of various types of property, especially intangibles (stocks, bonds, etc.) which yield different incomes, property in general no longer represents equal ability to pay taxes. The taxation of tangible and intangible property results in unjust multiple taxation. Many states, to avoid double taxation of corporations as compared to other types of business organizations, exempt from taxation the stocks of domestic corporations (but not foreign corporations). Nonresident stockholders are subject to unjust double taxation. There is a tendency, moreover, for competitive underassessment of property in each community by locally elected assessors in order to reduce the tax burden. Boards of equalization cannot correct all the resulting inequalities among tax districts. Furthermore, since intangible property and some forms of personal tangible property can be easily concealed, wholesale tax evasion develops. Since urban communities own proportionately more intangible property, an unjust tax burden is imposed upon rural communities. The owners of real estate are subjected to an increasing burden of taxation as other types of property fail to contribute to state needs.

Reform of State and Local Taxation. One improvement is the classified property tax. With this kind of tax, the assessment may be uniform with different tax rates for different types of property, or the rate may be uniform with different assessment values for different types of property. Since some types may be more easily concealed than others, lower rates for easily concealed property lessen the inducement for evasion and may lower the tax burden on immobile property, such as real estate. The classification may apply to all types of property, or only to certain designated classes with some classes, such as household goods (difficult to assess), exempt.

Another improvement of state and local taxation which is probably superior to the classified property tax is a state income tax system. A moderate tax on personal incomes with low exemptions would be imposed by the state in which the person receiving the income resides. Property would also be taxed by the state in which the property is located. (Intangible property could be completely exempt from taxation, or a classified property tax with a low rate on intangibles could be combined with the personal income tax.) A tax on net business incomes would be imposed by the state within which the business is conducted. An inheritance tax would also be included—tangible property taxed by the state in which it is located and intangible property taxed by the state of residence of the decedent. A few special sales taxes (e.g., on gasoline) may be used in this system. Under a state income tax system part of the revenue should be returned to the local government units on the basis of needs in order to compensate for their loss of revenue from property taxes. Under either system of improved taxation central administration by a competent tax commission is indispensable.

State and local (and federal) governments operate in an atmosphere of many levels. Decentralized planning is necessary, whereas efficiency can be improved by centralization. Because of jealousies and rivalries, the activities of the various government units are unco-ordinated. In the field of taxation there are many overlapping taxes, i.e., the same taxes are used by more than one unit of government. Thus a double cost of compliance and a double cost of administration are involved. Local government is badly in need of modernization, but this is most difficult to accomplish because of local loyalties, tradition, urban-rural antagonisms, the desire of office holders to retain their jobs, the resistance of taxpayers to reorganization for fear of an increase in their tax bills, the resistance of business groups receiving special favors, and the resistance of local units that might lose taxable resources. These local and state governmental units which resist centralization are unable adequately to finance their activities with the result that awkward devices, such as grants-in-aid, shared taxes, and tax crediting schemes, must be used.

Public Receipts from Loans. In order to maintain public credit, a long-run balance between revenues and expenditures is essential. Some countries have perpetual or indefinite maturity debts, but the amount of such debts may weaken their credit under emergency conditions. Public borrowing to be successful from a long-run point of view must be a temporary and supplementary source of revenue. In the main, public credit should be used to meet extraordinary or irregular expenditures.

Public borrowing to meet emergency conditions, such as wars and severe depressions, is legitimate.* The issue of paper money to finance a war is virtually a forced loan which may or may not be repaid. As much of war costs as possible should be met by increased taxation—the remainder by means of bonds. The sale of bonds for war purposes may be largely financed by bank credit and inflation results, but the effects of this type of inflation are to be preferred to paper money issues.

Public borrowing to finance government commercial enterprises is justifiable if the returns are deemed sufficient to cover all costs including interest on the capital invested. Public borrowing for public improvements which do not yield a money return is legitimate if the improvement represents an extraordinary expenditure for the government unit (i.e., a new school building for a small town would represent an extraordinary expenditure, but such expenditures recur regularly for large cities). The repayment of loans borrowed for extraordinary nonrevenue yielding improvements should be based on the probable duration of the improvement. For this purpose serial bonds rather than a sinking fund are preferred because sinking funds are more susceptible to political manipulation. For local government units, debt contraction and debt repayment should be supervised by some central authority of the state.

A major problem with reference to budgetary procedure concerns the unbalance characteristic of so many modern governmental budgets. While there is no adequate reason to keep a budget in balance over the whole period of business fluctuations, a greatly unbalanced budget aggravates the tax problem, weakens the chance of preparedness for future emergencies, and threatens the stability of money and prices. Many argue that there is no burden to debt as long as the public debt is held

---

* The national debt increased from 1 billion dollars prior to World War I to 24 billion in 1941 and to 269 billion in 1946. It was 275 billion in 1955.

internally. This statement must be qualified, however, because taxpaying is usually more general than bond holding and, furthermore, the greater portion of modern debt is held by the banking system. Thus retirement of debt involves a probable contraction of credit which may have deflationary consequences upon the entire economy.

The budget should perhaps be balanced over the whole period of business fluctuations rather than in any one year, and another prerequisite to an adequate counter-cyclical fiscal policy is the proper timing of taxes and, in some cases, the use of fluctuating rates, with the government taking responsibility for the elimination of defects, deficiencies, and maladjustments in the functioning of the economy.

GENERAL REFERENCES

Bastable, C. F., *Public Finance*.

Buehler, A. G., *General Sales Taxation*.

————, *Public Finance*.

Bullock, C. J., *Selected Readings in Public Finance*.

Ellis, P. W., *The World's Biggest Business*.

Groves, Harold, *Financing Government*.

Hansen, A. H., and H. S. Perloff, *State and Local Finance in the National Economy*.

Hubbard, Joshua C., *Creation of Income by Taxation*.

Kimmel, Lewis H., *Governmental Costs and Tax Levels*.

Lutz, Harley L., *Public Finance*.

Murphy, Henry C., *The National Debt in War and Transition*.

Poole, K. (ed.), *Fiscal Policies and the American Economy*.

Seligman, E. R. A., *Essays in Taxation*.

Shultz, W. J., *American Public Finance and Taxation* (3rd ed.).

CHAPTER TWENTY

INTERNATIONAL ECONOMIC RELATIONS

International economic relations constitute a field of study within the main body of economic analysis because of the existence of independent nation-states each having a government capable of pursuing an independent economic policy with respect to the rest of the world. International economic relations are concerned with those special problems which arise because of the existence of political boundaries and which do not arise within a country. In particular, it is concerned with the nature of trade between countries, the flow of investment funds between them, the commercial and monetary policies pursued by the various governments, and the different organizational arrangements made for the purpose of facilitating international trade and finance.

BALANCE OF INTERNATIONAL PAYMENTS

Nature. The balance of international payments of a country is a statistical statement of all commercial and financial transactions carried on between the citizens and government of that country and all other countries during one calendar year. It is a summary account of all selling transactions of a country abroad (credits) and of all buying transactions (debits) which indicates the changing economic position of a country in the world economy. The balance of international payments of the United States is prepared annually by the Department of Commerce.

The balance of international payments includes not only payments made or received for the purchase or sale of goods (the so-called "visible" items) but also payments made or received for such things as tourist and shipping services (the so-called "invisible" items). In addition, capital transactions—that is, international lending and borrowing—are shown as well as interest and dividend payments and gold movements. The total amount of selling (credits) is always theoretically equal to the total buying (debits)—that is, the sale of securities and short-term notes abroad (borrowing) and the sale of gold are temporary offsetting credits to any commodity and service buying in excess of selling.

Frequently, references are made to such items as American exports, French imports, and British borrowing. The references seem to suggest that the government or a country, in a collective sense, is conducting foreign trade. These convenient abbreviations should not obscure the fact that in most cases individuals are buying and selling and borrowing and lending. The figures that appear in balances of international payments represent the sum totals of thousands of individual transactions plus some government transactions. This is still true today in spite of the fact that in one country, the Soviet Union, the government has a complete monopoly of foreign economic relations and that in many others, including the United States, governments have on an increasing scale been engaging in buying and selling and lending and borrowing.

The notation should also be made that the oft-heard expression "balance of trade" has no practical significance. The physical merchandise trade of a country cannot be separated from its other "invisible" transactions any more than a family's expenditure on food and clothing can be considered without also taking into account money spent on movies, doctor's bills, and streetcar fares. What is important in both cases is the total volume of *payments* received and made. Many countries (e.g., Britain) regularly import more commodities than they export while others (e.g., the U. S.) export more than they import. The former situation is sometimes referred to as an "unfavorable" balance of trade and the latter as a "favorable" balance. These expressions are derived from 18th-century mercantilist thought when the importance of service transactions and other invisible items was underestimated. There is not necessarily anything favorable or unfavorable about the situations described.

Principal Items. The items appearing in a typical balance of payments may be grouped under three headings.

CURRENT TRANSACTIONS. These include merchandise trade, shipping services, travel expenditures, personal remittances and charity, and interest and dividends on foreign investments. Whether a debit or a credit balance will appear for these items depends on the situation of the country under consideration. Thus the United States normally has a credit balance of merchandise trade (i.e., sells more goods to foreigners than we buy from them) but a debit balance as far as shipping services are concerned (i.e., we pay more out to foreign shipowners for the use of their ships than foreigners pay us for the use of American ships). Britain on the other hand normally has a debit balance in her merchandise trade and a credit balance for shipping services.

CAPITAL TRANSACTIONS. These are the long-term and short-term capital movements in and out of a country. It might be noted here that it is possible for a country to be a creditor on long-term account and a debtor on short-term account at one and the same time.

GOLD MOVEMENTS. Although gold has value as a commodity, it has special significance as an international medium of exchange and is therefore treated separately in balances of international payments. Gold is at times an important "balancing" item and is shipped from one country to another to make up a deficit existing between receipts and payments. This was true in the 1930's when the United States received large quantities of gold.

Significance. A study of a country's balance of payments reveals much information about its economic status and development. For instance, a country with a large excess of commodity imports over exports and a heavy credit balance on long-term capital account (e.g., Iran) is likely to be an immature debtor, an undeveloped country that is borrowing foreign capital and using it to finance imports of capital equipment. A country with an excess of commodity exports over imports and with a large debit balance for interest and dividends (e.g., Argentina) is likely to be a mature debtor, a country that has developed its resources with the aid of foreign capital and is now in the process of paying off its debts by means of an excess of exports of commodities. A country with an excess of exports over imports and with a large debit balance on long-term capital account (e.g., U. S.) is an immature creditor, a country which is providing foreigners with capital which they are using to buy the lender's goods. Finally, a country with an excess of imports over exports and a credit balance for interest and dividends (e.g., Britain before 1939) is a mature creditor, a highly developed country living partly on the proceeds of its foreign investments which it uses to pay for a large part of its imports. Trends in the balance of payments of different countries provide the necessary statistical information for the formulation of international policy.

NATURE OF INTERNATIONAL TRADE
Development of International Trade Theory.

MERCANTILISM. In the 17th and 18th centuries the desirability of a country exporting more goods than it imported was stressed by many businessmen and economists. They thought that this would result in an influx of gold and silver which would strengthen the nation. Government regulation of trade was designed to achieve such a favorable balance and took the form of encouraging domestic industry by means of subsidies and tariffs and controlling imports. These ideas, which overemphasized the significance of money and ignored the effect of an influx of gold on the price level and thus eventually on the export trade, comprised the philosophy of mercantilism.

CLASSICAL THEORY. The classical theory of international trade was expounded in its early form by David Hume and Adam Smith in the late 18th century, developed in the 19th century by David Ricardo, Nassau Senior, John Stuart Mill, and others, and reformulated in its most sophisticated modern form in the 20th century by Frank W. Taussig. Although the theory is no longer generally accepted as an adequate explanation of international trade, it did emphasize correctly the fundamental advantages of specialization and freedom of trade in a peaceful and stable world economy.

According to the classical theory, countries will maximize their real incomes if they specialize in the production of those commodities which they are best fitted to produce and exchange them against the products of other countries. What each country will produce depends on the real costs of production (measured in terms of labor time) of the commodities concerned. Trade will take place not only when an absolute difference in real costs exists (e.g., when Brazil can produce coffee more cheaply than in the U. S., and the U. S. produce automobiles more cheaply than Brazil) but also when a comparative difference in costs exists (e.g., when the U. S. can produce two commodities, X and Y, more cheaply than Brazil but has a greater advantage in the production of X than of Y; the U. S. will then specialize in X in which her advantage is comparatively greater, leaving Brazil to specialize in Y in which her disadvantage is less). The trade possibilities between two nations are stated in the form of a barter comparison of the ratios of real costs (in terms of labor time) of each country which establishes a range within which trade may take place. (If the same labor time in the U. S. produces 20 units of X and Y; in Brazil, 10 units of X and 15 of Y, then a U. S. export of 10 units of X which exchanged for more than 10 but less than 15 units of Y from Brazil would be a gain for both countries.) The terms of trade (the actual trading *ratio* between the two commodities) and thus the gains to be derived by each country depend on the strength of the demand of each country for the other's product. Money was introduced into the classical theory through the medium of the specie-flow, price-level mechanism under which gold would flow from a country which was importing heavily, thus reducing its price level, and into a country which was exporting heavily, raising its price level. These changes in the price level were assumed to make money costs and prices reflect the differences in labor time costs and to bring about changes in the demand for goods that would result in the restoration of equilibrium in international payments for a country.

Weaknesses of the Classical Theory. The classical theory is based on untenable assumptions. Goods and services are not bartered, and to analyze trade if more than two countries or two commodities are introduced is difficult. It rests on the labor cost theory of value which has been discarded from modern economic analysis—that is, on the belief that price relationships can be determined by comparing the amount of real labor effort embodied in each product. Taussig's attempts to introduce capital costs into the analysis were not successful. The classical theory also assumes that the factors of production are perfectly mobile within a country but immobile between them, which is not true. In addition, it assumes free competition, the validity of the quantity theory of money, and the existence of the semi-automatic gold standard.

Interregional and International Trade. The modern theory of international trade is based largely on the theories of the Swedish economist, Bertil Ohlin, who holds that international trade is only a special case of interregional trade between different parts of one country, its special characteristics resulting from the existence of political borders, tariffs, different monetary systems, and so on.

According to Ohlin, different geographical regions (whether in the same country or different ones) are differently endowed with the factors of production. If each region concentrates on the production of those things requiring a large proportion of the factors which are relatively abundant in it, then trade can take place to the mutual benefit of all. Thus, China would concentrate on products requiring much labor, which is relatively abundant, and little capital, which is scarce. Belgium, however, would concentrate on goods requiring much capital equipment and relatively little labor. Money costs per unit of output would be kept to a minimum in this way and international trade would take place on the basis of the price differences which result. Thus the United States can produce automobiles cheaply because of the abundance of capital and skilled labor, and Brazil can produce coffee cheaply because of the abundance of unskilled labor and the right climate and soil. Trade between the two on the basis of the resulting difference in money costs is the same as between North Dakota and Florida with regard to wheat and oranges. The economic reason for trade is the same; the difference lies in the special factors arising out of the existence of independent states. Specialization (i.e., greater use of the relatively more abundant and hence cheaper factors) and international trade permit a more economical use of the world's erratically located human and natural resources and a maximization of real income for all. In this sense, international trade theory is no different from domestic price theory which has been discussed in previous chapters.

Real Differences between International and Domestic Trade. The differences between international and domestic trade are several.

FACTORIAL MOBILITY. While the factors of production are not completely mobile within countries and are not completely immobile between them, nevertheless there is a degree of difference. Within a country labor is fairly mobile with the result that there is migration from low-wage to high-wage areas. Immigration restrictions prevent labor from moving freely between countries, however, and hence marginal labor productivity and wage rates differ between countries. Since labor is highly organized in some places and unorganized in others, wages may temporarily be held out of line with marginal productivity (e.g., in Japan before World War II). Under these conditions low money wages may for a time assist one country to compete abroad, whereas high money wages may hinder another. Although labor cannot move from the low to the high wage areas, international trade in the long run will correct such discrepancies because exports are encouraged from the country with a depressed wage level causing an increased demand for labor in it and thus higher wages. In most cases, however, the differences in money wages reveal little with regard to competition since high money wages are usually the result of high productivity and consequently unit costs may be quite low. Capital is still much more mobile within countries than between them.

ARTIFICIAL BARRIERS. One of the principal differences between international and domestic trade is that in the case of the former, governments have erected artificial barriers which restrict or even stop the free flow of goods and services. The Constitution of the United States prohibits trade barriers among the forty-eight states but among nations there are not only tariffs, but also quotas, licensing systems, embargoes, arbitrary administrative restrictions, and other obstacles to the free flow of goods. These obstacles frequently explain why certain commodities are not traded internationally or only in small quantities.

MONETARY DIFFERENCES. International trade differs from domestic trade in that different countries use different currencies. The problem of the rate of exchange between the two is thus introduced. More important than the different currencies, however, is the existence of different monetary authorities and banking systems, each pursuing different policies with regard to price levels, volume of credit, and employment. The fact that France, Switzerland, and Belgium all use the franc does not prevent these currencies from having different values in each of the three countries.

OTHER DIFFERENCES. Differences in language, government regulations, trading customs, and laws, etc., distinguish international from domestic trade. Also political factors are often important, traders sometimes running a greater risk in operating under another government's jurisdiction than under their own. Transportation costs in international trade are sometimes greater than in domestic trade, and hence, certain types of industries are usually local.

The Importance of International Trade to the U. S.

The importance of international trade to the United States is often overlooked. Although imports comprise a smaller percentage of national consumption and exports a smaller proportion of national production in the United States than in many other countries, nevertheless qualitatively (i.e., for particular products) international trade is extremely important.

EXPORTS. The prosperity of American agriculture and of many American industries depends to a large degree on foreign markets. Normally 30 per cent of American production of tobacco, 28 per cent of cotton, 11 per cent of wheat, 22 per cent of office machinery, 17 per cent of farm machinery, and 14 per cent of automobiles and trucks, to mention only a few, are sold abroad. A loss of foreign markets would mean first unemployment and reduced incomes in the export industries and then depression in many domestic industries as the purchasing power of the affected persons declines. An Alabama cotton grower, deprived of his British market, has less money to spend on Texas grapefruit or on a suit made in New York.

A substantial export trade is essential if the U. S. is to enjoy full employment and a high level of national income.

IMPORTS. Many products must be imported into the U. S. from abroad because they cannot be produced at all within the country. These include tin, nickel, coffee, and bananas. Other products must be imported because insufficient quantities are produced at home to satisfy domestic needs—for example, wool, sugar, newsprint, and bauxite (for aluminum). Many of the natural resources are being depleted at a rather rapid rate and for this reason it may be necessary to import increasing quantities of such things as petroleum, copper, and lumber in the future. Finally, the U. S. imports many commodities which can be obtained more cheaply abroad than at home. This is true in cases where foreign costs of production are lower because of superior quality or location of natural resources, because of a more efficient labor supply, or because of greater abundance or suitability of certain kinds of capital equipment. In such cases the U. S. benefits by importing because the consumer pays the lower price while American labor, capital, and raw materials, which might otherwise be used in inefficient production of the goods imported, are released for employment in more efficient industries. Moreover, trade is a two-way proposition. If the U. S. does not buy foreign goods, then foreigners will be unable to buy from the United States except with special assistance.

FOREIGN EXCHANGE RATES

Nature and Significance. Since countries use different currencies, any economic transaction requiring payments among them necessarily involves exchanging one into the other at the ruling price or rate of exchange. It is important that the rates of exchange remain fairly stable; otherwise, trade and investment are discouraged by the possibility of losses incurred through changes in the rates. For example, if an American buys £1,000 worth of goods from a British exporter on six months' credit when the rate of exchange is $4.86 = £1, he may expect to have to pay $4,860 in order to obtain £1,000 to settle the debt. But, if the rate of exchange should move to $5 = £1, the American might find at the end of the six months that he actually had to pay $5,000 to obtain his £1,000. Since the exchange rate in part reflects the price levels of the various countries and since these are determined largely by domestic monetary policies, exchange rate stability is difficult to achieve. In order to maintain the value or purchasing power of a currency and its exchange rate, a deflationary money and credit policy may be required in a given country. Lower domestic prices tend to check imports and to expand exports which prevents an excess of demand for foreign currencies from depreciating the domestic currency. The deflationary policy, however, may aggravate domestic unemployment and may not be followed. Numerous organizational arrangements have been developed to achieve stability of exchange rates with varying success.

The Mechanism of Exchange. Foreign exchange dealings are merely one phase of banking. Exporters, for example, usually do not attempt to collect directly from foreign customers the money which they owe for shipments because the transaction can be more cheaply and conveniently arranged through banks. The exporter sells for domestic currency or bank deposits his claim (represented by a bill of exchange or draft) against a foreign customer to a domestic bank which specializes in foreign exchange. The domestic bank sends the draft for collection to a foreign bank which acts as its agent, and the amount of the collected claim is credited by the foreign bank to the account of the domestic bank. The domestic bank as a result has foreign currency or bank deposits for sale which importers buy in the form of drafts from the domestic bank to settle their debts abroad. The bank acts as a middleman and clearing house for international trade transactions. Ordinarily it attempts to buy and sell the same quantity of drafts in order to maintain its usual balances in different foreign centers. The bank makes a profit (or commission) by buying drafts at a lower rate than it sells. Because of Britain's important position in international trade, London banks and bill brokers have accumulated experience and facilities for dealing in foreign exchange. Consequently, many transactions between individuals in other countries were settled in terms of pound drafts before World War II.

The *rate of exchange* or the price at which banks buy and sell claims (drafts) to foreign currency and bank deposits depends upon the present and prospective supply of and demand for claims. There is no organized exchange market; each bank quotes its own rates. There are, moreover, various types of drafts and methods used in settling international transactions. Bankers pay more for drafts of short maturity (payable on sight or thirty-day bills) and good security (bills drawn against well-known merchants or banks) than for long-term bills (payable in sixty or ninety days) or doubtful security. Doubtful bills are usually not purchased, but are taken by the banks for collection on a commission basis. The rate of exchange, then, for any currency usually refers to the price at which bankers are buying and selling cable transfers (bankers' checks transmitted by cable) or sight bills of good security, very little interest or risk being involved in the transaction. The complex factors which determine the supply of and the demand for foreign exchange, and hence, the rate of exchange, vary with monetary conditions.

Exchange Rates under the Gold Standard.

MINT PAR OF EXCHANGE AND GOLD POINTS. The international gold standard, as it operated prior to 1914 and in a more limited way from 1925 to 1931, was the most successful system yet devised for maintaining exchange stability. Under it each of the major countries fixed the value of its monetary unit in terms of gold, permitted free convertibility of the currency into gold and allowed freedom of export and import of the precious metal. Since currencies were convertible into a specified amount of gold, a fixed ratio was established between them known as the mint par of exchange. For example, the pound was officially equal to 113.0016 grains of fine gold and the dollar to 23.22 grains. Therefore, $4.86 was equal to £1. Any American selling transaction with foreigners (exporting of goods or services, sale of securities, etc.) in terms of British money increased the supply of pound drafts offered for sale to American banks and tended to depress the price below par. Any American buying transaction with foreigners (importing goods and services, purchase of securities, etc.) in terms of British money increased the demand for pound drafts from American banks and tended to raise the price above par. If the volume of selling greatly exceeded the volume of buying for several months, the price of British money remained below par, but not much below $4.85 (lower gold point or gold import point). At this price American bankers found it more profitable to convert their balances in British banks into gold and to ship the gold home than to sell drafts against them to American importers. (The cost of shipping gold, i.e., packing, freight, insurance, and interest loss, between Britain and the United States was about one-half of one per cent of the value of the gold.) If the volume of buying greatly exceeded the volume of selling for several months, the price of British money rose above par, but not much above $4.89 (upper gold point or gold export point). At this price American bankers found it more profitable to build up their balances in British banks by shipping gold abroad, than to acquire balances by buying drafts from American exporters. The net result of this situation was that the exchange rate could not fluctuate more than a few cents above or below the mint par without eventually setting in motion a gold flow.

GOLD SHIPMENTS AND EXCHANGE RATE READJUSTMENT. These gold shipments were made almost exclusively by banks. The shipments were in large amounts—that is, the banks did not use this method of increasing or decreasing their balances abroad until the difference between the supply and demand for bills of exchange was more than sufficient to cover the cost of shipment. In other words, the banks postponed gold shipments until the supply and demand trends for bills of exchange definitely made gold shipments the most profitable way to increase or decrease balances abroad. Several factors were important in the postponement of gold movements. If in the above case American buying transactions exceeded selling transactions, the demand for pound drafts from American banks raised the rate of exchange on Britain. The slightly higher exchange rate tended to check American buying from abroad because the import price of some products would be increased enough to make it unprofitable. American selling, especially securities, was encouraged. If the excessive buying movement continued, the exchange rate might be forced slightly higher. American bank balances abroad would be depleted and, if the buying movement was expected to end in a few months, American banks borrowed short-term funds from foreign banks and continued to sell drafts rather than to export gold. The increased utilization of the American banks' credit facilities might increase interest rates slightly. Higher interest rates would encourage Americans to sell fixed income securities, such as bonds, to foreigners which would increase American bank balances abroad. Higher interest rates also encouraged American agents of foreign banks to offer pound drafts for sale in order to obtain dollars for short-term loans to Americans which increased the supply of pound exchange, and hence, checked its rise in price. These factors might prevent the exchange rate from reaching the gold export point for several months, or until the buying movement receded enough to make gold exports unnecessary.

Exchange Rates under a Paper Standard.

SUPPLY AND DEMAND. Under paper standard conditions rates of exchange can vary greatly. Since there is no convertibility, nor freedom of export and import of gold usually, there is no mechanism to keep the rates near a mint par. The supply of and demand for foreign currencies which develop from buying and selling transactions will determine largely the rate of exchange from day to day. The rates will also be affected by speculative buying and selling of exchange. Between 1932 and 1934, for example, the pound-dollar rate ranged from a low of $3.20 = £1 to a high of $5.05 = £1. During the 1930's these fluctuations in exchange rates were accentuated by day-to-day movements of "hot money"—that is, short-term funds moving from one financial center to another seeking security. Extreme movements in the exchange rate in time usually tend to correct themselves. If the volume of American buying of pound drafts should be steadily maintained in excess of the supply of them, the pound would become so much more expensive in terms of the dollar that American buying would be discouraged. At the same time British demand for American exports and dollars would be encouraged, thus contributing towards a readjustment in the exchange rate. During the 1930's many countries deliberately depreciated their currencies in order to stimulate their export trade.

PURCHASING POWER PARITY THEORY. Some economists have claimed that under paper standard conditions a par of exchange exists which is the ratio between the internal purchasing power of different currencies. It is calculated from index numbers of price levels of different countries. Changes in prices, or the value of money, affect trade and exchange rates between countries. If the dollar (paper standard conditions) buys more commodities when exchanged for pound drafts and used to buy British goods than when spent at home, buying abroad is stimulated. The buying transactions tend to raise the price of British money until a kind of parity with American money is reached. Stated differently, if an inflation scheme in Britain suddenly doubled British prices, the price of pound drafts for sale by American banks would tend to fall one-half in terms of American dollars. The par, however, is temporary and changes with every alteration of internal or external trade conditions. Any par statistically calculated for a given time and country is likely to deviate widely from actual exchange rates. Consequently, any attempt to calculate a normal purchasing par for a paper standard currency to determine if it is over-valued or undervalued as compared with actual exchange rates is misleading.

Government Control of Exchange Rates. The unsatisfactory experience of many nations with widely fluctuating rates of exchange under uncontrolled paper standard conditions after World War I and until the middle 1920's was the basis later for experiments in controlled currencies. In the 1930's to check deflation and to improve employment, all countries abandoned, or modified, the gold standard. Nearly all governments, however, resorted to direct or indirect controls over foreign exchange transactions. Many countries resorted to direct exchange control in order to prevent an official depreciation of the currency in terms of foreign currencies. Others resorted to indirect controls to prevent dislocation of the exchanges by speculative movements of short-term funds.

Direct Exchange Control. Germany was the most important country to impose exchange control in the 1930's. The government enforced a complete monopoly of buying and selling in the foreign exchange market. German exporters were forced to sell to German banks at an arbitrarily fixed rate any foreign exchange acquired by them. German importers had to obtain a permit before foreign exchange could be purchased from German banks, which thus gave the government complete power to determine the nature, origin, and quantity of imports. As time went on, exchange control was used by the government as a weapon of aggressive trade policy, and numerous exchange rates were established depending on the nature of the transaction. Foreign tourists wishing to visit Germany were permitted to buy marks more cheaply than were some of the would-be purchasers of certain German goods. This represented in effect a limited and controlled devaluation of the mark.

The results of exchange control were thoroughly undesirable. Countries selling goods to Germany were paid in "blocked marks" that could only be spent in Germany. As a result, Germany's creditors were often forced to buy goods from her that might have been obtained more cheaply elsewhere. This meant that to an increasing degree exports and imports between pairs of countries exercising exchange control tended to move towards a balance which meant a decline in normal multilateral trade. Foreign investment virtually ceased since capital was not permitted to leave a country which exercised exchange control, whereas foreign investors were usually unable to withdraw interest and dividend payments. Governments gained more and more control over all international transactions, and trade was distorted into uneconomic channels. Stability of exchange rates was achieved, but only on a basis of reduced trade and higher costs.

Not every country exercised exchange control as rigidly as Germany. Many South American countries had very simple forms of control which merely involved the rationing of scarce foreign exchange according to the greatest need. Denmark's control was designed only to prevent flights of capital. With the outbreak of World War II all the major countries adopted direct exchange control as a war measure.

EXCHANGE STABILIZATION FUNDS. Some governments sought to end the fluctuating exchange rates of the thirties by less drastic measures. Britain established an Exchange Equalization Account (£375,000,000) in 1932 and the United States an Exchange Stabilization Fund ($2,000,000,000) in 1934, both of which engaged in the buying and selling of foreign exchange in the open market for the purpose of offsetting any abnormal activity. For instance, if there was heavy buying of dollars in Britain which threatened to change the exchange rate, the British fund would sell dollars and if necessary borrow dollars from the American fund. Thus the effects of speculation and the movement of "hot money" could be offset. The huge government funds could easily dominate the market. Under the Tripartite Monetary Agreement of 1936, the British, French, and American stabilization funds were to be used in co-ordination to keep exchange rates stable. This was temporarily successful but ended with the outbreak of war in 1939.

International Monetary Fund. A major problem is how to maintain stable exchange rates and still avoid both the evils of exchange control and the rigidities of the old gold standard under which nations were often forced into painful deflation and unemployment in attempts to preserve exchange stability. The International Monetary Fund, established at the Bretton Woods Conference in 1944, represents the postwar attempt of the United Nations to solve this problem.

PURPOSES. The International Monetary Fund is intended to promote international monetary co-operation, eliminate exchange control, bring about stability of exchange rates, and provide for orderly change if conditions warrant it.

STRUCTURE AND FUNCTIONING. The Fund consists of $8,000,000,000 contributed by the forty-nine member countries, approximately 25 per cent of each member's quota being in gold and 75 per cent in its own currency. The Fund began operations in March, 1947, and the membership cited is that of November, 1950. Only part of the quota for each member has actually been contributed. The U. S. quota is $2,750,000,000. Voting power is allocated according to the size of a country's quota. Each country has fixed the value of its currency in terms of gold or the U. S. dollar, thus establishing a series of rates of exchange which cannot be changed by more than 10 per cent without the permission of the Fund. If the Fund finds, however, that a particular exchange rate does not reflect the fundamental cost-price situation in a country, then it can permit an orderly revaluation. The purpose of the Fund is to permit limited flexibility and yet to prevent the sort of competitive depreciation which took place before World War II. Any nation which is temporarily embarrassed by a shortage of any foreign currency may obtain that currency from the Fund in return for depositing an equal amount of its own currency. Thus one of the principal weaknesses of the gold standard is avoided—namely, that any country suffering from a shortage of foreign exchange inevitably lost gold and had to endure a painful deflation to bring about readjustment. The Fund will not support an exchange rate indefinitely in face of a fundamental disequilibrium, but it will provide the equivalent of a short-term loan to tide the country in question over a difficult period and give it time to solve its own problems. No interest rate is charged for the first three months; after that it rises steadily and the Fund can deny use of its resources to any member abusing its privileges. A parallel may be drawn with the Federal Reserve System in the United States where the Federal Reserve Banks will mobilize resources in support of a member bank that may be temporarily low on reserves instead of leaving each individual bank to face its difficulties alone.

Exchange control and multiple exchange rates are forbidden with two exceptions, although a transitional period is permitted during which members must be prepared for the abandonment of wartime restrictions. The two exceptions are that a member may impose restrictions on capital transfers (but not on current transactions) to prevent its flight abroad and on transactions in a currency officially declared "scarce" by the Fund.

EVALUATION. The Fund is not designed to take care of the abnormal postwar situation with its shortage of dollars. Its success will depend partly on whether certain objectives are achieved—particularly the lowering of trade barriers, the reconstruction of international investment, the maintenance of a high level of employment, and the establishment of greater economic and political stability in the world. However, ten years after the war the Fund was only partially operative. Nearly all nations retained exchange controls of the "transitional period." Convertibility of currencies was not imminent.

INTERNATIONAL INVESTMENT

Long-term Investment. The flow of capital funds from highly-developed countries into less well-developed areas is a normal and desirable process. The investment enables the borrower to develop resources and raise living standards while the lender benefits not only from the interest and dividends received but also from the expanded markets for goods which result from the increase in the borrower's purchasing power. Thus British capital before World War I helped to develop the resources of the United States, Canada, Argentina, and other countries, whereas today American capital is aiding in the development of Mexico, India, Brazil, and other areas. A healthy flow of capital between nations stimulates production and trade to the benefit of all.

Before World War I political and social conditions were relatively stable; the gold standard functioned smoothly providing a mechanism of exchange; barriers to trade were relatively low; in short, conditions were favorable to the free flow of investment funds and interest and dividend payments. After World War I and until 1929, foreign investment was renewed, particularly by the United States which poured billions of dollars into the rest of the world. Unfortunately, much of this lending was speculative in nature and only succeeded in concealing the fundamental weaknesses which had developed in the world economy as a result of the war. With the onslaught of the depression in 1929, American lending stopped, the gold standard broke down, the barriers to world trade were raised, and social unrest and political tension increased, culminating in war again in 1939. Conditions in the 1930's were not favorable to international investment which practically ceased, except for political loans by governments, with the result that some countries' development was retarded for lack of capital while others had idle funds that could not find employment. One of the major problems now confronting the world is how to revive international investment.

American Foreign Lending.

BEFORE WORLD WAR II. Before World War I, the United States was a net debtor nation to the extent of over three and a half billion dollars. In 1919, as a result of huge wartime lending accompanied by a liquidation of foreign assets in this country, the U. S. became the world's greatest creditor nation. By 1930, when long-term investment virtually ceased, the United States was a net creditor to the extent of ten billion dollars (excluding war loans). These rapid changes in the investment position of the country necessitated changes in various items in the balance of international payments. If a creditor nation is to receive payment of interest and dividends and eventually repayment of principal, it must be prepared to accept a larger volume of imports. This the United States was unwilling to do as evidenced by the three successive increases in the tariff between 1921 and 1930. Consequently, many debtors eventually defaulted. In addition, the American banking syndicates which floated foreign security issues were often more interested in making large commissions than in promoting sound investment. They stressed the physical productivity of the investment without mentioning the difficulties many countries were likely to encounter in transferring interest payments to the lenders. The general outcome was heavy losses for American investors. During the 1930's the market for foreign securities in the United States was stagnant.

POSTWAR INVESTMENT PROBLEMS. The end of World War II found Europe economically prostrate and only the United States capable of furnishing the capital for reconstruction. Billions of dollars have been poured out in financial aid by the United States since the end of the war both directly (Export-Import Bank loans, the $3,375,000,000 loan to Britain in 1946, etc.) and indirectly by means of contributions to such international organizations as the World Bank, the International Monetary Fund, etc. Even greater outlays were made under the Truman Doctrine and the Marshall Plan. Postwar investment by the U. S. may be wasted unless (a) it is used productively in a co-ordinated European reconstruction plan, (b) the barriers to world trade are lowered, and (c) some element of political and social stability is maintained.*

International Bank for Reconstruction and Development. This institution (known also as the World Bank) was established at the Bretton Woods Conference in 1944 and started operating in 1946. Its purpose is to bring about a revival of international investment in order to facilitate the reconstruction of war-ruined countries and the development of retarded though potentially rich areas.

---

* With the outbreak of the Korean War in 1950, American aid to western Europe under the Marshall Plan (ECA) shifted from recovery to defense measures.

STRUCTURE OF THE WORLD BANK. In 1950 the World Bank had forty-seven members and a capital fund of $8,348,500,000, of which the United States contributed $3,175,000,000. Only 20 per cent of the capital had been called up (2 per cent in gold, 18 per cent in currency of member country) with the remaining 80 per cent to be called only in case the Bank had to honor its guarantees of private loans. The authorized capital is $10,000-000,000. Voting power in the Bank is related to the size of the quota; the United States has about 34 per cent of the votes.

FUNCTIONING. The World Bank will carry out three basic operations.

1) The Bank will guarantee private investments made in foreign security issues. It will do this only after careful investigation of the purposes to which the loan is to be put and only after the government of the borrowing country has added its guarantee. The hope is that the Bank's power and prestige will be such that a guarantee will automatically ensure success of the loan. In this way the Bank will be able to introduce an element of stability into international investment, encouraging sound productive loans and preventing bad ones. The Bank may not guarantee loans in excess of an amount equal to its capital so that it can always meet its obligations. Its main purpose is to encourage sound private investment, not supplant it with government lending.

2) The Bank will make loans itself out of its capital in cases where investment may be desirable, yet where it is not possible to raise the money in the private capital market. The Bank's first loan in May, 1947, was of this nature—$250,-000,000 to France.

3) The Bank will sell its own securities to the investing public and lend the proceeds to deserving borrowers, thus acting as an intermediary between borrower and lender and as a medium for the assembly of small savings for purposes of international lending. The Bank's first bond issue in the United States ($250,000,000) was successfully floated in July, 1947.

EVALUATION. The World Bank can contribute materially towards the alleviation of the great dollar shortage at the present time. It may also promote sound investment policies and reduce speculation and unwise lending. Its success, however, will depend on the realization by all nations that the loans will be sound only if the goods which are produced as a result of the investments are able to move between countries with relative freedom.

Short-term Funds. Under the gold standard, short-term capital (liquid assets including bank balances and easily marketable securities) was an equilibrating force in international economic relations. A country losing gold because of heavy buying of foreign currency in the foreign exchange market would raise its discount rate. The consequent rise in interest rates would attract short-term capital from abroad and this demand for domestic currency would help offset the original disequilibrium and reduce or stop the export of gold.

In the 1930's, however, short-term funds increased in volume tremendously (as long-term investment declined, people held their assets in more liquid form) and proved to be a most disturbing factor in the foreign exchange market. They moved from one financial center to another seeking security rather than a high interest rate. A change of government, a political rumor, not to mention civil wars and revolutions, were enough to cause an abnormal demand for the dollar in particular as Europeans sought to remove their short-term funds to a place of safety in America. Between 1934 and 1939 no less than $3,895,-000,000 of this so-called "hot money" sought refuge in the United States. Its transfer was largely accomplished by gold shipments to the United States. One of the principal reasons for the establishment of the stabilization funds was to prevent dislocation of exchange rates by movements of "hot money." "Hot money" will be less of a problem in the future if its volume is reduced by an expansion of long-term investment and if the establishment of stable political and social conditions in the different countries enables higher interest rates to replace the desire for security as the motivating force in their movement.

DYNAMIC CHANGE AND ADJUSTMENT IN INTERNATIONAL TRADE AND FINANCE

Equilibrium and Dynamic Change. The modern theory of international trade, like that of domestic price, revolves around the concept of equilibrium, which may be thought of as a sort of norm toward the establishment of which economic forces are constantly working. The balance of payments of a nation may be said to be in equilibrium when the visible and invisible items and long-term capital items on the debit side cancel out or are equal to the same items on the credit side. In this situation there is no need for the movement either of gold or short-term capital since these are essentially adjustment items, and, when equilibrium exists, no adjustment is necessary.

Actually, however, the world economy is one of dynamic change, and new disturbing factors are constantly appearing to upset this equilibrium. Before the effect of one disturbing factor has been worked out and equilibrium has been restored, another disturbing factor has put in its appearance; consequently, long-run equilibrium is an ideal which could only be reached in a static world. The disturbing dynamic factors include changes in the nature of the demand for goods brought about by changes in population, custom, fashion, and tastes; changes in production costs brought about by new inventions and discovery of new natural resources; changes in transportation costs which enable new goods to enter international trade (e.g., the development of the steamship and railroads in the 19th century); and cyclical fluctuations in the level of prosperity in important countries affecting incomes and the demand for goods. All these dynamic factors affect important items in the balance of payments causing a disturbance in the previously stable relationships and necessitating readjustment. The mechanisms, through which these readjustments take place, are an important part of international trade and finance.

Readjustment under the Gold Standard. The way in which readjustment will take place after the injection of a disturbing new dynamic factor into the situation depends partly on the type of monetary system used. Under the gold standard, if the disturbance is mild (e.g., a temporary increase in the demand for foreign wheat by a country because of a domestic crop failure), then readjustment may be effected quite simply through a flow of short-term funds to the importing country from abroad which would provide it with the necessary foreign exchange. The short-term funds could be attracted by raising the discount rate, which would avoid gold exports. Thus short-term funds act as a short-run equilibrating force. The slight rise in the price of foreign currencies (higher exchange rate but not to the gold export point) for the wheat importing country would stimulate some of its exports and provide for the return of the short-term funds.

However, if the disturbance is a deeply rooted one, for instance the beginning of heavy long-term lending by country A to country B, then more fundamental changes would have to take place in the flow of goods and services between the two countries, in the uses to which the factors of production are put in both countries, and in the level of prices. Short-term capital movements and gold movements provide for a short-run adjustment in the balance of payments, but they would in time be exhausted by a large export of capital. A heavy flow of long-term capital from A to B, made possible temporarily by imports of short-term funds and by exports of gold on the part of A, would cause a reduction in A's purchasing power and an increase in B's. This would bring about a fall in some of A's prices which would increase A's exports (and thus B's imports), and a rise in B's prices, which would decrease its exports (and thus A's imports). This would mean that in A's balance of payments the increase on the debit side in long-term capital flow would in time have been balanced on the credit side by an increase in the volume of commodity and service exports, whereas in B's balance of payments the increase on the credit side in long-term capital inflow would have been balanced on the debit side by increased commodity and service imports. In A the factors of production would be attracted into the expanding export industries and away from the domestic goods industries. In B they would move out of the export industries and into the expanding domestic goods industries.

Large-scale foreign lending usually stimulates the domestic development of the borrowing country, which is the purpose of the loan (e.g., U. S borrowing in the 19th century), and also the export trade of the lending country (e.g., Britain in the 19th century, U. S. today). The repayment of the loan would simply reverse the movement of short-term funds and gold, and eventually B's increased exports of goods and services, because of price changes, would provide the means of repayment. All of this analysis assumes a stable exchange rate maintained through the operation of the gold standard with each country following a money and credit policy to facilitate the adjustments.

Readjustment under Paper Standard Conditions. Under paper standard conditions a disturbance in the balance of payments affects the rate of exchange which is free to move. The adjustment process takes place mainly through the medium of the exchange rate. Under paper standard conditions if country A, as in the example used above, started heavy long-term lending to B, A's currency would depreciate and B's currency would become more expensive, i.e., the exchange rate would rise. This would make A's goods cheaper in terms of B's currency and B's goods more expensive to A, which in turn would stimulate A's exports of goods and services to B but reduce B's exports to A. These changes would cause B's currency to become somewhat cheaper again to A, the degree of change depending on the elasticity of each country's demand for the other's goods following the initial change in the exchange rate. At all events, A's export industries and B's domestic industries would be stimulated with changes in their prices and a consequent reallocation of the factors of production. Thus the same final result is achieved as under the gold standard except that it takes place through the medium of sharp changes in the exchange rate instead of in price levels. A's balance of payments would show an increase in exports on the credit side and an increase in long-term capital outflow on the debit side, while in B imports would have increased on the debit side and long-term capital inflow on the credit side.

Foreign Trade and the Multiplier. Until the great depression of the 1930's, one assumption underlying most economic theory was that of relatively full employment of labor, capital, and natural resources. If this assumption is made in international trade, as it formerly was, then adjustment following the appearance of an equilibrium-disturbing factor must always involve price changes. Thus, for example, factors of production are transferred (say) from domestic to export industries because of changes in the prices of these products and consequently in the prices of the factors of production too.

This assumption of full employment appeared rather absurd in the 1930's when all countries had considerable idle resources; consequently, some economists have reformulated the theory of dynamic change in such a way as to include the new conditions. This involves the use of the concept of the "multiplier" and a new approach to traditional ideas through an analysis of changes in national income rather than of price changes, or in some instances both.

Suppose country A's demand for country B's exports increases, an autonomous change brought about by changes in consumer tastes in A. What effect will the increased expenditure in B have on national income and employment in that country (assuming the existence of idle resources that can be brought into use instead of their having to be attracted away from B's domestic industries by offering higher prices)? The increased expenditure in B will inject new purchasing power into the economy which will create incomes and new jobs as it circulates through the system. This increase in income and employment will not be infinite, however, because of certain "leakages" which will occur. Some of the recipients of the new income will not spend all they receive but will save a portion, thus reducing the income flow. Others may spend part of their new income not on domestic goods but on imports from A or elsewhere. And there may be other "leakages." These "leakages" will occur each time the new injection of purchasing power changes hands, thus reducing the amount which is passed on to the next recipients. But the rest of the income will circulate until the total "leakages" equal the amount of the original injection and its effect is thus exhausted. Idle resources will be drawn into use, and jobs will be created.

The multiplier, if the data were available, may be obtained by dividing the total amount of new income created by the original amount of the injected expenditure. Thus, if A's extra demand for B's exports amounted to an expenditure of a million dollars and the multiplier were three, this would mean that the total amount of new income created in B would be three million dollars. If the multiplier were larger, let us say six, it would mean that the "leakages" were smaller and that the total amount of new income created was greater (six million dollars). Other dynamic changes can have similar effects on a country's income and employment. And of course, the multiplier can also work in reverse. A decline in exports, for instance, can mean a reduction in expenditure, and the effect of this can spread through the economy.

CONTROL OF INTERNATIONAL TRADE AND FINANCE

International trade permits regional specialization in the use of world resources. It promotes the most efficient allocation of the factors of production and helps maximize the real income of the citizens which engage in it. Artificial barriers which restrict the free flow of goods and services between nations help to reduce real income and result in a relatively inefficient use of the factors of production. Nevertheless, many such barriers have been erected not only by governments but also by private business groups through the medium of international cartels. The justification for such artificial barriers is only in part economic; it also involves a knowledge of political, sociological, and military factors. At the root of them all lies the fact that the world consists of independent sovereign states; national sovereignty and the cultural background of organized social groups prevent a rational organization of world trade on the basis of purely economic considerations. Economic policy is influenced by politics both within nations and in the relations among them. Within nations, special interest groups are able to profit at the expense of the national welfare when they can, for example, persuade their government to impose a protective tariff on some commodity in which they are interested. In international relations, individual countries often believe that they can benefit from some particular policy, such as state subsidization of exports, even though the world economy as a whole suffers. In both cases the triumph of special interests over the general welfare usually occurs. This is the key to an understanding of many of the reasons for the prevalence of restrictive controls in international trade.

Tariffs. The tariff is the oldest form of protectionism. It consists of a tax on imports which results in the sale price of the foreign goods being raised in the importing country.

SPECIFIC AND AD VALOREM DUTIES. Specific duties are those expressed in terms of a specific amount of money per unit of import, e.g., 50 cents per square yard of cloth. Ad valorem duties are those expressed in terms of a percentage of the value of the import. The burden of a specific duty may become lighter if the price of the imported good rises but heavier if the price falls. An ad valorem duty on the other hand is more flexible in that the actual amount of duty collected will rise or fall with the price of the good, thus ensuring the same degree of protection all the time.

SINGLE AND MULTIPLE-COLUMN TARIFFS. While the United States applies the same tariff to all imports regardless of country of origin (except Cuba and the Philippines), some countries discriminate in their duties charging higher ones on the imports of some countries than on the same goods coming from others. The American tariff is a single-column one; the British tariff on the other hand gives special preferences to imports from British Empire countries, whereas the Canadian tariff before the war had three levels—a preferential one applying to British goods, an intermediate one applying to American goods, and a general one applying to countries with whom Canada had no trade agreement. While a single-column tariff will block the free flow of goods among nations and thus reduce real income, a multiple-column tariff will in addition distort the reduced amount of trade and force it into artificial and uneconomic channels. A multiple-column tariff is a weapon of discrimination in international trade and must be condemned. The United States is at present trying to eliminate such discrimination by pressing for the adoption of the so-called unconditional most-favored-nation treatment in commercial relations which means that each country would afford equal treatment to all others.

REVENUE AND PROTECTIVE TARIFFS. A revenue tariff is one that is imposed, like any internal tax, for the purpose of raising revenue for the government. A protective tariff is one that is imposed for the purpose of excluding certain imports, raising the prices of those that are imported, and thus encouraging domestic production through the elimination or reduction of foreign competition. The British tariff before 1931 was primarily revenue-raising in that duties were levied on commodities that were not produced in Britain at all (tea, wine, etc.). A revenue tariff also exists when an excise tax equal in amount to the import duty is levied on domestic production so that domestic producers receive no protection. The American tariff on the other hand is a protective one. Revenue from customs duties only constitutes about 4 per cent of annual federal revenues, and the prime purpose of the tariff is to eliminate as much foreign competition as possible. Most duties are extremely high although certain essential raw materials and foodstuffs that cannot be produced in the U. S. are admitted free. Statements often made to the effect that 60 or 70 per cent of all imports enter a country duty-free are misleading and do not mean that the tariff is low. On the contrary, it usually means in modern times that the duties are so high that only a few of the dutiable articles are imported at all. Thus, even higher duties on dutiable imports would exclude even more until 100 per cent of all imports were duty-free.

Although tariffs are still the principal form of protection in the U. S., in most other countries they have been reinforced or replaced by far more restrictive devices, such as quotas. Tariffs restrict trade by operating on the prices of traded goods; but they do not prevent some trade from taking place if consumers are willing to pay the higher prices that result. The revival of world trade depends today primarily on the elimination of quotas, exchange control, and other quantitative restrictions and only secondarily on the reduction of the more old-fashioned restriction in the form of tariffs. Since, however, tariffs are the traditional form of trade control, the following discussion of protectionism will be carried on in terms of the tariff.

Arguments For and Against Protectionism. The arguments used for and against protectionism are varied and are not all economic in nature.

NATIONAL DEFENSE. Many countries wish to protect and develop industries essential in time of war so as not to be dependent on foreign supplies in time of emergency. The development of the British chemical industry after World War I, the protection afforded the British farmer in the 1930's, the development of synthetic oil plants in Germany after 1933, and the current American interest in maintaining synthetic rubber plants are all examples of this. In a world where wars seem to be frequent and imminent, the economist can hardly argue against national security on the grounds that protectionism of this kind is uneconomic. It is in part a kind of insurance. The cost of losing a war is much higher than the costs to consumers of a protective tariff. The economist can point out, however, that the decline in trade which results from protective tariffs brings lower living standards and thus generates in part tensions which lead to war. From a military point of view, the British might have been better off during World War II if the extra money paid by the British consumer during the '30's for taxed food imports and higher-priced domestic products had been spent instead on strengthening the navy which convoyed the food ships across the North and South Atlantic.

INFANT INDUSTRIES. Promotion of *infant industries* is the most defensible economic reason for the use of protective tariffs. If an industry seems suitable for a given country because of its natural resources or easy access to raw materials and equipment, its labor supply, and its large home market, a protective tariff will restrict foreign competition and give domestic enterprises an opportunity to develop a new industry. This was the situation in the United States in 1791 when Alexander Hamilton published his famous "Report on Manufactures" advocating a tariff to protect the infant American industries against British competition. The same arguments are being used today by such countries as Brazil, Australia, and New Zealand.

At first the price of the new domestic product may be as high as the price of the imported foreign product plus the tariff duty—that is, imports decline until demand raises the price of the small domestic supply to that level. The exact effect of tariff duties on prices depends upon the time period and upon the supply and demand conditions both at home and abroad for the given product. The higher price enables the domestic enterprises to increase production of the protected commodity even though the costs of production are higher than those of the foreign producers. Consumers of the product are injured by the higher price and other industries may be adversely affected because the demand for labor and materials in the new industry increases their costs of production.

Over a period of years (say ten to thirty), however, enterprises in the new industry may train their labor force, improve their technique of production, develop large-scale operations, and consequently steadily reduce their costs. Enterprises abroad may assist the development by establishing branch plants in the protected market. The competition of domestic enterprises may then lower·the price of the product to a point where the tariff is no longer needed. The price may be low enough to permit exporting to other countries. The new industry, moreover, may have promoted research work which assists other industries in improving their efficiency. The burden, then, placed upon consumers and other industries during the early stages in the growth of the new industry, may be offset later by lower prices for consumers and increased profits in other industries. The volume and variety of employment for labor is increased.

The strongest argument against tariff aid for an infant industry is that vested interests develop and no industry is ever ready to admit that it has reached maturity and no longer needs protection. For this reason, an outright subsidy by the government (instead of a hidden one paid by the consumers in the form of higher prices) would be preferable to a tariff because it might be easier to remove. Tariff protection, moreover, for a few suitable new industries inevitably develops into *blanket protection* for nearly all industries. The new industries may furnish semifinished products which are the raw materials for other home industries. The higher price of these products during the early stage of development prompts the other home industries using them to obtain tariff protection which will compensate for the higher price.

THE BALANCED ECONOMY. Some countries may wish for *sociological and political* reasons to protect certain industries, even though production and consumption is lowered, in order to obtain a better balance between urban and rural population. Agricultural products, for example, may be protected in order to prevent a decrease in rural population. A larger rural population may be desired because of the higher birth rate in agricultural sections, because rural life is deemed healthful and picturesque, and because the rural population is more conservative politically. This argument was used in France for many years, particularly since the peasantry was considered a good source of recruits for the army.

BARGAINING AND RETALIATION. In the past, some countries believed that a tariff was necessary as a bargaining weapon, so that the offer of a reduction in duties could be held out as a concession if other countries would reduce their duties. The imposition of a tariff for such a purpose is not likely to succeed as evidenced by the experience of Britain in 1931, but the bargaining method used by countries with established tariffs appears to be the only hope of achieving an all-round reduction. It has been used successfully by the United States through the Reciprocal Trade Agreement Program. A tariff imposed in retaliation against another country's duties is not necessarily mere retaliation, but more likely an economic necessity since, if country A's income from exports is reduced by a foreign tariff, it has less foreign exchange available for imports and is thus forced to cut down on its imports. In this way tariff warfare feeds on itself.

"EQUALIZING COSTS OF PRODUCTION." One of the most superficially reasonable but economically unsound arguments for protection is the one which calls for a duty equal to the difference in the costs of production of the domestic and foreign producers of a commodity in order that the sale prices will be equalized and "fair" competition result. In the first place, there is no such thing as *the* cost of production of a commodity since an industry consists of many different firms with different costs. If the duty equalizes the cost of the least efficient producer with the foreign cost, then the more efficient would receive excessive protection. Secondly, such an equalization, if it were practical, would eliminate the only reason for international trade taking place at all, i.e., price differences. Presumably the less efficient the domestic industry, the higher would be the duty.

CREATING EMPLOYMENT. One of the strongest arguments in popular discussion, and one that is practically unanswerable in times of depression, is that imports put domestic workers out of work. Keep out foreign goods, and the unemployed can find jobs making the same goods at home. Of course, domestic workers can find work in the protected industry, and for a short period of time total employment may increase. The reduction in imports, however, will eventually bring about a reduction in exports also since the amount of foreign exchange put into the hands of the foreigners is reduced. Unemployment and a reduction in purchasing power will therefore develop in other sections of the economy. This is what happened in Britain in the 1930's when her new tariff created employment in domestic industries but unemployment in her basic export trades. Eventually, if the factors of production are mobile, they may move from the stagnating export trades, where prices are falling, into the expanding protected ones, where prices are rising, but the result is an increasingly inefficient allocation of productive resources. At the same time consumers are paying higher prices for the products; hence, real income is reduced.

This analysis, theoretically sound if the assumption of relatively full employment of resources is made, has been considerably modified in recent years. The great depression of the 1930's made many realize that permanent economic stagnation was a possibility. By being the first to reduce imports during a depression, a country had an opportunity to improve its employment at the expense of other countries. Moreover, there was the possibility that the initial increase in employment and incomes in the protected industries would stimulate investment and generally expand employment and income. Also any government expenditures designed to increase employment and income required some restriction on imports in order to retain fully the immediate benefits. Mass unemployment in capitalist countries made efficient allocation of resources seem a less important matter than how to get people jobs through pump-priming and other types of credit expansion. The theories of the multiplier showed the way to a solution of the most important economic problem of the time (unemployment) and made an allocation of resources of less than optimum efficiency seem a small price to pay. A solution for both problems, full employment and efficient allocation, is the desirable objective.

CHEAP FOREIGN LABOR. Another popular argument in favor of protection is that it is necessary to prevent the products of cheap foreign labor from undercutting domestic goods made by high-wage labor. High wages, however, are usually the result of great efficiency. American automobiles, for instance, are the cheapest and most efficient in the world although Detroit auto workers are among the highest paid industrial workers. The wage scale is low in India on the other hand because Hindu workers are for various reasons not very productive. Although a Hindu earns only a fraction of a Detroit worker's pay, nevertheless this "cheap labor" could not make an automobile to sell at American prices, much less below them. The important thing is that the labor force in a country be used in the most efficient way, and there is no economic gain for the U. S. to produce goods that require little capital and a great amount of unskilled labor when this combination of factors is present in other countries.

This analysis may be modified in exceptional cases, such as existed in Japan before World War II when a medieval social organization was combined with 20th-century industrialism. Normally, as cheap Japanese exports expanded, the prices of the factors producing them would have been bid up and wages would have risen as a result. But the semifeudal social structure of Japanese society prevented the formation of free labor unions which might have prevented labor exploitation. Consequently, the U. S. felt justified in restricting the entry of many Japanese imports.

TARIFFS AND POLITICS. The above arguments used in connection with the imposition of a tariff are not the only ones. In general, the arguments for protectionism, in so far as they are valid, rest on a series of special and extenuating circumstances. The advantages of regional specialization and trade on the other hand may be stated in the form of a general principle which is difficult to refute without bringing in political, sociological, and military arguments which are often contradictory. Many tariffs, particularly those of the U. S., have been imposed because of political considerations. Lobbying has always enabled well-organized special interest groups to achieve protection for particular products since there is no lobby for the general welfare. And logrolling, the procedure by which each congressman votes for the pet duties of his colleagues in return for their voting for the ones in which his constituents are interested, has resulted, with a few exceptions, in a steady raising of the tariff wall.

Quotas. A quota is an actual quantitative limitation on the amount of a commodity that can be imported. Thus it may be far more drastic than the tariff since the latter permits any quantity to be imported if the duty is paid, whereas the quota puts an end to imports altogether once it is filled. When quotas first became popular in the early years of the 1930 depression, they were usually global in nature—that is, a total quota was announced and whoever got his goods into the country before it was filled could take advantage of it. This resulted in discrimination against distant suppliers and was generally replaced by the allocated quota in which each supplying country received a specific share of the total imports allowed. Usually the distribution of quotas was calculated according to the relative importance of the various suppliers in some base year. This introduced a most serious inflexibility into international trade since some countries were unable to expand their sales even though their production was becoming more efficient whereas others continued to receive large quotas although their production was declining or becoming less efficient. Currently, the U. S. is trying to get other nations to eliminate quotas wherever possible.

Exchange Control. This has already been discussed from the point of view of the exchange mechanism. The important point to repeat here is that, when the government acquires a monopoly over the means of foreign payment, it automatically acquires also complete control of the nature, origin, and quantity of imports. This is the most drastic form of trade control of all.

Administrative Protectionism. Before World War II international trade was being more and more restricted by the arbitrary administrative devices of officials. For example, imports of meat into the U. S. from Argentina were restricted by means of a rigid interpretation of the sanitary regulation designed to keep hoof-and-mouth disease out of the country. A minute subdivision of tariff schedules enabled countries to discriminate among their suppliers. The use of arbitrary rates of exchange for determining the value of the goods for duty purposes was another device. The filling-out of countless forms, masses of detailed regulations, the requirement that licenses be obtained, and many other legal procedures, all were gradually reducing world trade in the interwar period.

State Trading. The Soviet Union has a state trading monopoly which handles all importing and exporting. Increasingly, however, in recent years, other countries have established government purchasing commissions and state trading agencies to deal in specific commodities. In 1945, for instance, the British government established a monopoly for cotton importing. This practice poses serious problems for a country like the United States which desires to keep trade in the hands of private enterprise. In the first place, it is difficult to maintain complete equality of treatment in commercial relations when the decisions regarding imports are made not by private individuals on the basis of price and quality, but arbitrarily by government officials. In the second place, private traders in the exporting country are at a distinct disadvantage since they are dealing not with other private traders but with a government monopoly. It is indeed a perfect case of monopsony. Increasingly too, trade is becoming a matter of negotiation between two state trading agencies, one selling and the other buying. There is no reason for supposing that the growth of socialistic controls inside countries will not be paralleled by a similar growth in international trade.

Government Lending. Before World War II international investment was passing partially into the hands of governments. Many loans were political in nature. Even in the U. S. large loans were being made by the Export-Import Bank, a government institution, for the purpose of stimulating our exports. The proceeds of the loans had to be spent in the U. S. Since World War II the bulk of international lending has been by governments. Perhaps the guarantee system of the World Bank will reverse this trend, which is making international finance a matter for political rather than economic consideration (e.g., U. S. loans to Greece and Turkey, 1947).

International Cartels. These are perhaps the most sinister form of trade regulation since control is exercised not by governments in the interests of their citizens, but by private producers for the sole purpose of increasing profits regardless of the effect on consumers. International cartels have usually been formed by monopolistic producers in big industrial countries and have resulted in the division of markets, price maintenance, the elimination of competition, and the restriction of production. They have been particularly prevalent in the production of chemicals, electrical equipment, and synthetic products like plastics. The control is usually exercised through the medium of the cross-licensing of patents which has in many cases resulted in the world-wide control of production and trade by what almost amounts to a private government. The holding-up of synthetic rubber production in the U. S. just before Pearl Harbor is a notable example. Currently the United States, which has always been more opposed to international cartels than other countries (some of which have encouraged them), is seeking to get international agreement on their control. The accomplishments, however, are very slight.

International Commodity Agreements. In the past these have usually involved agreements between producers of primary products covering such things as production, exports, division of markets, prices, and reserve stocks. They were formed between World Wars I and II to control rubber, sugar, tin, tea, and other commodities. Usually the consumer was not represented, and in the case of rubber in particular, this omission led to considerable opposition in the U. S., the principal consumer, when the price of natural rubber was being held up by the production controls of the Stevenson Plan. Although this type of commodity agreement is undesirable, commodity agreements can play a constructive role in world trade in the future if they are concluded for the purpose of preventing violent price fluctuations and promoting orderly marketing through "ever-normal granary" type of buffer stocks. Consumers, however, should be represented in the plan, and better still, the agreements should be concluded by governments in the public interest (e.g., the International Wheat Agreement, Inter-American Coffee Agreement).

WORLD TRADE AND FINANCE, 1919–1939

The 19th-century System. Prior to 1914 world economic conditions were relatively stable and orderly. International trade and investment had been expanding for almost one hundred years and had brought about an unparalleled rise in living standards. The gold ·standard was operating in the most important nations, and London served as an international money market with pound drafts as a kind of international currency. The barriers to trade in the form of tariffs were relatively slight. National economies were integrated into a world system based on regional specialization and exchange. There was a minimum of government interference in economic life, mass unemployment was not a problem as it later became, and prices and incomes were flexible enough to permit trade adjustment to take place through moderate gold movements.

Attempted Reconstruction after World War I. World War I shattered the well-integrated, 19th-century system. It destroyed financial stability in most countries and saddled the world with huge reparation payments and war debts with which the conventional trade adjustment mechanism was unable to cope. It hastened the industrialization of agricultural countries (e.g., Argentina, Australia) and led them to raise tariffs in order to protect their infant industries. At the same time many industrial countries tried to develop agriculture in order to be more self-sufficient in the event of another war. Agricultural production had been overstimulated by wartime demands, and surpluses accumulated which depressed world commodity prices. Britain returned to the gold standard in 1925 but stabilized the pound at too high a level (its prewar gold par) with the result that she was forced into a painful deflation involving unemployment and persistent gold exports. The U. S. had become a creditor nation but was unwilling to accept the responsibilities of such a position. Instead of accepting more imports, she raised her tariff three times in nine years. In all countries growing rigidities in the price and income structure, brought about by the growth of monopolies and labor unions, made the conventional trade adjustment procedure more difficult. Tariff barriers rose everywhere. The only thing which prevented the collapse of 1929 from coming earlier was the unprecedented outflow of private loans from the United States which permitted world trade to continue and at the same time concealed the fundamentally unstable situation that really existed.

Collapse and Disintegration, 1929–1939. The flow of American lending stopped in 1929 when the Wall Street stock market boom collapsed. Thereafter an increasing number of countries got into difficulties with their balances of payments and tried to remedy the shortage of foreign exchange by the imposition of import restrictions. These restrictions only reduced other countries' exports and forced them to impose further restrictions. One of the worst developments was the imposition of the Hawley-Smoot Tariff by the U. S. in 1930. The agricultural countries were hit first by the decline in the prices of raw materials and several let their currencies depreciate in 1929 and 1930. The Hoover Moratorium Agreement suspended for one year (July, 1931, to July, 1932) payments of German reparations and of Allied War Debts and paved the way for their discontinuance at the end of the period, but the relief came too late. The floodgates were really opened, however, by Britain's abandonment of the gold standard in 1931, which destroyed the mechanism which had given financial stability to the world during the 19th century, and which launched the world into a period of competitive currency depreciation in order to shift the burden of unemployment. The extensive use of quotas by France, the development of exchange control by Germany, and the establishment of a discriminating tariff system known as "imperial preference" by Britain contributed to the decline of world trade to about one-third of its predepression value.

The last chance the world had to take any collective action to restore world prosperity was at the World Monetary and Economic Conference held in London in 1933. The failure of the conference clearly revealed the divergence of national interests with respect to international economics and the unwillingness of nations to make any sacrifices for the sake of international order.

Since France had already devalued substantially the franc (stabilized at 3.9 cents in 1928 instead of prewar 19.3) with beneficial results for her gold supply and foreign trade, she favored maintenance of the gold standard by all countries. Great Britain opposed immediate stabilization of the pound because of her unfortunate stabilization experience in 1925 and because of the advantages gained since the abandonment of the gold standard in 1931. Both countries wished to discuss war debt reductions with the United States. The United States refused to discuss collectively the latter issue and opposed immediate stabilization of the dollar, which by the end of the year was devalued 41 per cent, because of her domestic program of public spending inaugurated to raise prices. The United States was willing to discuss general tariff reductions, but, without stabilization of currencies, tariff reduction could in part be offset by currency manipulation. Great Britain and the United States, moreover, could not agree, granting the general desirability of stabilization, on the relation of new gold pars (i.e., which should devaluate more relative to the other). The Conference ended, and the divergent policies continued until the fall of 1936 when a temporary and partial agreement was reached through the Tripartite Monetary Agreement already mentioned. In the later thirties, the huge expenditures on armaments, political loans, and the use of economic policy as a military and diplomatic weapon completed the disintegration of the world trading system.

U. S. Economic Foreign Policy between Wars. During the 1920's the U. S. pursued a contradictory economic foreign policy. The country had become a great creditor nation as a result of World War I, and huge postwar lending and prompt repayment of these loans as well as the World War I debts was expected. Yet the flow of imports into the country was restricted by means of three successive increases in the tariff (1921, 1922, and 1930) and thus foreigners were prevented from settling their debts to us in the only practical way, i.e., by selling us goods. This contradictory state of affairs was concealed for some years by further American lending which put dollars into foreigners' hands which they could use to repay old loans and buy American goods. The folly of the policy became apparent in 1932, however, when exports from the United States fell to less than one-third of their 1929 level and many foreign debtors defaulted in their loan obligations to the United States.

The first year of the Roosevelt Administration was marked by monetary experiments including the devaluation of the dollar and the refusal of the U. S. to consider exchange stabilization at the London Conference for the reason indicated above. Later the U. S. co-operated with Britain and France to maintain exchange stability. The Johnson Debt Default Act of 1934, an unnecessary piece of legislation, prohibited government loans to any foreign country in default in the payment of obligations owed the United States government.

The most constructive American policy started in 1934 when the Reciprocal Trade Agreement program was launched. This act gave the president the power to conclude trade agreements with other countries involving a reduction in American duties in return for a reduction in their duties. American duties could not be cut by more than 50 per cent of the Hawley-Smoot levels of 1930, and the benefits of all reductions were to be extended to all countries through the operation of the unconditional most-favored-nation clause, thus ensuring equality of treatment for all. Agreements were concluded with twenty-two countries up to Pearl Harbor (including Canada, France, Britain, Sweden, and Brazil), and there is evidence that the markets for American exports were materially expanded by the program. Particularly significant was the comprehensive agreement concluded with Britain in 1938. The Reciprocal Trade Agreement Program is evidence of the determination of the United States, expressed at the London Conference, to free trade from some of its restrictions. The president's powers to reduce duties have been expanded to permit a 50 per cent reduction in the 1945 level, thus permitting a maximum cut of 75 per cent in the Hawley-Smoot schedules in some cases.

In other respects, however, U. S. economic foreign policy in the 1930's was contradictory. For instance, domestic agricultural policy was designed to force up farm prices which hardly fitted in with the desire to expand agricultural exports. Eventually export subsidies were resorted to for wheat and cotton in order to reduce the prices to the foreign buyers.

WORLD WAR II AND POSTWAR PROBLEMS
Effects of World War II.

SHIFTS IN ECONOMIC POWER. One of the results of World War II was to eliminate Germany and Japan as industrial powers and seriously weaken the economic and financial strength of Britain and the rest of Europe, but to increase the productive capacity and economic power of the United States. At the present time, therefore, the United States is the only nation with the resources available for the reconstruction of the rest of the world.

CHANGED DEBTOR-CREDITOR POSITIONS. Britain entered World War II as a creditor nation with considerable foreign investments. She emerged from it a virtually bankrupt debtor owing billions of dollars to her dominions and colonies and with her economic resources so depleted that there is serious doubt whether she can ever finance essential imports of food and raw materials much less pay off her foreign debts. The United States on the other hand, after canceling forty billion dollars of lend-lease debt after the war, has poured out further billions to aid in postwar reconstruction.

THE GREAT DOLLAR SHORTAGE. The United States is the only country physically capable of supplying the reconstruction needs of the rest of the world at the present time, but there is a world-wide shortage of dollar exchange with which foreigners can pay for our goods. Their sales to the U. S. cannot expand rapidly. As a result the U. S. has had either to give a large part of the exports as gifts or to lend foreigners the money with which to pay for them. The supplying of dollars in this fashion by the U. S. not only is a matter of life and death to the recipients but also is the only way in which the huge volume of exports on which American prosperity partly depends can be maintained. In the long-run, the permanent reconstruction of war-wrecked economies, enabling them to produce and pay their own way, is the only real answer to this problem.

New International Organizations. The postwar period has seen the appearance of several important international institutions (in addition to the ones already discussed) designed to deal with specific problems in the field of international trade. Most of them are grouped together under the general supervision of the Economic and Social Council of the United Nations.

INTERNATIONAL TRADE ORGANIZATION. The Havana Charter signed by fifty-three countries in 1948, but not ratified for operation, proposes to establish an International Trade Organization. This would have as its objectives a reduction in the obstacles to international trade (tariffs, quotas, etc.), the establishment of a code of fair trading practices, the supervision of international commodity agreements and cartels, and the provision of a medium for international action in the field of trade development.

Also, the United States sponsored a General Agreement on Tariffs and Trade which reduced trade restrictions among twenty-three countries (Geneva, 1947). The GATT was expanded to include additional reductions and ten more countries at Annecy, France, in 1949 and a few improvements were made at Torquay, England, in 1951. A fourth general session of GATT (including 25 nations) for negotiating lower tariffs on a reciprocal basis was arranged for 1956 (Geneva). There was also the proposal to make GATT a continuous operating organization (Organization for Trade Cooperation) as a partial substitute for ITO which was not ratified.

The Trade Agreement Extension Act of 1955 authorized the President to negotiate reciprocal trade agreements with other nations until June 30, 1958. Duties in excess of 50 per cent ad valorem may be reduced to that level by equal amounts over a 3-year period. Any duty (as of January 1, 1955) may be reduced 15 per cent—5 per cent each year over a 3-year period. The Act permitted the President to impose quotas or other restrictions on any article if it is imported in such quantities as to threaten the national security. The Act also continues "peril point" provisions (i.e., Tariff Commission estimation of minimum duty rates required to prevent possible injury to domestic producers), and "escape clause" provisions (i.e., Tariff Commission investigation of complaints by a portion of an industry that existing duties are too low to prevent possible injury to a subdivision of an industry). In the latter case the President may increase duties and rescind trade agreement concessions.

Food and Agriculture Organization. This was established at the Hot Springs Conference, 1943, for the purpose of developing co-operation among nations in the field of agricultural production, nutritional standards, etc. Its purpose is to prevent a repetition of the situation in the 1930's when food surpluses piled up in some countries while people went hungry in others. It will also act as a central agency for all information in this field.

INTERNATIONAL CIVIL AVIATION ORGANIZATION. This organization grew out of the Chicago Civil Aviation Conference, 1943, and has sought to develop world-wide air communications with a minimum of obstacles to the free movement of passengers and planes. It also promotes co-operation between nations in the technical field.

None of the plans, however, for the reconstruction of world trade, including the Monetary Fund and World Bank, will be successful until the basic issue of world political security is solved. It is still true today that international trade is thwarted not by geography or technology but by politics. The prosperity of nations depends upon greater freedom and stability with regard to international trade and finance.

GENERAL REFERENCES

Commission of Foreign Economic Policy, *Report to the President*.

Ellsworth, P. T., *The International Economy*.

Haberler, Gottfried von, *The Theory of International Trade*.

———, *Survey of International Trade Theory*.

International Monetary Fund, *Balance of Payments Yearbook*.

Isaacs, Asher, *International Trade, Tariff and Commercial Policies*.

Kindleberger, Charles P., *International Economics*.

Krause, W., *The International Economy*.

Meade, J. E., *The Balance of Payments*.

Ohlin, Bertil, *Interregional and International Trade*.

Piquet, H. S., *Aid, Trade, and the Tariff*.

Public Advisory Board for Mutual Security, *Report to the President*.

Towle, L. W., *International Trade and Commercial Policy*.

U. S. Department of Commerce, *The United States and the World Economy*.

———, *The Balance of International Payments of the U. S.*

Viner, Jacob, *Studies in the Theory of International Trade*.

———, *Trade Relations between Free-Market and Controlled Economies*.

Young, John P., *The International Economy*.

FINAL EXAMINATIONS

PART I. TRUE-FALSE PROBLEMS

The first fifty statements are either true or false. The statement is false if any element of it is false. The correct answers are in the key on page 356.

Questions   *Check One*
                                               T–   F–

1. In an "economy of abundance" goods and services which satisfy human wants will remain scarce relative to total demand.   ✓ _____   _____

2. A substantial increase in production would eliminate the problem of allocation in the American economy.   _____   ✓ _____

3. Production is the process of creating various forms of utility; consumption is the process of destroying utility in the satisfaction of human wants.   ✓ _____   _____

4. Adam Smith's *Wealth of Nations* substantially supported mercantilism.   _____   ✓ _____

5. Various economic and industrial stages of development were often contemporaneous in the United States.   ✓ _____   _____

6. The main difference in economic systems appears in the mechanism for co-ordinating production and consumption. ✓ _____   _____

7. In the United States, prices which emerge from relatively free market transactions provide the main mechanism for co-ordination of production and consumption.   ✓ _____   _____

8. In the Soviet Union, state ownership is restricted to natural resources and the means of production in basic industries; individuals can own all kinds of personal property, engage in small private business enterprises, and operate small farms privately.   _____   ✓ _____

9. Free private enterprise in the United States is based on fundamental laws and customs which safeguard personal liberty, private property rights, and freedom of contract; certain government regulations define the limits within which the forces of the market operate.   ✓ _____   _____

Questions

10. An individual proprietorship has "limited liability" for business debts. ____ ✓

11. The corporation is a separate legal entity or person usually distinct from its owners. ✓ ____

12. The law of nonproportional returns is based on the use of a fixed factor of production and one or more variable factors. ✓ ____

13. For any enterprise using fixed and variable factors of production, the least-cost combination is never in the stage of diminishing returns. ____ ✓

14. The least-cost combination of factors is not always the most profitable output for an enterprise. ✓ ____

15. Economies of scale are related to variation in all factors of production in an enterprise. ✓ ____

16. In economic analysis marketing, risk-bearing, and transporting are not treated as part of the production process. ____ ✓

17. Real wages are calculated by dividing the index number of money wages by the index of consumers' prices. ✓ ____

18. Consumption in a competitive, private enterprise system, with some exceptions, is a guide to production and a reward for efficient production. ✓ ____

19. Only government agencies in the United States protect consumers in their purchases of goods and services. ____ ✓

20. In economic analysis markets are usually classified according to the number of buyers and sellers, the nature of the commodity (uniform or differentiated), and the conditions of entry. ✓ ____

21. Unitary elasticity of demand means that the quantity purchased by buyers varies directly with different prices. ____ ✓

22. All prices in the economy can be explained in terms of competitive, long-run equilibrium analysis. ____ ✓

23. The analysis of a competitive normal price provides, with some important exceptions, a useful standard for evaluating profits and for the allocation of goods and services. ✓ ____

24. Under semicompetitive conditions (monopolistic competition or imperfect competition, oligopoly, etc.) there are only a few possible adjustments of costs and prices for various commodities. ____ ✓

25. The supply of money includes cash, currency, demand deposits, and government bonds. ____ ____

26. Under existing monetary legislation in the United States, Gresham's Law is not an effective operating principle. ____ ____

27. Commercial banks increase their assets and liabilities when they make loans and discounts. ____ ____

28. Federal Reserve Banks are privately owned and publicly controlled. ____ ____

29. Member banks of the Federal Reserve System are required to maintain a 25 per cent reserve in gold certificates in the Federal Reserve Banks. _____ _____

30. The elasticity of note issue in the Federal Reserve System is now restricted to the amount of prime commercial paper arising from business transactions. _____ _____

31. A general change in prices indicates a change in the value of money and is measured by index numbers for a given date with reference to a base period. _____ _____

32. The equation of exchange $(MV + M'V' = PT)$ indicates the cause of price-level changes, but the quantity theory of money is a mathematical truism. _____ _____

33. Substantial doubt exists concerning the objectives in controlling secular price changes and the plans for achieving them. _____ _____

34. Investigation of business cycles involves correction of data for secular trend and seasonal variation. _____ _____

35. Functional distribution analysis attempts to explore inequalities in the receipt of income among individuals and families. _____ _____

36. Depending on the assumption of land being a general fixed factor of production, or a variable factor suitable for different uses, land rents are a result of prices paid for products or a cost influencing certain prices. _____ _____

37. The demand for loan funds (bank credit and savings) is based partly on their productivity in the purchase of capital equipment. _____ _____

38. Market rates of interest always have a close relation to a normal rate of interest. _____ _____

39. The demand for labor in the United States is closely related to its net marginal productivity. _____ _____

40. Pure profits are the result of dynamic conditions; minimum profits, the result of long-run (static), competitive conditions. _____ _____

41. National income is the estimated dollar value of all goods and services produced in a given year. _____ _____

42. A substantial majority of American employees do not belong to labor unions. _____ _____

43. The Labor-Management Relations Act of 1947 primarily favors unions by banning unfair labor practices by employers. _____ _____

44. A paucity of producers in a given industdy (oligopoly or industrial concentration) is a characteristic of many branches of manufacturing in the United States. _____ _____

45. The antitrust laws are based on the belief that competition is an effective regulator of most markets and,

Questions

with a few exceptions, that monopolistic practices can be
stopped by enforcing competition.   ____   ____

46. War costs, past and prospective, account for about 75
per cent of federal expenditures.   ____   ____

47. For fiscal adequacy any tax system in the United
States requires a diversity of taxes and some combination
of the benefit and ability principles of taxation. ____   ____

48. A country with a large excess of commodity imports
over exports and a heavy credit balance on long-term capital
account is likely to be an immature debtor country in an
undeveloped industrial stage.   ____   ____

49. Since the United States is relatively self-sufficient in
its production for domestic consumption, international trade
is of little importance for its prosperity and for a high
level of per capita consumption.   ____   ____

50. If approximately 70 per cent of all imports enter a
country duty-free, the conclusion is certain that the country
has few tariffs or very low tariffs on imports.   ____   ____

PART II. MULTIPLE-CHOICE QUESTIONS

This part consists of forty multiple-choice statements. For
each statement choose the numbered portion which most accurately completes the statement. The correct answers are in the
key on page 356.

Statement   *Selection*

51. The primary aim of economics is an explanation of
(1) how scarce means of production are allocated to satisfy
human wants of varying importance, (2) how to conserve
natural resources and to improve consumers' wants, (3)
how to select worthwhile social objectives for an economic
system to achieve.   _____

52. In economic analysis the method used is chiefly (1)
quantitative and inductive, (2) experimental with controlled
conditions, (3) qualitative, deductive, and statistical.   _____

53. A secondary aim of economics is an evaluation of
how well an allocating system operates with reference usually to an ideal type of competitive market allocation and
chiefly involves suggestions of policy for improving (1)
market adjustments, (2) specifications of social needs, (3)
principles of social justice.   _____

54. The English Industrial Revolution consisted basically

Statement *Selection*

of a change in (1) Britain's political institutions, (2) Britain's use of machines and mechanical power, (3) Britain's foreign trade operations.

55. In the United States government intervenes in economic affairs in order to (1) supplant the widespread failures of private enterprise, (2) supplement and control the operation of some private enterprises, (3) curb the growth of socialism.

56. In a corporation the owners of the enterprise are usually (1) holders of bonds and notes, (2) holders of common and preferred stock, (3) holders of notes and bills payable.

57. The balance sheet of a corporation usually (1) shows all the information needed to determine its financial position, (2) indicates detailed operations of receipts and expenses during the year, (3) needs to be supplemented by the income statement to determine its financial position.

58. The law of nonproportional returns indicates the nature of (1) technological changes, (2) physical input-output relations under certain conditions in a production unit, (3) economies of large-scale production, (4) least-cost combination of factors.

59. Entrepreneurs find it profitable to increase the variable factors in an enterprise as long as (1) no diminishing returns appear, (2) marginal costs are only slightly in excess of marginal receipts, (3) marginal receipts exceed marginal costs.

60. Hedging involves (1) cautious spot sales, (2) both spot and future contracts, (3) careful manipulation of "short sales."

61. Consumption in a private enterprise system is sometimes an ineffective guide for production because of (1) the influence of producers on the choices of consumers, (2) the complete knowledge possessed by consumers, (3) the adequate legal protection provided for consumers.

62. In a purely competitive market, firms (1) in the long run adjust output until the price is equal to the minimum average total unit cost, (2) in the short run try to maximize profits or minimize losses by holding marginal costs below marginal receipts, (3) in a brief market period sell only at a price which covers total average unit costs.

63. In the long run an increase in demand in a purely competitive market (1) would lower price slightly in a constant cost industry, (2) would increase price in an increasing cost industry, (3) would result in a competitive equilibrium price in a decreasing cost industry.

64. Under conditions of joint supply and joint costs

normal price for any one of the products is (1) equal to its average cost, (2) equal to its marginal cost, (3) not directly related to its cost.

65. In a purely monopolistic market the seller maximizes profit by (1) always operating at the output where the greatest difference between cost and price per unit exists, (2) never charging differential prices, (3) equating marginal costs and marginal receipts.

66. Capitalization of expected future incomes from production goods is the method (1) used by government in fixing prices during a war period, (2) used in part by businessmen in estimating the value of a production unit, (3) used by a monopoly in setting prices.

67. The money of the United States may be accurately described as (1) fiduciary or credit money, (2) standard or commodity money, (3) fiat money.

68. The control of money and credit is now (1) completely centralized in the Board of Governors of the FRS, (2) entirely a matter of fiscal policy, (3) a combination of monetary and fiscal policy.

69. An upward, secular price trend usually affects (1) creditors favorably; (2) debtors adversely; (3) the owners of common stock very little or favorably.

70. The quantity theory of money is open to criticism because (1) it ignores the causes of short-run changes in the demand for money for different uses, (2) it assumes that changes in prices are likely to be only approximately proportional to changes in the quantity of money, (3) it asserts that governments sometimes meet emergency expenditures by using bank credit or issuing paper money.

71. Business cycles are caused by (1) variations in agricultural output resulting from climatic changes; (2) profit-seeking as related to investment opportunities, leads and lags in purchasing power particularly among wage-earners, and hoarding of money income; (3) general over-production and under-consumption.

72. Business fluctuations cannot be eliminated, but they probably can be alleviated substantially by (1) appropriate monetary policy, (2) appropriate fiscal policy, (3) a unified program of monetary and fiscal policy and other related governmental measures.

73. The marginal productivity theory of functional distribution assumes (1) separate variation of homogeneous factors of production under conditions of perfect competition, (2) no changes in conditions of supply and demand, (3) no substitution of one factor of production for another.

74. Land rents are unearned and in a private enterprise economy should be (1) received by the government in the form of special tax revenues, (2) treated as one kind of possible unearned return inseparable from earned returns and subject to general taxation, (3) considered as indispensable in a private ownership system and hence not wisely subject to any governmental measures.

75. The short-term rate of interest may be largely the result of (1) equating the marginal cost of saving and the net marginal productivity of capital equipment; (2) liquidity preference, not time preference, and governmental monetary and fiscal policy; (3) private monopolistic control of loan funds and the time preference of individual savers.

76. The market rate of wages is largely the result of (1) monopolistic conditions in the sale of labor services, (2) monopsonistic conditions in the purchase of labor services, (3) a bargaining process (bilateral monopoly) between management and labor unions as modified by government intervention.

77. Oligopoly and industrial concentration have developed in the United States largely because of (1) economies of scale, innovations, and the desire for monopoly profits; (2) the absence of legislation for the control of monopolistic firms; (3) the interference of government in business.

78. The differential rates charged by a public utility should be based on the (1) value of service to different customers, (2) cost of service to different customers, (3) value and cost of service to different customers.

79. The general level of rates charged by a public utility should be based on the (1) present and prospective capitalized value of its net income, (2) spot valuation of its facilities, (3) prudent historical costs incurred by it as modified by special circumstances.

80. Public expenditures may be effectively controlled by (1) laws limiting the total indebtedness and tax levies of various governmental units, (2) proper classification of expenditures, responsible budget system, and centralization of fiscal administration, (3) a comprehensive program of reduction of taxes.

81. The tests of a sound tax system include mainly (1) standards for debt and tax limitations, the benefit principle of taxation, and the use of nonshiftable taxes; (2) the use of indirect taxes, the ability principle of taxation, and constitutional provisions prohibiting confiscation of property by taxation; (3) standards of fiscal adequacy, convenience, certainty, and justice.

82. Under gold standard conditions, exchange rates

among countries were determined by (1) current buying and selling of commodities in international trade, (2) substantial variations in exchange rates which equated international supply and demand, (3) mint pars of exchange and transactions involving gold points.

83. Under paper standard conditions, in the absence of governmental controls of trade and exchange transactions, exchange rates were determined by (1) the price of gold in black markets; (2) the approximate present and prospective purchasing power parity of various currencies; (3) the variation of gold output in the main gold-producing countries.

84. If the government of a given country controls the allocation of foreign exchange and its total international transactions, the exchange rate may be (1) completely stabilized; (2) forced up or down by changes in the price of gold; (3) forced up or down by changes in the purchasing power parity of its currency.

85. In modern times a nation's adjustment to international transactions usually involves primarily (1) its general level of prices, (2) its general level of prices and incomes, (3) its position in the production of gold.

86. Economically sound arguments for a protective tariff are primarily based on (1) national defense, (2) equalizing costs of production at home and abroad, (3) promoting infant industries during a trial period.

87. The United States should adopt a policy of admitting free of duty (1) only noncompetitive imports, (2) primarily agricultural products and minerals, (3) usually those products for which foreign countries have a comparative advantage in their production.

88. Relative conditions of free trade may be established by (1) import duties imposed only on products not suitable for domestic production, (2) comprehensive exchange controls, (3) quotas applicable to competitive imports.

89. A system of protectionism for home industries (1) benefits the entire economy, (2) discriminates against certain domestic industries, (3) assists both the import and export industries.

90. The freedom of international trade is improved greatly by (1) state trading, (2) international cartels, (3) international agreements concerning commodity and capital movements.

KEY TO FINAL EXAMINATIONS

PART I. TRUE-FALSE PROBLEMS

1. T	9. T	17. T	25. F	33. T	41. F	49. F
2. F	10. F	18. T	26. T	34. T	42. T	50. F
3. T	11. T	19. F	27. T	35. F	43. F	
4. F	12. T	20. T	28. T	36. T	44. T	
5. T	13. F	21. F	29. F	37. T	45. T	
6. T	14. T	22. F	30. F	38. F	46. T	
7. T	15. T	23. T	31. T	39. F	47. T	
8. F	16. F	24. F	32. F	40. T	48. T	

PART II. MULTIPLE-CHOICE QUESTIONS

51. (1)	59. (3)	67. (1)	75. (2)	83. (2)
52. (3)	60. (2)	68. (3)	76. (3)	84. (1)
53. (1)	61. (1)	69. (3)	77. (1)	85. (2)
54. (2)	62. (1)	70. (1)	78. (3)	86. (3)
55. (2)	63. (2)	71. (2)	79. (3)	87. (3)
56. (2)	64. (3)	72. (3)	80. (2)	88. (1)
57. (3)	65. (3)	73. (1)	81. (3)	89. (2)
58. (2)	66. (2)	74. (2)	82. (3)	90. (3)

INDEX

Acceptance, 131
Act of 1834, 122
Adult mortality, 216
Advertising: and competition, 106; and costs, 107; and demand, 91; influence of, on consumption, 82–83; in marketing, 72
Agricultural Adjustment Program (1933–1936), 229–230; second AAP (1938–   ), 230–231
Agricultural Marketing Act of 1929, 229
Agriculture: depression in (1920–1940), 225–228; and dietary habits, 227; in England, prior to the Industrial Revolution, 19; fixed costs in, 223–224; and freight rates, 227; and the government, 228–232; importance of, 222; and industrial monopoly, 227; and international trade, 312; long-run supply and demand in, 225–226; position of, in the economy, 222–225; and substitutes, 228; technological changes in, early, 15, 16; in the United States, 24, 222–233; and World War I, 226; in World War II and after, 232–233
Air transportation, and government control, 275, 346
Aluminum Company of America, 265
American Federation of Labor, 24–25, 238, 239; and the CIO, 243
Antitrust legislation, 264–265; evaluation of, 266–267
Arbitration: compulsory, 246; voluntary, 246
Assembling, in marketing, 71–72
Atomic power, 43
Autonomous economic order, 29

Balance of international payments, 305–308
Balance sheet: explained, 48; limitations of, 49–51
Bank notes, 120, 133
Bank of Canada, 144–145
Bank of England, 144
Bank of France, 144
Bankers, and the profit motive in business cycles, 165–166
Banker's acceptance, 131
Banking, functions of: clearance, 133; deposits, 132; loans, 131; note issue, 133
Banking Act of 1933, 134
Banking systems: in Canada, 144–145; in France, 144; in Great Britain, 144; in the United States, 135–144. *See also* Farm Credit Administration, Federal Deposit Insurance Corporation, Federal Home Loan Program, and Federal Reserve System
Banks: commercial, 131–134; failures of, 142; functions of commercial, 131–133; investment, 134; and loan funds, 185–186; savings, 134–135
Basing-point system, 261
Better Business Bureaus, 85
Bill of exchange, 131
Bimetallism, 122, 123, 126–127
Birth rate, 214–215; in the United States, 215
Black markets, 115
Blacklist, 236
Bland-Allison Act (1878), 123
Bonds and notes (corporation), 47–48
Boycotts, 245
Brassage, 122 n.

357